DISENCHANTING ALBERT THE GREAT

THE MAGIC IN HISTORY SERIES

General Editors
RICHARD KIECKHEFER AND CLAIRE FANGER

The Magic in History series explores the role magic and the occult have played in European culture, religion, science, and politics. Titles in the series bring the resources of cultural, literary, and social history to bear on the history of the magic arts, and they contribute to an understanding of why the theory and practice of magic have elicited fascination at every level of European society. Volumes include both editions of important texts and significant new research in the field.

A complete list of books in this series is located at the back of this volume.

MAGIC *in* HISTORY

DISENCHANTING ALBERT THE GREAT

THE LIFE AND AFTERLIFE
OF A MEDIEVAL MAGICIAN

DAVID J. COLLINS, S.J.

THE PENNSYLVANIA STATE UNIVERSITY PRESS
UNIVERSITY PARK, PENNSYLVANIA

Library of Congress Cataloging-in-Publication Data

Names: Collins, David J., 1965– author.
Title: Disenchanting Albert the Great : the life and afterlife of a medieval magician / David J. Collins, S.J.
Other titles: Magic in history.
Description: University Park, Pennsylvania : The Pennsylvania State University Press, [2024] | Series: The magic in history series | Includes bibliographical references and index.
Summary: "Examines the life and work of the medieval friar and magician Albert the Great, using his disputed reputation as a case study for the complex history of magic and its connection with science and religion"—Provided by publisher.
Identifiers: LCCN 2024016284 | ISBN 9780271097442 (cloth)
Subjects: LCSH: Albertus, Magnus, Saint, 1193?–1280. | Magic—History. | Magic—Historiography.
Classification: LCC BF1598.A5 C65 2024 | DDC 133.4/309—dc23/eng/20240424
LC record available at https://lccn.loc.gov/2024016284

Copyright © 2024 David J. Collins, S.J.
All rights reserved
Printed in the United States of America
Published by The Pennsylvania State University Press,
University Park, PA 16802–1003

The Pennsylvania State University Press is a member of the Association of University Presses.

It is the policy of The Pennsylvania State University Press to use acid-free paper. Publications on uncoated stock satisfy the minimum requirements of American National Standard for Information Sciences—Permanence of Paper for Printed Library Material, ANSI Z39.48–1992.

Michael J. Buckley († 2019) et John W. O'Malley († 2022),
sociis Iesu,
magistris amicis fratribusque suis,
hoc opus grato animo dedicat auctor

CONTENTS

LIST OF ILLUSTRATIONS / ix
ACKNOWLEDGMENTS / xi
LIST OF ABBREVIATIONS / xiii
TIMELINES / xv

Introduction: Telling a Medieval Magician / 1

1. Albert's Magic / 23
2. The Magical Albert / 46
3. Albertus Sanctus / 68
4. The Historical Albert / 94
5. The Encyclopedic Albert / 116

Epilogue: Disenchanted Albert / 141

NOTES / 151
BIBLIOGRAPHY / 177
INDEX / 201

ILLUSTRATIONS

1. "Albert Studies Nature." In (Pseudo-)Albertus Magnus, *Le Grand Albert et ses secrets merveilleux* (Paris: Le Bailly, 1865), iv / 19
2. Albert the Great, *De anima* 1.2.6. Munich, Bayerische Staatsbibliothek, clm 317, fol. 7r (detail) / 24
3. Excerpt from the vernacular poem *Semita recta*, Trinity College, Cambridge, MS R. 14. 44, fol. 16r (detail) / 56
4. Title page of *Legenda litteralis Alberti Magni* by Rudolph of Nijmegen, 1490. BSB-Ink R-284 / 81
5. "Albert the Great, bishop of Regensburg." Woodcut from Nicolaus Reusner, *Icones sive Imagines virorum literis illustrium* (Strasbourg: Bernhard Jobin, 1587), A-i-r / 100
6. Frontispiece for the Amsterdam edition (1721) of Naudé's *Apologie* / 127
7. "The Talking Head of Albertus Magnus." From John Henry Pepper, *Cyclopaedic Science Simplified* (London: F. Warne, 1869), p. 473, fig. 432 / 143

ACKNOWLEDGMENTS

This work took many more years to complete than I estimated upon realizing that Albert's reputation as a magician was more than just a fifteenth-century hagiographical problem. With the passage of that time, the weight of my indebtedness to others for their help and encouragement has grown exponentially. I wish to acknowledge that debt and express my thanks.

I am grateful to several scholarly foundations whose largesse supported this project. These include the Alexander von Humboldt Stiftung and the Gerda Henkel Stiftung in the early stages of research and the Helsinki Collegium for Advanced Studies for a recent year of writing. Several libraries and institutes proved themselves hospitable and intellectually stimulating places to work. These include the Albertus-Magnus-Institut (AMI) in Bonn, the Kulturwissenschaftliches Kolleg at the University of Konstanz, the Monumenta Germaniae Historica in Munich, the Société des Bollandistes in Brussels, and the Specola Vaticana in Castel Gandolfo.

I wish also to thank the many colleagues who offered extended counsel on points in this project related to their own specializations and who read chapters in draft: these include Henryk Anzulewicz (AMI), Owen Davies (University of Hertfordshire), Franklin Harkins (Boston College), Mark Henninger (Georgetown University), and Neil Lewis (Georgetown University). Georgetown's History Department organized a faculty seminar to discuss the completed draft; I am grateful for the afternoon of conversation about the manuscript and for the extensive reviews offered in writing by my colleagues Tommaso Astarita, James Collins, Elizabeth Cross, Amy Leonard, Jo Ann Moran Cruz, Tim Newfield, and above all the seminar chair, Alison Games. Ted Worm was, as an undergraduate research assistant, helpful to me at an early stage of research. If this project benefited from any magic at all, it was surely from the conjurations of the Interlibrary Loan Office at Georgetown's Lauinger Library in locating so many obscure journal articles and monographs for me, especially during the pandemic years 2020 and 2021. The anonymous referees provided by the press could not have been more meticulous in their reading of the manuscript in draft and thoughtful in their recommendations; Eleanor Goodman and the staff at the press were encouraging, conscientious, and cheerful partners in the process of turning a book project into a book. I am grateful to Richard Kieckhefer (Northwestern University) for his consistent readiness to talk about magic in all its forms, to Gabriela Signori (University of Konstanz) for her long-term confidence in the project, and to Martial Staub (University of Sheffield) for his ability to apply medieval insights to contemporary problems.

My year in residence at the Collegium in Helsinki occurred in the midst of the pandemic. I have often since wondered what life in that beautiful Nordic city would have been like had I been there in less unusual times. Regardless, I will always cheerfully associate my residence there with a Canadian couple: my colleague at the Collegium, Karen Knop (University of Toronto, d. 2022), and her husband, Ralph Glass (Veneveistämö Janne Pettersson Oy). As the city locked itself down ever more tightly, we three declared ourselves a bubble. For their friendship, constituted out of many memorable joint undertakings and hours of lively conversation about everything imaginable—from Marimekko to Eurovision, from Finnish gins to keelboat design, from sacramental theology to slaveholding reparations—in that bewildering year, I will always be deeply grateful.

Also in the category of personal debt, I wish to underscore my gratitude to the Jesuits of Washington, where I live, as well as of Bad Godesberg, Brussels, Albano Laziale, Munich, and Zurich, who so reliably provided a manner of home *in partibus*, one that included ready companionship and welcome distraction during the long solitudes otherwise necessary when one has lots of reading, thinking, and writing to do.

David J. Collins, S.J.
Washington, DC
15 November 2023

ABBREVIATIONS

EDITIONS AND SERIES

Borgn.	Auguste Borgnet and Émile Borgnet, eds. *B. Alberti Magni Ratisbonensis episcopi, Ordinis Praedicatorum Opera Omnia.* 38 vols. Paris: Louis Vives, 1890–99.
ed. Colon.	Albertus-Magnus-Institut, ed. *Sancti doctoris ecclesiae Alberti Magni Ordinis Fratrum Praedicatorum episcopi Opera Omnia.* Münster: Aschendorff, 1951–.
LCL	Loeb Classical Library. Cambridge, MA: Harvard University Press, 1911–.
Meyer	Ernst Meyer and Karl Jessen, eds. *Alberti Magni "De vegetabilibus libri VII."* Berlin: Georg Reimer, 1867.
Stadler	Hermann Stadler, ed. *Albertus Magnus "De animalibus libri XXVI nach der Cölner Urschrift."* Beiträge zur Geschichte der Philosophie des Mittelalters: Texte und Untersuchungen 15–16. Münster: Aschendorffsche Verlagsbuchhandlung, 1916–1920.

WORKS BY ALBERT THE GREAT

Abbreviations modified from Resnick, *Companion to Albert the Great*, xi–xv.

Abbreviation	Full title	Edition, volume
De anima	*De anima*	ed. Colon. VII/1
De animal.	*De animalibus*	Stadler
De cael.	*De caelo et mundo*	ed. Colon. V/1
De causis prop.	*De causis proprietatum elementorum*	ed. Colon. V/2
De causis et proc.	*De causis et processu universatis a prima causa*	ed. Colon. XVII/2
De fato	*De fato*	ed. Colon. XVII/1
De mot. anim.	*De motibus animalius*	Borgn. 9
De nat. loci	*De natura loci*	ed. Colon. V/2

De veget.	*De vegetabilibus*	Meyer
Ethica	*Ethica*	Borgn. 7
Gen. Corr.	*De generatione et corruptione*	ed. Colon. V/2
Metaph.	*Metaphysica* (1–5)	ed. Colon. XVI/1
	Metaphysica (6–10)	ed. Colon. XVI/2
Mineral.	*De mineralibus*	Borgn. 5
Phys.	*Physica* (1–4)	ed. Colon. IV/1
	Physica (5–8)	ed. Colon. IV/2
Somn. vig.	*De somno et vigilia*	Borgn. 9
Summa	*Summa theologiae* (qq 1–50a of Part 1)	ed. Colon. XXXIV
	Summa theologiae (complete)	Borgn. 31–33
Super Dan.	*Super Danielem*	Borgn. 18
Super Dion. Epist.	*Super Dionysii epistulas*	ed. Colon. XXXVII/2
Super Ethica	*Super Ethica*	ed. Colon. XIV
Super Ioh.	*Super Iohannem*	Borgn. 24
Super Isa.	*Postilla super Isaiam*	ed. Colon. XIX
Super Luc.	*Super Lucam*	Borgn. 22–23
Super Mt.	*Super Mattheum*	ed. Colon. XXI
Super Sent.	*Super Sententiarum I–IV*	Borgn. 25–30

WORKS ABOUT ALBERT

EDA Werner Rolevinck. *Tractatus de excellentiis domini Alberti Magni.* Berlin, Staatsbibliothek, Stiftung Preußischer Kulturbesitz. Ms. theol. lat. oct. 171, ff. 12r–19r.

LLA Rudolphus de Novomagio. *Legenda litteralis Alberti Magni.* Cologne, 1490. Gesamtkatalog der Wiegendrucke, M38537.

LVA Petrus de Prussia. *Legenda venerabilis domini Alberti Magni.* Cologne, 1486/87. Gesamtkatalog der Wiegendrucke, M32672.

TIMELINES

ALBERT'S LIFE

ca. 1200	Birth, Lauingen
1223 or 1229	Entrance into Order of Preachers
1233/34	Began teaching in German priories
1243–48	First residence in Paris, as student and teacher
1248	Returned to Cologne with Thomas Aquinas and takes leadership of studium generale in Cologne
1251	Began commenting on the Aristotelian corpus
1251–52	*Physica*
1254–57	Served as superior of the Teutonia province of the Dominican order
ca. 1254–57	*De mineralibus*, *De anima*
1256	*De vegetabilibus*, *De fato*, *Parva naturalia*
1257	Second lecturing tenure in Cologne
1257–64	Super Matthaeum and Super Danielem
1258–62/63	*De animalibus*
1260–62	Tenure as bishop of Regensburg
1270	Returned to Cologne
1280	Death

ALBERT AND PSEUDO-ALBERT AS A MAGICIAN

1265–72	Ulrich of Strasbourg, *De summo bono*
1470–91	Biographical writings about Albert in Cologne by Werner Rolevinck, Peter of Prussia, Rudolf of Nijmegen, and Jacobus Magdalius of Gouda
1625	Naudé, *Apologie*
1651	Jammy's opera omnia
1674	Moréri, *Le Grand Dictionnaire historique*
1697	Bayle, *Dictionaire historique et critique*

1751–65   Diderot and d'Alembert, *Encyclopédie*
1818   Shelley, *Frankenstein*
1890–99   Borgnet and Borgnet's opera omnia
1951–   ed. Colon.

ALBERT'S CANONIZATION

1280   Albert's death and burial in Cologne
1483   *Translatio* of Albert's remains in Cologne
1484   Pope Innocent VIII permitted Albert's veneration at Dominican priories in Cologne and Regensburg
1622   Pope Gregory XV permitted Albert's veneration in the diocese of Regensburg
1631   Pope Urban VIII permitted Albert's veneration in the city of Lauingen
1635   Pope Urban VIII permitted Albert's veneration to the Dominicans throughout Germany
1670   Pope Clement X approved November 15 as Albert's feast day within the Dominican order
1931   Pope Pius XI canonized Albert and declared him a doctor of the church
1941   Pope Pius XII declared Albert patron saint of natural scientists

INTRODUCTION
TELLING A MEDIEVAL MAGICIAN

The thirteenth-century scholar and churchman Albert the Great relied on magic. His commentary on Aristotle's *De anima* (On the soul) includes a straightforward acknowledgment of this. The question at hand was whether incorporeal entities, like souls and angels, could move. After outlining several arguments against this position, Albert raised the alternative possibility—that incorporeal entities can move—and affirmed, "We ourselves have verified the truth of this with the magical arts."[1] He elaborated little but promised to return to the matter in later writings. He offered further evidence of his familiarity with magic in other treatises and commentaries. Given a medieval presupposition linking the magical to the diabolical and the diabolical to the heretical, a twenty-first-century reader might expect Albert to have been censured or to have received an even harsher penalty for such a confession. He was not. To the contrary, he remained one of the most revered figures of his age, and his engagement with magic became the object of fascination, celebration, and even imitation.

This ostensible paradox warrants quick amplification. Albert's standing among the most highly regarded churchmen of his day remained unchallenged in his lifetime. He held many positions of trust within and outside his order before and after his authorship of the *De anima*,[2] which he wrote while he was provincial superior of the Dominican friars in Germany.[3] Other accomplishments contributed to the high regard in which his contemporaries held him, most of all his astute, innovative, and wide-ranging scholarship. He produced seventy treatises on theology, philosophy, and the natural sciences. Most of these titles advanced his Herculean project of commenting on the entirety of Aristotle's corpus, which was newly attracting scholarly attention in the Latin West. Albert was remarkable in the energy he devoted to understanding through an Aristotelian lens not only metaphysics and logic but also the workings of the natural world, including physics, botany, mineralogy, and zoology. In consequence of this breadth, one twentieth-century interpreter estimated Albert to have been "far more famous than Thomas [Aquinas]" during their overlapping lifetimes. Indeed, Albert was already called "great" in his own day, as well as being called by the professorial sobriquet *doctor universalis* (the teacher of everything). By the fifteenth century he was commonly referred to not only as Albertus Teutonicus (Albert the German) and Albertus Coloniensis (Albert of Cologne) but also Albertus Magnus (Albert the Great).[4]

This esteem did not develop because his writings about magic had been overlooked, ignored, or concealed. His own students celebrated this expertise, which was referred to in scholarship and legend with scarcely a hint of misgiving or word of correction for the next two centuries. In his own treatment of incorporeal beings, Albert's onetime student Ulrich of Strasbourg (ca. 1225–1277) lauded his teacher as one "who was inspired in his grasp of all fields of knowledge and experienced in the magical arts."[5] A generation later the Dutch chronicler Johannes De Beke (d. 1346) used one of the most ambiguous words in the high medieval glossary of magical terms, "nigromancy," in enthusing that Albert was "great in nigromancy, greater in philosophy, and greatest of all in theology."[6] In the late Middle Ages, anonymous authors began ascribing to Albert books that were not his, works of alchemy—some more learned than others—and so-called books of secrets that promised to reveal the innermost workings of the created world. New legends emerged as well, one telling, for example, of a voluptuous summertime feast he hosted in the dead of winter for the German king, and another of his conversion to a life of devotion after a youthful engagement with sorcery. If he had ever applied his knowledge of magic immorally, such legends piously intoned, Albert had repented early in life and this familiarity with magic aided subsequent critical analysis of magic in his serious scholarship.[7] Albert would not have recognized himself in much of this spurious writing.

Sustained objections to Albert as an avid practitioner of magic began to emerge in the fifteenth century, nearly two hundred years after his death and only after the more dubious dimensions of his reputation had established themselves in the imagination of elite scholars and popular storytellers alike. Efforts to correct this misshapen notoriety recurred intermittently over the next four centuries. The objections are noteworthy in three respects: First, those who weighed in—reforming churchmen in the fifteenth century, erudite libertines and skeptics in the seventeenth, and philosophes in the eighteenth—brought to bear defining trends in European intellectual history in evaluating the significance of Albert's thinking about magic. Second, their treatment of what Albert had actually written was not always more accurate than that of those they opposed. Regardless of what conclusions were reached on the matter, everyone was taking liberties with what Albert actually wrote. And third, with few exceptions, their goal was not to condemn Albert for taking a wrong stance toward magic but rather to clear him of any hint of the irrationality and misbehavior that association with magic could imply.

Serious concern over Albert's engagement with magic ended by about 1800, and more with a whimper than a bang. It was not that the fundamental questions—Did he practice magic or not, and of what sort? And should he be praised or condemned for it?—had been definitively answered, but rather that the research question had lost its attraction: Ecclesiastics and scholars who had since the fifteenth century found claims of his engagement with magic defamatory continued to regard most of Albert's corpus worthy of investigation, but not his uncontested writing on magic. Nineteenth-century historians newly interested in earlier approaches to the natural world included him as a serious representative of a surpassed paradigm. The Catholic Church canonized him with scarcely a glance at the magic that had seemingly disqualified him from canonization in earlier centuries. Romantic-era authors began deploying him as a stock character for the magician, but without deliberation over what he may or may not have written. Albert, as a serious scholar and practitioner of magic, whose works occasioned controversy and obliged analysis, had conjured himself away.

The aim of this study is to understand Albert's engagement with magic, the reputation it engendered, and the challenge that reputation posed in the context of European intellectual and cultural history. Albert wrote extensively about magic and intimated his practice of it in certain forms. His own words, scholarly pseudepigrapha, and popular fables fueled the development of his reputation as a magician in his lifetime and for centuries beyond. His words and that reputation often fostered admiration in elite and popular milieus. When they raised concerns, commentators on Albert did not censure the man himself but reinterpreted or refuted his reputation. Analysis of Albert's writings on magic and the reputation they inculcated thus not only draws attention to an obscure and possibly disturbing dimension of Albert's own life—significant in itself given Albert's renown as a thirteenth-century scholar and churchman—but also demonstrates the ambiguous, ambivalent, and unstable meaning of magic in the later Middle Ages and the early modern period. In the rest of this introduction I provide several dimensions of context—lexical, historiographical, and historical—before sketching the origin of Albert's reputation as a magician and the history of its treatment, as analyzed in the following five chapters and epilogue.

Telling a Magician: A Lexical Challenge

Magic is never and nowhere easy to define. Even narrowing our scope to "Albert's magic" does not point to an unambiguous subject of scholarly research. Furthermore, what Albert understood as magic and what others—whether they regarded him as a magician or not—understood as magic do not perfectly align. A preliminary consideration of terms and concepts associated with magic in Albert's day, however, raises into relief the problems about magic that are the heart of this book. *Magia*—the Latin noun for magic—might seem the natural place to start. It was, however, an uncommon word in the philosophical and theological lexicon of Albert's day, and in fact of the Middle Ages generally. Instead, references to specific kinds of magic and adjectives meaning "magical"—*magicus* or *magicalis*—predominated. Used substantively, *magic* could suggest books, people, practices, or, most commonly, knowledge. Latin Christianity's foremost thinker in late antiquity, Augustine of Hippo, for example, referred not to *magia* but to *artes magicae* (magical arts) in *The City of God* and *On Christian Doctrine*, where he developed his influential explanation of magic as fundamentally demonic.[8]

In the authoritative medieval reference work *The Etymologies* (ca. 620s), the scholar and prelate Isidore of Seville did not use the word in the chapter "On the Magicians" either. Rather, he distinguished and condemned two kinds of practitioner (*magi*), whose activities required the invocation of evil spirits. One, whom he labelled *maleficii* (translated commonly as witches or sorcerors, but meaning most literally evildoers), causes harm through the invocation of and with the assistance of malign spirits; *maleficii* "agitate the elements, disturb the minds of people, and slay without any drinking of poison, using the violence of spells alone." The other, whom he called diviners (*divini*), gives "certain knowledge of things to come and of things below," through the invocation of "evil angels"; astrologers and horoscope-casters number among the diviners. Isidore never subsumed these bodies of knowledge and corresponding practices under the single title *magia*, but only alerted his readers to their shared dependence on demonic participation.[9] Furthermore, Isidore drafted his chapter on magicians in the same section of *The Etymologies* in which he treated heretics, sibyls, pagans, and false gods. The problem that united the magicians to these others was flawed, or absent, Christian faith. What magicians knew and did shared, by Isidore's lights, its most important conceptual frontier with religion.

Such an alignment sets the stage for answering the question why natural magic—the form of magic closest to the heart of *Disenchanting Albert the Great*—was not represented in Isidore's taxonomy. Natural magic concerned itself with the workings of the natural world that eluded the conventions of scholastic natural philosophy but did not outright contradict Christian teaching.

Furthermore, natural magic's late emergence—only after Arabic scientific treatises started circulating in translation in the twelfth-century Latin West—serves as a reminder that changes within the millennium known as the Middle Ages can be at least as significant as the differences separating today's perspectives on magic from the medieval.

Credit for coining the term *natural magic* (*ars magica naturalis*) belongs to Albert's older contemporary William of Auvergne (1190–1249). As William used the term, natural magic encompasses natural phenomena of otherwise indeterminate cause. The proper field of natural philosophy relies on resemblances and contrarieties construed between the cause of a change and the observed change. The characteristic properties hot, cold, dry, and wet are, for example, central to ancient and medieval natural philosophy. Thus water's boiling in a pot can be explained with reference to the burning wood on which the pot sits. William was confident in the power of natural philosophy to explain nearly all natural phenomena and dismissed most of what was regarded as magical and wondrous in his day as ultimately explicable with natural philosophy. William's confidence has been taken to foreshadow the robust mechanism that defined modern science in the seventeenth century. Nonetheless, by William's reckoning, some natural phenomena have causes that are not based on similarity and contrariety. These are hidden causes. Examples of hidden causation include the generation of frogs and lice because these animals seemed to generate without parents. The power of rubies to dispel noxious fumes was similarly an occult one. While unexpected in the sense of not being explicable through conventional natural philosophy, such occult operations were taken to be fundamentally natural. William accordingly judged it permissible to take advantage of them, and he called the study and manipulation of occult forces the art of natural magic.[10] Although Albert and William briefly lived in Paris simultaneously, Albert did not adopt the term *natural magic* and developed his own similar concept differently from William, especially in his treatment of celestial influences.[11]

An alternative term Albert used for natural magic was *nigromancy*. Nigromancy is conventionally placed among the most disreputable words in the glossaries of medieval and early modern magic. In its vilest usage it referred to the conjuration of demons. In later centuries it connoted an exchange of the summoned demon's perverse aid for the conjurer's immortal soul. The word, however, has a frustrating history of shifting meaning. In its oldest iterations the word *necromancy*—from the Greek *nekros*, denoting dead, and *mantia*, denoting divination—indicated ceremonies for the conjuration of the dead. As a broad range of Arabic texts began being translated into Latin in the twelfth century, *necromancy* was used to translate an Arabic word for magic that did not necessarily insinuate conjuration.[12] Simultaneously, a fateful orthographical confusion emerged in Latin texts as *nigromancy* (now drawing from the Latin word for "black") began to be used interchangeably with *necromancy*. Now yet another, pernicious meaning was adjoined to the older one—namely, the conjuring of demons. In any given medieval manuscript from about 1100 onward, the word's meaning, regardless of the spelling, must be discerned from other indications in the text.[13]

Further confusing matters, some thinkers attempted to distinguish between good and evil forms of nigromancy. In his *Dialogues Against the Jews* Petrus Alfonsi (d. after 1116), a Jewish Spanish physician, astronomer, and Christian convert much influenced by the Arabic learning circulating in the Iberian Peninsula, classified nigromancy as a liberal art and divided it into nine parts. Four of them had to do with the elements—earth, air, fire, and water—and the remaining five concerned the conjuring of "wicked spirits."[14] Not long after, Dominicus Gundissalinus (1115–1190), a prolific translator of Arabic texts into Latin and much inspired by the tenth-century commentator on Aristotle al-Farabi, sketched eight particular natural sciences in *On the Divisions of Philosophy*. He placed what he called "nigromancy according to physics" (*nigromancia secundum physicam*) in his taxonomy of natural sciences alongside medicine, agriculture, navigation, and optics as well as the "science of images," astrology, and alchemy. In this sense nigromancy is the science of properties, which could be deemed natural, astrological, or magical. *On the Divisions of Philosophy* circulated widely, and its overview of natural sciences surfaced in other treatises on human knowledge across Europe. "Nigromancy according to physics" linked the natural sciences of medieval Dar al-Islam to the Latin West and informed early notions of natural magic. The challenge throughout the later medieval and early modern periods for theorists of natural magic would be to keep it clear of the scurrilous practices Isidore had condemned six centuries earlier.[15]

Gundissalinus's list of natural sciences included three more fields that Albert wrote about and that later interpreters of Albert sometimes struggled to evaluate as magic. The first is astrology, the study of the influence of celestial bodies and their movements on human society. Throughout the Middle Ages, celestial movements were observed, measured, and recorded so that future movements could be predicted and their influence anticipated. The claims that mathematical calculation undergirded astrological divination (called judicial astrology or judgments), that there were such celestial influences on the human world, and that they could be apprehended were regarded as legitimate and rational. The claim that certain readings of the future undermine human free will, however, was regarded as condemnable by Christian theologians, such as Isidore. The dividing line between legitimate and illegitimate astrology remained a lively and unresolved debate throughout the era.[16]

The second field is alchemy, which in contrast to astrology, became a subject of vigorous interest in the Latin West only with the reception of Arab learning in the twelfth century. The earliest treatises on alchemy describe the manipulations of material objects in ways that engendered skepticism when they seemed to contradict Aristotelian theories of the elements. As time went on, the metaphorical expressions its adepts used in describing procedures as well as the ritualistic appeals for spiritual aids in alchemical formulae and recipes made alchemy the object of ever greater critical scrutiny. Questions sharpened as to whose aid the alchemists sought to work their transmutations and to what ends they undertook their experiments.[17]

The third natural science, the so-called science of images, presupposed that the special emanations from celestial bodies could be harnessed to marvelous effect through signs drawn onto or engraved into objects such as gems. That the crafting entailed precise knowledge of the stars, objects like gems, and signs was in itself unproblematic. That the crafting sometimes entailed particular incantations and rituals smacked of wickedest nigromancy. Like the other two disciplines, the science of images was a disputed field. Albert and his student Thomas Aquinas disagreed on the question of the craft's morality. Albert, here and for topics like it, pushed the limit of the permissible further than his contemporaries. It is precisely his tenacity in seeking out natural explanations that attracted later experimenters in natural magic and caused confusion for later generations trying to make his thought flawlessly orthodox.[18]

Telling a Magician: A Historiographical Challenge

Modern scholarship ordinarily treats magic, in its many forms, in implicit or explicit conjunction with two other major fields of human endeavor, religion and science.[19] There are two main reasons for this, one having to do with shared content, the other with the modern scholarship itself. What magic, religion, and science share is an interest in understanding the natural world. This interest is of course definitional to the natural sciences. While less self-evidently so to religion, the interest is central to ancient and medieval religion as well. Not only Christianity but also the other monotheistic religions and many of the polytheistic religions and philosophical systems in Europe and the Mediterranean world hold some notion of a creating divinity. In consequence, thinking about nature has invariably led to thinking about the divine and vice versa.

Indeed, Christianity's dogma of creation was generally taken in the Middle Ages and early modern period to dignify the study of the natural world on its own terms, and it bore itself further out in the medieval effort to separate natural philosophy as an academic discipline in its own right from theology.

Modern scholarship on magic has maintained attention to science and religion as vital, if also sometimes anguished, partners. Within early sociology and anthropology, the triad of religion, magic, and science as rivalrous human approaches to the workings of the natural world emerged, each approach placed along a measure of rationality according to how it explains causation in the natural world. Early twentieth-century functional structuralism described the relationship among the three in evolutionary terms, but without unanimity among its theorists as to the ordering of religion and magic prior to the emergence of natural science. Subsequent scholarship into magic has reacted with skepticism toward evolutionary approaches for arriving at conclusions unduly shaped by the prejudices of researchers and for sacrificing precision in the drive to generate a general theory. Nonetheless, the legacy of this older scholarship still looms in the background of historical studies of magic today.[20]

The partnership between science and religion in the handling of magic is particularly germane to our purposes, as Albert observed in his own writings a distinction between theological and philosophical (scientific) assessments of what he identified as magic. By Albert's lights, how magic works is first and foremost a problem for the natural philosopher; whether it is good to practice is a problem for the theologian. Further, magic effected by celestial influences on the hidden properties of natural objects lends itself to testing against theories of the natural sciences; magic worked in concert with demons, however, warrants theological or ethical interpretation. He generally addressed the former issues in philosophical works like the *De mineralibus* (On minerals) and the *De vegetabilibus* (On botany), and the latter in theological works like his *Summa theologiae* (Systematic compendium of theology) and his *Super Sententiarum* (Commentary on the sentences of Peter Lombard). Albert shared such distinguishing efforts in principle with most fellow scholastics: Magic had a place on both sides of the frontier demarking what is proper to the philosopher versus the theologian. Moreover, even with very different notions of rationality, empiricism, and ethics, medieval and modern approaches to magic are roughly parallel: regardless of how different the overarching worldviews of medieval and modern scholarship can be, there is a shared tendency to evaluate magic against conceptions of what constitutes religion and science.

Measures of religions and scientific systems on scales of rationality have their own histories, and cautions against them in recent scholarship offer additional guardrails for our analysis of Albert's magic and his reputation as a magician.

Reacting to the hydra-like indomitability of calculated scholarly contrasts between the enchanted Christianity of the Middle Ages and the rational Christianity of modern Europe, the historian Alexandra Walsham offers her colleagues in the field of religious history a caution pertinent to historians of science and of magic. Each of us is, she opined, still "a product and a prisoner of [earlier] historiographical and epistemological trends" that instrumentalize the medieval for the sake of the modern; the temptation to craft new grand narratives for the sake of analogous agenda, she argued, remains.[21] The history of science has been similarly afflicted, and the historian of science and medicine John Henry, motivated like Walsham, laments a tendency among his colleagues to extract from historical sources—in this case, works of alchemy and astronomy—whatever rings modern and to leave aside the rest as tare to modern science's wheat. He proposes instead a comprehensive approach that evaluates even superstitious and irrational elements as potentially essential parts of the process of scientific development and thus necessary to integrate into overarching studies.[22] The danger of analyzing magic in history arises from the penchant to classify medieval understandings of nature that are wrong or that fail to correspond to the modern ones as irrational, superstitious, and magical and therefore are not worth further consideration.

At the intersection of the lexical and historiographical problems outlined so far is a rivalry between analyzing as magic what is presented in the historical sources as such and analyzing what appears in the sources to be magic according to a modern definition of magic.[23] Aligning with one side versus the other solves some problems only to cause others, and most historians try working with both approaches in some balance. Echoing Walsham's and Henry's critiques of their respective fields, the medievalist Isabelle Draelants blames the problem of defining magic on "the evolution of intellectual categories between the Middle Ages and the present day" and rejects as "useless" both the historian's view of "the progress of the sciences away from superstition" and the structuralist's "distinctions between science and magic."[24] In short, the aspiration to discern in the presumed diminishing history of magic an inevitable march toward greater human reason distorts the analysis of magic in history.

Investigation into Albert's reputation as a magician, as such, requires alertness to the shifting and ambiguous meanings of magic that separate what Albert meant from how his interpreters understood him, indeed from the thirteenth century to the present. It is a problem of contextualized understandings of magic in history not resonating. If magic could not avoid being diabolical, as a fifteenth-century Dominican could hold, what possible sense could be made of Ulrich's exuberant celebration of Albert's magic except to reimagine what Ulrich meant. Or, more subtly, as alchemy developed from a laboratory practice in the twelfth century to an evocatively mystical one in the sixteenth, the alchemical lab manuals of the earlier era could not help but come under new, hostile scrutiny. The change in judgment reflected not only changing contexts but specifically what was expressed and understood as magic in various historical moments. Along these lines, the historical study of magic is fascinating to religious studies scholar Bernd-Christian Otto not only for its range of referents but also for the range of dispositions brought to bear upon it, from the polemical and ostracizing to the forensic and the valorizing.[25] Attentiveness to such distinctions—in an approach he identifies as historical discourse analysis—helps unpack the recurrent renegotiating of Albert's equivocal reputation as a magician in two key respects.

First, it situates and obviates a challenge against regarding Albert as a magician at all. For example, Alain de Libera, one leading modern interpreter of Albert's philosophy, has remarked, "It must be said in the strongest possible terms: Albert's work has nothing to do with magic," and, "This tireless reader probably did not, as far as we can imagine, handle vials of chickweed, spurge, or houseleek juice, virgin boy's urine, bean blossom water, and bleak scales."[26] Leaving aside for the moment that Albert's studies of the natural world likely did bring him into contact with each of those ingredients, that very list is hardly the sole indicator of magical practice between the thirteenth and the eighteenth centuries. Furthermore, the very argument lends itself to polemics, sometimes in a valorizing mode vis-à-vis Albert's reputation as a magician, but here in an ostracizing one.

Second, Otto's contextualizing distinctions offer terms with which to understand two key turning points in this book: The first turning point occurs between the first and second chapters. In chapter 1 Albert's writings about magic are the principal focus and thus he is an active participant in the discussion over magic: what it is, how it works, and whether it is good to practice. Afterward, Albert's reputation as a magician is the principal focus, and he metamorphoses from participant to subject. Complicating matters, while Albert's writings constituted a reference for the later discourses, there was no undisputed canon of those writings, pseudepigrapha gained and lost legitimacy, and the range of topics he wrote about as magic expanded and shrank accordingly. The second turning point appears between the second and the third chapters. In the second chapter, the analysis focuses on historical figures and writings that assume magic works and is good to practice; chapter 3 examines those who thought to the contrary. What accumulates across these chapters is evidence of Albert's emergence as an instrument for partisan engagement in larger disputes over magic and more generally knowledge of the natural world. Just as knowing that the applied definition of magic helps us understand claims about Albert's magic, so studying

Albert's ambiguous and elastic reputation gives evidence of how what counted as magic changed.

That the famed schoolman earned a reputation as a magician in the thirteenth century and lost it in the eighteenth raises the question whether his history is one of disenchantment. The answer is not as straightforward as one might expect, and not only because *disenchantment* itself is such a fraught term. On the one hand, this investigation into Albert's reputation as a magician, in its broadest scope, exposes a diminished capacity in diverse European circles of learning to take someone seriously as a magician. Such developments across six centuries imply "disenchantment" in the sense of an increasing faith in reason and empiricism to explain natural phenomena without recourse to mysterious or supernatural forces. On the other hand, generation by generation Albert's reputation as a magician, viewed positively or negatively, did not progressively disappear; neither its support nor its opposition followed consistent, momentum-gathering strategies. Any assessment of disenchantment must begin with the recognition that on certain topics—for example, talismans activated by celestial influences—Albert was more likely to emphasize natural chains of causation (over demonic or miraculous ones) than many contemporaries as well as later devotees who claimed him as the precedent and inspiration for their identifications of magic. In turn, those who reacted against Albert's reputation often drew from contemporaneous approaches to magic that assumed much more demonic and miraculous interference in nature's common course than Albert had.

My analysis of Albert's naturalism and that of those who reacted to his engagement with magical topics has implications for the continuing evaluation and critique of the grand narrative of disenchantment in Western modernity. I have found the work of three scholars especially stimulating for my own thinking about disenchantment outside the now-fraught terms within which it has been traditionally understood in European history: Michael Bailey, who proposes the oscillating nature of superstition in its relation to skepticism in European intellectual history;[27] Alan Charles Kors, who, in an influential, revisionist history of the Enlightenment, locates the origins of much eighteenth-century thinking about secularism, atheism, and naturalism in expressly theological debates of earlier periods;[28] and Jason Ā. Josephson-Storm, whose expressed aim is to demythologize what he regards as the myth of disenchantment and who rejects a march of ineluctable progress from "enchanted ontologies and spiritualized orientations to nature" to the apprehension of "an unmediated cosmos . . . with the sparkling clarity of universal rationality."[29] While these scholars do not cleanly align with one another on questions of rationality and skepticism, and disenchantment and Enlightenment, in European history, they do collectively support what we in fact find by studying Albert's stance on magic and his evolving reputation as a magician: that both *magic* and *disenchantment* are ambiguous and elastic terms, and that when understood as such, they are all the more useful in making sense of debates over them.

Telling a Magician: The History—A Precedent?

The development of Albert's reputation as a magician is better described as labyrinthine than linear or even oscillating. Both those who approved of and those who rejected the practice of magic itself were consistent, though, in holding Albert immune from condemnation for his association with magic. This immunity begs the question whether Albert's treatment was unusual. He was certainly not the only learned figure of the Middle Ages associated with the practice of magic. The seventeenth-century librarian Gabriel Naudé composed an encyclopedic volume dedicated to exonerating many historical figures, from antiquity to his own day, falsely accused of sorcery.[30] The volume's table of contents reads like a roll call in honor of Mediterranean and European magicians. Albert is but one of forty-two cases Naudé addressed. The variety of figures on the list—from Numa Pompilius (715–673 BCE), the second king of Rome, who allegedly used demonic conjuring to subjugate the Roman people, to the reforming abbot and humanist Johannes Trithemius (1462–1516), whose *Steganographia*, a work on angelic cryptography, enemies denounced as itself diabolical—draws attention to the wide variety of ways magical powers were imputed to historical figures. In this group, Albert stands out as a practitioner of magic regarded as such in his own lifetime and based on his own acknowledgment. Examining the similar reputations of four other medieval figures—namely, those of the pope Gerbert of Aurillac, the philosopher Roger Bacon, the physician Peter of Abano, and the astronomer Cecco of Ascoli—draws Albert's distinctiveness into higher relief.

In the case of Gerbert of Aurillac (945–1003), like that of Albert, great learning drew him to study magic. But the accusations against Gerber, unlike those against Albert, predominantly involved demonic magic, emerged only after his death, and were aggravated by the charge of ecclesiastical ambition. Indeed, Gerbert ranks as the medieval sorcerer simultaneously most prominent and most vilified: prominent, because he held the papacy for four years under the name Sylvester II and because he left a substantial body of correspondence and scholarly writing extant to the present day;[31] vilified, because of the efforts taken to denounce him by factions in the Investiture Contest.[32] The earliest explanations for Gerbert's successes in the worlds of learning and power that pointed to magical proficiency date to the late eleventh century, long after his death. A German prelate, a certain Benno, perhaps of Osnabrück (1020–1088), drew a connection between the reforming pope Gregory VII (Benno's contemporary) backward to Gerbert as the later pope's teacher. He denounced them both as sorcerers. Sigebert of Gembloux (1035–1112) reiterated Benno's censure in his *Chronica*. He acknowledged Gerbert's learning but repeated the accusation of demonic conjuration, reported that the devil himself had beaten Gerbert to death, and urged his removal from the list of valid popes.[33]

The twelfth-century Anglo-Norman history writer William of Malmesbury gave the stories legendary form in his *Deeds of the English Kings*: Gerbert's accomplishments, he explained, were attained in an exchange with the devil for his soul. Gerbert's pact with the devil came, by William's account, during his studies in Muslim al-Andalus (not Christian Catalonia, as was more likely the case). Gerbert's lust for knowledge led him first to purloin a book of secret knowledge, the one most valued in the collection of his Saracen tutor. Trapped by rising floodwaters on his flight back to France, he turned to the book, conjured a demon, and exchanged his soul for the powers he needed to evade capture. By the same means, once home he acquired new depths of knowledge, insinuated himself into circles of spiritual and temporal authority, and won ecclesiastical dignities all the way to the papacy. Once regarded by those who favored his nomination to the papacy, including the emperor Otto III, as a committed reformer and imperial loyalist, Gerbert numbered, by William's reckoning, among the most depraved figures in all Christian history.[34] Papal chroniclers defended both Gerbert and Gregory through the centuries, but William's version of Gerbert's sorcery was repeated in influential places, including in the thirteenth-century compendium *The Mirror of History* by Vincent of Beauvais.[35]

The emergence of Roger Bacon's reputation as an Oxford magus likewise emerged only after his death even though he had written extensively and largely disapprovingly of magic. Bacon (1220–1292), Albert's younger contemporary, referred to magic in his *Opus maius* and *Opus tertium* and composed a work known under the title "On the Secret Works of Art and Nature and the Nullity of Magic." As he used the term, magic is mainly deceptive and illusory, even in the rare moments when he allowed for the possibility of spirits' cooperating with conjurers. The wonders of nature, he argued, surpass the illusions of any magician, even if the two kinds of phenomenon are easily confused. Bacon himself regarded magical arts as illicit and misused knowledge.[36] While his explanation of magic rendered anything like good or white magic nonsensical, his idea of experimental science corresponded in part to what contemporaries saw in natural magic.

Groundwork for his reputation as a sorcerer was laid in a late fourteenth-century Franciscan chronicle that recorded a vague allegation that Bacon's own Franciscan order had condemned him for writing about certain "novelties." Afterward another friar, Peter of Trau (fl. 1385), reported that Bacon had created a mirror that allowed his students to see what people were doing anywhere in the world. While Bacon's authentic works were consulted, quoted, and sometimes plagiarized in the later Middle Ages, additional works on magic were being composed and falsely attributed to him. Listing several of these spurious titles in his *Famous Writers of Great Britain* (1548), the English churchman and religious controversialist John Bale (1495–1563) denounced Bacon as an "enchanter and conjurer."[37] Although Bale later reversed his judgment and called the charge of conjuring a defamation, the sixteenth-century accusation left a consequential paper trail.[38]

As in Albert's case, fictional literature spread Bacon's reputation as a magician. Indeed, Bacon's conjurations made their most influential appearance not in a learned treatise but in a play, Robert Greene's comedy *Friar Bacon and Friar Bungay* (1592). Greene drew most of his material from the less successful and anonymous *Famous Historie of Fryer Bacon* (ca. 1590). The plays put in circulation a set of stories about Bacon as a magician: that he used a mirror to reveal a secret romance to a jealous lover, transported people inexplicably from one place to another, summoned the ghost of Julius Caesar to contend with that of Pompey at a royal banquet, and strove unsuccessfully to construct a talking head with the aid of celestial and demonic powers. In the play, Bacon ends his magical investigations when two students fight each other to the death after witnessing a duel between their fathers in his magical mirror. Bacon, appalled, renounces magic and leads ever after a life of penance.[39]

Again, as in Albert's case, a defense of Bacon finally emerged: in 1557 John Dee composed an essay, no longer extant, that defended Bacon as the consummate Christian and his accomplishments as free of any diabolism. Naudé numbered Bacon among history's misunderstood geniuses. Late seventeenth-century attempts within the Royal Society to collect and publish Bacon's scientific works, though unsuccessful, still drew serious attention to Bacon as an experimenter and inventor.[40] Bacon receives multiple mentions in Denis Diderot and Jean le Rond d'Alembert's *Encyclopédie*. These references are fewer and generally less exuberant than those to Albert, but sometimes, as in the article on chemistry, comparison turns in Bacon's favor. A brief biography of Bacon is included in the article on scholasticism. Bacon, the author reported, "took the habit of a Franciscan, but wasted his time neither arguing nor languishing. He studied nature, sought its secrets, and devoted himself entirely to astronomy, chemistry, optics, and mechanics. He made great progress in experimental physics such that one can see in him the hints of several discoveries that were made only in centuries much later than his own." The article concludes with an account of the accusations of magic against Bacon and his sufferings at the hand of his order: "The favor of the pope did not reduce his enemies to inaction: they turned to his order's superior, who condemned his doctrine, suppressed his works, and threw him into a dungeon."[41]

Born fifty years after Albert but already in his twenties and advanced in his studies at Constantinople when Albert died, Peter of Abano (ca. 1250/57–1315/16) was a Paduan physician and philosopher. His major work was the *Reconciler of the Differences Between Philosophers and Physicians*, in which he addressed issues pertaining to astral influences and astrology.[42] Several additional treatises on astral influences and astrology—the *Illuminator of the Doubtful Things of Astronomy*, *On the Movement of the Eighth Sphere*, and *On Images*—enjoyed more limited circulation.[43] He wrote well-received treatises on poisons and physiognomy as well. His medical insights were founded on Ptolemy, Galen, and Avicenna and earned favorable citation up to the seventeenth century.

His perspective on several points of cosmology coincided with Albert's, and he likewise gained a reputation as a magician. Peter regarded the influences of celestial movements on humans as a significant part of the study of nature. Peter saw in astrological influences the effects of the celestial realm's perfection on the terrestrial realm's imperfection. Like Albert, he was reluctant to explain remarkable phenomena in the world with reference to the intervention of angels and demons. Both Peter and Albert distinguished the science of the stars from anything diabolical, which they repeatedly condemned. Along these lines, both men accepted the crafting and use of talismans as benign in principle. Both were inclined to natural understandings of hidden properties and in this regard drew from interpretations of Aristotle developed in the Muslim world and newly arriving in the Latin West in the twelfth and thirteenth centuries.[44]

More like Bacon's reputation than Albert's, however, Peter's reputation was related to an ambiguous set of interactions that he had had with ecclesiastical authorities and that became disparaging only after his death. The nature of Peter's conflict with ecclesiastical authorities remains unclear. He alluded to it in his own writing, and terms in his will have been interpreted as stratagems to protect his property for his family should he be condemned. On the one hand, his astrological determinism, rejection of the conventional association of demons with mental illness, explanation of saintly miracles as wondrous, and extensive treatment of the effectiveness of medically therapeutic incantations could all have attracted official inquisitorial attention. On the other, he affirmed in the *Reconciler* an important distinction between his philosophical speculation and his unreserved adherence to Christian doctrine. He likely appeared before ecclesiastical tribunals on two occasions. The first court acquitted him, but he died during the second trial and that court posthumously condemned him. The court then ordered his body be exhumed and burned. When his body was not found, he was burned in effigy. Michele Savonarola

(1385–1466), a physician, humanist, and history writer, as well as a grandfather of the ill-fated Dominican reformer Girolamo, provided an unreliable link between Peter and the pseudepigrapha in a story that focused on the hostility of Parisian Dominicans toward Peter for dabblings in illicit magic.[45] The foremost modern scholar of Peter's life and thought, however, has declared the circumstances surrounding his death and attempted *damnatio* a mystery.[46]

Much like Albert's reputation, Peter's hung on the reception of both authentic and inauthentic writings that circulated in subsequent centuries. In the fifteenth century Peter's authentic medical works enjoyed multiple printings, and multiple treatises on conjuring and divination, misascribed to him, began appearing, too. *Experiments with Rings*, for example, was an illusionist's handbook based on an Arab notion of the moon's twenty-eight mansions (segments in its rotational path in the sky around the Earth),[47] and the *Commentary on Magic* was a compendium of astral magic and conjuration published under the title "Heptameron" in Heinrich Agrippa's *On Occult Philosophy* in 1565.[48] Moreover, Marcilio Ficino was convinced of Peter's sorcery, and Giovanni Pico attacked Peter's medical astrology in his *Disputations Against Divinatory Astrology*.[49] Trithemius was more cautious: in a paragraph that followed one in which he defended Albert against any necromantic insinuations, he allowed that Peter may not have written such works as the *Commentary* but affirmed that the author, also of other books under Peter's name, was "vain and superstitious in all things."[50]

Naudé defended Peter in the *Apologie*, enthusing that Peter ought to be numbered among the brightest figures in an otherwise ignorant age and that his *Reconciler* should be considered among the most insightful works on medicine and astronomy.[51] Naudé's exoneration of Peter is as exuberant as the *Encyclopédie*'s is stingy. In the latter's entry on scholasticism, Peter ranks among the movement's minor figures. The contributor drew attention to the accusations of magic against him, as he also had for Bacon but not for Albert, and sarcastically opined, "It is not clear why he was given this honor. Today he would only be thought a miserable astrologer and a ridiculous charlatan."[52]

The sharpest contrast of the four figures under consideration to Albert is found in the case of Cecco of Ascoli (1257–1327), who, as a self-professed conjurer, was executed for nigromancy in 1327. Cecco taught astronomy at Bologna and earned renown in his day for a commentary on the thirteenth-century astronomical work *The Sphere of the World* by Johannes de Sacrobosco as well as for handbooks on cosmology and astrology. Despite his attracting hostile attention from church authorities, the duke of Calabria hired him to make astrological forecasts for him in 1326.[53] Less than a year later, his fortune turned: inquisitors charged, tried, and condemned Cecco, and he was burned at the stake on 26 September 1327. Once again, incomplete records make the exact charges a matter of some speculation today. His commentary on *The Sphere* contained passages on astrological nigromancy, a form of demonology that places demons within the cosmic sphere and accessible through ceremonies to humans. Such writings, let alone activity, would easily have attracted the censure of ecclesiastical authorities. His nigromancy drew on the learning newly reaching the Latin West from the Muslim world, and he tapped magical traditions allegedly originating with the biblical Solomon. Parts of his writing also indicate tendencies to astrological fatalism regarding human judgment and astrological determinism regarding sacred events. His condemnation followed so closely upon Pope John XXII's condemnation of ritual magic in *Super illius specula* that it is hard not to conclude that Cecco was executed to make of him an example during the bull's early implementation.[54] Cecco received scant attention in later centuries. Naudé listed him with Socrates, Iamblichus, and Julius Caesar Scaliger (1484–1558)—that is, among those whose greatest inspirations came from their own particular genii—but offered scarcely a word specific to his life or writings.[55] The editors of the *Encyclopédie* passed over Cecco in silence. Girolamo Tiraboschi (1731–1794), the librarian to the duke of Modena and Reggio, linked Peter and Cecco as astrologers in his famous review of Italian literature, *The History of Italian Literature*. He retold the story of Cecco's condemnation for conjuring and evaluated favorably Cecco's "Acerba," a poetic work of some five thousand verses on nature, morals, and philosophy that touches on astrology and the occult.[56]

These four cases offer a sketch of the diverse and unpredictable routes by which learned medieval figures earned reputations as practitioners of magic, sometimes during, sometimes after their lifetimes. In all four cases the scrutiny they attracted as reputed practitioners of magic was predominantly hostile, and in two cases it led to judicial condemnations (Peter and Cecco). Concern for demonic associations, however contrived, has a part in each of these stories. Albert's own reputation for thinking about and practicing magic developed in the same intellectual and cultural landscape that these four figures inhabited. Yet, unlike them, Albert traversed it unscathed. Adding Albert to the group underscores how ambiguous, capricious, and elastic the links were between what particular thinkers wrote and their reputations as magicians in a given moment and what the implications of that judgment could be.

Telling a Magician: The History

With this context now set, we turn to the outlines of the analysis that follows, chapter by chapter. Each chapter takes aim at a phase in the development of Albert's reputation as a magician from his own day to, by the epilogue, our own.

Chapter 1, "Albert's Magic," lays the groundwork by outlining Albert's own understanding of magic, beginning with an analysis of his affirmation of magic in *De anima* and expanding to include his treatment of magic, natural and demonic, in his philosophical and theological works. Chapter 2, "The Magical Albert," traces the emergence of Albert's reputation as an expert in magic, beginning during his lifetime and following its positive expression in the fifteenth century. This chapter draws into consideration early life-writing about Albert as well as the composition of legends concerning his magical activities, the emergence of pseudepigrapha and early debates over his genuine bibliography, the effects of new understandings of magic on understandings of what Albert had written, and, most important, how little concern his evolving reputation as a magician attracted from ecclesiastical and academic authorities.

The next three chapters follow the critical approaches to Albert's reputation for magic in stages. Their subjects share the aim of making Albert's thought less "magical," but they achieve this through different means, first moralizing, then historicizing, and finally, scientific. They tap, each in their own way, into discourses of magic's ostracism. Chapter 3, "Albertus Sanctus," analyzes the beginnings of an unease with his reputation as a magician. That unease can sometimes be detected in an oblique defensiveness, as when the Dominican theologian Luis de Valladolid prepared a list of Albert's authentic writings around 1414 that accented Albert's opposition to diabolical magic. Sometimes it took a disapproving stance, as when the distinguished theologian and university chancellor at Paris Jean Gerson, in a rare word of direct criticism, judged Albert's supposed treatment of astrology "unworthy of a Christian thinker" in 1419.[57] A full-scale effort was finally mounted late in the century to scrub Albert's reputation of any blemish of magical proclivity. The participants in this campaign hoped to settle the matter once and for all with his canonization, and in consequence more biographical writing about Albert was composed in the two-decade period beginning in 1470 than in the preceding two centuries. Study of the canonization efforts uncovers new, high stakes to settling the question of what Albert had been doing in the thirteenth century now in the era of burgeoning witch trials. By the lights of his Dominican advocates, what Albert really wrote and all the more what others wrote about him and put under his name put his sterling reputation in jeopardy and had to be, as necessary, rewritten and refuted. What their efforts demonstrate, in comparison with the history of the preceding chapters, is that as much purposefulness could be applied to excising certain ideas and activities from Albert's résumé as imputing them to it.

The concerted fifteenth-century attempt to rescue Albert's reputation not only failed to achieve his canonization; it also failed to snuff out curiosity about his alleged sorcerous propensities. The circulation of legends and pseudepigrapha

Fig. 1. "Albert Studies Nature." In (Pseudo-)Albertus Magnus, *Le Grand Albert et ses secrets merveilleux* (Paris: Le Bailly, 1865), iv. The image places Albert the Great in both the foreground—in a makeshift laboratory that includes alchemical equipment— and the background, in the field studying animals. A biographical chapter in the volume is devoted to "Albert the Sorcerer."

continued in the sixteenth and seventeenth centuries, much buoyed by the printing press. *The Grand Albert*, a book of secrets with medieval roots ascribed to him, for example, remained a publishing favorite into the nineteenth century (fig. 1).[58] The title was sufficiently representative of magic and superstition in the early modern period that the French priest and satirist Laurent Bordelon placed it next to *The Lesser Albert*,[59] a similarly famous book of conjurations, on the bookshelf of the hapless protagonist of his *History of the Ridiculous Extravagancies of Monsieur Oufle* in 1710, noting such books were "in credit among fools."[60]

Arguments continued across all epochs of European intellectual history over what the magic of earlier generations had meant, and Albert's connections to magic surfaced again and again as a case worth examining. In contrast to the late fifteenth-century objections to Albert's reputation for magic, the later authors who turned to address Albert's magic expressed little interest in the ecclesiastical or moral implications of what Albert might have thought and done. Whereas fifteenth-century arguments emphasized Albert's piety hand in hand with his rationality as characteristics mitigating against the possibility of his practicing magic, the later inquirers were more concerned with what Albert had written about the natural world in comparison to the natural sciences of his own day and theirs. Rather than drawing Albert's scholarly integrity from his moral character, as the generation who had sought his canonization had done, these investigators were interested in assessing how Albert explained the natural world in the first place.

Chapter 4, "The Historical Albert," evaluates the first of the two secular attempts to resolve the problem of Albert's reputation for magic. It takes Gabriel Naudé's seminal text in this regard, *Apologie pour tous les grands personages faussement soupçonnez de magie* (A defense of all great persons falsely suspected of magic) (1625).[61] Naudé's volume comprises sections on the nature of magic and on history writing. Naudé applied these theoretical points to a set of cases to exculpate the "falsely suspected." Naudé acquitted Albert with a two-pronged argument deployed throughout the volume: first, that envious contemporaries had maliciously confused brilliance with superstition, and second, that allegations of magic too easily allowed lazy history writers to titillate foolish readers. While making cursory allowance for Albert's moral integrity, Naudé established a framework for understanding advances in the natural sciences and emphasized Albert's commitment to natural-scientific knowledge and the principles of rational, empirical discovery, which gave cause for admiration but also excused Albert even when, from the perspective of later science, he might have been wrong. Naudé's *Apologie* became the locus classicus in treatments of magic and its practitioners for the next two centuries. Scarcely a scholarly work on magic can be found in the seventeenth and eighteenth centuries that does not rely on Naudé's *Apologie*.

Among the writings that were most dependent on Naudé's work and approach was the quintessential repository of learning in the eighteenth century, the encyclopedia. In that era of great philosophical accomplishment and contest, the encyclopedic genre was as much a tool of propaganda as of reference and education. The genre found fertile soil across Europe and proved itself a reliable, supple, and effective instrument for every side in an era of heightened religious, philosophical, and national rivalries. In this respect, the most famous of encyclopedias, Diderot and d'Alembert's, is but one of many such works.[62] The fifth chapter, "The Encyclopedic Albert," turns to these encyclopedias precisely because they demonstrate the era's intellectual and cultural complexity. What its investigation finds is that despite the captiousness of the times and even as Albert's thought was judged to be surpassed, encyclopedia authors of every stripe handled him with consistent respect: Albert was a man learned in matters of the natural world, perhaps even worthy of association with the naturalists of the most recent periods. Scholarly contributors to Diderot and d'Alembert's *Encyclopédie* treated Albert's accomplishments no less graciously than did the Jesuits in their *Dictionnaire de Trévoux*, even as they acknowledged inadequacies in his work when judged against the natural sciences of the eighteenth century. While Albert's own students lauded him for his expertise in magic and two centuries later Dominican confreres denounced the calumny, two centuries still later philosophers and Jesuits passed over Albert's magic and analyzed instead the knowledge of the natural world he attained. Albert's learning was still, by many measures, great, but his magic had become immaterial.

Across the approximately six centuries under review in *Disenchanting Albert the Great* and in each of the next five chapters and epilogue, different dimensions of Albert's rich and multifaceted scholarship rise into and sink out of view. The almost effervescent quality of this variation reflects not only what Albert thought about the complex topic of magic but also the ideas, ever-changing among his readers, about what magic could be, how it worked, and whether it was good to practice. Judgments changed across time, as did the content of what was being evaluated as magic. *Disenchanting Albert the Great* can be taken therefore as a case study in the history of both magic and disenchantment across the six centuries under review. The study is about one leading medieval thinker's relationship to magic and the history of reactions to it. Extracted from Max Weber's well-known thesis that links processes of rationalization, disenchanted approaches to the natural world, and Western modernity, the search for disenchantment in Albert's reputation as a magician has implications for understanding what disenchantment could mean in intellectual history, but in a twofold, upended sense. First, *Disenchanting Albert the Great* is an analysis of one scholastic philosopher's naturalizing tendencies in treating forces shaping the natural world, of which many were deemed inexplicable according to the conventional approaches of his own day. For Albert identifying certain phenomena as magic was not about expanding the realm of the mysterious and unknowable, but quite the reverse—namely, keeping these phenomena and their causes within the sphere of the natural. They were, as it were, knowable unknowns.

Second, it is a history of how that disenchanting approach to natural phenomena inspired responses that in turn enchanted and reenchanted Albert and his thought. We see this in the tendentious appeals to Albert's legacy as an endorsement for kinds of magical arts that the *doctor universalis* would have neither recognized as magic nor approved of. Critical interpretations followed as well, sometimes analyzing what Albert himself had written, sometimes critiquing what others had written about or ascribed to Albert, and then turning to other matters altogether. Responses of this latter sort constituted a kind of disenchantment, however unevenly, until discussion of Albert's magic passed across the threshold of 1800. Then, a scholarly interest in ascertaining his contribution to and place in a history of natural sciences managed to displace interest in his magic qua magic. What lingered as a reputation for magic thereafter no longer had to do with what he had actually written or done, or even what his contemporaries thought he had done. At long last, the Albert who had worked as a natural philosopher to disenchant the cosmos but who ended up himself enchanted, was disenchanted and recognized as a master of natural knowledge, which is what he had, in fact, aspired to all along.

1

ALBERT'S MAGIC

A passage from Albert's commentary on Aristotle's *De anima* draws attention to the friar's experience with magic. The passage is located within an extended reflection on the movement of souls. While movement in this philosophical context could refer to many kinds of change, in this passage Albert was concerned with locomotion and the question of how an incorporeal entity can itself move or be the agent of movement.[1] After considering an argument against souls' movement,[2] Albert remarked that an alternative opinion—that "incorporeal entities such as angels and demons, as the ancients called gods, and souls separated from bodies move from place to place"—had also been articulated. He attributed this position to ancient figures—the Athenian philosopher Socrates and the mythical Greco-Egyptian sage Hermes Trismegistus—as well as to "diviners and spell-casters in the present day." He then affirmed, "We ourselves have verified the truth of this with the magical arts" (fig. 2).[3]

The confession startles. A formidable, learned tradition in the ancient and medieval worlds held magic in contempt. Augustine of Hippo (354–430) had laid the foundation for its denigrated status in Western Christian circles of learning and power centuries before Albert: humans succeed at magical operations always and only in concert with malign spirits.[4] Closer to Albert's own day, Hugh of Saint Victor (1096–1141) condemned magic for masking itself as learning: "Magic is not part of philosophy but stands outside it, professing falsehoods. It is the mistress of all iniquity and evil, lying about the truth and truly injuring souls."[5] This tradition situates Albert at the heart of a paradox. On the one hand, Albert's acknowledgment suggests not only a personal skill in magic—which ample documentation indicates many medieval churchmen studied and practiced, at times openly—but also his reliance on magic in determining contested philosophical points. On the other hand, Albert's unimpeachable orthodoxy and moral integrity precludes his practice of magical arts.

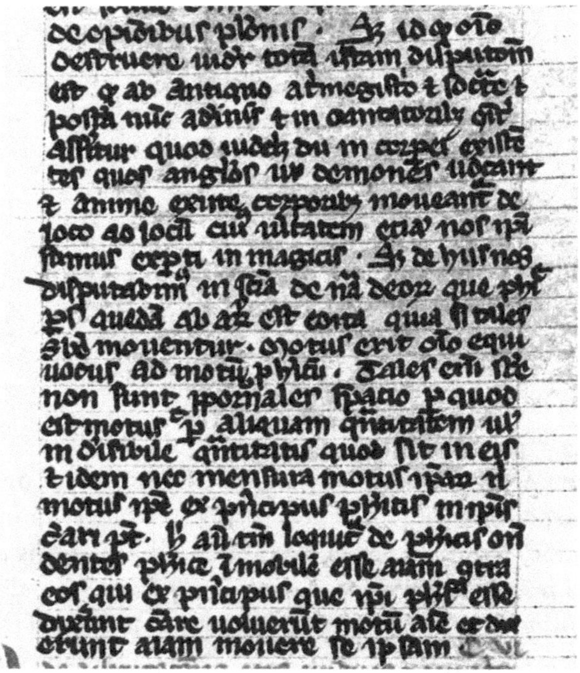

Fig. 2. Albert the Great, *De anima*, 1.2.6. Munich, Bayerische Staatsbibliothek, clm 317, fol. 7r (detail). Taken from a thirteenth-century manuscript of Albert's *De anima*, this detail includes Albert's acknowledgment of relying on magical arts to verify the motion of incorporeal entities.

What could this trailblazing philosopher, revered theologian, and trusted churchman have meant by testifying to the truth of a philosophical claim with reference to magic?

Unfortunately for both medieval and modern readers, Albert elaborated neither here nor elsewhere in the commentary. Moreover, he did not compose a treatise explicitly on magic, and there is no other frank acknowledgment of his use of magic to resolve a philosophical dispute. This does not mean, however, that Albert had nothing else to say about magic. References to magical arts can be found throughout Albert's corpus. Expanding the catchwords to include related terms—*nigromancy* and *divination*, for example—and specific practices—*suffumigation* (uses of incense) and *spell-casting*, for example—increases the amount of material pertaining to magic in his writing.[6] In the face of this diffuse abundance, many scholars have focused on particular subthemes in single treatises or across a select set of related ones. Albert's *De mineralibus* (On minerals) has garnered the most attention in this regard because of the open stance

Albert took toward talismans and the so-called science of images[7] and for the treatise's contribution to theories of alchemy.[8] Astral influences and divination often intersected with the healing arts, modern scholarship into which has less often looked at Albert alone than included consideration of him in comprehensive works.[9] Albert proposed ways of understanding how "fascination" worked, the capacity of one person to impede the actions of another by force of will and popularly known as the evil eye,[10] and authoritatively cited Hermes Trismegistus as a figure representative of ancient and magical learning across multiple works.[11]

Whether Albert had a comprehensive stance on magic is a question of a higher order. Popular assessments consider the possibility favorably, but they draw into their fields of view many writings on magic that have been misascribed to Albert and fables with tenuous links to Albert's biography.[12] Serious scholarship has responded ambivalently. The historian of medieval science Lynn Thorndike discouraged pursuit of the question in his magisterial *A History of Magic and Experimental Science*,[13] and the historian of medieval philosophy Alain de Libera has argued, "It must be said in the strongest possible terms: Albert's work has nothing to do with magic."[14] In contrast, Henryk Anzulewicz, a senior scholar at the Albertus-Magnus-Institut, developed a working definition of magic from Albert's writings: "the knowledge of the forces at work in nature as the tool of supralunary intelligence, and the art of manipulating them."[15]

The studies allowing for Albert's sympathetic treatment of magical arts offer evidence that Albert took a naturalizing approach to kinds of knowledge and practice understood in his day as magical. Calling his approach naturalizing foregrounds his efforts to explain magic—whether as theory, practice, or phenomenon—as comprehensively as possible according to principles of natural philosophy and without appeal to divine, supernatural, or miraculous forces. Magic thereby encompasses properties and changes that, on the one hand, were in his own day judged natural but, on the other, not explainable via the accepted, ordinary rules of the natural sciences. Albert's contemporaries varied in their own judgments of when to appeal to magic as a reasonable explanation. Albert worked to keep his explanations as congruent as possible with the general rules governing nature as it followed its common course. In identifying phenomena as magical, Albert was not suggesting anything necessarily superstitious, immoral, diabolical, or even miraculous about it.[16] Rather magic, as Albert most commonly addressed it, denotes a knowledge of celestial influences on the properties of objects in the sublunar (i.e., terrestrial and human) world and the application of that knowledge by human agents to their advantage.

At the same time, Albert condemned many practices and desires for knowledge that fall under the rubric of magic. He rejected activities in which demonic cooperation is necessary or invited and which human concupiscence makes attractive. While his use of the term *nigromancy* was ambiguous, he denounced it unequivocally when its referent included rituals and demons.[17] When he rejected activities as magical, he was taking the term as used by others, such as Augustine and Peter Lombard (1096–1160). This is the case, for example, when, in his commentary on Peter's *Four Books of Sentences*, he turned to a question about magical powers and denounced as apostasy any appeal for aid from demons with rituals incorporating "invocations, conjurations, sacrifices, suffumigations, and adorations."[18] Albert expounded on such problems more extensively, it should be noted, in his theological writings than in his philosophical ones, the previous example being a case in point.

To elaborate Albert's perspective on magic, this chapter takes its structure from components of his acknowledgment in the *De anima*. This particular affirmation offers a prompt, as it were, to examine references to magic in all its forms across his writings, and our close reading of them draws into relief the distinctiveness of Albert's understanding of *magica* in comparison to the tradition following Augustine. Three aspects of the *De anima* passage are taken as broadly indicative: first, for the attention it draws to incorporeal entities and their influences on the terrestrial and human world; second, for the kind of cognitive success he denoted with the expression "aliquid in magicis experiri" (to verify something with magic); and third, for the kinds of magical expertise he appraised and the ways he did so.

It bears reiterating a caution already touched on in the introduction: Albert used neither the Latin word for magic (*magia*) nor the expression *natural magic* (*ars magica naturalis*) as coined by William of Auvergne. Albert's preferred term, *magica*, was also not his own. Augustine applied it to divinatory practices, certain healing practices, and astrology. While Augustine condemned comprehensively all of what he called *magica*, Albert did not. Albert was not the only one to use such words differently from Augustine, and later writers used such expressions in distinctive ways. Such shifting usages in the medieval and early modern periods require that an eye be kept peeled for key moments when the expressions have unexpected referents or when phenomena one anticipates would be called magical were not. Practices commonly regarded as magic in Albert's own day included the ritual summoning of spirits; the exploitation of natural forces identified in symbolic terms (e.g., sympathy and contagion as explained by James G. Frazer); and the direct, expressed willing of external effects into being without external mediation.[19] Albert treated all three practices as possible, and he addressed dimensions of them, in some respects to reject them, in others to provide naturalizing explanations for them. He did not regard all of them as properly magical. Attentively allowing for magic's changing and equivocal meanings is essential to assessing what Albert himself thought about magic as well as what later generations made of Albert's thought. Certain kinds of knowledge that many thirteenth-century thinkers excluded from the realm of the magical were what later generations considered—sometimes favorably, sometimes lamentingly—constitutive of it. These differences over time made Albert look sometimes more, sometimes less like a magician than he had looked in his own day. For example, though neither Albert nor his contemporaries regarded alchemy as a form of magic, by the fifteenth century, alchemical writings ascribed to Albert threatened his reputation as a serious and moral scholar. Aspects of his astronomy were judged similarly. Pointing out these activities in this chapter further defines Albert's perspective on magic and establishes a baseline to help evaluate his legacy as a magician and his treatment as such, even when, or especially when, the retrospection distorted what Albert had actually held and written.

Gods and Souls, Spheres and Forms

For Albert, the 1250s was a decade of sustained and fertile thinking about the natural world. By the time he turned to the *De anima*, he had already composed several substantial commentaries on other writings of Aristotle. These included commentaries on central works of natural philosophy, such as the *Physica* (Physics) (1251–52), *De generatione et corruptione* (On generation and corruption) (1251–54), and *De caelo et mundo* (On the heavens and the earth) (1251–54). At roughly the same time as his *De anima*, he composed commentaries on what became known as the *Parva naturalia* (Short treatises on nature) (1256), a collection of Aristotelian writings on body and soul linked to themes of the *De anima*, as well as three encyclopedic works on natural objects. Study of the natural world belonged to the philosophical discipline "natural philosophy." Albert, like many others, also wrote on the "natural sciences" and "physics," both concerned with being in motion. For Aristotle, the soul (*anima*) was the principle of animation. In this sense "soul," too, had to do with the workings of the natural world and was decisive to the subdiscipline of natural philosophy that attended to living being in motion. Albert's aim was to make the soul, and indeed all created immaterial entities, objects proper to philosophical reflection.[20]

While Albert tended to follow the Aristotelian text closely in his commentaries, he made a digression, identified as such, in an early section of the *De anima* to expand on Aristotle's review of older philosophical opinions about the soul. In it he laid out an understanding of the kinds of movement that exclude the possibility of the soul's physical motion. Then he turned to a contrary opinion, which he attributed to ancient Hermes and Socrates as well as the diviners and spell-casters of his own day: that incorporeal beings, known variously as gods, angels, demons, and the souls of the dead, move "from place to place."[21] Albert varied in his commentaries between representing the positions of others and claiming them as his own. Here he suggested that such movement was not explicable with the usual principles of Aristotelian movement but could be with magical theory and that he had tested it successfully in that latter manner. He did not explain what he had actually engaged in; his words could encompass something as banal as working with a magnet or as scandalous as a summoning a spirit. He himself must have realized how remarkable this statement was because he promised he would return to the topic of such movement elsewhere in conjunction with "knowledge regarding the nature of gods."[22] It is not clear whether he is here referring to a planned work of his own or to another specific treatise on which he planned a commentary. He used the same expression—regarding the nature of the gods—elsewhere, for example, to designate Hermes's *Asclepius*[23] and a particular work of Cicero's.[24] The further reference to Aristotle's "first philosophy"[25] links the problem to metaphysics—that is, the study of being itself, a subdiscipline of philosophy that Aristotle sometimes also called theology, sometimes simply wisdom.[26] Albert completed his commentary, the *Metaphysica*, around 1264, but without returning in it to questions of magic and the movement of incorporeal beings.[27]

It would thus seem that a problem of physics brought Albert to a point where magic offered a mode of knowing that rendered an answer accessible to him. The gods and their movement are challenging to understand in several respects. In the tradition of ancient belief that the scholastics inherited, the gods have theological implications as the objects of pagan worship and philosophical implications as the movers of the celestial bodies. In his *Super Ethica*, written circa 1262, Albert explained his understanding of this very difference: the gods must be understood in two senses, according to theology as angels and saints, and according to philosophy as intelligences (also called separated substances and incorporeal entities), effecting the movement of celestial bodies.[28] His treatment varied accordingly in his writings. While in his philosophical works the gods are incorporeal beings that have a part in the operations of the cosmos, in his theological works Albert addressed "gods" as the object of false worship.[29] From Albert's point of view, the intersection of the two conceptions of "gods" in ancient thought was a serious intellectual mistake, and in his *De caelo et mundo* he even mockingly cast an image of gods bumping into one another as they pushed around multiple spheres in multiple universes.[30] But not all ancient thinkers conflated the two ideas: with no reference to the mythical pantheon, Aristotle had proposed that each celestial sphere had an immaterial intelligence that was external, separate, and distinct from it. Albert christianized this idea by explaining the celestial intelligences responsible for such movements as instruments of the one unmoved mover—that is, the one, true God of Christian faith.[31] While the human soul gives form, perfection, and purpose to the body that it enlivens as well as possesses its own understanding and will,[32] by Albert's reckoning celestial intelligences do not possess body or will. Albert's promise of later elaboration on gods' movement in a work of metaphysics underscores the philosophical concerns of the passage. The magic he explained himself to have relied on thus sheds light on the philosophical issues pertaining to the gods of celestial movement, rather than theological ones pertaining to the gods of false belief.

While Albert never realized plans to compose a *De natura deorum*, his passing reference to the gods and demons of ancient philosophy and his treatment of separated substances (incorporeal entities) in the *De anima* could not have but drawn the medieval reader's attention to the issue of celestial spheres, their movement, and the influence of their movements on the sublunar world. The general premise—that the celestial region influences the terrestrial and the human—could not have been more self-evident to Albert and his scholarly contemporaries. Given that he raised these issues with recourse to the magical arts, the questions emerge, What are the influences of celestial movement on the sublunar world, and how does Albert's understanding of them divide between influences that could be explained in ordinary cosmological terms and influences that required reference to the magical arts? Albert accepted that celestial movements influence growth and decay in the sublunar world. While ancient and medieval philosophers argued over how such influence worked, the basics are intuitive. The sun is, for example, the celestial body whose influence would be the most obvious to these thinkers, as it is to us, its effects being at the heart of their conceptions of life and growth, and diminishment and death, or as commonly summarized in ancient and medieval philosophical literature "generation and corruption" in nature. The sun's instrumentality (like that of other celestial bodies) is threefold: it is effected through motion, light, and influence.[33] When Albert discussed "influence," he meant a power that works like light but is imperceptible and which reaches places light cannot, for example, to the seed sprouting underground. Ultimately, Albert argued, celestial forces instigate all generation and corruption in the sublunar world. Here marks the logical starting point of astrology, understood as the prediction of the effects of the motion of celestial objects.[34]

Medieval philosophers generally analyzed terrestrial objects according to properties yielded by a mixture of the properties—heat and cold, and dryness and moisture—that characterized them. Celestial influences could change the balance of these properties, as for example the sun's capacity to remove moisture from a grape, turning it into a raisin. In this example, the causes of the change and the changing properties themselves are, according to the reigning theory of elements, "manifest." Some objects have properties that cannot be accounted for in this way, properties that often vary in their detectability by time and place. Scholastic philosophers regarded such causes and changing properties as occult (hidden) rather than manifest. Since every motion in the lower world is accordingly linked to movement in the upper world, occult properties and change necessarily correlate to movements of the celestial spheres and their intelligences.[35] Drawing on the Neoplatonic work of Avicenna (980–1037), one of the Muslim world's most influential philosophers on the Latin West, scholastics such as Albert concluded that the celestial spheres emanate "special forms" that could be received by terrestrial objects, thereby activating their occult properties.[36] Such emanation is natural to the extent that it occurs in the created world, but it is other than ordinary insofar as the accepted principles of medieval physics could not account for the results.

Albert remarked in his *Physica* that the celestial movements are "not from nature but from intelligence."[37] These celestial movements are precise, regular, and constant, and their influence on Earth—summoning it to greater perfection—is fitting: it is in the nature of superior entities, such as the celestial bodies, to influence inferior entities, such as the objects on earth.[38] At the same time, predicting the workings of these celestial influences falls short of certainty: the celestial spheres and the terrestrial objects move relative to one another and at a distortingly far distance. In the end the one who tries to understand, calculate, and anticipate such effects cannot attain the precision and attendant certainty that constitute the more rigorous standards of a natural science.[39] Albert's assessment made the magical arts a legitimate mode of understanding the natural world, but a speculative and imprecise one.

Aliquid (in magicis) experiri

The next phrase in Albert's acknowledgment inviting scrutiny is "experti sumus," translated here, "we have verified."[40] In classical Latin the verb *experior* could mean "to test," "to experience," or "to endure." The substantives *experimentum* and *experientia* derive from *experior*. In medieval Latin these substantives could connote "experience" and "test." These words appear (in various grammatical forms) throughout Albert's works, and especially in philosophical writings, suggest a firsthand familiarity with the experience or test[41] that in most instances complemented, validated, or reinforced what Albert had already asserted with reference to established authorities.[42] In short, Albert used *experiri* to intimate the confirmation of knowledge through sense experience.[43]

Albert placed "truth" (*veritas*) as the direct object of *experiri* only twice: in the *De anima* passage on magic and in his consideration of the interpretation of dreams in *De somno et vigilia* (On sleep and sleeplessness).[44] Albert more frequently put specific characteristics of natural objects and phenomena as the object of the verification. Examples include the effects of planetary coldness on plants in the *Meteora*,[45] successful techniques of grafting in *De vegetabilibus*,[46] and the reactions of fish to the odor of sulfur in *De animalibus*.[47] He used "videre" (to see) in a similar way in his *De mineralibus* to indicate having "learned with [his] own eyes."[48] Although a modern experiment involving the testing of hypotheses according to the scientific method is not what Albert had in mind, he used *experiri* to indicate lessons gained from arranged testing. For example, in explaining the hardness of a woodpecker's beak in *De animalibus*, he explained, "We have verified this often by using an almond to block a hole the woodpecker had made. It then returned and pierced it while we were watching."[49] *Experiri* had bearing on cognitive success beyond the strict limits of physics: in a passage on alchemy, for example, he called upon *experti*, who could verify for him from their own experience something he could not: "I have learned for certain from men experienced in these matters that [these metals] are frequently found distinct from the substance of the stone, just as grains of gold are found in sands."[50]

Albert also distinguished for his readers conclusions supported by firsthand sense experience from those reached abstractly with logic and the application of laws and principles to circumstances. He used *probare* to indicate either mode of conclusion. Sometimes he ascertained the properties of, say, plants with experiments (see below). In another instance he offered the capacity to be "proved" (*probare*) as the standard physics meets but the magical and necromantic sciences miss: "These things cannot be proved by physical principles, but it is necessary to know the sciences of astrology and magic and the necromantic sciences" to explain them.[51]

Beyond his use of a particular vocabulary, *experiri* was also foundational to a strategy of verification. As he explained in the early chapters of *De vegetabilibus*, "to consider well and meticulously what has been said, it is necessary to make conjectures and tests (*experimenta*) so that we understand the nature of trees per se . . . and similarly small plants, vegetables, bushes, and mushrooms. . . . We inspect what the ancient experts (*experti*) have written, in order to take in correctly what they have said. For by ourselves we could scarcely or never verify (*experiri*) all these things well."[52] Experiments, he explained, are particularly suited to verifying the properties of plants. "Some of what we assert we have ourselves verified (*probavimus*) by tests (*experimento*), and some we report from what others have said. But it is not easy to make such claims unless they have been verified with tests (*probata per experimentum*). Where, regarding particular natures, syllogism fails, experiment alone can confirm."[53] Anticipating the weakness of results achieved inductively through experiments, he underscored repetition and variation as ways of strengthening experimentally won conclusions. "Much time is required to verify what has been tested, so that one is not mistaken in any way. As Hippocrates put it, 'Life is short; art, lasting; experiment, fallible; and judgment, difficult.' It is therefore important to verify an experiment not just in one way but according to all circumstances, and so at the outset a work will be certain and correct."[54] Albert also admitted what he could not verify by experiment and experiences: In recording the unusual claims of Hermes about the effects of fertilizing roses and other plants with human blood, Albert qualified his report with the admission he had "not verified this with a test."[55] In another case, he distanced himself with the expression "they say" from a claim regarding the magical use of lodestone to detect a wife's infidelity.[56] In short, Albert used *experiri* to describe something he had done himself or had watched others do; he did not use the word *experiri* to indicate what he had read elsewhere.

Albert produced three treatises in the mid-1250s on kinds of natural objects, the *De mineralibus* (1254–57) on metals and minerals, the *De vegetabilibus* (1256), and the *De animalibus* (1258–62/63). These volumes cataloged the relevant objects with descriptions of their properties taken from authoritative older works. He sometimes expanded and verified these descriptions on his own, and he indicated as such those properties accessible through the magical arts. Volumes from the *corpus aristotelicum* inspired the latter two works, even as he incorporated many other works into his treatises as well. However, he found little in the Peripatetic tradition for his treatise on minerals: at the beginning of the *De mineralibus* he expressed regret that he had only selections of Aristotle's writings on minerals to work with, and what insights he found in Avicenna he judged unsatisfactory.[57] Still, he had no shortage of thinkers to rely on, Hermes most approvingly. And in compiling his alphabetic list of individual minerals and describing them, he drew from the well-known and highly regarded works of Marbod of Rennes, Arnold of Saxony, Bartholomew of England, and his own student Thomas of Cantimpré.[58]

Of all Albert's works, the *De mineralibus* is closest to being a manual on the magical arts. It belongs to a genre—the lapidary—with roots in Near Eastern antiquity and that became popular in the thirteenth-century Latin West as scholars tried with new energy to determine the distinguishing properties of everything in the natural world.[59] The *De mineralibus* took principles related to the change through celestial bodies, movements, and influences as developed in *Physica, De caelo et mundo, De causis proprietatibus elementorum*, and *De generatione et corruptione* (as sketched above), and applied them to metals and minerals. Thus, "the first principle in this science is that everything which comes to be by nature or art is moved at first by celestial powers."[60] The boundaries separating medieval understandings of astronomy, astrology, and the magical arts are murky: on the one hand, the three areas of knowledge were related; on the other, what they constituted differed from thinker to thinker and changed over time.[61] Albert was not unique in the connections he made between supralunary movement and sublunary change. This relationship explained how extraordinary properties could be taken full advantage of by those with magical knowledge. The making of talismans was such a skill. Experts inscribed images into suitable gems at opportune times to aid in the capture of celestial influences, the imposition of special forms, and the activation of hidden properties. In *De mineralibus* Albert spelled out that knowing about images was a science and how to use images in making talismans was an art, both being ancient and natural: "Therefore also in considering the craft of making gems and metallic images in the likeness of the stars, the first teachers and professors of natural knowledge recommended that the carving be done at duly observed times, when the heavenly force is thought to influence the image most strongly, as for instance when many heavenly powers combine in it. And they worked wonders by means of such images."[62] As celestial movements were a decisively influential variable in the making of effective talismans as well as effecting other kinds of magic, knowing astronomy and its corresponding mathematics was essential to magical expertise. As far as Albert was concerned, the knowledge and the craft were still natural and rational, and thus also wholesome.

Albert turned from the general to the specific when he remarked, using *nigromancy* in the sense of *secundum physicam*, "the nigromancy of images and seals" is "good doctrine," albeit a knowledge mastered by few. His Dominican confreres, he reported, were expecting more on the topic from him. The crafting of talismans required understanding in "astrology, magic, and the sciences of nigromancy."[63] Magi preserved and cultivated this knowledge among their sciences, and Albert named Magor the Greek, Germa the Babylonian, Hermes, Ptolemy, Geber of Spain, and Tebith as authorities.[64] By common reckoning in the thirteenth century, the right stone, marked at the right time and in the right way, with the right sign, could harness celestial powers and activate hidden properties. Based on authoritative writings, he explained what powers gems, as engraved, could have. For example: "Near the North Pole [Polaris] in heaven there are pictured two Bears [the constellations Ursa major and Ursa minor], and between them is placed a twisting Dragon [Draco]. And if this is engraved upon a stone that gives wisdom and skill, it will increase cunning and adroitness and bravery."[65]

Albert's dispassionate acceptance of talismans' operations follows from his framework of celestial causation. Thus their crafting and use could be judged not simply morally neutral but also as a form of artistic creation and application. They represent the capturing of celestial influences whose best end is the drawing of any person or thing to its true end: "The starting point of this science is that everything whatsoever, whether made by nature or by art, receive its first movement from celestial powers. In nature there is no doubt of this. In art it is also the case, because the human heart must be stirred, in the right way and not before, into making something. And this can only be by a celestial power."[66] As the art thus derives from nature, the figures as inscribed in the talismans are echoes of what is first generated by the celestial bodies: "What is first in kind and order pours its causal ability into everything that follows in a way proper to each."[67] He continued, "It is necessary to conclude from this that if a figure is impressed upon matter by nature or by art and with heed to the heavenly configuration, some force of that configuration is poured into that work of nature or of art. Hence wise Ptolemy proposes that heed be given to the celestial configurations in undertaking all actions, comings and goings, and even dressing and undressing."[68]

That heavenly powers have effect through the arts, even the magical arts, as in nature calls to mind Albert's distinctive axiom that "the work of nature is a work of intelligence" (*opus naturae est opus intelligentiae*). He included the phrase in whole or in part several times in De mineralibus.[69] Anzulewicz, in his study of magic in Albert's writing, proposes that this precept be taken in conjunction with one from Aristotle's *Physics* that "art imitates nature in its operations." Together they provide a framework in which to understand Albert's naturalizing disposition toward the magical arts. Magic constitutes a legitimate means of participating in cosmic dynamics. The magician's very inspiration to perform magic belongs to the natural order, and the magician's crafts are as natural as any force of generation and corruption, and change and movement, shaping the created world.[70]

Albert's perspective on the "good doctrine" of talismans and his use of the term *nigromancy* in Gundissalinus's sense distinguish him from the anonymous author of the *Speculum astronomiae* (here identified as the Magister Speculi) and even more so from Thomas Aquinas. The Magister Speculi offered an overview of works of astronomy and astrology in thirteenth-century circulation and distinguished between licit and illicit practices as well as between properly scientific works and works of magic.[71] The Magister drew distinctions between three kinds of talismans, two of which he condemned as nigromantic and the third he called the "imago astronomica." Aquinas accepted the naturalness of talismanic powers but rejected the possibility of their crafting or use without demonic assistance. By his lights, talismans were unavoidably nefarious.[72]

As for the properties of stones Albert described in his *De mineralibus*, why he designated some stones as magical is not always clear. In this respect, his description of the magical usefulness of *lippares* is illustrative. In ordinary circumstances, he reported having heard, any wild animal that runs to it will remain hidden and protected from pursuing hunters and their dogs. "If true, this is quite marvelous," he remarked, explaining that this property "is without a doubt to be accredited to celestial power."[73] Lippares exemplified, by Albert reckoning, an insight into the naturalness of magic that he ascribed to Hermes, namely, "that there are wondrous powers in stones, in plants as well, powers by means of which one would be able naturally to achieve whatever one does by means of magical sciences, if these powers are well understood."[74] Other passages distinguish ordinary from magical properties more clearly, even if the distinction is not explained. In ordinary circumstances, for example, *jaspis* has coagulant and contraceptive effects; in the hands of magicians reciting incantations, it also dispels fevers and dropsy.[75] Lodestone (*magnes*), in ordinary circumstances, attracts iron and even transfers its power to iron so that the iron becomes attractive as well. But when used with spells and signs "according to the teachings of magic," it can cause hallucinations.[76] Emeralds, in ordinary circumstances, incline a wearer to chastity, increase wealth, confer eloquence, and cure epilepsy. They are also good for divination, and thus are "sought after by magicians."[77]

Other writings extend Albert's naturalizing approach to the magical properties of plants and animals. *De vegetabilibus* and *De animalibus* included encyclopedic sections that follow the model of *De mineralibus* in distinguishing between ordinary and magical properties. Composed after *De mineralibus*, both rely on the earlier work's theoretical reflections and do not much expand on them. In *De vegetabilibus* (1256) he underscored the basic physical and metaphysical principles behind magical properties: the uncommon effects worked with particular plants and stones were due to properties imparted through the separated substances (the intelligences) associated with celestial bodies and movements as well as the consequent special forms; this knowledge and its application were the métier of the magician.[78]

The *De vegetabilibus* is Albert's commentary on *De plantis*, a work likely by the first-century BCE Jewish philosopher Nicolaus of Damascus and misascribed in the Middle Ages to Aristotle by both Muslim and Christian scholars.[79] Albert completed the commentary in 1256, after the *De anima* and the *De mineralibus* and two years before the *De animalibus*. The commentary is expansive and includes a loose paraphrase of Nicolaus's text, definitions of key concepts, and digressions in which Albert developed his own positions. The work, comprising seven books, is an invaluable repository of medieval botanical knowledge. The first and fourth books follow the *De plantis* most closely. Albert called the second, third, and fourth books his own digressions. Books 6 and 7 he devoted to special and applied botany and drew on works beyond the *De plantis*, such as Avicenna's *Canon of Medicine* and Matthaeus Platearius's *Book of Simple Medicines*.[80] Albert referred to his own experience—*aliquid experiri*—throughout to affirm claims he made about plant life. Such verifications pertained to changes in the growth of plants—for example, the transition of a tree from "tender grass" to "great tree"[81]—the effects of grafting peach branches on to the trunk of a plum tree,[82] the effects (some good, some bad) of different fertilizers under grape vines,[83] and the effects of timing, with the obvious allusion to celestial influences, on gardens, wheats, and grasses as they are planted and harvested.[84] These changes are natural and are effected by celestial powers in unremarkable ways, as he explained in early sections of the commentary.[85] Other powers of plants require magic to take effect, or rather, it is magicians, working out of their own expertise, who have determined the real and natural but also hidden powers of plants. "Those who apply themselves to magic," he explained, have determined that the grass of the bee-eater can open closed locks,[86] and that figs can tame ferocious bulls.[87] Many magical vegetal properties concern libido, conception and contraception, and childbirth: the seed of the willow, drunk in a liqueur, extinguishes libido and makes women infertile,[88] and the mature, acidic root of a pear tree, if held above a woman, can either impede conception or ease childbirth, as required.[89] Sticklewort, which Albert identified for its coldness and dryness, "has many uses in medicine and magic, especially against wounds, and ulcers";[90] and the ashes of the same pear tree whose root eases childbirth can be used topically to cure infections on the skin.[91]

Albert singled out incantatory uses of plants for attention. He noted, for example, that certain kinds of incense are effective in conjuring the gods (*dii*) in conjunction with the right "characters, signs, and sacrifices."[92] In another instance, he remarked that a kind of hedgenettle, "with a flower of blue and long and somewhat broad leaves," is effective in divination when plucked to the "spells of Asclepius."[93] Those who apply themselves to "enchantment and physical ligatures" know how to use ebony at a cradle to protect an infant from nightmares.[94] Enchanters know how to make fighting staffs from the wood of the medlar tree,[95] and the juice of the poplar leaf has contraceptive powers.[96] Ceremony is, by Albert's reckoning, at the heart of the distinction between magic and necromancy (in the sense of diabolical magic). Magic allows one to deploy the fig to tame the wildest bull and to use pear root contraceptively. Nigromancy, in comparison, offers knowledge of which fragrant plants aid conjuring the louder spirits and how to gather such plants for most effective application. The enchanter would seem to align, at least in *De vegetabilibus*, more closely to the magician than the nigromancer. Regardless, Albert appears disinterested in his handling of these cases of nigromancy and incantation. He was writing, here and in all these natural philosophical treatises, not to condemn but to highlight plants as means to achieving certain effects. Albert's *magica* were ultimately natural and nondemonic.

Albert referred less to magic in his *De animalibus* than in his other two encyclopedic works. When he did, animals are more often magic's victims than its ingredients. Nonetheless, he noted, for example, a particular fish—the so-called ship-in-irons (*detinens navim*)—has the astonishing power to hinder a ship's movement, but could also be employed by magicians to inspire love or hate in the human heart.[97] Augurers are particularly keen, Albert reported, on the nuthatch, a bird whose call and flight lend themselves to meaningful decipherment.[98] Nigromancers also benefit from certain animal byproducts. In one of the stranger cases, he described the nigromancers' interest in the "hychomindez," a lump, frog-like in shape and manure-like in consistency, that is expelled from the wombs of possessed sows. Called the "animal of cleverness" in Greek and "harpa" in Latin, it was useful, so Albert claimed based on nigromancers' testimony, for controlling the minds of women.[99]

Aside from such single-entry animals, some animals with magical implications appear across several works. His treatment of the hoopoe is one such case. The bird had a venerable association with magic in ancient literature, especially sacred texts: Condemned in the Pentateuch as unclean,[100] the hoopoe converses intelligently with Solomon in the Quran.[101] Hoopoes also appear in Aristophanes's *The Birds* and Ovid's *Metamorphoses*, in both instances as Tereus of Thrace transformed. In the former he plays the part of a garrulous travel companion; in the latter, a violent autocrat.[102] These references catapulted the hoopoe into learned discourses of all sorts, religious and profane, across the medieval world. As these discourses intersected, outlines of the hoopoe as dirty, cunning, and occultish emerged. Albert's treatment of the bird cautiously blends this reputation into the zoological purpose of his writing. Thus Albert used the hoopoe as an example of general phenomena, such as distinctive feathers, especially at the head, in which respect he placed the hoopoe with the peacock.[103] Like the bat, it sleeps through the winter.[104] Like all nesting birds, it has customary practices for keeping eggs warm, and dung is its nest-insulant of choice, especially human dung as a prophylactic against poisons.[105] Magical associations are raised at two points: once in the *De mineralibus*, where Albert indicated that a particular mineral, *quiritia*, itself useful for magical purposes, is to be often found in the hoopoe's nest, and then noted that magicians and augurers value the bird as an aid to enchantment and divination.[106] The other passage is in *De animalibus*, where he confirmed that the blood of the hoopoe, spread on the temples of one sleeping, causes nightmares. He elaborated, "Enchanters search for the bird and its parts, especially its brain, tongue, and heart. Here, however, we will not turn our attention to this, for investigations into it are proper to a different science."[107]

Two areas of magic, as commonly understood and here not yet touched upon, are fascination and the diabolical. Albert addressed both, but not in exactly the same terms as the *magica* he predominantly investigated in the three encyclopedic treatises. Fascination, also sometimes called bewitchment or the evil eye, is the putative power of one person to interfere with the thought and actions of another by force of will. Ancient thinkers took feelings of envy or love to constitute simple forms of fascination and developed physical explanations that identified the cause of such feelings as small particles exuding from one person (the envied, the loved) to the other (the envious, the enamored). The physician Galen considered fascination in terms of imbalances in humors in both the perpetrator and the victim, and the Platonizing Christian thinkers of late antiquity added a demonic dimension in their search for causation.[108] Avicenna discussed fascination in terms of the human soul acting outside its body, an idea that was appropriated into thirteenth-century Latin Christian debates as suggesting that the human imagination could have power over a distance.[109] In many medieval treatises, the power of fascination encompassed any causation between animate beings at a distance, such as the poisoning effects of an electric ray and the clouding effect on a mirror of a menstruating woman's reflection. The lethal gaze of the basilisk and the power to drive "men and camels" into ditches and to emaciate flocks of sheep and cattle were likewise effects of the evil eye.[110]

Aristotle's rejection of influence at a distance made fascination a problem for scholastic thinkers. Albert agreed that fascination could certainly not be the soul's exiting the body and hindering another's action.[111] He proposed handling "imaginatio" equivocally as all the faculties of the soul[112] and focused on powers the body exercised on itself rather than on a distant body.[113] Albert did not engage the classic examples, such as the gaze of the basilisk or menstruating woman, but instead limited himself to the theoretical issue of how a person could have certain kinds of influence mentally over a distance. His solution focused on the fascinator more than the fascinated, and he associated the fascinator's talent with power gained at birth due to various celestial circumstances.[114] Albert ultimately regarded the fascinator less as a magician than as a philosopher, the result of a natural, even mechanistic, explanation of fascination that minimizes a soul's influences beyond the body to which it is united and implicitly rejects the idea of fascination having anything to do with supernatural or demonic intervention.[115]

Albert exhibited a different kind of concern for the devil and "diabolical magic." *Maleficium*, that is, witchcraft and sorcery, in contrast to the forms of magic with which most of this chapter has been concerned, is very much a matter of theological concern, and Albert's substantive treatments of it are in his earliest and his latest works, his commentary on the *Sentences* and his *Summa theologiae*. In the commentary he addressed maleficium through questions posed by Peter Lombard and in reference to the biblical episodes in which it appears. Albert's positions follow Peter Lombard's closely. In an article that rejects the use of maleficium to repel maleficium, for example, he used language whose sharpness—he called nigromancy (here used in the sense of demonic magic) a "noxious art" (*ars pestifera*)—has no parallel in his philosophical writings.[116] In discussing various healing arts, some of which seem to operate in the penumbra of superstition and diabolism, he unequivocally affirmed legitimate medicine as God's gift, having nothing in it to do with demons.[117] In short, Albert restricted his consideration of malign demons to his theological writing and even there his handling of them was sparse. He was scarcely concerned with the ritual magic that became in later centuries a matter of great concern, including to members of his own order, as we return to in subsequent chapters. He developed no notion of a pact with the devil even though others in this period did, including his student Aquinas, who discussed it recurrently and already with some subtlety, distinguishing, for example, tacit from express pacts with the devil that undergirded various forms of divination.[118]

Authorities and Practitioners

Albert's acknowledgment in *De anima* ascribes the opinion of incorporeal movement "from place to place" to four figures—two specific people and two kinds of magical practitioners—whose associations with the magical traditions of antiquity and the Latin West are substantial. Analysis of them sheds further light on Albert's stance on magic. The Athenian philosopher Socrates and the mythical Greco-Egyptian sage Hermes compose the first pair. Socrates has been best known through the philosophical dialogues of his student Plato, but few of the Platonic dialogues featuring Socrates were available in Latin in the thirteenth century.[119] The character of Socrates was known in the Middle Ages through other references. Albert's sources for what Socrates thought are the same Neoplatonic writings that influenced so much of his analysis of Aristotle. The writings of the Christian Neoplatonist Pseudo-Dionysius (ca. 500)[120] and the *Book of Causes*, which was an epitome of the thought of the pagan Neoplatonist Proclus (412–85) and was misascribed in Albert's day to Aristotle,[121] were among the works Albert read at Paris. He referred to the *Book of Causes* throughout his writing, and his authoritative commentaries on the Pseudo-Dionysian writings immediately preceded his turn to the Aristotelian corpus.

The thrice-great Hermes loomed large in the medieval scholarly imagination as a deeply learned philosopher and theologian and as the author of a body of writings, known as the *Hermetica*, that covered astrology, magic, medicine, and alchemy.[122] While Hermes was admired for his learning in the Middle Ages, he became more famous and controversial in the early modern period, especially as his biography and his authorship of the texts came into question. In Albert's day, however, the legendary person and his writings were taken at face value.[123] Much of the *Hermetica* was translated into Latin from Greek and Arabic in the twelfth century and was present in wide circulation within learned circles in the Latin West by the thirteenth century. The *Asclepius* was the single most important of the hermetical writings to Albert, as to so many scholastics, and he appealed to it when discussing divine nature, fate, human anthropology and psychology, and the intellect. Much of the *Hermetica* also promised to reveal nature's most hidden secrets and founded itself on the astrological correspondence of the heavens and the earth. Such writings made Hermes an important figure in the West's conversations about magic. Albert placed Hermes at the beginning of the history of philosophy and in a triumvirate of great ancient thinkers alongside Socrates and Plato. Albert's notion of celestial causality and his understanding of occult properties emerged in part from his engagement with the *Hermetica*. Albert's explicit treatment of the legendary figure concentrates more (and more favorably) in his philosophical than his theological writings.[124]

Complementing ancient endorsement of the movement of "incorporeal entities ... from place to place," Albert also linked the opinion to "diviners and spell-casters ... to the present day." The identification of diviners and spell-casters in this passage calls to mind rough outlines Albert sketched of magical practitioners in his biblical commentaries on the Gospel of Matthew and on the Book of Daniel, both written between 1264 and 1268 alongside many other biblical commentaries. In *Super Mattheum*, occasion for the outline is the story of the magi, where he grappled with the question whether the magi's understanding of the star of Bethlehem was licitly gained or demonically inspired.[125] He started with the theological opinion held since Christian antiquity that the magi were not sorcerers but legitimate astrologers.[126] He had touched on this issue briefly in his earlier commentaries on Pseudo-Dionysius, in which he wrote, "Magi are called greatly wise in astrology, because this science is about the greatest of matters."[127] Albert then took the opportunity to explain at some length what magi in general are and are not: "Indeed, magi, mathematicians, spell-casters, sorcerers (or nigromancers), soothsayers, augurers, and diviners are different from one another."[128] The mathematician, he continued, is of two sorts: one who studies "separation and abstraction" as is associated with the quadrivium,[129] and one who prophesies from the movement of celestial bodies.[130] The former practice is "praiseworthy rather than objectionable." The latter is "sometimes good and sometimes bad," depending on whether the prophecy was offered as necessary or probable and on the nature of the knowledge's occultness. Uncovering a maliciously placed poison would, for example, be useful and good, but predictions can also be the work of quacks, he reminded his readers, and such fraud deserves condemnation.[131] He then explained the caster of spells (*incantator*) as using animals, herbs, stones, and images to achieve extraordinary effects. The nigromancer divines from the dead or from demons. The augurer divines from birds; the haruspex, from the entrails of sacrificed birds and animals. Albert addressed four mantic arts together—geo-, pyro-, hydro-, and aeromantics. Over and above these, there are fortune tellers, both simple (*sortilegi*) and pythonic. None of these received revelation of the Christ Child; only the magi did, from which he concluded the goodness of their learning.

This passage in Albert's commentary is not the oldest such taxonomy of magical practitioners in the Latin West. The standard outline had been sketched six centuries earlier by Isidore of Seville in his encyclopedic work, *The Etymologies*. Between the two, Hugh of Saint Victor (ca. 1096–1141) offered an outline that followed Isidore's closely.[132] Albert's position on magic diverged from theirs at telling points: Albert, for example, did not follow Isidore's fundamental distinction between ceremonial magic and divination. Isidore's taxonomy encompasses a wider range of magician than Albert's. Albert drew no specific attention to the magicians of the Bible and classical literature, such as the Egyptian magicians, whom Moses battled, and Circe, the Greek goddess of magic. Isidore's explanations of the kinds of divination is fuller: he includes, for example, *harioli*, whose knowledge, Isidore described, comes from conjuring demons. Among astrologers, Isidore not only included *mathematici* and magi but also referred to *astrologi*, who read the stars, and *genethliaci*, who draft natal charts.

Albert and Isidore defined several kinds of magician differently. Isidore used "magi" as an umbrella term for all magicians and diviners, and he judged magi wicked by definition, even as he allowed for the goodness of the biblical wise men who followed the star to Bethlehem. The context of Albert's remarks may explain his narrower focus on the magi's wholesomeness. He was, after all, consciously trying to show how the gospel magi are not wicked in their learning or practices, as their appearance and role in the scriptures had to be justified. Isidore treated magi more generally and subsequent to their appearance in scriptures and placed them without hesitation into the category of magicians who do evil. He explained, "Magi are those who are popularly called evil-doers because of the magnitude of their crimes."[133] Later he touches on the discrepancy between the magi of the Bible and the magi in his taxonomy: "Now originally interpreters of the stars also used to be called magi, as we read of those who announced the birth of Christ in the Gospel; afterward they went only by the name *mathematici*. Knowledge of this art was permitted up to the time of the Gospel, so that after Christ had been born, no one ever again should interpret anyone's horoscope from heaven."[134] Albert's more benign treatment of magi in his biblical commentary follows from this historical, philosophical understanding of what magi know and practice.

Albert's other treatment of magi, in his *Super Danielem*, hews more closely to Isidore's. Magi have a different role in Daniel: rather than diviners of a great revelation, they are the foil against which the virtue of Daniel and his companions shine at a time when the Jews suffered under the rule of the Babylonian king Nebuchadnezzar II. Astrology itself, it should be noted, was not the problem. Albert explained it neutrally, as he had in Matthew 2, as "the learning and language of the Chaldeans." Daniel and his companions learn astrology and other occult forms of knowledge in Babylonian captivity. Their efforts earn God's favor, the scriptures record, and Daniel in particular is given "understanding of visions and dreams."[135] This power of discernment is put to the test when Nebuchadnezzar calls Daniel along with the royal "soothsayers, magi, sorcerers, and Chaldeans"[136] to interpret his dreams. Albert, in his *Super Danielem*, emphasized the wickedness of sorcerers, who make human sacrifices and use human blood for their divinations.[137] He distinguished between Daniel's virtuous learning and the magicians' wicked application of their learning. A similar distinction is maintained in his *Super Isaiam*, where destruction of wicked diviners, sorcerers, and soothsayers is promised as part of Israel's liberation.[138] Albert here harmonized philosophical insight and biblical commentary, as he affirmed that magi were primarily men of great learning, "like teachers, who philosophized on all matters," in particular astronomy and in such a wise manner that they were able "to uncover the future in the stars."[139]

Alchemists do not appear on either list of magical practitioners. Albert exhibited a sustained interest in alchemy, which he understood as the art of transmuting metals, throughout his career.[140] Aristotle had not written a treatise on alchemy, to Albert's expressed disappointment, but Albert found an endorsement of the practice in the *Meteorology* and Aristotelian principles that were relevant to it.[141] In his early theological works, such as the *Sentences* and the *Super Ethica*, he emphasized the limits of what could truly be changed through alchemical practices.[142] Quoting Avicenna in his *De mineralibus*, he rejected the alchemical possibility of complete transmutations of one substance to another, as he had in his commentary on the *Sentences*. He allowed, nonetheless, for more limited changes: "Let the practitioners of alchemy know that it is not possible to change the species of substances, but only to make something similar, for example, when they color a red metal with yellow so that it appears to be gold, or to whiten it until it be similar to silver or gold or whatever substance they want. I do not believe that anything else is possible, such as applying a different species to a substance by an ingenious means. What is not impossible is to remove accidental properties or to reduce a gap between them."[143] In this respect, the closer alchemy was to the acceptable, practical science of metallurgy, the better.[144]

In the final analysis, Albert regarded alchemy as something belonging neither to the natural sciences nor to the magical arts in the strictest senses. He explained, "The transmutation of these bodies and the change of one to another is not determined by physics but by the art called alchemy."[145] Like magical operations, alchemy suffered from an imprecision in experimental determinations that prevented its inclusion as a part of physics. Where he dealt with magical arts, such as *De mineralibus*, he wrote of alchemy as its own body of knowledge.[146] Albert thus stands with his high medieval colleagues who engaged the alchemical writings coming from the Muslim centers of learning without concern for mystical, spiritual, or diabolical underpinnings, such as became characteristic of concern over it in later centuries.[147] In consequence of such explicit openness to alchemy's possibilities, multiple pseudepigraphal volumes on alchemy appeared under his name, especially in the fifteenth century. On the one hand, the ascriptions reflected his genuine interest in the theory and practice of alchemy, and the works often drew heavily from Albert's own writing. On the other, often their contents incorporated ideas that were not Albert's but were colored by the mystical dimension that was so characteristic of Renaissance alchemy. In these later centuries, the pseudepigraphal volumes caused unease among scholars and churchmen who had their own new concerns about magic and demons in society.[148] These pseudepigraphal works, not always recognized as such, would influence Albert's reputation as a magician and reactions to it centuries later, which is a theme for later chapters.

By way of summary, the foregoing allows for five generalizations about Albert's magic that point to at least a partial teaching on magic. First, magic of the kind Albert devoted most attention to had to do with phenomena in the natural world. It encompassed a body of knowledge and a set of skills based on the ways that the celestial spheres were assumed to influence the sublunar world. The influence of the celestial spheres on the sublunar world is at the heart of his natural philosophy generally. What constituted the magical arts for Albert were a particular mode of celestial influence—the emanation of specific forms, the hiddenness of the properties that were thus activated, and the role of a human expert in linking celestial influence to hidden property. The magical arts accordingly verged on natural philosophy, but they were distinguished from it insofar as the phenomena could not be accounted for with reference to the mainstream theory of elements, and the operations themselves fell short of the standards of certainty and precision Albert demanded of the natural sciences.

Nonetheless, Albert regarded the magical arts as fundamentally natural in that their causes and effects were fully encompassed in the natural world, a world created by God and open to rational discovery. The magical arts are a form of participation in the divinely ordained workings of the natural world. Following from this confidence, if a phenomenon requires divine intervention to explain it, then it numbers among the miracles and is the object of theological reflection. The magical rather expresses an aspiration to perfection in the sublunar world such as is already found in the celestial world. Although Albert did not use the term *natural magic* and while his Neoplatonic notion of emanations and specific forms distinguished him from many contemporaries, Albert worked along lines similar to William of Auvergne in naturalizing his explanation of hidden properties and magical effects.

Second, the most unambiguous telltale of his naturalizing understanding of the magical arts is his recurrent use of the verb *experiri*. The word connotes the use of the senses in ascertaining facts about the natural world. He used it in the *De anima* to explain his learning of a particular truth that clarified the question of the movement of angels and demons. His use of *experiri* clearly indicates the sense experience of change in the natural world, whether pertaining to magical, hidden properties or ordinary, manifest ones. As Albert understood them, the magical and the (naturally) scientific further abut on not only metaphysical and cosmological grounds but also epistemological ones.

Third, Albert took a discrete and disaggregated approach to what some thinkers treated in aggregation. He did not take *magia* as a comprehensive term. Instead, he distinguished kinds of magic and their practitioners and evaluated them individually on their own terms. He laid these distinctions out in the taxonomies in his biblical commentaries and especially in his treatment of occult properties, which he deemed discoverable by the magical, nigromantic, and alchemical arts. All of these, by Albert's lights, were themselves natural, that is, constitutive of the created world. They were also all natural even though the corresponding bodies of knowledge lacked the rational certainty that would qualify them as part of natural philosophy. He made and appealed to the distinctions along these lines with a flexibility that suggests overlapping understandings of what was, in fact, strictly magical and what was narrowly philosophical.

Fourth, Albert distinguished between philosophical and theological approaches to magic. In the main, what he identified as magical arts (as well as alchemy and nigromancy) he scrutinized in his philosophical treatises, not his theological treatises. The principal questions he addressed in his philosophical treatises had to do with the effects of the magical arts and whether and how sense could be made of magical phenomena as natural. Practices that incorporate the ritual invocations of demons and other ceremonies also warrant philosophical reflection in as much as they effect change in the natural world and to the extent that their operation resembled the magical arts proper. Nonetheless, he restricted his extended reflections on their moral wickedness and their incompatibility with revealed truth, as well as condemnation of them, to his theological treatises. His most energetic condemnations of magic (in the overarching sense) appeared not in his own most original writings but rather where he reflected on older Christian authorities such as Augustine and Peter Lombard.

Fifth and finally, Albert's thought on magic is most remarkable for its "naturalizing" tendencies. These tendencies allowed him to acknowledge with calm confidence his own use of magic in resolving a controverted point of incorporeal physics, and they provide a contrast to the rich tradition of Augustine brought forward in the writings of, among others, his student Aquinas. It would be incorrect to suggest that Albert—or William of Auvergne or even Roger Bacon—rejected Augustine's stance on the diabolical. Albert regarded as self-evident real commerce between humans and demons that manipulated the workings of the natural world to nefarious ends, and he condemned such unequivocally. Nonetheless, Albert found amid the catalog of wondrous causes in the natural world an ever-larger portion that warranted rational, natural explanation. The irony, as we shall see, is that Albert's naturalizing tendencies—which we might also cautiously call disenchanting—laid the groundwork for an ever-more enchanted Albert during his life and posthumously. The story of that enchanted Albert, his rise and fall, is the subject of the remaining chapters.

2

THE MAGICAL ALBERT

Testimony to Albert's skill in magic appeared in his lifetime. Ulrich of Strasbourg, a Dominican friar, Albert's onetime student, and a respected scholar in his own right, enthused that his teacher was "a man, who was inspired in his grasp of all fields of knowledge and experienced in the magical arts."[1] The line appears in his *De summo bono* (On the highest good), a treatise on theology and philosophy, that Ulrich wrote while Albert was still alive. At this point in the treatise Ulrich was addressing the operations of angels and demons, their possible embodiment, and their interactions with humans, including the feasibility of demons' mating with humans. "Knowledge of this subject matter derives in great part from the magical arts."[2] In citing Albert, Ulrich not only expressed a student's enthusiasm for a respected teacher—"the wonder and miracle of our day"—but also insinuated that his position on the operations of angels and demons aligned with Albert's own.[3] Albert, however, was not reflecting on demons and angels as objects of moral or social concern in the *De anima*. Furthermore, he scarcely ever touched on the topic of succubi and incubi—that is, demons who feign sexual intercourse with human beings, commonly in dreams—and his lengthiest treatment of them is in a brief response to the matter as raised in Peter Lombard's *Sentences*.[4] In short, Albert's treatment of spiritual beings and the magical arts does not offer support for Ulrich's interest in demons, and it is hard to imagine that Ulrich did not realize that. Appeal to respected authorities is of course a common kind of argument, in our own day no less than in Ulrich's. But this passage puts Ulrich at the head of what became a long tradition of appealing to Albert to justify innovative, controversial, and unconventional ideas, especially ones having to do with magic, and even ones not consistent with Albert's own thought.

During his life and for about two centuries thereafter, affirmation of Albert's expertise in the magical arts took a variety of forms. First, authors of historical and biographical texts often commented on Albert's piety and learning with emphasis on his knowledge of the workings of nature, magical arts included. Although no full-length vita of Albert appeared until the fifteenth century, written details about his life accumulated in the meantime in histories of the Dominican order, usually in conjunction with the life of his most famous student, Thomas Aquinas. Three facts stand out about this body of writing. First, this literature sometimes includes reference to Albert's knowledge of the magical arts, with varying degrees of specificity and accuracy, but never in a bothered manner. Second, Albert was placed in the role of magician in a series of late medieval fables. These include, for example, moral tales that present his practice of magic as that which he renounced before becoming a holy friar and bishop. These legends associate Albert with magic in a variety of forms, sometimes demonic and sometimes in ways that Albert would scarcely have understood. Appearing in both Latin and vernacular texts, these fables straddled the lines that divided elite and common culture and suggest ways that elite concerns and interests could take popular form.

Finally, Albert became an authority in discussions about magic with reference both to scholarly works he had actually written and to a growing body of pseudepigrapha. Ulrich made his point, for example, with reference to the authentic *De anima*, and Albert's single most popular work, measured by the number of surviving manuscripts, its later use, and its quotation, was the *De mineralibus*. The latter contained Albert's most sustained commentary on magical arts, alchemy, nigromancy, and divination. The pseudepigrapha reinforced and extended Albert's authority on questions of magic. Indeed, one twentieth-century interpreter of Albert remarked that "works falsely bearing [Albert's] name ... achieved a far wider circulation and thus greater impact than the genuine ones,"[5] and most of those spurious works, but certainly not all, pertained to magic and related arts. These misascribed works must be handled here with care for a number of reasons: First, the determination of attribution across the pseudepigraphal works falls, as it fell, along a spectrum of certitude. On the one end, it is still possible today to find scholarly supporters, in addition to opponents, of Albert's authorship of the *Speculum astronomiae*.[6] On the other, there were works like the *Experimenta Alberti*, a book of spells, that could not be more fraudulent. Second, taken as a group, the pseudepigrapha appealed to a broad spectrum of readers; individual pieces each enjoyed their own readerly appeal. Third, to interpret them with an eye to understanding Albert's shifting reputation as a magician requires an appreciation of how magic itself was conceptually a moving target: magic did not mean the same thing to Albert, the composers of the pseudepigrapha, and the later readers of Albert and the pseudepigrapha. Thus a treatise understood as harmless or even quite erudite in one generation could be taken as diabolically inspired in another. Accordingly, the many alchemical texts that appeared falsely under Albert's name in the late Middle Ages are introduced and investigated in this chapter because later the defenders of Albert's reputation found alchemy a despicable, often diabolical activity despite that Albert himself, along with his Christian contemporaries and Arabic sources, had generally not regarded alchemy as a magical art in the strictest sense, let alone a diabolical practice.

The aim of this chapter is thus to sketch the emergence of Albert's reputation as a magician with reference to this complex set of writings. Sometimes the kernel of Albert's authentic thinking can be identified in these developing claims; sometimes the claims were quite contrived. Sometimes the magic associated with Albert was naturalizing and enhanced what can be identified in his genuine works; sometimes it was quite malign. Of central importance, however, is what we will not find—namely, that Albert fell into disrepute on account of these new assessments and writings.

Albert and Magic in Life-Writing and Fables

The earliest historical references to Albert tend to affirm his learning rather than to offer biographical detail. Early affirmations of his learning, usually in conjunction with his piety, can be found in writings by the Dominicans Gerard de Frachet (1195–1271), Thomas of Cantimpré (1200–1270), and Ulrich of Strasbourg; the Franciscans Bonaventure of Iseo (d. 1273) and Roger Bacon; and the unknown author of *On Ecclesiastical Writers*. Frachet offered scant introduction to Albert in *The Lives of the Brothers* (1255–60), an official collection of anecdotes intended to record the early history of the Dominican order for the sake of its new members. In it Albert is described simply as "excelling in natural philosophy" (*physica*).[7]

Thomas decorated these sparse biographical details with more affirmations of Albert's moral integrity. As a friar, Thomas studied under Albert in Cologne and afterward spent several years studying in Paris. His *Book of Bees* (1256–63) is one of two major works that stand as markers of Aristotle's growing influence on thirteenth-century natural and moral philosophies. Thomas referred to his teacher twice in *The Book of Bees*. In the first reference, he recounted Albert's dismissing a demon from his room with the sign of the cross. In the second, he introduced "Master Albert" as the learned occupant of a chair of theology and a man of deep prayer, advanced in knowledge, holy, and intact in virtue. The conjunction of learning and devotion, by Thomas's reasoning, explains Albert's easy rejection of the demon's blandishments.[8] Albert also appears in *The Book of Bees* as a narrator of stories that later readers retold with Albert cast not as the narrator but as the principal character. For example, Thomas reported Albert's telling the story of a person who first chose and then regretted taking three days in purgatory over one year of sickness.[9] By the fifteenth century, Albert's defenders denounced a rumor, derived from this tale, that Albert had requested from God a visit to purgatory so that he might understand it better and treat it more accurately in his writings.

Ulrich's enthusiastic appeal to Albert's magical expertise had an influence beyond what Ulrich could have imagined: "My teacher the Lord Albert, bishop of Regensburg, a man inspired in his grasp of all fields of knowledge—so that he is appropriately called a wonder and the astonishment of our time—and experienced in the magical arts, from which knowledge of this material greatly depends, holds opinions that diverge from all that precedes. He says for instance that the apparition of angels does not happen through the assumption of bodies but through the likeness of bodies, which they (angels) heap upon the bodily senses in the manner discussed above."[10] One hears Ulrich's enthusiasm for Albert especially in the expression "a wonder and astonishment of our time," a phrase that echoes a similar expression used for the emperor Frederick II (1194–250), whose learning was also admired.[11] The association of magic with knowledge about the limits of angelic bodiliness harkened to Albert's actual ideas and even to aspects of that problem as discussed in the *De anima*. Here in the passages that follow on human sexual commerce with demons Ulrich bypassed the sharp distinction Albert made between philosophical and theological approaches to angels and demons and ultimately treated at length a topic that Albert had not.[12]

The *Liber compostelle* was a late thirteenth-century alchemical encyclopedia that included references to Albert and the practice of magic. The author was likely the Franciscan Bonaventure of Iseo.[13] Unresolved manuscript variations put most of the *Liber*'s composition between 1256 and 1270, but parts of some manuscript texts appear to be composed as late as 1280, a dating that complicates authorship since Bonaventure's uncertain year of death is placed between 1273 and 1284.[14] There are two distinct presentations of Albert, and both of them would have been written in Albert's lifetime. In one, the author identified himself as "a close, personal friend of Friar Albert the German of the Order of Preachers," and referred to "the knowledge and experiences of the secret of secrets such as nigromancy, alchemy, et cetera" that they together collected.[15] The other, seemingly later variation, adds Thomas Aquinas to the list of the author's collaborators who with him investigated "the wisdom of wisdom." In this later version, the cooperative study of secrets is absent, but elsewhere the author clarified: "In those days, the friar Albert had permission from the pope, because of his reputation for holiness, intelligence, and prudence, to learn, examine, study, and test all the fields of knowledge, good and bad, to praise books of truth and condemn all books of falsity and error. Hence, he worked hard to complete the books begun by Aristotle and made new compilations of books in many fields of knowledge such as astrology, geomancy, nigromancy, precious gems, and experiments of alchemy."[16] Although the latter version of the *Liber* has a defensive tone unlike the former, the two versions correspond in their calm acceptance that Albert was skilled in magic and related fields of knowledge, which included alchemy, nigromancy, and other divinatory arts. The latter version elaborated in a way both apologetic and intellectually decisive that this work was done in conjunction with the larger project of understanding Aristotle, which suggests the philosophical underpinnings of the project. The results of Albert's studies, as described in this passage, have been taken to allude to the *Speculum astronomiae*. Furthermore, Albert's engagement with this work, even to the extent it brought him in contact with wicked and false books, was itself praiseworthy. In this respect, Bonaventure's references to Albert's magic were consonant with both Ulrich's and Thomas's.

A more critical assessment, albeit not quite touching on magic, can be found in an entry on Albert in a collection of "lives of illustrious men." The author, long but incorrectly thought to be the secular canon and theologian at Paris Henry of Ghent (d. 1293), acknowledged Albert's reputation as among the most learned of men, one who "writes and has written" much. Nonetheless, Pseudo-Henry continued by lamenting that "when [Albert] excessively followed the subtlety of secular philosophy, he obscured the splendor of theological purity."[17] That very implication—that philosophical interests and energies undermine the more important study of theology—was a criticism also laid at Albert's feet by his acclaimed contemporary Roger Bacon. Albert and Roger may have come to know each other when they lived simultaneously in Paris between 1245 and 1248. Both were accomplished commentators on Aristotle. Like Albert, Bacon wrote on the topic of magic and related fields, was interested in distinguishing rational natural studies from the superstitious, irrational ones that often took the label of magic, and earned a lasting reputation for having practiced these arts.[18]

Bacon is most famous for his *Opera*, three treatises on the reform of education, written for Pope Clement IV (r. 1265–68). His judgment on Albert in these works is complicated. On the one hand, he wrote of Albert in the *Opus minus*, "He was devoted to learning. His discernment was boundless. What he pondered, he understood. He was thus able to draw together many useful things from the boundless ocean of writers."[19] Responsibility for the fallen state of education, however, Bacon laid at the feet of two fellow scholastics: Alexander of Hales (1185–245) and an "unnamed master," taken to be Albert, who "made himself an authority . . . and composed this and that great volumes on natural philosophy."[20] Bacon also denigrated Albert in his *Compendium of the Study of Philosophy* (1271–72), in which he took the mendicant orders to task for admitting boys too young; neglecting their education in languages, the arts, and rudimentary philosophy, and rushing them to the study of theology. He named Albert and Thomas Aquinas as examples of the problem.[21] The consequences, accumulating across the generations, were dire, by Bacon's lights, allowing for "a reign of unlimited errors, . . . God permitting, the devil actualizing."[22] As Jeremiah Hackett has pointed out, "It is the polemic and persuasive side of a very important debate on the principles of philosophic and scientific method in the schools of thirteenth-century Europe."[23] The irony is that where magic and natural philosophy aligned, Albert and Bacon had far more uniting them in the face of the more hostile views toward magic held by most of their contemporaries, than dividing them.

While no vita was composed in the years immediately following his death, references to Albert continue to appear in a variety of writings.[24] These mentions continued to stress Albert's piety and learning, especially in philosophy and in the knowledge of the natural world. The Dominican author Ptolemy of Lucca (1236–1327), for example, dedicated several sentences to Albert in his *New Ecclesiastical History*: "Albert attained the highest level of excellence among doctors for the breadth of his knowledge and the gift of teaching. He has commented on all Aristotle's logic and natural philosophy, and he has handed on his special experience of nature with greatest clarity and excellence."[25] William of Tocco (1240–1323), who authored the first vita of Thomas Aquinas, established the custom of including a few remarks about Albert in relation to his student, associating the breadth of his learning and the vigor of his piety to Thomas's accomplishments.[26] While William avoided making a relative judgment on the two scholars, such a ranking was inevitable. The friar Henry of Herford (1326–1370) made the first ranking in his *Rather Remarkable Matters* (after 1355), dutifully praising both and then analogizing them as sun (Thomas) to moon (Albert): theology, Thomas's forte, is to the day, as philosophy, Albert's, is to the night.[27]

Even as official chroniclers and history writers of the Dominicans developed the key points of Albert's learning and piety with an emphasis on his study of the natural world, a number of tales were emerging that drew attention to specific magical activities, sometimes inspired by innocent remarks in the earliest of writings, sometimes developed more freely. Thomas of Cantimpré's account of Albert's casting a devil out of his room, a moral tale giving evidence to Albert's capacity to resist temptation, gave rise to another tale in the vernacular *Saxon World Chronicle* (1314–16). In the latter work, Albert, now bishop of Regensburg, faces a demon, whom he dismisses from his chambers. The chronicler explained Albert's ability to do so as a function not of his moral integrity but rather of his accumulated experience in summoning demons, which he had practiced for the sake of learning "hidden matters" for the good of Christianity.[28] In the *Chronicles* of Johannes de Beke (d. 1346), another ambiguous story is introduced with a description of Albert as "great in nigromancy, greater in philosophy, and greatest of all in theology." *Nigromancy* here could only refer to the variety that was associated with physics. The story that follows tells of a dinner Albert hosted for William of Holland, king of the Germans (r. 1247–56), on the winter feast of Epiphany in the priory's garden. To the amazement of the king and his entourage, as they repaired to the cloister gardens, the sun broke through the clouds, the temperature rose, the snow melted away, the plants became fragrant and fruited, and birds began to sing. Then, upon completion of the feasting, the summer departed as quickly as it had arrived, the snow and cold returned, and the guests "who had removed their coats for the meal, raced back in confusion to the fires of the dining room."[29] Much later accounts explained the story with appeal to the priory's operation of a greenhouse.

Albert's knowledge of the natural world and particular skill in working with it also appeared in works that had no historical aspirations but in which episodes from Albert's life served other purposes. One of the most famous such stories about Albert has to do with his reputed creation of a talking head. *The Rosebush of Life* (ca. 1363), which the prominent Florentine businessman Matteo Corsini (1322–1402) may have written at the peak of his family's influence in ecclesiastical and imperial politics, is a collection of essays on virtues and vices, composed in an Italian vernacular.[30] Corsini proposed the story of Albert's talking head, animated as it was supposed to have been by astral forces, in a chapter on wisdom. Suggesting the intersection of motifs from the very first line, the chapter takes as its theme a verse from the Book of Wisdom: "For Wisdom is more beautiful than the sun, and above all the order of the stars: being compared with the light, she is found before it."[31] Additional quotations, in this case, about wisdom and knowledge from Isaiah, Seneca, and Socrates follow. The lengthiest part of the chapter consists of the story of Albert's talking statue: "By great wisdom he made a metal statue according to the courses of the planets and with such rationality that it spoke." Albert's achievement did not require, Corsini explained, "diabolical art or necromancy (*negromanzia*)," which kill body and soul and the faith forbids. One day when Albert is absent, the story continues, an unnamed friar knocks on Albert's door and the statue calls him in. Seeing the statue talk and assuming it is "an idol of wicked rationality," the friar smashes it to pieces. When Albert returns and learns of the destruction of the statue, he grieves over the loss of "thirty years to build it and with a science not known among the friars." When the friar begs forgiveness and suggests Albert build another, Albert explains an insurmountable difficulty: the full set of necessary celestial movements will not recur for another thirty thousand years.[32] Strikingly, Corsini drew a solid moral line to separate this permitted use of astral forces to animate the statue and any forbidden applications of diabolical arts.

Automata were objects of great fascination in the ancient, medieval, and early modern worlds, but Albert had only rare occasion to address them in his commentaries[33] and never discussed the crafting of a talking head. He was not alone, however, among medieval scholars and churchmen in having such a story told about him. Creation of talking heads was attributed to at least three other learned figures from this period, Gerbert of Aurillac (Pope Sylvester II, 945–1003), Robert Grosseteste (1168–1253), and Roger Bacon. All three were famous for their knowledge of the natural world and were rumored to have practiced magic. William of Malmesbury's account of Gerbert's construction of a head established a precedent for such storytelling.[34] After describing Gerbert's aims in Spain to learn "all that human curiosity has discovered, good or evil," his surpassing "Ptolemy with the astrolabe, Alandreus in astronomy, and Julius Firmicus in judicial astrology," his success at learning divination from "the singing and the flight of birds" and how "to call forth spirits from hell," his theft of one teacher's most protected and prized "book full of all the arts known to him," and his summons "of the devil, and binding himself to him forever in return for aiding his escape," William remarked, "probably some may regard all this as a fiction, because the vulgar are used to undermine the fame of scholars, saying that the man who excels in any admirable science, holds converse with the devil." Once back in Christian Europe, William continued, Gerbert "cast the head of a statue, by a certain inspection of the stars, when all the planets were aligned, that responded when queried and pronounced the truth, either in the affirmative or the negative." When Gerbert asked, for example, whether he would become pope, the statue replied, Yes. The principal components of the learned man's talking statue—the association with men of great learning, especially in natural philosophy, celestial influences, demonic assistance, and moral turpitude—for the medieval Latin West were set.[35]

The construction of a talking head by Robert Grosseteste, a leading cosmologist in his day, an early commentary writer on Aristotle's *Physics*, and the bishop of Lincoln,[36] first appears in a vernacular "poem of consolation," a genre that relates an anxious person's search for insight and peace. John Gower wrote *The Lover's Confession* (1386–93) for King Richard II of England. He included Grosseteste in the poem as an example of sloth, a habit that works against love,[37] and he situated the relevant verses between accounts of Ulysses tarrying at Troy over Penelope and of the Foolish Virgins in the gospel parable. The poem presumes familiarity with Grosseteste's learning, introducing him simply as "the grete Clerc." He was working seven years on a head of brass to "make it forto telle / of suche thinges as befelle," but he fails to animate it by delaying "half a Minut of an houre," thus missing the one necessary celestial moment.[38] Gower's disapproval was thus not directed at the celestial knowledge needed to animate the statue, which is only alluded to, but rather at the indolently missed timing.[39] The Benedictine monk Richard Bardney (fl. 1485/86–1519) developed the theme of Grosseteste's mastery of the natural sciences at greater length in an early sixteenth-century verse "Life of Robert Grosseteste, Bishop of Lincoln." In it Bardney explained that the astral powers were needed to animate such a head, a task summarized as the "arts of wisdom" conquering "the power of nature." The Grosseteste story thus generally includes the importance of learning and power of celestial influences, but the diabolical and morally depraved elements of the Gerbert story are replaced with a milder lesson against laziness.[40]

Roger Bacon, a closer contemporary to Albert, was the last to have the fable of a talking head incorporated into his popular biography.[41] Composed amid England's religiously violent sixteenth century, the prose romance *The Famous Historie of Fryer Bacon* (ca. 1555) provided the opportunity to castigate this Catholic friar and papal confidant for sorcerous activities. Aided by an impious servant and another friar, Bacon crafts a brazen head, hoping to empower it with speech. At first unsuccessful, he conjures a devil and forces him to explain how to animate the head. The devil explains that at a key moment of early animation further actions must be taken, otherwise the whole effort would be lost. In an echo of the Grosseteste story, Bacon, exhausted by his sorcery, decides to take a nap, during which the head suddenly begins to speak, first to say, "Time is," then "Time was," and finally "Time is past." At the last of these utterances, it "therewith fell downe, and presently followed a terrible noyse, with strange flashes of fire, . . . : At this noyse the two Fryers awaked, and wondred to see the whole roome so full of smoake, but that being banished they might perceive the Brazen-head broken and lying on the ground: at this sight they grieved."[42] Learning, craftsmanship, and fatigue remain part of the story, and the diabolical returns. Among these stories, then, the Albert version distinguishes itself on key points pertaining to natural philosophy and magic: he succeeds at animating the head and needs only his own wits to build the apparatus and harness the astral forces; demonic assistance has no part. In Corsini's version of the story, the making of the talking head exemplifies not a weakness but the gift of wisdom, and only the impetuous assistant who least understood the workings of the natural world and confused the head for an idol appears foolish, not the master whose knowledge and labors succeeded at the goal.

Along similar lines, Albert's knowledge and talents became a feature in a set of late medieval poems suggestive of a remarkable translation of ideas from elite scholarly circles to a larger circle of readers, and in ways similar to what one finds in hagiographical writings, composed with the complementary goals of entertaining and edifying.[43] A striking example is found in the German vernacular poem "There Was a King in France."[44] The oldest manuscript of the poem dates to the early fifteenth century. The poem recounts how a lecherous student in Paris, from Lauingen (Albert's hometown in Swabia), named Albertus Magnus, uses "the black arts" to kidnap a royal princess and assault her nightly.[45] The distressed princess confides what is happening to her mother, who in turn tells the king. Exposed by a trail of red paint left by the princess and leading to his apartments in a city whitewashed on the king's orders,[46] the student is arrested, convicted, and condemned to death. He escapes in the nick of time thanks to a magical ball of yarn.[47] Eventual remorse leads him back to Paris, where the king pardons the now contrite student.[48] Having abandoned his sorcery and devoted himself to a life of holiness, Albert becomes the bishop of Regensburg.[49] The poem concludes with the moralizing reassurance that even the gravest of sins can be forgiven the repentant.[50] The storyline possibly traces back, once again, to Thomas of Cantimpré, who recounted in *The Book of Bees* that Albert told the story of a count's daughter, cared for in a convent, whom her brother, a Franciscan friar, rescued from nightly kidnapping by demons.[51]

This story may have led to an adjustment in another poem that also put a crafty Albert at center stage. In the sole surviving poem of the German balladeer Martin Schleich (fl. ca. 1500), "A Beautiful Song of a Queen of France," the tale is told of a queen who, undetected, seduces and then murders nine men in succession. A tenth prospect, the young student Albert, though captured, manages "through his art" to escape. In hiding, he makes her crimes public by attaching notes to the beaks of obliging birds, which release them across city and countryside. After her arrest and indictment, Albert leads the prosecution at the trial. Sentenced to a life of penance, she dies after eighteen years in a convent and is led to heaven by angels. Escape was a common purpose of magic, and these are the arts, as is explained in the poem, with which Albert evades the queen. But as in "There Was a King in France," the point of the story is less to dwell on Albert's "art" than on the salubrious effects of contrition and penance. A slightly older, similar story likely known to Schleich identifies the tenth victim as Johannes Buridan, a leading fourteenth-century scholastic in Paris; a later adaptation of the material by the Franciscan satirist Thomas Murner (1475–1537) was probably written independently of Schleich.[52]

A third example in verse draws attention to Albert's mastery of alchemical arts, a theme he touched on in *De mineralibus* and a mastery that inspired more

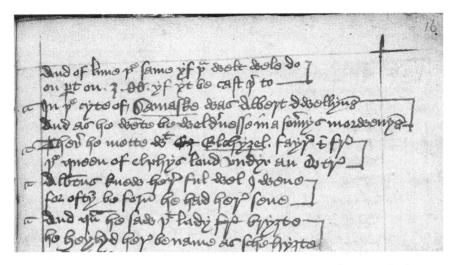

Fig. 3. Excerpt from the vernacular poem *Semita recta*, Trinity College, Cambridge, MS R. 14. 44, fol. 16r (detail). "Albert was dwelling in the city of Damascus / and he went into the wilderness on a summer's morning / There he met with Elchzyel, fair and free, / the queen of the elven lands under an Elder tree." The fifteenth-century poem presents Albert as a scholar with marvelous sources for his knowledge of the natural world.

pseudepigraphic texts than any other. The title of a fifteenth-century Middle English verse "The Right Path, Albert Bears Witness," appeals to the title of the most widely distributed alchemical tract ascribed wrongly to Albert, the *Semita recta* (Right path), to which we will turn shortly. The verse tract bears no resemblance to its namesake, and the two compositions have no passages in common.[53] Whereas the original is an alchemist's laboratory manual, the verse tract describes an encounter between Albert and Elchyzell, a queen of the elves, that takes place in Damascus (fig. 3). The queen instructs Albert how to produce an alchemical elixir that aids in the production of silver and gold. As she explains the recipe, Albert poses questions. The poem indicates the author's familiarity with basic alchemical principles. It follows certain late medieval conventions in alchemical tracts, such as the inclusion of anagrams and codes, that were not part of the original *Semita*. While the principal ingredients in the recipe, silver and mercury, and the goal of producing silver and gold from less noble metals were usual parts of alchemy for Albert, other parts of the poem are creative and anachronistic signs of the mythical dimensions his reputation as a master of the natural world had achieved. Here this mastery brings him to the Levant and into conversation with an elven queen.[54] Furthermore, the poem's language and provenance indicates the broadening geographical expanse of Albert's magical regard beyond the western continent and into Britain.

In another literary instance, Albert appears as an authority rather than a character in the mid-fifteenth-century vernacular poem "The Defender of Ladies." The French-language poet Martin Le Franc (1410–1461) composed the 24,000-verse poem while a secretary to the antipope Felix V and a prebended canon in Lausanne.[55] It includes an 823-line discussion of witchcraft between the "Foe" and the "Defender." At a certain point in the conversation, the speakers arrive at a disagreement over the reality of witchcraft's effects. The Defender makes a common argument for their illusory quality, citing church fathers and the *Golden Legend* to argue that demons are incapable of causing such events as the sabbat, enabling witch's flight, or engaging in sexual commerce with humans, except as illusions. The Foe offers the refutation that demons could have these powers with God's permission, points to classical and biblical examples, and cites Augustine and Albert.[56] The Foe further suggests Albert's approving interest in the *Secreta secretorum* (Secrets of secrets). That work is an encyclopedic reference that touches on good governance, morals, healing arts, magic, alchemy, numerology, and many other related topics. At its core is a contrived letter of Aristotle to Alexander the Great. Although its origins are obscure, the oldest, extant Arabic versions—known as the *Sirr al-Asrar*—date to the tenth century. It was popular once it arrived in Latin Christian Europe in the mid-twelfth century, and in the thirteenth century Roger Bacon, much more than Albert, took inspiration from the work. Bacon prepared his own edition of it, appending a preface and glossing the more obscure passages.[57] For Le Franc in the fifteenth century, however, Albert's interest was the more authoritative, at least in the hands of the Foe.

Pseudo-Albert

It bears recalling the conjecture that Albert's pseudepigrapha had more influence than his authentic works. They are of many different kinds, but most of them had to do with magic and other fields peripheral to natural philosophy. Some pseudepigrapha were likely written by students and others in learned circles close to Albert, thus making it all the harder to distinguish from his authentic works. False authorship was usually credited to a master, in Albert's case and so many other medieval cases as well, not in order to deceive outright but in homage, as well as to enhance the seriousness with which the writing would be taken and to protect its contents from rejection or condemnation. Misascription by later generations could also be as much a matter of mistaking authorship as contriving it. All these reasons for incorrect authorial ascription can be found among Albert's pseudepigrapha. So many pseudepigrapha, like the biographical writings and the legends, affirm Albert's mastery of knowledge about the natural world. The pseudepigrapha contributed to Albert's reputation as a practitioner of magic and even the dark arts. The effect of a particular text in this regard can change over time. None of the pseudepigrapha seems to have emerged with the intent of defaming Albert; yet over time some were taken that way. In the next few pages treatises are introduced that initially raised little or no concern for Albert's disciples and devotees. The gap between their contents and what Albert actually wrote can seem small and the potential for controversy minimal. In subsequent chapters, however, we return to many of these texts on account of the strong rejections or defenses they receive from scholars and churchmen trying to make sense of Albert's supposed authorship of them. What will have changed was generally not the pseudepigrapha themselves but the lenses through which they were evaluated. Given how much of the pseudepigrapha reflects knowledge of the natural world and how central such knowledge was to the shifting medieval and early modern understanding of magic, reaction to Albert's pseudepigrapha can be demonstrative not only of Albert's thought but also of a later reader's understanding of the magical and natural sciences.

Among the most widely disseminated pieces of Albert's pseudepigrapha having to do with the hidden properties of natural objects is the *Liber aggregationis*. This book is a combination of two works: the *Liber de virtutibus herbarum, lapidum, et animalium* (Book of the properties of herbs, stones, and animals), which explicitly claims Albert as its author, and the *De mirabilibus mundi* (On the wonders of the world), whose authorship was often assumed under the claim of the former. In fact, the *De mirabilibus* had as its principal source the *De proprietatibus*, a Latin version of *The Great Book of Properties* by the tenth-century Muslim physician Ibn al-Jazzar.[58] Across the seventy-six Latin manuscripts of the *Liber aggregationis*, the oldest of which dates to the 1290s, as well as hundreds of printed editions in Latin and vernaculars, there are variations: the text lent itself to revision and extension.[59]

The *Liber de virtutibus*, which sometimes also appears under the title *Experimenta Alberti* or *Secreta Alberti*, is itself a collection of three books dedicated, one each, to the magical and medicinal powers of sixteen plants, forty-six stones, and eighteen animals. The section on stones resembles Albert's *De mineralibus*, especially as a guide to experiments. *De mirabilibus mundi* takes the form of a "books of secrets." This genre, popular in the Middle Ages and early modern period, consists of recipes with which the hidden powers of natural objects could be exploited to the users' advantage, usually financial. An appeal to the ancient origins of its contents is also common in such works. As Greek and Arabic writings on magic and alchemy arrived in the Latin West from the twelfth century onward, books of secrets were increasingly ascribed to leading philosophers as well, but none more than Albert.[60] Sometimes the two parts present magical effects that are not quite in concord, as for example, the hoopoe heart that assures a keenness in marketplace dealings in the *Liber* but which makes the mind forgetful and dull in the *De mirabilibus*.[61]

The *Liber de virtutibus* is structured encyclopedically, much as we saw in Albert's own writings, and the *De mirabilibus* comprises short recipes. Both, however, propose *experimenta* as a means to access hidden power, and among the recurrent phrases throughout is the author's own telling confirmation: "ego expertus sum." This recalls Albert's own use of the expression in his natural philosophical works, especially his acknowledgment in the *De anima*. There is an echo of the nigromancy that Albert himself accepted as "scientific," that is, as a kind of natural knowledge applied to practical effect. The desired effects tend more to the psychological (for example, the powers of the hoopoe heart) than the therapeutic. Despite these echoes of the real Albert, the *Liber aggregationis* likely emerged not from Albert but from Dominican circles close to him.[62]

The *De secretis mulierum* has similar origins and also promises its readers the revelation of hidden knowledge, that is, "to manifest lucidly things private and hidden about the nature and condition of women." Although several distinct works appearing under the title have added to the confusion over authorship, a follower of Albert's likely wrote the treatise in the thirteenth or early fourteenth century. The student drew from Albert's own writings on generation, and certain corresponding passages in his *De animalibus* buttressed the conclusion that he had written the whole work. The commentaries that often appear with it in manuscript and print commonly reiterate Albert's authorship. If the work's use was primarily for study, as the commentaries suggest, the characteristics of its contents leave unclear whose use was intended. It seems less likely to be useful for faculties of medicine at the universities than for readers in monastic settings and possibly even literate households.[63]

The *De secretis*'s account of human generation represents thirteenth-century medicine inconsistently well, and the mode of inquiry into operations and pathologies is often more philosophical and theoretical than medical and practical. The author distinguished between philosophers and doctors of medicine, and Aristotle, Avicenna, and Galen are among the most cited authorities. Divided into thirteen chapters the book explains conception, embryonic development, birth, deformed or monstrous births, signs of virginity and chastity, and the relevant bodily fluids of menses, semen, and blood. Gender reveal being no less intriguing in the Middle Ages than our own day, chapter 8 proposes ways to determine the sex of a fetus.[64] A full chapter and many additional passages are devoted to the celestial influences, especially Saturn's, on all the processes described in the volume, and especially as affecting in the fetus aspects of its future physical appearance and psychological characteristics.[65] While much more specific in coverage here than in in Albert's authentic writings, the contents correspond to Albert's own ideas about these powers' impact on motion and change, through form and substance, in living and inanimate objects. Astrology, more than witchcraft, nigromancy, or other interest in the diabolical, features in the treatise.[66]

None of these three works was included in the official bibliographies of Albert's works that Dominicans compiled. None was included in the opera omnia of 1651. Yet among a general readership and in the popular press the association of these works with Albert the Great proved irresistible. In the late fifteenth century these three works began appearing in single-volume anthologies, first in Latin and quickly thereafter in vernaculars. In modern scholarship the compilation is often referred to by its French title, *Le Grand Albert*. Across nearly three centuries of manuscript and printed-book reproduction, the component parts varied, with other works being added to and subtracted from the Pseudo-Albertan works, for example, excerpts from Pliny's natural history, Galen's medical writings, and the seventh-century Byzantine physician Paul of Aegina's medical compendium.[67]

No single subject produced a greater variety of pseudepigraphal treatises under Albert's name than alchemy. This is an effect of the *De mineralibus*, which itself was widely reproduced and disseminated in the later Middle Ages, in which Albert expressed himself generally favorably to alchemy and which was singular in its contents and usefulness to aspiring alchemists. Albert treated alchemy as a body of knowledge and a craft distinct from but with similarities to magic. It was a science he took seriously thanks to encouragement he took from writings of Aristotle and Avicenna in particular. The most famous of the pseudepigraphal treatises on alchemy was the *Semita recta*, whose title was reused in the story of the elven queen. The *Semita* relies on the high medieval understanding of alchemy as a particular kind of metallurgy.[68] It begins with a brief introduction to the alchemical arts, followed by a description of the necessary equipment for alchemical practices, the usual materials and their properties, and the operations. A concluding paragraph addresses the critical question of how to effect transmutations of lesser metals into gold and silver. Its final phrase offers a concession: "the Lord willing."[69]

Such content made it logical for the *Semita* to be paired with the *De mineralibus* as the latter's lab manual. Other indications of influence, such as *The Height of Perfection* (*Summa perfectionis*) by Pseudo-Geber, suggest an author familiar with the alchemical theory and practices of the thirteenth century, perhaps even a student of Albert's. The oldest manuscript dates to about 1300 and names Albert as the author. Its popularity is testified to by thirty-five extant

Latin manuscripts as well as by medieval and early modern translations into English, German, Greek, and Italian, and a first printed edition in Basel in 1561.[70] Through the seventeenth century, the Dominicans themselves disagreed over the *Semita recta*'s ascription to Albert. In the later Middle Ages, it was routinely credited to Albert, but late fifteenth-century Dominican life-writing about Albert rejected his authorship. Along with several other works of dubious origin and now judged inauthentic, the text appears under the title *Libellus de alchimia* (Little book of alchemy) in the last volume of Albert's 1651 opera omnia, edited by Dominicans in Lyon.[71] Another pseudepigraphal treatise, the *Alkimia minor* (Lesser alchemy), follows the *Semita* closely and expands on it.[72]

By including a mystical dimension to its alchemical descriptions, the *De occultis naturae* (On the hidden things of nature) diverges from the manual style of the *Semita recta* and *Alkimia minor* as well as from the sober alchemical approach of Albert himself in the *De mineralibus*. The work claims Albert as its author and is fashioned as a letter to a concerned "reverend father." It contrives a foil of conflicting alchemical ideas that can be resolved by returning to the ancient masters—Geber, Rasis, Avicenna, and Hermes, among others. Later thinkers like Pseudo-Geber, Pseudo-Arnold, Pseudo-Lull, and Roger Bacon are also influences. The last section of the *De occultis naturae* is structured as a florilegium, a collection of the author's favorite passages from the works of others, many of them originally in Arabic. Objects and procedures are described in metaphorical language, especially with medicalized and sexualized imagery: silver is phlegm, gold is blood, and the conjugal union of sulfur and quicksilver yields the philosopher's stone. The author expressed with certitude that alchemy provides a means to change a mineral's actual species, an idea Albert rejected. The *De occultis naturae* instead represents strains of later medieval alchemy—ubiquitous reference to Arab works and the use of metaphorical language suggest, for example, the fourteenth century and later—but not Albert's own.[73]

Other alchemical pseudepigrapha fall similarly along scales of closeness to the *De mineralibus*. The *Calistenus* is like the *Semita* in its adherence to the metallurgy of *De mineralibus* and the principles of celestial influences.[74] The *Compositum de compositis* (Compound of compounds) distinguishes itself by its religious imagery, which not only distinguishes it from the *De mineralibus* but also is at odds with Albert's scrupulous distinctions between philosophical and theological reasoning and reflects new strains of alchemical thinking more characteristic of the early modern period than the medieval.[75] Focusing on gold and silver to the exclusion of any other material's relevance, the *Propositiones artis alchemiae* (Propositions of the art of alchemy) departs in purpose and scope from the *De mineralibus*.[76] The *Secretorum tractatus* (Tract of secrets) builds on certain foundational insights of the *De mineralibus*, such as the central importance of celestial influences and a reserve as to the possibility of real transmutation of species. Distinctively in this work, the author considered various kinds of false alchemy and rather than associating it with ignorant and incapable practitioners, as was customary in Albert's own day, rejected it as sorcerous.[77]

The alchemical tracts wrongly attributed to Albert did not cast him in the role of magician, good or malign. Rather, they affirm Albert's intimate expertise in all aspects of the natural world. Some of them also reiterate cautions and affirm limits on what might be morally and naturally accomplished through magic and other forms of engagement with the natural world. Some transgress the boundaries the real Albert set, such as the appeal to religious imagery and theological argument in certain texts. Others offer evidence of an alchemical thinking and process foreign to Albert's own day but characteristic of later generations. Testimony to and encouragement for *experiri* in alchemy and related magical practices by the Pseudo-Alberts are more prevalent in the pseudepigrapha than the authentic writings; indeed, the how-to dimension of many pseudepigrapha finds little parallel in the authentic writings. In short, whereas the authentic writings give indications that Albert engaged in some magical and related practices and relied on the practices of others for information he includes in them, some pseudepigrapha are actual manuals for magical and related practices.

Finally, we turn to a work, the *Speculum astronomiae*, that is taken in this book as not Albert's but for which there continues to be scholarly arguments for its authenticity. If the resilience of a claim were evidence of its accuracy, then surely the *Speculum*'s ascription to Albert would be true. Ascertaining with certainty the treatise's authorship, however, has proved a vexatious challenge.[78] Its earliest manuscripts are anonymous, and its oldest extant attribution to Albert dates only to 1339,[79] later by decades than the attributions of many pseudepigraphal works. The attribution, once made, however, proved compelling. In the centuries that followed, Giovanni Pico della Mirandola (1463–1494) was one scholar of note to call Albert's authorship into question, which he did in his *Disputations Against Divinatory Astrology*, albeit without much explanation.[80] Others drew from the work without naming an author.[81] Although the earlier bibliographies of Dominican works did not list the *Speculum* as Albert's, the seventeenth-century opera omnia included it.[82] In the nineteenth century, new approaches to the critical editing of medieval manuscripts encouraged the development of alternative hypotheses.[83] Bernard Geyer excluded the *Speculum* from the prospectus of the Cologne opera omnia because, among other reasons, Albert appeared nowhere else inclined to anonymity in addressing even controversial subjects.[84] For the time being, the neutral designation of the author as the Magister Speculi seems to have achieved a level of scholarly acceptance.[85]

In the face of these disputes, Lynn Thorndike cautioned that the designation of a particular author is less important than the recognition of the circles in which such writing traveled. Indeed, the contents are of great significance, regardless of the treatise's actual authorship. Many ideas are similar to Albert's own writings: The *Speculum* distinguishes between the mathematical study of celestial motions and their effects. This distinction, between astronomy and astrology, was kept fairly consistently in the Middle Ages, even if the terminology for the parts was not, as also by Albert. Certain forms of astrology could be nigromantic, that is, shaped by diabolical influences, but need not be. In this regard, the *Speculum* sets out to distinguish between licit and illicit books, inspired by a regret that many wholesome, scientific books had been condemned with the wicked. The lists of books offer unparalleled glimpse into medieval thinking about these fields.[86] The Magister's encouragement that the nigromantic books be set aside rather than destroyed is noteworthy, and its motivation inspired considerable conjecture.[87] Nowhere in Albert's other writings is there the sustained treatment of either natural or judicial astrology. Astrological practices like horoscopes, nativities, and interrogations are accepted in many respects and explained. The dangers of nigromancy, however, are taken as real, and the degree of concern, appropriate to the topic of the work, complements the philosophical writings on celestial movement and influences known to be Albert's. The distinctions drawn by the author followed principles laid out in the *De mineralibus* and other authentic works, but the Magister devoted effort to denouncing particularly contemptible practices that Albert rejected only in passing. For example, from Albert's authentic works we know he rejected ritual magic that included incense and invocations to demonic figures. Where he did so only in passing the *De mineralibus*, the author of the *Speculum* did so in detail. At several points the Magister and Albert diverge, such as the former's greater concern that demonic assistance spoils the making of talismans. But the differences do not always make the Magister sterner. On the topic of divination, for example, the Magister made a series of distinctions that Albert did not. While the Magister regarded none of the mantic arts as a genuine science, he did accept that geomancy was a licit form of astrology and chiromancy was an acceptable form of physiognomy.[88] Such distinctions are compatible with a reading of Albert on celestial influences. But when Albert described the practitioners of mantic arts in his commentary on the Gospel of Matthew, he dismissed them all as wicked, excepting only, of course, the magi themselves.[89]

In the fifteenth century a set of battle lines were drawn that crossed the *Speculum*, which is assayed in the next chapter. Here the reactions of three important fifteenth-century thinkers serve to round out this introduction to the *Speculum*. The first two reactions are the opposing views of two distinguished Parisian conciliarists and successive chancellors of the university, both of whom regarded the *Speculum* as Albert's. The first, Pierre d'Ailly (1351–1420), wrote, "Albert the Great published a very useful tract, in which he distinguished the books of true astronomy and those of the magical arts according to their principles and ends so that one would be able to separate astronomical truth from magical vanities."[90] The other, Jean Gerson (1363–1429), d'Ailly's successor as chancellor of the University of Paris, faulted Albert for a disposition toward superstitious subjects—generally in his treatment of the Peripatetics' writings and specifically in the *Speculum*—"unworthy of a Christian teacher." As regards the treatment of superstitious topics, Gerson compared Albert unfavorably with Thomas Aquinas and associated him with such otherwise revered ancient teachers as Hermes, Plato, Porphyry, and Apuleius.[91] A third formidable fifteenth-century thinker, the Florentine Platonist Marsilio Ficino (1433–1499) likewise regarded the *Speculum* as Albert's, but treated Albert as one authoritative voice among many whose divergent and often irreconcilable views on magic and related issues required discerning interpretation. Accordingly, for example, in his *Three Books on Life*, he reported the *Speculum*'s measured approval of talismans because they attracted celestial, not demonic powers, but favored Aquinas's greater skepticism.[92]

Albert the Renaissance Magician

Despite critics like Gerson, reactions to the *Speculum* indicate that admiration for Albert's mastery of the natural world, even when it might be magical, could find enthusiasts beyond the Middle Ages and include early modern humanists and Neoplatonists. Albert's association with the magical arts did, too. Ficino, a key figure in the history of magic in the Renaissance,[93] offered approving consideration of the use of celestial forces to activate hidden properties in inanimate objects in an echo of Albert's own notion of magical arts.[94] Ficino even considered the possibility of statue animation, such as was imputed to Albert in the stories of the brazen head.[95] Another leading writer of the period on magic, Henricus Cornelius Agrippa von Nettesheim (1486–1535), used Albert as an authority in his *Three Books of Occult Philosophy* (written 1510, published 1533). The work was an eclectic mix of Neoplatonic, hermetic, kabbalistic, and Christian ideas that combined traditions of magic, medicine, and theurgy. Agrippa cast a cosmology in which a universal soul sustained all creation and revealed itself in the magical properties of natural objects. Agrippa presented Albert among the most important experts in the workings of the natural world, naming him alongside Aristotle, Hermes, and Avicenna. While Albert was generally mentioned only by name, the *De mineralibus* and the *Speculum* are works Agrippa valued, drew from, and quoted indirectly. In his "Retractiones," printed as an appendix to the *De occulta philosophia* in 1533, Agrippa offered some clarification of his ideas about, among other topics, "natural magic." Albert, it will be recalled, never used the term *natural magic*, but Agrippa's definition of it—the use of celestial influences to draw out the hidden properties of terrestrial objects—fell close to Albert's description of magical arts in *De mineralibus*. In proposing a list of its practitioners, Agrippa placed Albert with other important figures in the medieval tradition of celestial magic—Arnold of Villanova, Raymond Lull, Roger Bacon, Peter of Abano, and the author of the *Picatrix*—as well as a larger set of ancient figures pagan, Christian, Jewish, and Muslim.[96]

Another use of Albert's reputation in the period was in defense of particular magical activities and against accusations of sorcery. The reforming abbot and humanist Johannes Trithemius (1462–1516) pointed to Albert as a warning against how common people often mistook interest in laudable kinds of magic for diabolical kinds.[97] In response to the demon theorist Johannes Weyer's attacks[98] on Trithemius for diabolism in the humanist monk's study of angelic cryptography,[99] the Paracelsan naturalist Jacques Gohory (1520–1576) appealed to Albert, along with other learned figures, as a model of orthodoxy in his practice of similar arts.[100] Pico made a similar appeal to Albert in endorsement for "natural magic" in his *Nine Hundred Conclusions* (1486). Pico's *Conclusions* were a call for a debate in Rome over his new all-encompassing system of knowledge, in which natural magic served as the linchpin. Pico devoted one section of the *Conclusions* to philosophical theses taken from Albert, none having to do with the magical arts, but Pico had incorporated aspects of natural magic, as understood at the time, and the Jewish mystical discipline Kabbalah into the *Conclusions*. Ecclesiastical authorities intervened to stall the debate, and in his defense of the project, the *Apologia*, he argued for the wholesomeness of natural magic by citing numerous respected learned figures from antiquity and the Middle Ages who by Pico's lights practiced it. He discussed William of Auvergne and Roger Bacon at length, and Albert as well: "The catholic and most holy Albert the Great was not ashamed to say that he himself had sought to attain this natural magic, and had learned much through experience in these things."[101]

This chapter begins with reference to Ulrich's writing on the intervention of angels and demons in human affairs. A concluding Renaissance figure returns us to that subject. Pietro Pomponazzi (1462–1525), an innovative and committed Aristotelian, drafted a treatise, *On Incantations* (1520), that circulated as a manuscript for thirty-five years before its publication in 1556.[102] A letter responding to a medical doctor's question about healings through magical, medical, and miraculous means offered the inspiration behind the work's composition. In it Pomponazzi disparaged explanations of healings, however seemingly miraculous, that made reference to the power of demons and angels. In place of such preternatural causation, Pomponazzi proposed a system of natural causes. Albert is among the authorities Pomponazzi cited most in the treatise, as he attempted, in effect, to apply to miracles something analogous to the naturalizing tools Albert applied to magical processes.[103]

Acknowledgment of Albert's naturalizing tendencies thus provided the bedrock for the development of any subsequent reputation he would enjoy, from the most orthodox to the most controversial. This bedrock was constituted out of his distinctive competence in natural philosophy and a mastery of its practical application. Even when he was forced to bask in the glow of a more greatly esteemed student, it was his natural philosophical insights that brought him there. But no sooner was his natural philosophical acumen brought into the light than his mastery of knowledge that lay beyond the strictly philosophical came into view. His real mastery inspired acclaim, even when, as we saw in the case of Ulrich's exclamation, that acclaim went beyond what Albert actually wrote. That readiness, or at times susceptibility, to go beyond the most surefooted interpretations of Albert's work ultimately became not only commonplace but largely unchallenged.

Accordingly, Albert stood for subsequent scholars as a figure who was philosophically authoritative and trailblazing. The precedent he set validated theoretical considerations and corresponding practices that were peripheral to, indeed beyond, what was in other circumstances regarded as strictly philosophical, natural, rational, and orthodox. Much of this, and in increasing scope, was regarded as magical, and yet for Albert's fame it was not deemed a hindrance. Gerson's disapproval of Albert as reputed author of the *Speculum astronomiae* is the exception that proves the rule. What Albert wrote was sometimes more, sometimes less relevant to aspects of his general reputation. The alchemical texts, taken as a group, demonstrate that variety. Reaction to them changed, as did the idea that Albert had learned anything through magical arts. In the case of Albert's brazen head, the story was remarkably tweaked so that, in contrast to other versions, the diabolism was excised and Albert's participation was rendered expressly scientific and certainly moral. When in the literary contributions acts of wicked magic were imputed to Albert, these set the stage for a dramatic conversion, once again drawing attention to the piety accompanying his brilliance.

Albert's precedent-setting became even more important as Renaissance thinkers developed their ideas about magic. For some Albert's precedent became an outright defense. But it was not just a vague notion of Albert as pious and orthodox that attracted thinkers even three centuries later to take Albert's own ideas seriously: Albert's real and pseudepigraphal works offered material with which to buttress their own notions of a "natural magic," as they moved well beyond what medieval figures like Albert, who never used the expression, and William of Auvergne, who did, had worked out in the thirteenth century. Hand in hand, however, with Albert's increasing popularity in certain learned circles and beyond, concerns emerged as well. Misuse of Albert was to be taken as the reflection of a deeper problem, and how the symptom was treated developed along with how the underlying problem was understood. What the problem was, who saw and attempted to treat it, and what their ultimate goals were are the subject of the next chapter.

3

ALBERTUS SANCTUS

Mid-lecture, the story goes, Albert lost his train of thought. His students reacted with astonishment at the uncharacteristic lapse. Albert, however, recalled the promise of the Blessed Virgin Mary in his youth that he would be granted boundless understanding and faultless memory until shortly before his death. Then at the end of his life, the Virgin had explained, he would be returned to childlike innocence. Realizing that the moment of reversion was upon him, he offered a profession of faith, recanted anything in his writings that might be found contrary to the faith, and departed the aula to his tearful students' laments. He never returned to the podium and spent the next years in quiescence till his death in 1280.

The story appears in the preface the friar preacher Luis de Valladolid attached to his index of Albert's authentic works, the *Tabula*. He composed the work during a two-year tenure of teaching at Paris (1412–14). While such indices had been compiled before—the oldest, the Stams catalog, may have originated in early fourteenth-century Paris[1]—the *Tabula* marked a new effort at comprehensiveness, especially regarding Albert's philosophical titles.[2] Biographical details are taken from earlier official writings, especially those of Thomas of Cantimpré, but reflect the same interest in thoroughness and include accounts of visions and such pious stories as this one of Albert's final years before death.[3]

Luis's contribution to Albert's fame, however, is more than just a matter of scope. The story of his memory lapse, for example, offers not only a possible glimpse into what geriatric dementia looked like to medieval observers but also a new, challenging perspective on Albert's learning. Nothing in the story suggests that Albert's scholarly accomplishment was other than intellectually and piously worthy. Indeed, his capacity for learning, it appears, had been supernaturally vouchsafed. Yet with such learning came, it would seem, the ultimate need for relief, the return to a childlike innocence in preparation for death and judgment. Such breadth of knowledge as Albert's, the story insinuates, puts salvation in jeopardy. Evidence of this ambivalence is to be found in other aspects of Luis's writing about Albert. Although the *Tabula* aspired to a new precision in cataloging Albert's philosophical titles, Luis drew little attention in the vita to Albert's philosophical accomplishment and left his great achievement in natural philosophy unmentioned. When Albert's philosophical efforts do come up, they are placed in explicit subordination to theology. In the course of recounting a particular vision of Albert's, Luis quoted Albert's explanation that the philosophical works had been written "for the defense of the faith and the elucidation of divine wisdom." And yet, Luis also compiled a longer list of philosophical titles in the *Tabula* than can be found in any previous such index. In regard to Albert's learning, one notes in Luis's writings a justification and a limit that emerged with new intensity across Dominican writings of the fifteenth century: the justification is in the emphasis on the service of Albert's philosophy to theology, an emphasis that was new in degree more than kind; the limit appears with Albert's absolute opposition to demonic magic, which was defined decidedly more broadly at the hands of the fifteenth-century authors than Albert himself had, and without much attention to what might be excused or even celebrated as natural magic. A passing indicator of such reinforcement on Luis's part can be seen in the listing of the *Speculum astronomiae*. In the earlier Stams catalog, it was listed under the title *Against the Nigromancers' Books*, a noteworthy interpretation of the book's purpose since the author himself had expressed concern that good works were being condemned indiscriminately with wicked ones.[4] Luis highlighted its denunciatory purpose yet more boldly, listing it as "the book in which Albert intended to reject the magical sciences of the nigromancers—namely, nigromancy, geomancy, hydromancy, aeromancy, pyromancy, soothsaying, horoscopes, divination, witchcraft, fortune-telling, and sleight."[5] And yet, the Magister Speculi, precisely on the matter of the various mantic arts, made distinctions lost in Luis's description.

Another early fifteenth-century writing offered another version of Albert's final days that also intimated a concern over the moral jeopardy in which his earlier intellectual pursuits could have put him. Hermann Korner (1365–1438), a friar in Lübeck, introduced Albert in the entry for the year 1265 in his *New Chronicle* (1423, 1435) as a second Aristotle, "or even one greater than Aristotle," "very erudite in the natural and dialectical arts," and particularly grounded in both testaments of the Bible. What he had written on "theology; moral, natural, and rational philosophy; astronomy; astrology; geometry; and arithmetic," Korner enthused, filled "about 160 volumes." But then on the matter of nigromancy Korner reflected that Albert may have turned to that field out of a not-quite wholesome longing to know everything, such that with the "maturity of old age" and the "sanctity of a tested life" he thankfully rejected "any such thing." Shortly before his death, Korner further related, a sickly Albert had himself brought before senior members of his priory to address them: "For a long time, dearest fathers, an ugly rumor has circulated about me that, practiced in art of nigromancy, I worked many strange and scarcely believable things with it. Many are therefore of the opinion that I have not walked along the way of salvation but of reprobation and am in a state of damnation." Albert then protested that whatever he had read, written, or done regarding nigromancy had been "for the sake of ascertaining whether there be some truth in it," and only "out of a desire to study everything knowable to the human mind." He finally promised them the following sign: on the third day after his burial, the fathers should reopen his grave and inspect his body: "If you find me lying supine in the customary position for the buried, then you will know I am among the damned. If you find me kneeling and facing east in prayer, you will know that I am either enjoying eternal bliss or on the way thereto." Shortly after this exchange, he died; by Korner's account, when Albert's grave was reopened three days after his burial, the friars found his corpse, facing east, kneeling in prayer.[6]

These two writings, composed contemporaneously in opposite corners of the empire by two of Albert's Dominican confreres, indicate a new strain of concern about Albert's learning and the place of the demonic within it. Luis and Korner shared admiration for the breadth and depth of his learning but insinuate that such knowledge was achieved at a risk. Neither denied Albert's engagement with magic, even with diabolical magic, but both justified it as the means to condemn the nigromancy itself. Nigromancy, as referred to in these writings, no longer denoted anything in the line of physics, in Gundassalinus's sense, but rather collaboration with demons. Luis insinuated the danger of such an undertaking: Even one as unquestionably devout as Albert benefited from a purifying return to childlike innocence and ignorance in the face of divine judgment. Korner handled the same general unease with the assurances implied by the posthumous sign. On the one hand, Albert's learning had, as we have already seen, not been immune from criticism: Bacon had criticized Albert's training and what it betokened, and Gerson found Albert's presumed work on the *Speculum astronomiae* unseemly. Both, however, were exceptions to a tradition that held Albert as devout, learned, and practical, even if in not entirely consistent and internally compatible ways. On the other hand, Luis's and Korner's writings suggest a new set of concerns regarding Albert's scholarly accomplishment. It is possible to read these new expressions of concern and the requirement of some resolution—the sudden quiescence according to Luis, the wondrous repositioning of Albert's corpse according to Korner—not only as a way to assure the concerned reader of Albert's eternal bliss but also as a discreet admonition to readers curious about magic in unwholesome ways. In exactly these respects, Luis and Korner stood at the beginning of a trend.

This chapter investigates the emergence, first of concern, then of hostility toward the suggestion of religious heresy or moral depravity in Albert's learning. A new apologetic interpretation emerged in full force in the final third of the fifteenth century. It consisted of a concerted effort to refute the possibility that he had practiced magic, to assert Albert's vigorous condemnation of magic, to portray Albert as an exemplary instance of learning and piety in conjunction, and to settle any controversy on the matter with his canonization. These efforts emerged most strongly where two entities with a special claim on Albert intersected: the city of Cologne and the Order of Friar Preachers. As we shall see, however, the urge to clarify who Albert was, what he had accomplished, and why he deserved to be raised to the altar was more than a matter of municipal and congregational pride. Albert's rescue, as these factions saw it, was a serious priority in the face of a new social and religious agenda that Albert's reputed engagement with magic appeared to contradict. The movement is represented in three key compositions, all originating in late fifteenth-century Cologne and all aimed at achieving Albert's canonization. This chapter examines them and situates them within a social context in which it was necessary not only to get the record straight regarding what Albert had and had not done but also to recast magic along more diabolical lines. These three document are the *Tractatus de excellentiis Alberti magni* (Tract on the outstanding qualities of Albert the Great) by the Cologne Carthusian Werner Rolevinck (1425–1502), composed in the early 1470s;[7] Peter of Prussia's *Legenda venerabilis domini Alberti magni* (Legend of the venerable lord Albert the Great), published in 1486 or 1487; and Rudolf of Nijwegen's *Legenda litteralis Alberti magni* (Written legend of Albert the Great), published in 1490.[8] A metrical vita by Jacobus Magdalius was appended to the last of these. Peter, Rudolf, and Magdalius were Dominican friars in Cologne.[9]

The Cologne Hagiography

Werner Rolevinck (1425–1502), who authored the *De excellentiis*, was a celebrated author of works on biblical, devotional, and historical themes. The most successful of his many titles was the universal history, *A Bundling of Dates*, that enjoyed over fifty printed editions in Latin and multiple vernaculars between 1474 and 1726. His style and approach bore the marks of Renaissance humanism.[10] Rolevinck's exact inspiration remains uncertain. The Charterhouse of St. Barbara, which Rolevinck entered in 1447, operated one of Germany's most important early printing houses and was a center of learning in a learned city. The Dominican presence in the city and at the university ensured contact and allowed collaboration in ordinary times. The destruction by fire of the Carthusian library in 1451 required the monks' reliance on other libraries in the city, the Dominicans' among them, to continue their own work and rebuild their collection. Their prior, Hermann of Appledorn (r. 1457-75), was particularly invested in that project in the 1460s.[11] Certain leitmotifs in the intellectual life of the charterhouse also drew attention to Albert. Multiple Carthusians at St. Barbara worked on Pseudo-Dionysius in the fifteenth century, including most famously the mystic Denis Ryckel (1402-1471), and Albert's commentaries on Pseudo-Dionysius were standard references in the later Middle Ages. Of particular relevance, Hermann of Appledorn assigned the charterhouse's leading calligrapher, Peter Kaltyser (d. 1477), to prepare an anthology of Albert's works in the 1460s. The university rector, Peter Rinck (1429-1501), financed the project. Whether Kaltyser completed the work is unknown, but the project offers the possible explanation that Rolevinck's *De excellentiis* was composed as its preface and increases the likelihood that the *De excellentiis* was composed in the late 1460s or the early 1470s.[12]

The *De excellentiis* is first and foremost a laudatory discourse on Albert's virtue. While it follows Albert's biographical timeline only loosely, it frames the important events in Albert's life and his achievements in a historical context. The work consists of four parts: a moralizing introduction on the rarity of individuals blessed with both great learning and good morals,[13] a gloomy sketch of Albert's own era as one marked by turmoil in church and empire,[14] an explicit refutation of the claims of Albert's practice of sorcery,[15] and a concluding encomium on Albert's life such as would justify his canonization.[16] Across these four sections, Rolevinck's pleading took three general forms: he associated Albert with other great men of faith beginning with Adam; he discussed Albert's own particular virtues, singling out his particular strengths in learning, devotion, and trueness to the church; and he engaged in several meticulous examinations of texts to demonstrate the morality both of Albert's study of magic and his teachings on it.

Throughout the *De excellentiis*, Rolevinck's favored literary devices are contrast and pluricolon. Thus in the first section his assertion of the difficulty in finding people who are both learned and devout sets up the opportunity to highlight how the church through the centuries has been blessed with men of learning and devotion who are raised up to confront the challenges of the day. Late antiquity set the standard, by Rolevink's lights, for a period in which the church was threatened by imperial persecution but was graced by such church fathers as Augustine, Gregory, and Jerome.[17] Albert's own century—torn asunder by the antipapal policies of Emperor Frederick II (r. 1220-50), the military threats posed by North Africans from the south and pagans in the Baltics, and the chaos and confusion sown by Albigensians in southern France[18]—was even more challenged, and so all the more in need of figures of heroic virtue and uncommon learning. Albert was such a man, along with other "scholastic doctors," such as Alexander of Hales (1185-1245), Bonaventure (1221-1274), and Thomas Aquinas (1225-1274).[19] Rolevinck noted that of these four figures, two each came from the two great mendicant orders. Rolevinck also situated Albert in a momentous trio of friar preachers along with Dominic and Aquinas. Rolevinck even made a trinitarian comparison on this point: Dominic was the Father for his decisiveness; Thomas, the Spirit for his gentleness; and Albert, the Son for his wisdom.[20]

In the middle of the treatise Rolevinck addressed the claims—what he characterized as defamations—that Albert had immorally studied and practiced magic. These include that he was "given to astrological images more than is decorous for a religious," "disguised himself in women's garb to learn the secrets of women," and "like another Solomon, disputed about the stars, the elements, stones, and so on, including the hyssop that grows from walls."[21] Rolevinck rejected all these claims. He turned to Ulrich of Strasbourg's infelicitous celebration of Albert as "unsurpassed in all knowledge and experienced in magical arts." Ulrich's own orthodoxy and friendship with Albert was indication enough for Rolevinck of the strictly innocent meaning of the sentence.[22] "Experienced," Rolevinck proposed, could only have meant that he had appropriately studied magic through reading. Rolevinck praised the *Speculum astronomiae* for setting a standard of orthodoxy against which any other claim against Albert could be tested for authenticity.[23]

Rolevinck remarked admiringly on Albert's learning and understanding. These were the fruit of effort and of grace, and it made him uniquely suited to defend the faith against the challenges of his age. Albert's *scientia* distinguished his talents from the confusion of the magical arts. Echoing Luis, Rolevinck underscored that such learning was put to the service of the faith. Albert's singular knowledge was the reason for his greatness, singular in fact and singular in name. To call Albert "the Great," Rolevinck explained, was warranted but not required. Although referred to as "magnus" already in the thirteenth century, in the fifteenth century Albert was still more commonly referred to as "the German" (Albertus Teutonicus). Rolevinck, arguing in favor of both, observed that in sacred history there are such great figures as John the Baptist and in profane history, Alexander the Great. Perhaps, he opined, it would be seemly for there to be one designated "great" for his learning.[24]

The *De excellentiis* ends not with an explicit call for Albert's canonization, but rather with an endorsement of learning. It is a learning of a particular kind and undertaken with a specific goal, a learning that has no value independent from moral virtue and must necessarily be accompanied by moral fortitude. Learning pursued in virtue and in service to the Christian faith places Albert, Rolevinck enthused, alongside the prophets, evangelists, ecclesiastical doctors, and scholastic doctors as defenders of the faith. "Laborious study" is to be joined with humility and meekness. Only thus, he admonished, will one win at the end "glorious contemplation and rest."[25] Rolevinck took this general counsel to Albert's expertise in magic and arrived at a justification for it similar to Luis's: Albert's engagement with magic was never as an end in itself but for the sake of its refutation, and by refuting it to bolster the Christian faith.

What became of Rolevinck's work after its completion is unclear. Although multiple manuscript copies are known to have existed as late as the eighteenth century, the text was never brought to press. The one surviving copy appears to have been kept within the precincts of the charterhouse until the end of the eighteenth century. Nonetheless, within a decade of its composition, in Cologne other writings about Albert appeared that shared its enthusiasm for Albert's learning and virtue and its characterization of Albert as magic's stalwart opponent. The two most substantial of these works are two freestanding vitae, the first such devoted to the thirteenth-century scholastic and offering substantial biographical description.[26] Both were composed by friars of the Cologne priory between 1483 and 1490.[27] They rely on a common set of earlier written sources,[28] which include chronicles of the Dominican order and the diocese of Regensburg.[29] Biographical details likewise appear again that were first recorded piecemeal in Ulrich's *De summo bono* and Thomas's *De apibus*, as well as Ptolemy of Lucca's *Historia ecclesiastica nova* (1313),[30] John of Colonna's *De viris illustribus* (ca. 1330),[31] and Henry of Herford's *Liber de memorialioribus* (after 1355).[32]

The first legend of these new vitae was the friar Peter of Prussia's *Legenda venerabilis domini Alberti Magni* (Legend of the venerable lord Albert the Great), published in 1486 or 1487.[33] It includes the story of Albert's life from his birth to death as well as a description of his burial, a small number of posthumous miracle accounts, and a report of the translation of his remains on 11 January 1483, celebration of which, the author explained in the prologue, was the occasion for the life's composition.[34] Less than two years later, in 1488, the second vita of Albert was presented at the chapter meeting of the Teutonian province of the Dominican order at Pforzheim in Baden. The vita was read aloud to the assembled friars, who proposed amendments to it and ultimately gave it their approval. Its author was Peter's confrere in Cologne, Rudolf of Nijmegen. In 1490 the revised version of the second vita appeared in print under the title *Legenda litteralis Alberti magni* (Written legend of Albert the Great).[35] In its prologue Rudolph described the differences between his own and Peter's works as an abbreviation and a "change of color."[36] Beyond a common subject, the second legend bears limited resemblance to Peter's. Verbatim correspondences are few, and the styles of writing, the overarching structures, and the manner in which Albert's research into the magical arts is addressed are distinct.

Appended to the 1490 printing of Rudolph's work is another original composition, the *Legenda compendiosa et metrica venerabilis domini Alberti Magni* (Legend of the venerable lord Albert the Great, abridged and versified) by the humanist poet and friar Jacobus Magdalius.[37] The 250 dactylic hexameters do not retell in verse the biography expressed prosaically in Rudolph's work, but rather highlight in a ceremonious style key events and insights into Albert's greatness. The poem recounts the Virgin's promise of great knowledge, it celebrates the virtue of his religious devotion, and it repeats Albert's encounters with and temptations from the devil, all of which Albert handily exposed and resisted. It underscores the association between Albert and Thomas.[38] It tells the story—*proh dolor!*—of Albert's loss of memory at the end of his life.[39] It concludes with an account of a posthumous apparition to a confrere in Cologne, at the end of which Albert highlighted the association between gems and celestial influences.[40]

The publication of so much life-writing about a single historical figure, in the same city and religious house and within a short period, is even more unusual than the two hundred years separating Albert's actual life and the composition of these first full-length vitae.[41] The Carthusian's early participation, while noteworthy, keeps the ambit of interest still tight. That the Dominican vitae were sent to press suggests a corporate or hierarchical approval that would militate against ongoing revision or replacement. Determining where and how the portrayals of Albert overlapped with and differed from each other, as well as ascertaining points of overlap with the Rolevinck work, could shed light on how the friars construed the later works to be improvements on the earlier (aimed at different readerships) or responses to new problems. Both printed vitae inform the reader, for example, of a large, common set of biographical and historical details describing Albert's youth, his entrance and life in the Order of Preachers, his course of studies, his tenure as bishop of Regensburg, his abundant and erudite scholarly oeuvre, and the prominent people with whom he worked. The vitae also endeavor to establish a certain religious temperament for their subject, and so describe Albert's devotion to the Blessed Sacrament, the Blessed Virgin Mary, and the wood of the Cross. Both express a disappointment that he had been neglected for canonization. The range and nature of the similarities do not suggest that the authors were targeting different audiences (say, one for Roman curial cardinal, the other for itinerant Rhenish preachers) or that between the first and the second accounts new biographical information had been discovered.

Albert and the Magical Arts

The most striking differences between the two lives have to do with how the authors address Albert's scholarly association with the magical arts. Both lives begin with an assertion that Albert's good name and scholarship were being misused to defend certain magical investigations that he had in fact condemned. Both stress in contrast that Albert's investigations had been for moral and orthodox purposes. The two vitae make this point differently. The differences—between the points the authors made and the ways they made them—merit careful examination. Peter began by offering a historical background that echoes both Luis's and Rolevinck's. According to him certain heresies had sprung up in the twelfth century, manifesting themselves in the form of "superstitions," encouraged by "a great throng of damnable nigromancers" who had won the admiration of the people by "false miracles." Even university professors had been led into "various erroneous opinions." In the search for an orthodox response "all turned their attention to Albert, the interpreter of the entirety of philosophy" so that "the precious might be separated from the vile" and "the true from the false." Albert thus approached the ancient texts not out of "curiosity"—denoting here an idle, self-serving interest in mastering hidden knowledge—but rather to solve the immediate problem of the heresies and the charlatanism occasioned by the misinterpretation and misuse of texts as well as to put even the most exotic of sciences better at the service of theology. Peter denounced as the fruit of ignorance and envy what subsequent generations, especially Peter's own, had accused Albert of: being an actual *magus*.[42]

Peter then moved from historical description to analysis and apologia. Peter asserted that careful scholarly examination can distinguish good from evil writings; this noble goal, easily distinguishable from the idle acquisition of knowledge, justified Albert's study of magical texts. "Albert studied the books," Peter remarked, "not in sin but as a work of virtue so that he could reject them," and elsewhere, "So that the head of Goliath might be removed by his own sword," an analogy taken from 1 Samuel 17:51 and commonly used by Christian theologians in late antiquity to justify the study of Greek philosophy for the insights it would bring to Christianity itself.[43] Peter also emphasized Albert's humble ability to distinguish between that which could be definitively rejected and that which appeared wrong to him but was still open to argument, thus resulting in "determinative" and "disputative" interpretations of the problematic texts.[44] An emblematically scholastic confidence that dialectically applied reason could discern the true from the false shapes in these passages. It is a style that was indeed suitable to the specific problem, but hardly typical of medieval life-writing about saints, an issue to which we will shortly return.

Peter also drew distinctions within the subject of Albert's study. The first distinction lies between true natural philosophy and various peripheral sciences. Peter allowed that alchemy and astrology were genuine sciences, but ones especially vulnerable to misuse.[45] In fact, Peter was convinced, with Albert, that they often were. Peter distinguished between two modes by which the sciences might be investigated and applied, approving one and rejecting the other.[46] The former encompassed reflection on the divinely ordered structure of the universe; the latter, its manipulation. The former was the work of a philosopher; the latter, of a nigromancer. Peter imputed this opinion to Albert, but at the same time expressed doubts that the distinction could be followed by even the best intentioned and trained student. The devil, Peter explained, was simply too adept at masking his own evil designs.[47] So, too, the reprobate alchemist and astrologer. Peter warned, "Having fabricated their revelations of this sort, they are believed to have transmitted divinatory knowledge to their followers, mingling some observations from astrological knowledge so that the hidden falsity appears less. Albert, therefore, correctly spoke about these diviners in his commentary on Isaiah 44."[48] Peter also acknowledged Albert's recognition that alchemy and astronomy were among the tools of charlatanism, itself not diabolical but certainly immoral. Peter highlighted Albert's mistrust of dream analysis, and his resistance toward correlating the capacity for language to higher rationality: even Indian parrots and African pygmies can be taught to speak, Albert argued, though neither possesses human reason.[49]

A further distinction Peter described separates out fields of investigation that might be used for good or for ill from those fields that are inherently evil on account of demonic participation in terms of study and practice. With Albert, Peter condemned this latter category, identified as nigromancy, absolutely. But as we saw, Albert expressed himself sparingly on nigromancy, and when he did, he did so principally in his theological writings. Peter made the topic of central importance. In a concern increasingly characteristic of the fifteenth century, Peter cautioned that humans' manipulation of the natural order to the advantage of a client almost always involved depraved commerce with demons. The advantages might be material, as in the case of alchemy; psychological, as is the case with love potions; or intellectual, as is the case in prophesying and divination. Peter reiterated the classic condemnation of the nigromancer's evil vanity. He drew from an older condemnation in Augustine's *City of God* when he listed as examples magic for the seduction of women, the opening of sealed documents, the rendering immobile of ships, and the inducement of fear in others.[50] Peter was also concerned to enlist Albert's support in denying nigromancy any claim to true philosophy. The difficulty of distinguishing diabolical mantics from legitimate astronomy in the texts of ancient pagan Greeks and their Muslim and

Jewish interpreters was precisely the justification for Albert's lengthy study of such writings: only thus could the nigromantic be sifted out from the scientific.[51] Yet Albert never addressed the possibility of human pacts with the devil, even though the issue was emerging as an important one already in his own day.

Peter's final distinction regarding the subject of study is that between the immoral and the heterodox. One way practitioners of alchemy and astronomy place their souls in danger is by the immoral frauds they perpetrate against unsuspecting and foolish clients.[52] Peter also identified certain practices as outright evil and argued that they should not be learned. They lead the practitioner to heresy, apostasy, and idolatry and thence to eternal damnation: "All these things as narrated by Albert, recognize for yourselves, so that you might know the impiety of nigromancy and that you might recoil from incurring the crime of apostasy."[53] Peter here sketched Albert's classification of kinds of divination: geomancy, aeromancy, pyromancy, hydromancy, chiromancy, and garrimancy. Expanding on what he took as Albert's from the *Speculum*, he explained that chiromancy as a kind of physiognomy could be considered true but is superstitious when one studies the lines of the hand to tell fortunes, as practiced by "old women and gypsies."[54] Such divination is especially dangerous for giving the false "appearance of being defensible with reason."[55] Concern for souls lost to the faith, Peter averred, was Albert's motivation for turning to nigromantic texts: like Saint Paul illuminating for the Athenians the altars of the demons and the sayings of the poets, Albert set himself the task of exposing the errors of the nigromancers.[56]

The most sophisticated part of Peter's argument consisted of his frequent and careful reference to a body of theological, philosophical, and historical texts, most importantly Albert's own writings: Peter signaled the reader already in the prologue that his vita would make its argument on the basis of Albert's own words, a surer proof of his sanctity than even miracles.[57] In the eleven chapters dedicated to addressing Albert's association with the magical and related sciences, Peter cited Albert's own works—both in natural philosophy and in other genres such as biblical commentary. His treatment of Albert's stance on geomantics in chapter 13, "Why engravings on stones according to the aspect of the stars are prohibited, and how these engraved stones cannot speak," is typical of how Peter proceeded. He began by sketching erroneous positions regarding engraved stones. He presented Albert's philosophical counterassertion—namely, that stones do not have souls and thus no power to effect wonders. Without souls, Peter explained, stones can only "speak" with the assistance of demonic powers. Peter then cited Peter Comestor's gloss on the second chapter of Genesis, in which mantics with stones are defended with reference to an apocryphal story of Moses's fashioning of rings of remembering and forgetting. Then Peter identified counterarguments in Albert's *De mineralibus*: first, that the nature of the art inclines toward idolatry; second, that the practice itself is too often applied to the "vain and evil" ends of the magician, such as the seduction of women; and third, that the art itself is difficult. This section of the vita concludes with a summary warning that those tempted to practice the art should be dissuaded first by its difficulty and then by the church's prohibition. Peter reinforced Albert's point with quotations from Thomas Aquinas's *Summa contra gentiles*.[58] The problem here of course is that Peter has not represented Albert's position and the divergences between it and Aquinas's accurately. As we see in chapter 2, Albert held the crafting and use of talismans, while susceptible to abuse, to be based on "good doctrine."

Peter also made use of biblical arguments regarding the practice of magic. In one instance, he followed Albert by turning to the first line of the biblical Book of Daniel in order to show that occult knowledge can be God-given: "God gave the boys knowledge and discipline in every book and wisdom, but to Daniel he gave understanding of all visions and dreams." With reference to Saint Jerome and Albert, Peter proposed that the interpretation of dreams, to be sure a magical art, might be licit. It was among the passages that Peter used to clarify Ulrich's assertion that Albert was "experienced in magic."[59] Furthermore, the passage is highly reminiscent of the thematic style of mendicant preaching, an elaboration on an introductory biblical verse for the sake of a theological or pastoral point. It complements the more structured, dialectic arguments we find elsewhere, and highlights both the complexity of Peter's strategy to exonerate Albert and the work's mendicant character.

Out of Peter's sustained refutation of so many defamations of character and misuses of scholarship emerge two complicated but important questions: the first has to do with Peter's use of Albert's writing; the second, with Peter's characterizations of Albert's opponents. Despite the wide circulation of Luis's *Tabula* and its predecessor indices,[60] Albert's authentic canon was still under dispute. Not only was such a genre inchoate in the fifteenth century, the custom of authors' taking passages from their masters' works, expanding on them, and then releasing them under their masters' names posthumously made the constructing of such indices especially challenging. Consequently, there was no shortage of Albertan pseudepigrapha, as we see in the previous chapter. Peter, it appears, followed Luis's *Tabula* closely but not exactly as to the determination of authentic texts.[61] On his own, Peter rejected outright the *Semita recta*, *De mirabilibus mundi*, *De virtutibus herbarum, lapidum, et animalium*, and *De secretis mulierum*. Concerning the last of these, Peter flatly remarked, "Prudent men know without difficulty that it is under no circumstances ascribable to Albert."

Peter was particularly exorcised over the misattribution of the *Semita recta*.[62] Here and elsewhere, his refutation involved two kinds of argument. First, he claimed that material arguments concerning alchemy in the *Semita recta* contradicted the arguments in the *De mineralibus*, whose authenticity was unquestioned. He wrote:

> The alchemists claim that this book is Albert's. But because Albert condemned the *Semita recta* with his opinions and because he knew all things contrary to those said in the *Semita recta*, the alchemist's claim is simply false.... The *Semita recta* proposes that it is possible to make gold from stone and many other things. It approves all things, which Albert refuted and he said that these were stupid claims. If you simply inspect the *De mineralibus* of Albert and the *Semita recta*, you will say: the *De mineralibus* condemns and obliterates the *Semita recta* above all.

Second, Peter distinguished the books by formal aspects of their arguments. By his reckoning, for example, the two books could not have come from the same hand: "It does not even have the style of Albert, and therefore those who desire to know read the two books and they know what I have said is true.... Thus by logic it is to be noted that the *Semita recta* is not Albert's, as already proved."[63]

Rudolph addressed a similar set of problems and developed the concern over Albert's appropriation by magicians (fig. 4). Like Peter, Rudolph named envy as the source of the calumnies. He reiterated what other writers had already expressed about Albert—namely, that he was an orthodox and moral interpreter of magical texts who read them so as to combat evil more effectively. Echoing Peter, he drew the analogy between Paul at Athens and Albert before the magicians, he accused the envious of rodent-like gnawing at the vulnerable flock of the faithful, and to defend Albert's use of nigromantic texts to defeat the nigromancers, he poetically appealed to the young poet-king David, stealing "the warlike arms of an unfriendly king."[64]

Rudolph also reinserted and addressed issues first raised by Rolevinck but passed over by Peter, such as the rumor that Albert had disguised himself as a woman so as to apprentice to a midwife.[65] How else could he have been able to write so expertly about human embryology, gynecology, and obstetrics?[66] Midwives themselves did attract suspicion, of course: no occupation was as close to the mysteries of conception and birth, and their manufacture of love potions, proconceptives, contraceptives, and abortifacients could arouse significant animosity.[67] But cross-dressing itself, for lack of a better term, was not absolutely or consistently condemned in the Middle Ages. Religious and civil

Fig. 4. Title page of *Legenda litteralis Alberti Magni* by Rudolph of Nijmegen, 1490. BSB-Ink R-284. Rudolph's life of Albert the Great emphasized traditionally pious parts of the Albert biography, such as his identification of the young Thomas Aquinas's great intellectual promise, as represented here on the title page of Rudolph's work.

legal understandings and enforcement varied from place to place through the centuries. There was a tradition of cross-dressing holy women, for example, stretching back to the earliest generations of Christianity. On the specific matter of wearing clothes associated with the opposite gender for a purpose other than sexual activity, the concern was greater for illicitly dressing as a man than as a woman.[68] Herein lies the distinctiveness of Rudolph's rejection of Albert's midwifery.

Without explicitly addressing the authenticity of *De secretis mulierum*, as Peter had, Rudolph began with the acknowledgment that Albert had indeed been an expert in the secrets of conception, fetal development, and childbirth. He then turned to the reasoning of Albert's detractors: Albert's copious writing about the generation of animals and the secrets of nature did not, by Rudolph's reckoning, allow one to conclude that he had been a trained midwife.[69] He elaborated, "Was he a gardener because he wrote about plants; a mechanic because he wrote about machines; a sailor, field hand, weaver, or hunter because he spoke about matters that concerned these occupations. Hardly. These would not be valid conclusions. It is indeed malformed to hold that only a woman can know of these things, a notion defeated with the reasons above."[70] This example also represents a noteworthy stylistic difference between the two vitae: Rudolph clearly favored the persuasive devices of a rhetorician in crafting the *Legenda litteralis Alberti* to the dialectic structures deployed by Peter. The above examples rely above all on the enthymeme, a partial syllogism favored in classical rhetoric that builds on possibilities rather than logical certitudes. Another indication of Rudolph's "rhetorical" rather than "dialectic" approach in his reference to Albert's other acknowledged specialties—navigation, agriculture, textiles, hunting, and so on. Reference to these other fields, which Albert wrote about expertly without practicing, reinforced the primary enthymeme. While the dialectician would regard the accumulation of similar cases an inferior argument, the rhetorician regarded such repetition and induction as subtle tools in the art of persuasion.[71]

Peter and Rudolph distinguished themselves further in their references to historical figures who, like Albert, read widely, even in that which they disagreed with so that their arguments might be more effective. Peter repeatedly cited the principle that one might best defeat an enemy by knowing him and illustrated that principle with reference to, for example, Paul in Athens and Thomas Aquinas. Rudolph, in contrast, tended to emphasize cases in which examples imply principles. For example, Rudolph invoked the many church fathers who had written about carnal sins: surely, Rudolph proposed, one may not conclude that because they wrote about carnal sins they had therefore committed them.[72] In a passage of graceful name-dropping drawn from Eusebius of Caesarea's

Church History[73] Rudolph recalled for his readers that the greatest apologists of history were effective only because of their familiarity with what they opposed—Justin Martyr, Anatolius of Laodicea, and even Julian, the fourth-century Arian cleric turned apostate emperor who "knew the utility of knowledge and who fortified himself with these arms through study of philosophy, the zeal of philosophy not for the Catholic faith but for the pagan, so that he was learned in that which was interdicted to Catholics."[74]

The Problem of the Demonic

The question naturally arises why attention to Albert's magical expertise turned from admiration to indignation as it did, when it did, and where it did. There were of course other controversial figures, in and before the fifteenth century, whose potential associations with illicit magic raised concerns. But Albert is unique in the energy and focus of the new displeasure he occasioned.[75] Why then in the later fifteenth century, and why in Cologne rather than any other city that claimed association with him? In fact, the setting, instrumentalization, and aims of the vitae find initial explanation in the association of Jacob Sprenger with their composition and printing. Sprenger was prior of the Cologne Dominicans, and it was under his authority that Peter wrote the vita in the early 1480s, that the vita was printed in 1486/87, that Rudolph was set to the task of writing a new vita, that the provincial chapter in Pforzheim in 1488 took up Rudolph's vita to evaluate it, and that it was published with Magdalius's verses in 1490. Sprenger's participation in these activities is noteworthy because Sprenger was clearly associated with two movements whose traces run through both vitae: first, his association with the composition, printing, and ecclesiastical approval of the witch-hunter's manual, *Malleus maleficarum* (Hammer of witches) (Speyer 1486/87), situates him among those convinced that demonic magic posed a significant and immediate threat to Christian society. Second, he was a leader in the fifteenth-century reformist wing of the Order of Preachers called the Observants. The connection of the vitae to Sprenger and through him to increasing late medieval worries about the demonic magic and Dominican Observantism offers a clue to understanding the origins of and purposes behind the composition of the vitae and their new treatment of Albert's experience in the magic arts.[76]

The scholarship in search of an explanation for how later medieval developments in the understanding of magic shaped, on the one hand, the witch hunts of the early modern period or, on the other hand, the rise of modern science, is copious if also inconclusive.[77] Nevertheless, a rough outline of developments here can shed light on the specific case at hand and on correspondences between the two effects. In short, late medieval intellectuals were increasingly worried about the real workings of the devil in Christian society and convinced that it was through the practice of magic by humans that the devil was most effective at working toward his destructive ends.[78] The conviction grew concomitantly that such borderline fields of natural philosophical study as alchemy, astrology, and divination were feasible only with diabolical cooperation. Albert himself did not refer to these as magic and employed the term *magical arts* with narrow precision, but the learned ecclesiastical circles of the fifteenth century held less tightly to such a distinction. Instead, the concerns among reformers, scholars, prelates, and princes in this period resulted in the emergence of a new concept of witchcraft that blurred the difference between common magical practices and the nigromancy of learned treatises and that conceived the witches' most malign powers to be the reward for their abandonment of the Christian faith and surrendering of their souls to the devil.[79] Nigromancy, which was considered in Albert's new vitae, distinguished itself from witchcraft (*maleficia*), which was not, as elite from common magic. The new linkage between concerns over learned magic and common magic, nevertheless, explains how, in the person of Jacob Sprenger, the worries about both could occupy someone simultaneously and with astonishing consequences.

Sprenger was of course not the only friar inspired by the fifteenth-century furor over demonic magic. Indeed, many Dominicans shared in it. The friars Nicholas Eymeric, John Nider, and Henry "Institoris" Kramer were among the most influential advocates for the vigorous eradication of nigromancy and witchcraft. All three were Observant Dominicans. Nider's *The Anthill*, composed 1436–38 and first printed in Cologne in 1475, is one of the earliest books describing methods of investigating and prosecuting sorcery; in fact, its author conceived it primarily as a text on religious reform.[80] John Vinet, who composed the *Against Those Who Invoke Demons* in 1450 while an inquisitor in Carcassonne, was an Observant friar.[81] And, the most notorious witch-hunter's manual of all, Kramer's *Malleus maleficarum*, was also the product of Observant friars. The book is crucial for associating apostasy with all magic. Innocent VIII's bull "Desiring with great ardor," issued on 5 December 1484, and printed with the first editions of the *Malleus*, linked witch-hunting and inquisition for the first time at this powerful ecclesiastical instance. The bull specifically commissioned two Observant Dominican inquisitors we have just encountered, Kramer and Sprenger, to pursue witchcraft as a theological delict.[82]

As to the witch-hunting frenzy, the ways that both life-writers confront the slanders against Albert fit seamlessly into the new concerns about dark magic that developed in the fifteenth century and set the stage for the great witch hunts of the sixteenth and seventeenth.[83] For example, the charge of apostasy was central to the new condemnations; indeed, Peter, it will be recalled, made the connection explicit between the kind of magic Albert's detractors defended by locating it in the writings on apostasy.[84] Does this mean that the emerging conflation of two very different magical systems—the learned nigromancy of a clerical elite and the common magic practiced more broadly and associated with some of the magical arts Albert had in fact written about favorably—fueled the concern to exculpate Albert from the charge of magic? Were Peter and Rudolph concerned only about the misuse of Albert by a certain kind of magically inclined intellectual, clerical and learned, or did their concern to make Albert's study more conventional extend to some threat posed by the popular belief in and uses of magic?

While the references to astral influences and gems at the end of Magdalius's versified vita hearken to the older, stricter limits on which magic was most susceptible to diabolization, the two prose legends identify threats of heresy and apostasy in kinds of magic previously not regarded as demonic. Peter, for example, did criticize the popular curiosity in magic, especially when that curiosity was directed toward learned types of magic, which included by his lights alchemy and astrology. This curiosity, by Peter's reckoning, led in the direction of heresy and apostasy. Rudolph, though he made less of the magical concerns than Peter and referred to heresy but not apostasy, came closer to this convergence when he focused on the problem and implications of "obstetrics." The concern for apostasy and heresy served Sprenger well, as only on those grounds could an inquisitor such as himself or Kramer involve himself in the prosecution of sorcerers and witches.

Reform in Head and Members: Rebuilding Albert

Limiting and justifying Albert's study of magic were first steps toward exonerating him, but pruning his reputation back to a more ordinary form of extraordinary holiness was another. What then was he, and why should he be canonized? Peter's and Rudolph's answers were straightforward: Albert was a bishop, mendicant, and scholar, virtuous in every respect. On the one hand, Albert's service as bishop of Regensburg had warranted the passing attention of earlier chroniclers, and "holy bishops" were attracting renewed enthusiasm in the final decades of the Middle Ages. On the other, mendicants and scholars were not common subjects of vitae sanctorum in the fourteenth and fifteenth centuries.[85] Rolevinck's celebration of Albert's mendicant learning and piety Sprenger could take as reconnaissance in developing his own tactics of making Albert unmagical and "Observant." A glance to the emergence of the reforming movement in Cologne and Sprenger's contribution to it raises the latter tactic into high relief.

The origin of the Dominican Observance can be traced to central Italy around 1300. Like reform movements in other orders, the Dominican Observants desired to refashion what they perceived as corrupted religious life by strictly interpreting and enforcing the obligations of community living and the rules against private property. A new master general, Raymond of Capua, fully endorsed the movement and required in 1390 the establishment of at least one "Observant" priory in every province of the order. The first priory to adopt the Observance in the empire was in Colmar in 1389.[86] Given the prestige of the Dominican studium generale in Cologne, this priory's adoption of the Observance in 1465 was a significant gain for the movement. When Jacob Fabri of Stubach (ca. 1420–ca. 1489), the provincial superior of the Teutonia province and an advocate for the Observant movement within the order, was summoned to Rome in 1485 following the untimely death of a master general,[87] the trusted assistant who served as acting provincial was Jacob Sprenger,[88] as he served again from November 1487 after Fabri's resignation from provincial office until his own election as provincial at the chapter meeting in Pfortzheim the following May.[89]

Evidence of Dominican interest in Albert's canonization before the implementation of the Observance is sparse.[90] The Cologne priory's adoption of the Observance corresponds exactly to Kaltyser's compilation of Albert's works at the St. Barbara charterhouse and to Rolevinck's likely composition of the *De excellentiis*. Peter's and Rudolph's vitae express their desire for Albert's canonization with apologies for its absence. The lack of canonization, Peter pointed out, echoing Rolevinck, could not in itself suggest a shortage of sanctity on Albert's part. Indeed, "it is probable that there are more excellent, noncanonized persons in beatitude than canonized ones."[91] Rather conventionally, Peter vaguely blamed "the resistance of wicked prelates" and "negligence of the friars" for the oversight.[92] Furthermore, Peter encouraged private devotion to Albert and suggested that the length of time intervening since Albert's death was hardly such as to hinder the working of miracles through his intercession.[93] Peter pointed out that in a letter from Pope Pius II to the Turks the fifteenth-century pontiff cited "Albertus Teutonicus" as if already among the canonized.[94] Rudolph reiterated these points and added miracles. He blamed the brevity of certifiable miracles on fraternal negligence and assured readers that in any event miracles were dispensable evidence of sanctity: John the Baptist, for example, performed no miracles in this life or the next, but surely, Rolevinck continued, the abundance of miracles credited to Saint Dominic might compensate for the paucity of Albert's own. What posthumous miracles and apparitions he could conjure up Rudolph listed just the same.[95]

Twentieth-century historians recognized that Observant friars were behind the unsuccessful push to have Albert canonized in the 1480s, but they did not go the further step of concluding that a purpose of the vitae was to turn him into an Observant Dominican avant la lettre. When the legends of 1486 and 1490, however, are compared with Luis's vita (1414) and another brief vita written contemporaneously, the so-called Cologne Legend (mostly before 1421), the differences—additions, excisions, and alterations—suggest exactly such a transformation. This is especially apparent in the descriptions of Albert as a friar and provincial. That Albert was an inspired member of his order and true to its rule reflects a trope for clerical and religious saints. Thus that both Peter and Rudolph, with material reworked from Rolevinck, reported that the Blessed Virgin Mary had appeared to the adolescent Albert, who preferred praying in church to playing with friends, and called him to "flee the world" and enter the Order of Preachers, "'directed in most recent times by my son for the salvation of the world'"; that he excelled in studies and in the spiritual life; and that he was one of many spiritually gifted men drawn in those days to the order are all characteristics that can be found in many legends of religious, and not just members of "reformed" communities.[96]

Particular emphases on how he governed the Teutonian province as provincial and how he led his life as a senior friar, particularly as expressed in stories that are not drawn from the early lives, turn Albert more tendentiously into an Observant. In Peter's *Legenda*, the reader learns about the spirit of poverty out of which Albert governed the province. Peter emphasized as well how widely the friar preachers spread out across central Europe under Albert's guidance, and how Albert traveled to them all by foot "without a coin in his purse, begging for bread from door to door along the way with the other friars: he was the emulator of apostolic perfection, desiring to be observed by the friars in everything." These assertions and stories are repeated in Rudolph's *Legenda*.[97] As provincial, Albert enforced a strict reading of the friars' rule, lest, as Peter reported, "from small transgressions the friars fall into greater ones." The asceticism of the Dominicans in this period distinguished the friars, Peter remarked, from the laxity and indifference of other religious and secular clergy. Peter dramatically recounted how Albert, out of regard for the order's vow of poverty, ordered the exhumation of a deceased friar whose private accounts, held in violation of the vow, had been discovered only after his interment in a Dominican church.[98]

A final Observant ideal Peter highlighted is the appreciation of community life. The Observants considered living outside cloister a serious yet common corruption of religious life. Peter addressed this by including several scenes of Albert in community, reclining at table with his confreres, for example; sensing from afar the untimely death of his student, colleague, and friend Saint Thomas; and yearning to return to the simple life of the Dominican priory while serving as bishop of Regensburg and then in fact returning to his own great joy and that of his fellow friars. In contrast, his governance as provincial did not play more than a passing role in the earlier vitae.

The authors let Albert's deeper desires to be a simple mendicant academic shape their telling of his Albert's episcopal experience (at Regensburg from 1260 to 1262). This yearning extended to the life-writers the opportunity to speak about the dangers of the world outside the cloister, such as would surround a bishop.[99] The trickiest subject the authors were challenged with was his resignation from office in 1262. A medieval legend suggested that Albert's alchemy had solved the financial distress under which the see suffered, thus allowing Albert to return home. The fifteenth-century life-writers pointed to other holy prelates who had stepped down honorably from ecclesiastical office to pursue the life of perfection without worldly distraction. Both mentioned, for example, Peter Morrone, that is, Pope Celestine V (ca. 1209–1296, r. 1294): While Dante placed Celestine in hell's antechamber for his "Great Refusal," Peter and Rudolph recounted succinctly his unhappy four-month papacy, his happy subsequent foundation of an eremitical order, and his canonization under the name Peter, rather than Celestine, in 1313. In a similar manner, the friar authors reported, Albert's return to the Cologne priory, complete with papal permission, occasioned great rejoicing.[100]

From Sorcery to Sanctity

More than a decade elapsed between Rolevinck's *De excellentiis* and the translation of Albert's remains in 1483; three more years before the publication of a first vita, and four more until the second, along with its poem. At this point we may cautiously summarize how interest in Albert developed within German Dominican circles in the late fifteenth century, why Albert's centuries-old association with magic in particular needed reframing, and briefly consider an aftereffect of the failed canonization efforts. Reform impulses, constituted necessarily by heightened ideals and sharpening critiques of the status quo, were astir in religious milieus across Europe. As they arose in the vibrant monastic and mendicant culture of fifteenth-century Cologne, they inspired the Carthusian local historian Werner Rolevinck to panegyrize Albert the Great in the *De excellentiis*. A component of these reforming ideas, one that caught the attention of Observant Dominicans in general and their Cologne superior Jacob Sprenger in particular, was the priority of extirpating sorcery from Christendom. All the more scandalizing to these reform-minded friars, practitioners of magic appealed to one of their order's greatest learned personalities, imputing to him the reputation as a sorcerer, and a lecherous one no less, popularly known to consort in the Near East with elvish queens. These reformers conceived a proper vita as the means both to refute the calumny and, in fact, to redeploy this revered Dominican scholar against the diabolic forces at work against Christendom and for ongoing reform. The Dominican Observants, Sprenger included, were devoted, after all, to a particular kind of reform in the church and their own order. Albert's activities as prior, provincial, bishop, and papal legate put him in positions where he could exemplify the kinds of reform they favored. More ambitious still, the canonization, to which end the vita would be put, would highlight beyond the order and to the whole church the goals of reformed religious life and a society free of magic. Albert was an all-the-more suitable candidate given that he lay buried in Sprenger's own church, and the location of that church in Cologne increased the chance of a canonization. Cologne was a center for the veneration of saints in the empire. The presence there of the Dominican's studium generale and the empire's largest university further enhanced the city's significance in ecclesiastical and academic circles. That an elector archbishop governed the city reflected its political and ecclesiastical significance in the empire. All indicators suggested to Sprenger that the biographical fashioning of Albert, along with his canonization, was an opportunity too good to pass up for the order, the church, and Christian society.

By 1483, Sprenger could point to the relics, a limited cult, and the backing of his order and Cologne's university. Still, he lacked a vita, an essential element in a petition for canonization. Given Albert's reputational difficulties in certain learned circles, a distinctive aspect of the vita needed to be conspicuous: it needed to show that Albert was no magus, and to the contrary that what Albert wrote supported the largely antimagical position being contemporaneously staked out by Sprenger, the university's theology faculty, and his confreres in the order. Peter of Prussia, a friar of the Cologne priory, was set to the task. He relied on the textual resources to be found in Cologne, which he interpreted and supplemented in light of the concerns of his confreres regarding the horrifying loss of souls to heresy and apostasy through the practice of magic and related commerce with the devil. Work on the book corresponded to other important events in the development of a cult of veneration, most notably the solemn translation of Albert's remains in 1483, the presence at which by the Dominican master general Salvo Cassetta gives evidence of the whole order's commitment to Albert's canonization.[101]

By 1486 Peter's work was completed and sent to press. Although its publication indicates the text's approval among the Dominican leadership, it must have become quickly clear to those seeking Albert's canonization that simply refuting Albert's bad reputation, though a necessary claim, was insufficient for canonization. Peter's vita might have offered a valiant rebuttal to those nigromancers who appealed to Albert in justification of their scurrilous practices, but for a canonization the Dominicans needed a vita that presented Albert in a recognizably edifying and laudatory fashion. The *Legenda venerabilis* followed in course. The Cologne Dominicans tapped Rudolph of Nijmegen—whose writing style suggests a personality characterized by both tact and wit—for the new task. The resulting vita takes the success of Peter's earlier forensic efforts as a given and emphasizes instead the virtues and piety of Albert as friar, prelate, and teacher. Rudolph needed to address only one problematic issue passed over by Peter: the offensive notion that Albert had learned hidden things about women, though the practice midwifery should be expressly rebutted.

In 1488 Sprenger—already acting provincial superior, suspecting his own election as full provincial superior, eager to marshal all possible support for Albert's canonization, and satisfied with Rudolph's progress—brought the unfinished work to the biennial province chapter. His goal was to attain the assemblage's approval. As it happened, he was concurrently working for the university's approbation of the *Malleus*. The province chapter in Pforzheim gave its approval, suggesting at the same time revisions. Sprenger, now newly elected provincial superior, returned to Cologne where Rudolph revised his work over the ensuing two years. In 1490, with Sprenger's backing, the revised work was sent to press. As a further nod to the latest trends in learned society, a classicizing, 250-line vita metrica by a leading humanist poet and Observant friar Jacobus Magdalius was appended to the printed book. These efforts resulted in a qualified success: by the end of the fifteenth century the Holy See had permitted veneration of Albert within the Dominican order and in the diocese of Regensburg.[102]

While Albert had to wait another three centuries before a successful petition for canonization was mounted, Rome expanded its permissions for veneration over that period. Dominican concern for keeping Albert's reputation pristine continued, notwithstanding the failure of the early canonization efforts or even whatever distraction from a single medieval thinker that the sixteenth century's religious tumult might have induced. Looking ahead, even as ecclesiastical authorities—the Supreme Sacred Congregation of the Roman and Universal Inquisition was founded in 1542; the Sacred Congregation of the Index, in 1571—sharpened their scrutiny into teachings and activities that had been accepted or tolerated, Albert escaped censure.[103] The Spanish Dominican theologian Alfonso Chacón (1530–1599), for example, accepted Albert's authorship of *De secretis mulierum* and defended its contents in the face of its condemnation by the Spanish Inquisition and doggedly worked to keep the title off the Roman

Index. After Gonzalez Ponce de Leon, a consulter to the Index, rejected Albert's authorship during an updating of the Index in the 1590s, the Dominicans were charged with producing a corrected edition of the treatise, and Federico Borromeo (1564–1631), the cardinal archbishop of Milan, advocated successfully for its removal from late drafts of the Index that appeared in 1596. In 1604 it was replaced on the list but without ascription to Albert.[104] In short, so long as Albert was tethered to the treatise through presumed authorship, it evaded censure. Meanwhile, a host of others associated with related magical theory and practice found themselves and their works condemned and placed on the index, Arnold of Villanova and Peter of Abano to name just two.[105]

The significance of the fifteenth-century events rests on three key points: the first has to do with the part that late medieval religious reformers imputed to magic, in learned and common forms, in the corruption of Christian society. As the preceding analysis shows, the instigators of the fifteenth-century canonization campaign for Albert belonged to a particular faction within the Dominican order. This faction, the Observants, was committed to reversing a perceived moral decay, initially, within the order, and then, within all Christendom. Historians are newly discovering striking links between these reforming friars and the first concerted efforts to condemn many kinds of learned and popular magic as demonic that ecclesiastical and civil authorities had either tolerated or considered benign in previous centuries. A sharp distinction between *magic* as an overarching term and *sorcery* (or *nigromancy*) as its malign form made little sense in this mindset. That it was Observant friars in Germany who first promoted the canonization and expressed concern for Albert's misuse by sorcerers and nigromancers makes it impossible to explain the new fashioning of Albert's life and scholarship as an innocuous and general attempt to bolster a particular devotion. Rather, it must be related to a larger program on the part of these reformers qua reformers to delegitimatize and prosecute thinking and experimentation that were labeled *magic* and *nigromancy*. These late fifteenth-century hagiographical writings did not review the range of learned practices that Albert himself most often and favorably addressed as "magical arts," nor his acknowledgment of forms of nigromancy and alchemy that, according to content and circumstance, he regarded as rational and benign sciences. This body of life-writing stands as evidence of an association in the minds of these late medieval reformers between ideals of holiness, the reform of Christian society, and an exclusion of anything "magical" from the rational and the moral. It marks instead a new manifestation of an old Christian idea that the magical is always diabolical.

An attendant fifteenth-century concern for thirteenth-century natural philosophy is at the root of a second problem that emerges from the canonization efforts. Albert was only one of many thirteenth-century figures who were highly regarded scholarly authorities in their own day and beyond and whose writings touched on areas regarded as tangential to natural philosophy in the narrow sense. High medieval texts on subjects such as alchemy, astrology, and certain forms of divination appeared in striking numbers in the fifteenth century.[106] New philosophical interests at the universities and new printing technologies drove this trend, and the milieus where natural philosophical works were produced were identical to those where the magical works were. That many of the latter works were spuriously attributed to thirteenth-century authorities is more about enhancing the significance of the work than it is deflecting attention from the real author.

We see in consequence the new fifteenth-century attempts to establish official lists of authentic thirteenth-century works. Lists, indices, and *tabulae* were the genres of legitimizing and delegitimizing. To the extent that Albert's name carried weight among natural philosophers and theologians alike, these pseudonymous magical writings are a case in point. The variations across these lists suggest that the newest conceptions of legitimate natural philosophy and magic being developed at the universities were prejudicially guiding the hand of those compiling the official catalogs. Analysis of the fifteenth-century life-writing by Observant Dominicans sheds light on the manuscript and printing history of the texts on natural philosophy and the magical arts circulating in the fifteenth century and invites further consideration to determine how competing parties used and misused the thirteenth-century scholarship in the debates that foreshadowed the concern about magic that was peculiar to that and subsequent centuries.

Third and finally, the concerns associated with the failed canonization efforts to exonerate Albert from any hint of untoward magical interest and the effort to recharacterize and deploy him as magic's uncompromising adversary moves the history of his reputation as one "experienced in magic" through a decisive new threshold. Whereas up to this point, this reputation was largely ignored, repeated calmly, and regarded as benign, in the eyes of the late fifteenth-century reforming Dominicans it was scandalous. Furthermore, the correction it required was a methodical recasting of the person and his work, such as no previous generation had been inspired to undertake. Albert continued to have a place in the larger conversation about what magic was and whether it was good to practice, but now more equivocally including not only the sympathetic researcher into and occasional experimenter with magic, but also by parties with more disapprovingly discriminating viewpoints on magic as its model opponent. New ideas about magic, what it is and whether it is good to practice, made this enlargement and complexification of his reputation possible, and the new ambivalence made Albert the potential instrument of both those who sought to legitimize magic, especially in certain contested forms, and those who sought to its delegitimization.[107]

The transforming and expanding treatment of Albert's reputation for magic thus opens a view simultaneously on to the diabolization of magic and its naturalization: the late fifteenth-century Dominicans reclaimed Albert after all by proscribing the invocation of demons and enervating ritual actions. These Observants were creating—at least for the natural philosophers and practitioners of the magical arts and nigromancy—a less enchanted world, one in which conjured demons and magical incantations were simply off limits, but not their workshops and experiments. Albert, whose efforts in the thirteenth century at naturalizing what was by others regarded as necessarily demonic, was thus himself disenchanted in the fifteenth, but at the price of diabolizing some of what he had attempted to naturalize. As the next two chapters nevertheless show, the Dominicans did not have the last word on what Albert's experience in magic really meant, how these matters should be handled, or what reputation Albert should in the final analysis enjoy, and even among those who saw in him no ally to magic, superstition, and the diabolical.

4

THE HISTORICAL ALBERT

With reference to the mythical Greco-Egyptian sage Hermes Trismegistus, the French polymath Gabriel Naudé (1600–1653) suggested that to call Albert simply "the Great" is to shortchange his accomplishment: Were the title "very-great" (his translation of *trismegistus*) not by tradition reserved to Hermes, surely it would belong to Albert as well.[1] Indeed, Albert has not only been shortchanged, Naudé continued, he has also been defamed with allegations of practicing magic endlessly repeated and "now maintained by the ignorance of the common people against [his] happy memory." Albert was not alone in suffering this notoriety. In his *Apologie pour tous les grands personages faussement soupçonnez de magie* (1625) (A defense of all great persons falsely suspected of magic), Naudé identified Albert and forty-one additional cases, drawn from antiquity, the Middle Ages, and Naudé's own time, who deserved exculpation.[2]

Blame for the aspersion—against Albert and the others—Naudé laid at the feet of two kinds of writer. The first were historians, who, he explained, "never represent pure things to us but twist and mask them according to the appearance they wish to make them take." He pointed to multiple examples, including "the gentiles and idolaters" who had attacked the early Christians; Imperial chroniclers, who "have uttered a thousand villainies against the popes"; and the English, who "describe the Pucelle d'Orléans as a witch and magician" (151–54).[3] The other kind were demonographers, whose writings were "fat and blistering with so many fables that they almost suffocate the truth" and "resemble the great Colossus of Rhodes that was ruined by its own vast and prodigious height" (379). Throughout the *Apologie* he cited many of the era's most highly regarded experts on demon theory and witch-hunting, among them, the Spanish-Netherlandish Jesuit and humanist Martin Anthony Delrio (1551–1608) and the Bordeaux jurist Pierre de Lancre (1553–1631). Their distortions, according to Naudé, mangled a more illustrious history, that of human genius, which could manifest itself in forms political, philosophical (including the natural-scientific), and literary.

In addition to handling specific cases of false accusation, Naudé's treatise included a general theorizing about both magic and history writing. His theoretical reflections on magic encompassed an interpretive review of what magic was, how and why its practice became an aspersion, and why the misrepresentation proved so resilient. The logic of his exonerations followed from this analysis: genuine magic is exceedingly rare; the claim that someone has practiced it, generally fraudulent; and the claim's most common "proof," its repetition. Turning to the accusation of practicing magic as a historical claim, he argued that authors repeat the fraudulent claims out of a lazy aversion to testing their sources or out of malice and envy toward the accused. Readers prefer being tantalized by untoward stories to hearing the truth. Once tantalized, the mass of uneducated people is prone to frenzied agreement. Naudé pleaded instead for the rejection of such historical claims unless they be "recognizable as fair and sensible [*juste et raisonnable*] through conscientious investigation [*une diligente recherche*] and meticulous review [*une exacte censure*]."[4]

Relying on these principles, Naudé divided his treatment of cases into fifteen chapters in which he acquitted forty-two cases of magicians wrongly accused. In addition to devoting the eighteenth chapter to Albert, paired with the thirteenth-century Oxford natural philosopher Robert Grosseteste, Naudé cited Albert throughout the volume. In the dedicated chapter Naudé dismissed as spurious a set of books wrongly ascribed to Albert; singled out problems related to alchemy, astrology, and magic in general; and dealt with the legend of the animate brazen head. Based on inconsistencies between authentic texts and pseudepigrapha, the testimony of specialists, and his own assessment of the sheer unlikelihood of the claims, Naudé concluded that Albert cannot be attainted of anything but the most rational attempts at understanding the natural world, some aspects of which Naudé approved as "natural magic" (331–41).

Naudé's exoneration of Albert echoes the work of the Cologne Dominicans a century and a half earlier. Naudé and the friars shared an appraisal of the calumny's complex origins, partly in learned commentary, partly in vernacular fable. They shared a confidence in the possibility of discovering the truth through the comparative analysis of documents. Although the textual analysis of the earlier Cologne writings with their humanist undertones drove the *Apologie* all the more, Naudé's work could hardly be taken as the product of the fifteenth-century Rhinelandish friars. Naudé exhibited little interest in Albert's ecclesiastical or moral accomplishment beyond a curt expression of confidence that Albert had been a good friar and bishop of Regensburg. Naudé's argument— regarding Albert and the other natural scientists—presumed an evident and decisive distinction between demonic and natural magic, one the Cologne authors regarded as secondary in their attempt to purge any taint of magic from Albert's study. Finally, Naudé, unlike the Dominicans and despite a sympathy he may have harbored for Aristotelianism,[5] never argued that Albert's philosophical ideas were correct, no more than he obliged himself to the equivalent on behalf of the other *grands personnages*. Verifying the truth of Albert's natural philosophy was as incidental to Naudé purposes as that of Numa Pompilius's religion and Heinrich Cornelius Agrippa von Nettesheim's occultism as raised elsewhere in the *Apologie*. Rather, Naudé was concerned to show that their thought was, whether correct or incorrect, reasonable and not superstitious.

Naudé's work, understood on its own terms and drawn into contrast with the earlier approach, invites consideration of what kind of work the *Apologie* was, what problems motivated Naudé to compose it, and what intellectual allegiances guided his handling of the alleged magic of these *grands personnages*, Albert in particular. To discern the new phase through which Albert's reputation as a magician was passing, understanding what the *Apologie* was, reflected, and contributed to is as important as what it specifically argued about Albert. Whether the *Apologie* should be counted as the first history of magic, as it sometimes has been, is arguable.[6] Regardless, in the menagerie of seventeenth-century books about magic, Naudé's *Apologie* ranks among the most comprehensive and influential, as its lengthy publication and translation history[7]—and, more strikingly still, the reliance of eighteenth-century thinkers on it (as the next chapter details)—confirm.

This initial sketch of the work draws into relief the skepticism and historicism that made it so distinctive and ultimately so attractive to later thinkers. They are Naudé's principal tools of exoneration. Along with the accompanying theoretical framework, the *Apologie* undermined the univocal and self-evidently derogatory significance of calling something or someone magical. In this respect Naudé developed the attack of the fifteenth-century friars against Albert's sorcerous reputation. In this chapter, we turn first to Naudé's theoretical argument about the accusation of magic in general and as applied to Albert and other alleged magicians, then to the networks of learning that were Naudé's intellectual milieu and within which certain questions were so contested (What is magic, and is it rational and good to practice?), and finally to the larger issue of Naudé's historicizing as that which most definitively made Albert's reputation a defamation, and thus made Albert neither a magician nor even, as Cologne Dominicans hoped, a saint, but one step closer to being a natural scientist.

An Apology for Albert: History Writing and Magic

Naudé laid the groundwork for his defense of Albert and the other *grands personnages* by outlining how history should and should not be written. Good writing about famous men and events requires the experience, reflection, observation, and impartiality of an author (148). These are prerequisites to the "conscientious investigation and meticulous review" that result in "fair and sensible" judgments. Naudé's employment as the librarian to Henri de Mesmes (1585-1660), a president of the Parlement of Paris, introduced him to vibrant circles of learning and culture in early seventeenth-century Paris[8] and offers a preliminary explanation for the expansive and learned set of historians he offered for emulation: some ancient—Seneca, Quintilian, Plutarch, Thucydides, and Tacitus; others, humanist—Erasmus (1466-1536), Juan Luis Vives (1493-1540), Michel de Montaigne (1533-1592), and Antonio Possevino (1533-1611). He emphasized that skills beyond the literary also helped in the writing of good history, praising Girolamo Cardano (1501-1576) and Francis Bacon (1561-1626) for the scientific expertise they brought to their history writing (149). Nations, too, benefit from suitable (or "perfect" as he called them) models of historical writing, as for example what Polydorus Virgilius Castellensis (1470-1555) provided the English; Beatus Rhenanus (1485-1547), the Germans, and Paulus Aemilius Veronensis (1455-1529), the French (148). Unsuitable history writing, too, can be found in all abundance, he lamented, pointing to reliance on the biblical books of Esdras and the Apocalypse for historical insight. And he rejected the works of several medieval and humanist historians, including those of the Danish author Saxo Grammaticus (1160-220), the Swabian humanist and chronicle author Johannes Nauclerus (1425-1510), Olaus Magnus (1490-1557), author of the celebrated *History of the Northern Peoples*, and "an infinite number of others" (150, 152). And why, he bemoaned with something of a caricature, would anyone take silly and untested stories as true, such as Turnus's throwing pieces of mountains at his enemies simply because Ariosto retells the story, or the apostles' playing cymbals at the Virgin Mary's funeral because painters included such touches in their art. The repetition of such anecdotes in popular writings, Naudé warned, was scarcely grounds for a reader or history writer to accept them as true, let alone repeat them.

The principles of good history writing do not, by Naudé's reckoning, destroy magic's legitimacy but rather should allow for its more careful assessment. He divided magic into four kinds, each based on a different principal agent for its effectiveness (156): divine, angelic, demonic, and natural. Divine, or sacred, magic works through God's grace and comprises "prophecy, miracles, and the gift of tongues." Its practitioners have included biblical figures like Moses and the apostles as well as later wonder-working saints. Naudé judged divine magic valid but, especially in the postbiblical period, misidentified and misunderstood. Because it is also rare, divine magic was deemed by Naudé to have scarcely ever come up in true history writing. The second form of magic—theurgy—works with the help of angels. Naudé explained that theurgic—or white—magic is associated with a practitioner's ascetic manner of life, which aids "the soul who desires communication with superior deities." Naudé judged theurgic magic, like divine magic, genuine and licit but uncommon. Addressing an argument between Julius Caesar Scaliger (1484–1558) and Cardano on the relationship between astrology and theurgic magic,[9] Naudé proposed that the conflict could be defused if they recognized that what they were really arguing over was sometimes divine, sometimes natural magic, neither of which required the interference of superior, spiritual intelligences, be they angels or demons. Another challenge in the determination of theurgic magic, by Naudé's lights, was distinguishing it from the third sort, demonic magic. "Goetia," he explained, "requires no necessity of specifying more particularly" and damages in proportion to how much it is discussed. Quoting Ovid, he warned, "When the torch is waved, I have seen flames flare up. But once stilled, nothing again."[10]

Naudé placed Albert among the thinkers whose work legitimates the fourth category of magic, natural magic. By Naudé's definition, it requires only human reason and no special grace or spiritual aid (161–63). Natural magic is "what the Persians called wisdom, the Greeks philosophy, the Jews Kabbalah, the Pythagoreans the science of formal numbers, and the Platonists the sovereign remedy giving tranquility to the soul and equilibrium to the body." Natural magic, he explained, is applied natural philosophy; following Francis Bacon, he included "practical physics" in this category as a "contemplative magic." Citing Avicenna, he numbered medicine, chemistry, astronomy, and physiognomy among the forms of natural magic, to which he added the readings of palms and foreheads plus the interpretation of dreams and geomancy. Medieval writers sometimes included mantic arts among the sciences as well, but the real problem natural magic faced according to Naudé was a confusion between it and demonic magic. His thought about natural magic drew inspiration from the Dominican philosopher Tommaso Campanella (1568–1639), especially his *De sensu rerum et magia* (1620),[11] which itself notices Albert only with passing mentions of the brazen head and the possibility of demonic interference in astrological prediction.[12]

Naudé offered several reasons why practicing demonic magic had become such a common defamation. First, some *grands personnages* claimed it about themselves. This, Naudé proposed, was a misleading tactic to bolster one's own authority among superstitious people, as for example, the English kings' claims to be descended from Merlin, the Prophet Muhammad's claim to be descended from the angel Gabriel, and the claims of philosophers from Socrates to Campanella of having spiritual familiars (163–67).[13] The sickly appearance many talented persons acquire from grueling labor, Naudé bemoaned, insinuates nigromancy (167–73). Mathematicians, among all specialists in the quadrivium (the four liberal arts pertaining to number in space and time), Naudé regarded as particularly vulnerable to the suspicion. Mathematics was associated not only with the study of celestial movements, which lent itself from time immemorial to charges of demonic commerce but also with the building of mechanical devices, especially automata such as Albert's brazen head, that amaze simple people. Naudé provided contemporary examples—the magnetic ointment of Rudolf Goclenius, Joseph Duchesne's panacean powder, Jean Beguin's fulminating gold—as sophisticated applications of quadrivial expertise wrongly confused with invoking demonic interference (174). Naudé thus concluded: the prejudices and irresponsibility of the authors—historians and demonographers—who retell such stories of demonic magic and the credulity of readers who prefer being entertained to learning the truth conspire against the recognition of authentic quadrivial brilliance (185–94).

Apologizing for Albert: The Defendants

With this theoretical groundwork laid, Naudé turned to the cases. His basic argument is that each accusation originally emerged from some misapprehended or misrepresented accomplishment. The fourteen chapters are organized with reference to chronology, occupation, and kind of accomplishment (of the last, there are three main kinds—philosophical, literary, and political). While medieval churchmen number among those he defended, he exonerated none of them on the grounds of theological learning or heroic virtue (fig. 5). The most ancient figures—Zoroaster, Orpheus, Pythagoras, and Numa Pompilius, each in his own chapter—appear first. Others treated individually in chapters include the sixteenth-century German polymath Agrippa von Nettesheim (the eighth chapter in the section) and the Roman poet Virgil (first century BCE), who for reasons to be touched on later Naudé handled last. Other chapters bring together multiple cases that share a common accusation. Naudé treated Socrates, Aristotle, Plotinus, Porphyry, Iamblichus, Chicus Aesculanus, Scaliger, and Cardano together in the seventh chapter for allegedly receiving "the extraordinary assistance of some genius or familiar demon" (256). Merlin, whom Naudé took to be a sixth-century poet and seer, Savonarola, and Nostradamus are linked as prophets (301–18). Joseph, Solomon, and the biblical magi are convened as dreamers in the

Fig. 5. "Albert the Great, bishop of Regensburg." Woodcut from Nicolaus Reusner, *Icones sive Imagines virorum literis illustrium* (Strasbourg: Bernhard Jobin, 1587), A-i-r. The image presents Albert as bishop of Regensburg, clothes him as a friar, and identifies him as a master of the natural sciences. The couplet reads, "I was a great teacher of Wisdom and a bishop. The hidden power of nature is known clearly by me."

thirteenth chapter (355–64). The popes Sylvester II (r. 999–1003) (Gerbert of Aurillac) and Gregory VII (r. 1073–85) are paired as victims of unseemly ecclesiastical politics, not for any similarities in the magic they might have practiced or accomplishment they might have achieved in office (341–54).

The seventeenth and eighteenth chapters focus on figures from the central and later Middle Ages, the majority of whom are friars: treatment of Thomas

Aquinas, Roger Bacon, Thomas Bungay (1214–1294), Michael Scot (1175–1232) and Johannes Trithemius as well as the layman Giovanni Pico della Mirandola constitute the seventeenth chapter (318–31); of Albert the Great and Robert Grosseteste, linked as bishops (of Regensburg and Lincoln, respectively), the eighteenth (331–41). Naudé lauded these thinkers for bridging learning from the time of Boethius (477–524), Symmachus (345–402), and Cassiodorus (485–585) to the fall of Constantinople (1453), the latter taken to mark a new threshold in the history of the Latin West's engagement with antiquity. Implicitly responding to a dispute on this point, Naudé was silent on the adoption of Aristotle in this period, as Aristotelianism did not readily accommodate notions of malign spirits.[14] Naudé's defense of the first set of figures focused on their licit expertise in the quadrivium, especially in astronomy. For example, Aquinas he praised for arguing against astral magic, and Pico for distinguishing "in reason and in morals" chemistry from alchemy, and natural from demonic magic. Naudé rejected the suggestion of the demonologist Johannes Weyer (1515–1588) that Pico practiced demonic magic, citing "three famous English authors" who argued the contrary. In defending Trithemius, Naudé first identified the evidence brought forward by those accusing the abbot of sorcery: a book on astral images, frequent references to magic in letters, and finally his work on angelic cryptography that had inspired his denunciation in some quarters in his own lifetime.[15] Naudé rejected all of these as inadequate to the charge of sorcery and denounced Trithemius's defamers, including the demonographers Weyer, Delrio, and Johann Georg von Gödelmann (1559–1611) as well as the Franciscan cosmographer André Thevet (1516–1590): "How they wither with perpetual infamy the memory of a man on the poor grounds of such feeble conjectures, which are totally vain, false, and unfounded" (329). In response, Naudé simply listed earlier authorities that had rejected the charge and explained steganography as nothing more than "a new and much more certain way of writing and communicating ... by means of an invention which could not be deciphered except by one who had its key" (330).

Naudé turned to Albert in chapter 18, after a quick introduction to Grosseteste taken from the chronicler Matthew of Paris (1200–1259), as "a holy prelate, loyal adviser to the king, reformer of monks, director of priests, teacher of clergy, provider to scholars and students, preacher to the people, and hammer against vice" who composed a "great number of books, of which we have some in philosophy" (332). Naudé explained the epithet *magnus* with reference to the history writer Paulo Giovio (1483–1552) and the political thinker Giovanni Botero (1544–1617) as well as emphasized the breadth of Albert's learning "in letters, fields of knowledge, and things," citing Trithemius and Thevet. Naudé opined that Albert would be at least as celebrated as his student Thomas Aquinas had only the master's works been as well disseminated as the disciple's (332–33). He raised and dismissed the claim that Albert had invented the "canon, musket, and pistol." As Naudé pointed out to the reader, the first author to make the claim did not bother to address the many eminent authors who had already written about "the invention of 'fire sticks'" without mentioning Albert at all. Citing the Dominican chronicler Giovanni Cornazzano (d. 1335), Naudé proposed instead a "German monk named Berthold Schwarz" or "a chemist who lived in Cologne" (332–33).

Albert's reputation as an alchemist posed a more serious problem. While alchemy in Albert's day had been a practice related to mineralogy and physics, by Naudé's time it had developed cosmological, medicinal, and mystical dimensions that associated it more closely with magical activity. Naudé allowed for the rationality of a transmutational alchemy as taken from Arabic sources and developed by scholastic philosophers as a form of applied physics but rejected the later developments. Naudé's stance on alchemy appears to have taken form during his studies of medicine in Paris and Padua: His medical studies with René Moreau (1587–1656), his lifelong friendship with Guy Patin (1601–1672), sometime dean of the medical faculty in Paris, and his citations to medical authors such as Nicolaus Guibert (1547–1620) and Jean Riolan (1577–1657)[16] tip his hand in favor of the established tradition of Galenic medicine over the avant-garde iatrochemistry (medicinal chemistry) of Paracelsus (1493/94–1541). The latter was ever-more defining of how alchemy was understood in the sixteenth and seventeenth century.

Naudé's presentation of the history of alchemy is somewhat haphazard. Before he turned to Paracelsus, who has his own chapter in the *Apologie*, Naudé inserted a history of alchemy into chapter 14 that nodded to the interactions of Christian and Muslim thinkers central to the field's development. He placed early in this history, for example, the Persian polymath Jabir ibn Hayyan (ca. 721–ca. 815). Naudé dedicated more text to the possibility of Jabir's Christian origins than to analyzing the disputed list of alchemical texts Jabir may have written and were studied in the later medieval Latin West. It is also not clear that Naudé knew to distinguish between the medieval Persian Muslim and thirteenth-century Latin scholar Geber, who followed closely Albert's mineralogical theories and whose *Summa perfectionis* was a much-celebrated alchemical handbook (276–78). Roger Bacon, whose alchemical works anticipated the expansion of transmutational alchemy into anatomy and medicine but were surpassed at least in the short term by the mineralogical and metallurgical traditions of alchemy favored by Albert and Geber, stands out for how little he and his alchemical ideas appear in Naudé's excursus (322–23).

Arnold of Villanova (1240–1311), a Catalan physician and another principal in chapter 14, likely wrote no alchemy; yet his association with the Spiritual

Franciscans attracted millenarian disciples who aligned him with their Christological alchemy. Arnold himself, Naudé emphasized, "was no ignorant friar or beguine, ... or some miserable, wandering chemist as we are told. ... On the contrary, he was the most gifted physician of his time ... and [who] gave sufficient proof by his writings of what he knew of the sciences of mathematics, medicine, and philosophy, the practice of which made him agreeable and necessary to Pope Clement and Frederic, king of Sicily. These would never have wanted to use him if they had recognized him as an enchanter and magician" (282–84).

The alchemist John of Rupescissa (ca. 1310–1366/70), whose *Book of Light and Quintessence*, Naudé reminded his reader, was often falsely ascribed to Albert, features only in passing, despite his writings' influence on Paracelsus in the development of iatrochemistry as a replacement to Galenic medicine.[17] Indeed, as Naudé wrote, the followers of Paracelsus were vigorously working toward that end, and the publication of Paracelsus's collected works in the 1590s is an impressive marker of their enthusiasm.[18] Naudé's defense of Paracelsus, however, was restricted to the specific issue at hand, namely, that Paracelsus may have, through alchemy, practiced demonic magic. Naudé rejected the assertion, but beyond that harbored no sympathy for Paracelsus. Indeed, he was uniquely contemptuous of Paracelsus and sarcastic in his defense: "The great heresiarch ... who today is the zenith and rising sun of all alchemists" is best defended from the charge of magic by appeal to "the novelty of his conceptions, the difficulty of his style, and the obscurity of a great number of words in his books." In other words, Paracelsus was so confusing it is impossible to figure out whether, at any given point, Paracelsus was talking about "a turd or a pill, a stone or a loaf of bread, the devil or nature." While "the depravity of his religious opinion" gave both pope and Luther ample grounds to condemn him as a heretic, to baffle a student, Naudé submitted, is not to practice sorcery. Rather, Paracelsus, while innocent of practicing demonic magic, stood in the long tradition of medical grifters (288–90).[19]

Naudé's reflections on alchemy, however haphazard, laid the groundwork for the second of a two-step defense against alchemy used as part of the sorcerous charges leveled against Albert and others—namely, that not only was the claim of practicing alchemy false but also that what was being leveled against Albert and others as alchemy was not the alchemy that had inspired thirteenth-century curiosity. Furthermore, because of the widespread currency of Albert's reputation as an alchemist, Naudé's tactics included of necessity both exposing the pseudepigrapha as such and denouncing malformed, contemporary appeal to Albert as an adherent of the newer alchemical theories. Naudé accordingly took as his example Michael Maier (1568–1622), a physician at the court of the Hapsburg emperor Rudolf II and the author of the alchemical treatise *The Symbols of the Golden Table of the Twelve Nations* (1617). *The Symbols* included a full chapter on Albert's alchemical activities, including stories of his learning alchemy from Saint Dominic, his teaching alchemy to Saint Thomas, and his using alchemy to return the diocese of Regensburg to financial solvency.[20] Naudé then rejected three "books of chemistry" as misascribed to Albert with references, first, to their absence from Trithemius's sixteenth-century index of Albert's works, and then, to an ascription of one, *De quinta essentia*, to Albert by Gianfrancesco Pico della Mirandola (Giovanni's nephew, 1469–1533) that was so egregiously misguided as to delegitimate the authenticity of the other two. Naudé dismissed Albert's contribution to more mystical forms of alchemy with a terse indignation worthy of Peter of Prussia: "Albert could not have dreamed of doing so."[21] With a nod to the possibility of confusion rather than malice and sloth on the part of the history writers, Naudé proposed that the least culpable explanation for this particular defamation could derive from a confusion between the writings of John of Rupescissa and Albert that once recorded was mindlessly repeated. Still, sharper minds should take their cue from Francis Bacon and Nicholas Guibert (ca. 1547–ca. 1620), who wrote to expose the alchemical writings of Albert and Aquinas as counterfeit and elsewhere to condemn as delusional those of John of Rupescissa, Roger Bacon, and Paracelsus.[22] Albert had, after all, mocked the alchemists and their transmutations in *De mineralibus* (333–34).

Naudé followed up on the problem of alchemy with the problem of magic, by drawing attention to three volumes, *De mirabilibus*, *De secretis mulierum*, and the *Speculum astronomiae*, which he argued are all wrongly ascribed to Albert. Naudé handled them much as the earlier critics had, pointing to internal inconsistencies, contradictions vis-à-vis other writings of Albert's, and the judgments of learned authorities. Despite Naudé's unease with much of Delrio's demonography, he cited him along with Gianfrancesco Pico in rejecting Albert's authorship of *De mirabilibus* and *De secretis mulierum*.[23] As for the *Speculum*, Naudé brought up what Gerson, Agrippa von Nettesheim, and Pico had written as reasons against Albert's authorship. Citing Giovanni Pico's evaluation of Roger Bacon's *On the Faults Occasioned by the Study of Theology* (*De viciis contractis in studio theologie*), Naudé proposed Bacon as the *Speculum*'s author instead. Bacon's "devotion to judicial astrology" would also seem, by Naudé's reckoning, to make him the more likely author. In the end, Naudé allowed an uncertainty about the authorship and opined that the work serves as a useful record of astrological ideas for inquisitors and others involved in the condemnation of error, especially of "libertines and atheists" (334–37).

Naudé then turned to legends: "All that remains now is to refute the error of those who believe that under certain constellations brazen heads can be forged, which give answers and serve those who possess them as guides and conductors in all their affairs" (337–41).[24] Accounts of their manufacture and use were legion,[25] and Naudé listed among their reputed creators the Spanish nobleman and astrologer Enrique de Villena (1384–1434), the poet Virgil, Pope Sylvester, Grosseteste, and Roger Bacon. By Naudé's calculation, no one has been more defamed by the claim than Albert, and he pointed to the repetition of the claim in works of the Spanish theologian Alonso Tostado (1410–1455),[26] the Franciscan friar and kabbalist Francisco Giorgio Veneto (1466–1540),[27] Delrio, the Dominican theologian Bartholomaeus Sibylla (d. 1493),[28] the Paduan cleric and mathematician Giorgio Raguseo (1580–1622),[29] De Lancre, and "others whom it would be boring to name."[30] Naudé proceeded to denounce Tostado's credulity in this and other fables, blaming "a black patch of his humanity." He looked to other "more rational accounts" not for the animation of the figure but for the origin of the fable, which he blamed in the end on Jewish superstition. As for the theoretical possibility of inventing a talking head, Naudé rejected it with appeal to Aquinas and Aristotle. It was easily possible through steam and whistles to create a figure that emitted pleasant noises, he observed, but the idea that speech could be re-created, or even achieved by a demon using the figure, was biologically and philosophically impossible. Spiritual entities cannot, he explained, manipulate the physical organs necessary for the production of sound, let alone speech. In short, Albert "could not make by superstitious magic a statue that could respond in intelligible and articulate voice to the doubts and difficulties proposed to it." To the extent anything in this vein would be possible, it would have to be "similar to the one of Memnon, which made a small pleasant sound and murmur when the rising sun came by its heat and made the air that had thickened and condensed in the cold of the night come out through small pipes." In short, whatever could be achieved would have to be achieved within the limits of "natural magic, which depends on mathematics." Simply because of the impossibility of its achievement, no other kind of "android" should be imputed to Albert or any other learned person, and historians who did so were pandering to simple readers. Naudé rounded off his admonition with another quotation from Ovid: "Rumor rejoices in mingling the false with the true, and through lying grows in size out of very small things."[31]

An Apology for Albert: Seventeenth-Century Occult Forces

As meandering as Naudé could be across the nearly seven hundred pages of the *Apologie*, the defense rested on the three tactical legs of skepticism: historical contextualization, confidence in reason against credulity, and confidence in reason against malice. This tripartite approach to intellectual problems was not, for Naudé, anomalous to the *Apologie*. Linked, these ideas composed an intellectual program, one applied by him to a breadth of matters related to and beyond the false accusation of magic. Investigating the broader program in Naudé's work uncovers a network of connections in Europe's culture of learning, which helps explain what was at stake in the *Apologie* for Naudé and his contemporaries as well as lays the groundwork for appreciating the *Apologie*'s influence on later generations. Albert's exoneration emerged in this context. The incipient program shaped his two earlier works: *Le Marfore* (1620),[32] which defended the king's favorite, the Duke of Luynes, against the rumors of political rivals,[33] and the *Instruction à la France* (1623),[34] a tract that denounced the Rosicrucians as a hoax and ridiculed the hysteria the movement inspired.[35] In fact, his treatment of the Rosicrucians, especially for their associations with the occult and ancient mystical traditions, applies tactics of historical contextualizing and skeptical rationalism that anticipate the arguments he later used in the *Apologie*. Moreover, the *Instruction* draws attention to certain intellectual alliances that also shape the *Apologie* in its refashioning of magical accusation, such as those leveled against Albert.

The Rosicrucians (frères de la Roze-Croix, brethren of "the Rosy Cross") constituted a reputedly mystical movement long in existence but only newly visible in the early seventeenth century thanks to a set of manifestos—*The Sayings* (*Fama Fraternitas*), *The Creed* (*Confessio Fraternitas*), and *The Chemical Wedding* (*Chymische Hochzeit*)—that originated in Germany and spread across Europe beginning in the sixteenth century.[36] However, these earliest Rosicrucian documents actually originated in a small circle of German acquaintances in the sixteenth century,[37] and the same Michael Maier who, to Naudé's disgust, had drawn Albert into his alchemical work *The Symbols of the Golden Table* wrote for the Rosicrucian movement as well. His *Laws of the Fraternity of Rosicrucians* was published in the same year as Naudé's *Apologie*.[38] The writings sourced the movement's foundation to a fifteenth-century doctor who had traveled to the Near East to learn hidden knowledge and there adopted Sufi mysticism. Upon returning to Europe, he collected around himself disciples who were to preserve his insights until such time as they could be safely revealed. The early seventeenth-century manifestos announced the impending emergence of this circle of learned and mystically inspired men and the dawning of an age of cultural, religious, and intellectual renewal. The pamphlets' contents show signs of familiarity with Renaissance alchemy, Kabbalah, and other forms of mysticism that circulated across Europe at the time.[39]

Secret societies whose constitutions mingled mystical philosophies and political innovation were objects of considerable concern to political and ecclesiastical authorities, perhaps in no place or time more than in early modern

France. With some independence from any real assessment of the threats posed and even of their actual existence, such societies could inspire vigorous denunciation; in the resulting controversialist literature, the perceived threat could lead to the most fantastic conflations of ideologies and movements. In the first three decades of the seventeenth century, the Rosicrucians earned exactly this kind of attention; by 1624, the year Naudé's *Instruction* appeared, the "brethren of the Rosy Cross" were linked to Alumbradism, atheism, libertinism, Paracelsianism, and Protestantism.[40] Some feared in the movement a Calvinist plot to unite Protestant powers on the Continent with England.[41] Such anxieties could be put to political use, as did the controversialist Jean Boucher (1548–1646), who hoped to mobilize Catholic rulers against Protestant states and the Turks by accusing the Rosicrucians of attempting to overthrow Catholic states from within in his *Mystical Crown* (1623).[42]

A number of Jesuit controversialists took an interest in the Rosicrucian threats. The Luxemburgish Jesuit Johannes Roberti (1569–1651) had been involved in an extended debate with Rudolph Goclenius (1572–1621) over a form of sympathetic healing that required the application of an ointment made from a wounded victim's blood on to the wounding instrument. The practice was promoted in the *Archidoxis magicae*, a grimoire attributed to Paracelsus. Roberti argued that the therapy could hardly be natural, but was rather demonic or supernatural, and Goclenius's defense smacked of atheism. Be that as it may, in his *Self-Tormenting Goclenius* (1618) Roberti included a chapter on the Rosicrucians that condemned them as Paracelsian.[43] The label *Paracelsian*, it should be noted, was an equivocal term. It could refer to a mix of medical, cosmological, and chemical ideas derived from Paracelsus or, as in this case, was a term of abuse that conservative thinkers directed against a novel mystical, magical approach to medicine and natural philosophy also derived from Paracelsus's writings.[44] Another Jesuit, Jacques Gaultier (1562–1636), included his own denunciation of the Rosicrucians in his *Chronological Table*.[45] Gaultier, among the most prolific controversialists of the period, had composed this elaborately annotated chronology of ecclesiastical and theological history to demonstrate the organic connections between heresies and idolatries across time. He regularly revised the oft-republished volume. In the French edition of 1621, he inserted a section on the Rosicrucians as a pernicious movement inspired by the pernicious thought of "Erasmus of Rotterdam, Luther, Philip Melanchthon, Paracelsus, Tyco Brahe, etc." and enhanced by the satanic powers of "empiricism and magic, so as to better deceive fickle and curious spirits."[46]

The third and most formidable Jesuit controversialist to become involved was François Garasse (1585–1631). In *The Strange Teaching of the Best Minds of Our Times* (*La doctrine curieuse*) (1623) Garasse made his target a *bon esprit*,[47] whose following he described as freethinkers who denied the existence of God, regarded the Bible as nonsense, took fate alone as the governing principle of human action, and rejected all moral standards. They pursued their interests with devious discretion to avoid punishment from the authorities or offending the simpleminded. Garasse divided these freethinkers into two principal categories: libertines and atheists. The former were united in "the confraternity of the bottle," and their softness rendered them less malign than the latter. Paracelsians and Alumbradans, practitioners of a form of Christian mysticism regarded as heretical by the Spanish Inquisition, moved easily among them, but Huguenots, Garasse conceded, would be as offended by them as Catholics. The immediate occasion for the work was the appearance in print of a collection of iconoclastic poems, *An Anthology of Satirical Poets*, in 1622—several of which were by the baroque poet Théophile de Viau (1590–1626)[48]—but Garasse's list of enemies was long and included the essayist Michel de Montaigne (1533–1592), the ethicist and Montaigne-enthusiast Pierre Charron (1541–1603), and the Neapolitan naturalist Lucilio "Giulio Cesare" Vanini (1585–1619). While the last two were Catholic clergy, Vanini was condemned to death by the Parlement of Toulouse for blasphemy and atheism. The Jesuit controversialists were not alone in their contempt for Rosicrucianism nor in finding its demonization useful. What emerged from the polemical denunciation was an alliance in menace of Rosicrucians, Protestants, Alumbradans, and Paracelsians, tangled together by secrecy, mysticism, heresy, and magic.

This association constitutes the backdrop to the dramatic events of the summer of 1623 that led to Naudé's composition of the *Instruction*: anonymous posters appeared across Paris announcing the Rosicrucians' imminent arrival to save humanity from error and death. The incident has since been proved a local hoax, but at the time the posters provoked distress across the city and a frenzy of pamphleteering. The messy association of Rosicrucians with dangerous movements earlier embedded in the Jesuit tracts became screaming headlines in the pamphlet war. The pamphlets pithily linked diabolism, decadence, and atheism to Rosicrucianism.[49] Prominent figures entered the fray. The savant Nicolas-Claude Fabri de Peiresc (1580–1637) initially shared Garasse's concern about the subversive poetry of the *Anthology* and denounced the libertinism of the Rosicrucians.[50] A volume of collected documents, ascribed to the publisher Jacques Dupuy (1586–1656), correlated investigations into magic with letters by Théophile and descriptions of Rosicrucianism.[51] Boucher's *Mystical Crown*, appearing that same summer, expanded denunciation of the Rosicrucians as veiled Protestantism and Paracelsian diabolism. In effect, Boucher synthesized the anti-Rosicrucian rhetoric of both Roberti and Gaultier, taking the antimagic attack from the former and the dread of Protestantism from the latter.[52]

Naudé himself stepped into the fray with his *Instruction à la France*, published with the *privilege du roy* in December 1623.[53] His expressed aim was to undermine Rosicrucianism's reputed mysterious origins, but his subversions encompassed the faulty associations of Rosacrucianism with the other movements, alarming by Jesuit lights, like Protestantism and Paracelsianism.[54] While somewhat scattered across the treatise's 117 pages, Naudé's argument followed two tracks: first, he rejected the history of the Rosicrucians as unproved. There was, in Naudé's judgment, no evidence for any of it outside of what was claimed in their own tracts or imputed to them by their critics. He noted with sarcasm that the strongest evidence in favor of their existence was the energy the French people expended worrying about them.[55] In a rambling review of the limits of human rationality, he opined that assertions made even in such important fields as law, religion, and science need always be taken with skepticism given how common disputes among experts are even on central points.[56] Conflicting opinion, even among learned men, is the foundational justification for doubting authority and testing sources.[57] This review of conflicting opinions and the poor testing of sources thus constitutes a first reason to reject Rosicrucianism as a hoax.[58]

His second line of argument picks away at Rosicrucianism's association with the other threatening movements. He put Paracelsianism under particular scrutiny, and his rejection of it extended beyond the matter of its association with Rosicrucianism. He did not, after all, deny the existence of the Paracelsians, who advocated the very medical alchemy he rejected. The medical faculty of the University of Paris had in previous decades several times ruled against Paracelsian approaches to the healing arts, and several of Naudé's mentors and friends were among the faculty members most hostile.[59] Foreshadowing a critique he incorporated into his chapter on Albert in the *Apologie*, he rejected as nonsense Maier's Paracelsian alchemy.[60] While his objections to Paracelsians aligned him in a certain respect with the Jesuit controversialists, Naudé had different grounds and was thus led to dispute claims made by each of them. He did so often by name; in the *Instruction* Garasse was Naudé's principal bête noire.[61] *Instruction* can thus be summarized with reference to its three targets and its primary method of dispute: mob-inciting pamphleteering, Paracelsianism, and theologically driven anti-Parcelsianism. Such claims require direct evidence, Naudé demanded, and there was none to be found in the polemics leading up to and constituting the panic over Rosicrucianism.[62]

Such arguments in the *Instruction*, along with what we have also already seen in the *Apologie*, draw Naudé's intellectual sympathies into relief, including his elitist concern over the easily agitated Parisians, the confidence he expressed in the historical testing of sources, the hard delimitation of theology from philosophy, the lack of interest in ecclesiastical politics, and his general rejection of magic as useful explanatory tool except in a form that was practically synonymous to natural philosophy in theory and physics in application. Ideas such as these and a specific set of professional relations led the historian René Pintard to situate Naudé among his "tetrade" of erudite libertines in his seminal work *Le libertinage érudit* (1943), allied with the archempiricist philosopher and Catholic priest Pierre Gassendi (1592–1655), the iconoclastic poet and royal tutor François La Mothe Le Vayer (1588–1672), and the Genevan lawyer and diplomat Elie Diodati (1576–1661).[63] This tetrade itself came into contact with other circles of elite learning through the "cabinet" fostered by the brothers Pierre and Jacques Dupuy.[64] These then brought Naudé, as testified to in correspondence and other documents, into collegial contact with the mathematician, philosopher, and friar Marin Mersenne (1588–1648), the Dutch manuscript collector Isaac Vossius (1618–1689), and Peiresc. Further lines of intellectual engagement can be traced from Naudé to René Descartes (1596–1650) and the Jesuit polymath Athanasius Kircher (1602–1680).[65] Naudé's association with Gassendi, Mersenne, and Descartes puts him in an orbit of skepticism, particularly toward forces designated magical: Mersenne's mechanistic philosophy, Gassendi's theory of physics, and Descartes's dualism of matter and spirit all undermined explanations for change in the natural world that relied on magical, hidden forces.[66]

In origin the term *libertine* was pejorative, and Naudé himself used it negatively in both *Instruction* and *Apologie*. But by the end of the seventeenth century an approbatory use emerged, and Pintard coined the designation "erudite libertinism" to carve out a literary style from a moral indifferentism in order to draw connections between early seventeenth-century intellectuals and the eighteenth-century philosophes.[67] Under this rubric, the tetrade emerged. Pintard's thesis has inspired a considerable literature.[68] While Pintard aligned the libertines with strains of atheism, Richard Popkin identified in Naudé and others an undertone of Catholic skepticism toward the fideistic, such as strains of seventeenth-century French Catholicism were adopting from Protestantism.[69] Recent evaluations of the Enlightenment's antecedents have made it all the more difficult to assess anything ringing of atheism in earlier thinkers except in relation to internal Christian theological debates.[70] While the identification "libertine" as a movement or a category of individual thinker is today largely avoided,[71] Naudé's biographers highlight in him a philosophical ideal, common in the learned circles of Paris in his day, of liberation from social conventions, religious foremost among them.[72] This ideal encompassed a vigorous skepticism toward arguments from authority, a predilection for and expertise in ancient literature, a greater interest in secular and natural philosophy than in theology, and a confidence in human reason applied to problems in the natural world. Precisely these characteristics in the writing of Naudé led Paul O. Kristeller to link Naudé and Pierre Bayle (1647–1706) and to place them "between Renaissance humanism and the Enlightenment." We turn to such assessments of Naudé's significance in greater detail in the next chapter.

This contextualizing backdrop of ideas allows relevant aspects of the *Apologie* to be drawn into higher relief. The opening pages include poems dedicated to Naudé, in a manner typical of Renaissance literature and as a marker of the repute the young Naudé was gaining in certain circles. The clergyman, orientalist, and astrologer Jacques Gaffarel (1601–1681) provided poems in Hebrew and Latin to celebrate Naudé's efforts, raising them up to heaven like Horace's first ode on angelic wings.[73] The Parisian medical professor Guy Patin celebrated him in a four-line verse as Apollo's agent to kill Python.[74] Guillaume Colletet (1598–1659), who had contributed to *Le Parnasse*, which also provoked the trial of Théophile, penned a sonnet in which he declared Naudé the real sorcerer for so charmingly defending all antiquity against the false charge of sorcery.[75]

The obligation to protect ancient writers from the false charge of sorcery is the first, but not only, justification for composing the *Apologie*. At the beginning of the preface, Naudé explained how troubled he was by a certain "Invective Against Homer and Virgil"[76] that accused these favored ancient poets of sorcery and nigromancy. The invective stood at the conclusion a longer work whose author, unnamed by Naudé, was none other than the Jesuit Garasse. That lengthier work was a reply to criticism elicited by *The Curious Doctrine*,[77] some of which had emerged from the circle of thinkers linked to Naudé through the Dupuy cabinet.[78] The "Invective" repeated a series of legends about both poets' practice of nigromancy and tapped an idea with a long pedigree in Western literature that spiritual powers had something to do with poetic inspiration.[79] Virgil attracted the harsher commentary as Garasse underlined both the poet's own conjurations and the poor example of literary characters from works like the *Aeneid*, who often gained from idolatry and conjuring.[80] That even Virgil from his high pedestal in the monastic and humanist curricula could be drawn into the fracas offers a taste of Garasse's willingness to be incendiary.

Naudé extended his expression of frustration beyond Garasse's "Invective" to what he identified as its source, a work of the Bordeaux jurist De Lancre, *The Faithlessness and Unbelief of Magic* (1622).[81] Both *Faithlessness* and the earlier *Inconstancy of Evil Angels and Demons* (1612) appealed to his experiences as a prosecutor of witchcraft in the French Basque country, a task King Henry IV (r. 1589–1610) commissioned him to and he fulfilled with alacrity in 1609. These volumes sealed his fame among the foremost demon theorists and witch hunters of the early seventeenth century. *Faithlessness* differs from *Inconstancy* in the later book's defensive posture toward the question of demonic power. As De Lancre explained in *Faithlessness*'s opening letter to King Louis XIII (r. 1610–43), it was urgent to reject the "new academics," jurists in particular, "who subscribe to the idea that . . . everything is only an illusion."[82] Virgil fell into De Lancre's sights, in addition to the reasons taken over by Garasse, because of the *sortes virgilianae*, a practice attested since antiquity of using books of Virgil's poetry for divination.[83] Virgil's putative reliance on spirits for his own inspiration motivated the bibliomancy. De Lancre interests us here, however, not for his particular demon theory and worries over the mantic arts, but rather for the *Apologie*'s concern, beginning with De Lancre, about demonographers as the source of bad information about the practice of magic (144).

While Naudé never named Garasse in the *Apologie*, he referred throughout the work to De Lancre and numerous other authors of prominent works of demon theory, among them the Clevish court physician Weyer,[84] the political philosopher Jean Bodin (1520–1596),[85] the Spanish-Flemish Jesuit humanist Delrio,[86] and the Saxon diplomat Gödelmann.[87] Within their writings are a range of ideas about witch-hunting, some more skeptical, some more convinced. Naudé judged that even in their skepticism none of these authors, including Gödelmann and Weyer (both among the more skeptical demon theorists), had gone far enough. To take Gödelmann's work as one example: While he never rejected the power of the devil in human society, he repudiated on natural philosophical grounds many of the claims made about witches' flight and the occurrence of sabbats.[88] Naudé generally took a critical stance toward these demon theorists, but not tout court. Delrio's *Magical Investigations*, a widely disseminated witch-hunting manual in the seventeenth century, included cases of false magical claims, which Naudé cited as authoritative, including those in Albert's favor.

While the reprintings, translations, and dissemination of the *Apologie* during and after Naudé's lifetime suggested widespread approval, Naudé's skepticism toward demon theory and its judicial applications in particular attracted criticism. Among the most strident critics was the Capuchin polemicist Jacques de Chevanes (ca. 1608–1678), who devoted a substantial section of his *Wise Disbelief and Ignorant Credulity* to refuting the *Apologie* in 1671, almost two decades after Naudé's death.[89] De Chevanes work is a revanchist attempt at reinvigorating belief in demonic threats at a time when, particularly in France, the courts, secular and ecclesiastical, regarded their menace ever less seriously. On the one hand, he rejected Naudé's distinctions between licit and illicit magic, collapsed angelic magic into demonic, and divided natural magic into demonic magic and natural philosophy. This reorganizing of practices allowed him then to claim that most of what Naudé had excused as natural magic was in fact demonic.[90] On the other hand, he judged the defense of Albert, Aquinas, and other orthodox Catholic thinkers as gratuitous: "Their knowledge is the fruit of their watchfulness and of their assiduity in study. It is a gift of the Holy Spirit, which is communicated to them for the church. Far from dealing with demons, their conversation is in heaven. The ancient philosophers have slipped the precepts of black magic into their writings, but these illustrious scholars have taught the worship of the true God."[91] In short, De Chevanes walked away from the secular defense that Naudé mounted and toward the argument for Albert's innocence based on learning, orthodoxy, and virtue that Peter of Prussia had laid out two centuries before.

Just as his version of skepticism distinguished Naudé from Peter and De Chevanes in how it drove him to discern in magic some rational endeavor, by historicizing magic Naudé could identify in it developments in human thinking about the natural world. What the historian's "conscientious investigation and meticulous review" and the "fair and sensible" judgments achieve in both the *Apologie* and in the *Instruction* in the first instance is a debunking of illegitimate histories rather than the construction of alternate ones. While Naudé ended *Instruction* with the reputed Rosicrucian history in tatters, he hinted at, without fully developing, an alternative to a history of magic in the *Apologie*—namely, that in particular times and places political, religious, and scientific ideas were mischaracterized as "magic" through ignorance and opposition, and that Albert's magic needed to be associated with applied physics rather than confused with the diabolical. He arrived at both conclusions with reference to learned writings and their critical reading. Years later he wrote to Dupuy, "I concluded a long time ago that most wonderful things would not be so highly esteemed if one could know the impostures or the lack of judgment of those who report them."[92] Naudé demonstrated these as his strengths: an encyclopedic familiarity with ancient and modern literature (imaginative, philosophical and scientific, and polemical), and a skepticism toward the neatly told tale. The *Apologie*, which he wrote at age twenty-five, already puts these defining interests in writing.

On the matter of historicized skepticism, Walter Raleigh's treatment of magic in his *History of the World* (1614) offers an illuminating contrast to Naudé's. Its frontispiece sets a learned tone: The Mistress of Life raises up a globe under the all-seeing eye of Providence. She stands on personifications of Death and Oblivion. Experience stands to her right; to her left, Truth. Four Pillars—Witness of the Times, Messenger of Antiquity, Light of Truth, and Life of Memory—frame them. It shouts out the learning of the age, but the contents, in the final analysis, are in the traditional form of a universal history, beginning with the creation and covering the first twelve books of Genesis (up to the birth of Abraham) in the first book of the first part. The section on biblical history considers Zoroaster as the inventor of magic and astrology; distinguishes "magicke," conjuring, and "witcherie"; and favorably quotes from authors ancient and modern, among the latter, Ficino and James VI of Scotland. Raleigh allowed for natural magic and distinguished between licit and illicit divinations. Raleigh's consideration of Albert in this regard surfaces in his sketch of "magicke" as "the whole philosophie of nature... which bringeth to light the inmost vertues, and draweth them out of Natures hidden bosome to humane use,"[93] a definition resonant with the long traditions of a natural magic. In form, Raleigh's approach was no less encyclopedic than Naudé's. But in contrast to Naudé, the collating of sources lacks any attempt at critical insight. Raleigh's *History* naively included marvels worked with angelic and demonic assistance, repeating what its author found in his sources. In this respect, Raleigh's history of magic was exactly the kind of history writing that Naudé rejected.

While Naudé's treatment of magic, especially when placed next to Raleigh's, seems avant-garde, his tactics of "diligent research" and "accurate censorship" draw from contemporary developments. His extensive references in the early chapters demonstrate such links and the sources for his standard of "fair and reasonable" for establishing claims made about historical figures.[94] Among the history writers he offered as examples are several who are commonly placed at the advent of modern history writing: Philippe de Commines (1447–1511), Francesco Guicciardini (1483–1540), and Johann Sleiden (1506–1556), among them. In advocating for the exclusion of supernatural explanation from historical event, Naudé pointed to Vossius's and Bodin's historiographical works, *The Historical Art* (1623) and *The Method for the Easy Understanding of History* (1566), respectively.[95] His application of the tripartite standard—diligent research, fairness and reasonableness, and final scrutiny—reached a highpoint of intricacy in another work, when he waded into the debate, raging in the mid-seventeenth century, over the authorship of the fifteenth-century spiritual classic, the *Imitatio Christi*, which he attributed to Thomas à Kempis rather than the leading alternative, Jean Gerson.[96] Whether examining religious works like the *Imitatio* or scientific and magical ones, as throughout the *Apologie*, Naudé contributed to a new category of history unfolding, in Donald Kelley's evocative phrasing, "not *sub specie aeternitatis* but in the cycles of generations."[97]

While not a first history of magic, the *Apologie* is the product of a skeptical, historical perspective such as was emergent in and beyond the milieu in which Naudé worked. Magic, by Naudé's lights, whatever the claim or accusation, obscured rather than clarified what it labeled. Even as Naudé granted that magic existed, albeit rarely, the aim of the *Apologie* was to erase it as a working concept except in the rational and natural form described by Campanella. Naudé was willing to classify Albert's achievement, alongside that of certain others taken from antiquity and the Middle Ages, as "natural magic," but such magic was so removed from the other three forms—divine, angelic, and demonic—as to render their lexical association accidental. In effect, Naudé's approach reconstrued Albert not as a magician, but instead as a master student of the natural world. Thus the Dominicans' and Naudé's Alberts were both acquitted of practicing magic, except in the specific sense of natural magic, which allowed both to draw attention to natural philosophy and applied physics. But even among the Dominicans there was some ambivalence, it will be recalled, over how far to esteem his accomplishments in natural philosophy. Hence, the two Alberts diverged in terms of their ultimate accomplishment: for the one, in his learned piety, for the other, in his natural learnedness; and for the one, *sub specie aeternitatis*, for the other, in the progress of generations. In the final analysis, the friars wanted a saint; the historicizing skeptic, a thinker, philosopher, and scientist.

5

THE ENCYCLOPEDIC ALBERT

Denis Diderot (1713–1784) and Jean le Rond d'Alembert (1717–1783), editors of the premier eighteenth-century European compendium of knowledge, the *Encyclopédie*, thought a lot about magic. In the taxonomical sketch that Diderot designed for the project's prospectus in 1750, "The Figurative System of Human Knowledge [*connaissances*],"[1] he designated "natural magic" along with alchemy, metallurgy, and chemistry as forms of physics, which are in turn forms of the "science of nature." "Black magic" he paired with divination as forms of the "science of God." These two sciences—of nature and of God—fell under "reason," which itself complemented two other forms of understanding (*entendement*), memory and poetry (*poesie*). D'Alembert repeated this categorization of magic in the *Encyclopédie*'s introduction a year later.[2] The editors further designated eight headwords under the category of magic—from *ananisapta*, a kabbalistic acronym, to spell-casting (*sortilege*)—and made divination a category of its own. The *Encyclopédie*'s contributors raised magic in over a hundred entries, but never in conjunction with Albert the Great.

The absence of a magical Albert in the *Encyclopédie* could leave us in an unsatisfying cul-de-sac. Two related aspects of the *Encyclopédie*'s contents, however, illuminate the absence of the magical Albert as a culmination point in his afterlife. First, multiple contributors evaluated the practice of magic by other historical figures, among them Albert's fellow scholastics Roger Bacon and Arnold of Villanova. And second, the encyclopedists drew attention to Albert in entries on other learned topics, in twenty-two entries ranging from *androide*, a reference to the legend of his brazen head, to *zingnites*, a stone to which, the Baron d'Holbach recorded, "all sorts of amazing virtues are attributed and which is said to have the transparency of crystal."[3] The goal of this chapter is to figure out the transmutation of Albert from a figure whose association with magic led necessarily to its praise, blame, or refutation up to the eighteenth century to a figure whose older associations with magic could be ignored in favor of other scholarly accomplishments. The *Encyclopédie* offers a striking case of that transmutation, but it is not original to it, nor is it as simple as the encyclopedists picking up where Naudé left off.

By way of evaluating Albert and his magic in the encyclopedias, two points of background require preliminary consideration: the first has to do with Naudé's influence and the other has to do with two genres of scholarly writing that shape Albert's reassessment in the seventeenth and eighteenth centuries, the encyclopedia and the opera omnia. To the first of these, several eminent historians over the last half century have highlighted Naudé's place in early modern European intellectual trends. They have done so in the context of discerning the lines, such as they may be, connecting the Renaissance to the Enlightenment. Accepting the coherence of these periods for the sake of argument, we find several serious attempts place Gabriel Naudé along such lines. These take Naudé's skeptical, historical perspective as representative of late Renaissance thought and anticipatory of the early Enlightenment. Paul O. Kristeller, for example, placed Naudé and the French philosopher Pierre Bayle (1647–1706) on either end of a metaphorical bridge connecting the Italian Renaissance and the French Enlightenment.[4] Richard Popkin in his study of skepticism named Naudé among the early seventeenth-century thinkers who constituted the link between Michel de Montaigne (1533–1592) and Bayle.[5] And the revisionist successor to René Pintard on libertinism, Anna Lisa Schino, identified Naudé's skeptical, source-critical approach in the *Apologie* as the prototype for Bayle's *Dictionnaire historique et critique*.[6] Naudé's conspicuous placement in such important historical studies is striking, especially in the insistent connection between him and Pierre Bayle, once dubbed "the spiritual leader of the Enlightenment."[7]

In fact, Bayle appealed to Naudé many times in his *Dictionaire*, among his most complex and influential works. The *Dictionaire* includes an entry on Albert in which Bayle cited the *Apologie* nine times. Whenever Bayle addressed rumors of Albert's questionable activities in the entry—the alleged midwifery, the pursuit of the philosopher's stone, the construction of a speaking head, and so on—his footnotes point to the *Apologie*. After citing Naudé to dismiss such stories as fables, he, as was his wont, turned with a critical eye to what and whom Naudé cited, in the end verifying and underscoring the librarian's points. Investigating Bayle's reliance on the *Apologie* as regards Albert and magic promises to shed light on one strain of the connections Kristeller, Popkin, Pintard, Schino, and others have attempted to make between the Renaissance and the Enlightenment. Investigating how others drew from the same body of opinion as they grappled with the magical dimension of Albert's learning promises in turn to shed light on a dimension of the problem of how magic was related to and distinguished from rational religion and study of the natural world in the eighteenth century.

Bayle's work also draws our attention to the first of the two genres of scholarly literature that are central to assessing the seventeenth- and eighteenth-century developments in Albert's reputation as a magician. The encyclopedia has become as closely associated with the Enlightenment as any single idea that emerged from it. The genre's aspiration to topical completeness makes it an especially promising resource in the search for perspectives that are temporally and culturally specific. A survey of seventeenth- and eighteenth-century encyclopedias for historical interpretations of Albert in particular and magic in general bears this out. But before turning to specific findings in a range of encyclopedias, we must briefly consider the the genre in general and the way it can be useful to this study. The encyclopedia was in key respects then what it is now: a written work, often of multiple volumes, in which editors arranged, often alphabetically, extensive information drawn from many branches of knowledge. An encyclopedia was often the product of significant scholarly efforts and many years of preparation. While compendia of knowledge encompassing fields can certainly be found in antiquity and the Middle Ages, in the late seventeenth and eighteenth centuries the encyclopedia became a common genre as never before. In the same period, the nomenclature for the genre itself was still not standardized, and the terms *encyclopedia* and *dictionary* were interchangeable across European languages. Diderot and d'Alembert deployed both terms in their project's full title, *Encyclopédie, ou Dictionnaire raisonné*. Comprehensiveness was a goal, but in tension with focus; thus editors used prospectuses and prefaces to explain their chosen scope. Editorial trends transformed the encyclopedia from a collection of definitions and etymologies to a topical compendium of arts, sciences, biography, and so on. Accordingly, while the earlier, smaller encyclopedias tended to be authored by a single person, the later and larger encyclopedias tended to be the product of many expert contributors.[8]

Understanding the influence of the editorial hand opens up the encyclopedias' usefulness to historical investigation. While in our own day the genres of encyclopedia and dictionary commonly (if also naively) connote objectivity in representation and neutrality on contested matters, in the early modern period editors conceived of encyclopedias and dictionaries as purposeful vehicles of particular political, cultural, and philosophical programs. As vernacular languages gained against Latin in literate communities, linguistically distinct, national traditions emerged. Even as the French dominated the genre, Ephraim Chambers's *Cyclopaedia* (1728) enjoyed pride of place in its day in England, as did Johann Heinrich Zedler's *Universal-Lexicon* (1732–54) in Germany.

Publishers solicited subscriptions not only from scholarly readers but also from eighteenth-century elites, newly emergent and intellectually earnest, such as state officials, diplomats, courtiers, and professionals, along with their wives and daughters. Encyclopedias that enjoyed market success were revised and reissued, sometimes multiple times over many decades.[9]

The flexibility of the genre and increasing demand for it led to a fascinating and relevant development. Learned and popularizing, encyclopedias were developed and deployed in the service of the era's most pressing philosophical, political, and cultural rivalries. Hardly a philosophical faction or cultural program shaping the intellectual landscape of the eighteenth century was left unrepresented by its own encyclopedia. For our purposes, such struggles included those touching on the bounds of human understanding, the rationality of politics and religion, and matters of natural causation, such as would have to be addressed in explaining matters of magic and superstition. For precisely such questions, Diderot's encyclopedia can be read as representative of one voice of Enlightenment thinking, just as, say, the *Dictionnaire de Trévoux* can be taken to represent another one, Catholic, conservative, and at least on some points, critical of the former.[10] While there is little reason to expect conflicting treatments across the encyclopedias of the mineral borax, we may anticipate emblematic differences across their treatments of thirteenth-century theology; on the matter of magic—in general and in Albert's practice of it—careful scrutiny of the continuity and variation across the encyclopedias promises significant results.

The goal of this chapter is thus to scrutinize the treatment of magic and, to the extent it is addressed, of Albert's practice of it across the philosophical tumult in the era's most important encyclopedias. Louis Moréri's *Le Grand Dictionaire historique* (1674) is commonly regarded as the era's first, and Bayle's references to it in his own *Dictionnaire* demonstrate the inspiration it offered the genre. Comparative analysis of several rival French encyclopedias that drew on one another and were revised multiple times in the late seventeenth and eighteenth centuries complicates any assumption of particularly Catholic, Protestant, or secular perspectives on the era's matters of great moment, including on rationality, natural science, magic, and superstition.

The chapter concludes with Diderot and d'Alembert's *Encyclopédie* (1751–72), in which Albert's appears in more than twenty entries on all manner of theological, philosophical, and scientific themes, excepting magic. On the one hand, these many entries give evidence that the editors of and contributors to the *Encyclopédie* recognized Albert's discrete contributions to particular fields according to their standards of philosophy and the natural sciences. On the other hand, the contributors to the *Encyclopédie*, in this singular expression of

Enlightenment thought, treat the accusation, in effect, as unworthy of consideration. Examination of the antecedent and rival encyclopedias from this era brings this development into focus, first about Albert and then about magic, a development across an era of raucous intellectual exchange that demonstrates more striking conformity on the issue of magic than one would anticipate.

The other genre that newly affected seventeenth- and eighteenth-century scholarship, especially in the fields of philosophy, theology, and study of the natural world, is that of "collected works." Collected works, often ambitiously titled *Opera omnia*, brought together for a single author not just the titles of what they had written—as we saw emerging in Albert's case in the fifteenth century and making various cases for what writings qualified as authentic—but the writings themselves. Dominicans published Albert's first opera omnia in 1651 in Lyon, at the halfway point between Naudé's *Apologie* (1625) and Moréri's *Grand Dictionnaire* (1674). The Lyon opera omnia was a resource without analogue in the medieval period, and after 1651 the encyclopedists who wrote about Albert in whatever capacity used it, despite recognized editorial flaws and ongoing debates over the genuineness of certain texts.

The importance of a consistently edited, comprehensive collection of a single author's works was not self-evident in this period, and so the production of an opera omnia for Albert is itself notable. Scholarly interest in producing opera omnia in general began increasing in the sixteenth century, a fruit of the value Renaissance humanists placed on source use and philological precision. Accordingly, the authors who most warranted sixteenth-century opera omnia were ancient poets such as Horace and Ovid. Among theologians, those from late antiquity were initially more popular than medieval or Reformation thinkers, and spiritual writers were more popular than dogmatic theologians.[11] Interest in producing the collected works of scholastic thinkers was not initially strong. The first opera omnia of Thomas Aquinas, the *Editio Piana*, published in Rome in 1570 was an exception, sponsored by the Dominican pope, Pius V (r. 1566–72), who declared Aquinas a doctor of the church.[12]

The Dominican pursuit of an opera omnia for Albert emerged in the context of a renewed interest in his sainthood, expressed at a general chapter in 1601 and reiterated in 1629. In response to the latter, the friar Bernardino Gauslini sketched a biography and bibliography in 1630, sending only the former to press.[13] Responsibility for developing a petition for canonization fell again to the order's Teutonia province as Albert's onetime home and the custodian of his remains. While the papacy acceded to several requests for regional veneration within the Holy Roman Empire, the long-term effects of the Reformation and the ongoing Thirty Years' War kept the province undermanned and distracted. The project languished until a new master general, the theologian Thomas Turco (r. 1644–49), turned in 1644 to the French—specifically, a friar at Grenoble, Pierre Jammy (d. 1665)—for help. Little is known of Jammy beyond his teaching of theology and philosophy at the friars' local school and his authorship of a treatise on grace.[14] At the time, Lyon was an active center of book production,[15] and the friars there were already preparing the collected works of Spanish exegete Tomas Malvenda (1566–1628), which appeared in twelve volumes in 1650.[16] To inspire subscriptions to Albert's opera, the order published and circulated a prospectus in 1646 that included an index based on Gauslini's,[17] and in 1647 the order took a collection within the order to help underwrite the project. Friars in Lyon ultimately solved the financial challenge by striking a deal with local booksellers, who agreed to publish Albert's volumes in return for exclusive printing rights in the city over all the books of the order for the following ten years.[18]

The Jammy opera omnia comprises sixty-nine titles in twenty-one volumes. Jammy planned, but never drafted, an additional four volumes. The authenticity of seventeen incorporated titles is rejected today, including the *De alchimia* (*Semita recta*), the *Speculum astronomiae*, and several collections of sermons, devotional works dedicated to the Blessed Virgin Mary, and commentaries on the Psalms and on the Apocalypse. The Jammy edition includes the authentic works, important to the debate over Albert's association with magic, too: *De mineralibus*, *De animalibus*, *De vegetabilibus*, as well as the *De anima*, and others. Jammy's apparatus was sparse: there were few citations or cross-references and no commentary on the writings themselves. Jammy flagged Albert's perplexing passage on magic in the *De anima* in the margin, but added no comment.[19] The front matter of the first volume includes an unremarkable letter of dedication to the reigning pope Innocent X (r. 1644–55), tables of contents, and two elogia, one to Albert, the other to Thomas Aquinas, penned by the Jesuit rhetorician Pierre Labbé (1594–1680).[20] Jammy inserted a brief vita as well, derived from familiar, older works, Peter of Prussia's and Rudolph of Nijmegen's most prominently. The vita included several stories, stock to the repertoire, of Albert's devotion to the Virgin Mary, in particular regarding her promise to him of knowledge and understanding. But there is silence on Albert's alleged practice of magic.[21] By adopting Jammy's index of authentic work in their *Scriptores ordinis praedicatorum* (1719–23), the Dominican bibliographers Jacques Quétif and Jacques Echard bolstered its authoritativeness.[22] While this canon was never unquestioned, encyclopedists, among all other kinds of scholars, now had what earlier writers had lacked—namely, titles and texts together as a common reference for reconstituting Albert's thought.

Albert as Entry

Louis Moréri's *Grand Dictionnaire*, arguably the first of the early modern encyclopedias,[23] offers a baseline for our analysis of the encyclopedias in two respects: in its handling of Albert's practice of magic and, more fundamentally, in the sources it relies on. Moréri (1643–1680), educated at the Jesuit college in Aix and ordained as a secular priest in Lyon, published volumes of his own poetry and enjoyed success as a preacher before turning to *Le Grand Dictionnaire historique*. This work first appeared as a single volume in 1674, and Moréri was bringing a second, revised, two-volume edition to press when he died in 1680.[24] He spent the last five years of his life in Paris, tutoring the children of Louis XIV's foreign minister and traveling in Paris's vibrant circles of learning. Biography, theology and philosophy, history and literature, and geography fell within the work's ambit. Relatively few entries are devoted to the sciences and technology. Mercury, for example, appears as a Greek god but not as a planet or chemical element. In the preface to the first edition, Moréri pointed out his most valued sources and models, which encompassed the particular histories of regions, dynasties, and religious orders as well as earlier specialized works on literature, theology, and sciences.[25] Jean Leclerc (1657–1736), a Calvinist theologian and philosopher from Geneva, took over the task of revising *Le Grand Dictionnaire* after Moréri's death. Under his direction, the sixth edition comprises four volumes.[26] Subsequent revisions were undertaken until the twenty-fourth edition, of ten volumes, appeared in 1759. Louis-Ellies Dupin (1657–1719), a Jansenist theologian and philosopher at Paris, followed Leclerc and oversaw later revised editions. By the mid-eighteenth century, there were adaptations of the *Grand Dictionnaire* in English, German, Dutch, and Spanish.

Over this period, the entry for Albert underwent little change; the topic of magic, some. In Moréri's first edition a brief entry touches on the friar's scholarship, appeals to endorsements of his erudition and devotion from Trithemius and the sixteenth-century Jesuit theologian Robert Bellarmine (1542–1621), and continues, "It is also useful to note his beautiful knowledge of the secrets of nature, which allowed him to make many ingenious and admirable things, but also made him esteemed a necromancer [*negromancien*]. This was only in a century of ignorance, and good people have always had more advantageous feelings for such a great man, whose body is still preserved without corruption."[27] The last sentence draws attention to a kind of distinction between bad magic and good religion that other encyclopedias did not take as self-evident. On this point Moréri made his most significant amendment in the second edition, where he expanded direct reference to Albert's alleged practice of magic and replaced the earlier reference to necromancy with the more general term *magic*: "Some Authors have accused him of magic, of having discovered the secret of the philosopher's stone, of having invented gunpowder, and of having formed an android, that is to say a head of bronze forged under certain constellations, which responded to his demands. We are [today] quite removed from such ridiculous ideas." As in the passage from the first edition, Moréri asserted here that what legend imputed to Albert is irrational and incorrect. None of the examples he offered can be traced to the authentic writings of Albert. Furthermore, Moréri took issue with aspects of Jammy's opera omnia, noting that it includes "some treatises that are not by this great man" and neglects "others attributed to him."[28] Subsequent editors left this revised entry on Albert as it was.[29]

The replacement of *negromancie* with magic in the second edition points to new ideas about what these terms and practices encompassed. Neither of the first two editions includes an entry on necromancy (or nigromancy) or magic, but *mages* is a headword in both. The entry offers a history of *mage* as a learned vocation with its origins among "the priests and philosophers of the Persians." It associates these ancient sources of wisdom with the magi of Saint Matthew's Gospel. Moréri cited Naudé on this point, who had included a chapter on the biblical magi in the *Apologie*.[30] Moréri followed Naudé's *Apologie* also in regard to Roger Bacon, Giovanni Pico, and Trithemius. While there is no entry on magic in the volumes, the term comes up some forty times in other entries, most commonly to describe the activities of ancient philosophers and early Christian heresiarchs. Leclerc's revision of 1692 finally included an entry on magic. By his reckoning, magic was a means of accomplishing something that could be good or wicked. Like Naudé, Leclerc distinguished between natural, artificial, and diabolic magic according to agency: natural magic produces its extraordinary and marvelous effects through the forces of nature alone; artificial magic produces the same through human industry; and diabolical magic, or black magic, produces effects beyond the powers of nature alone and only with the aid of demons. The definitions and the examples he offered are taken from Naudé's *Apologie*.[31] Leclerc's 1692 entry on magic remained largely unchanged through the 1759 edition. An entry on necromancy first appeared in the 1718 revision by the Jansenist Dupin. His definition includes no hint of the natural connotations with which Albert had been familiar: it is "a magical art," superstitious and pretended, in which practitioners rely on rituals and demons to consult with the dead. He established the practice's antiquity with reference to a Dutch classicist, Samuel Pitiscus (1637–1727), and the German-Swiss Hebraists Johannes Buxtorf the Elder (1564–1629) and the Younger (1599–1664).[32]

Just before Leclerc's first revision was issued, another encyclopedia appeared, controversially at the time, but much consulted by subsequent encyclopedists.

Antoine Furetière's *Le Dictionaire universel* emerged out of a conflict between the author and the Académie Française. Furetière (1619–1688) was a member of the learned society, but the Académie saw his dictionary as a plagiarized rival to its own, not-yet-completed dictionary. Furetière had outlined the scope of his project in the *Essais d'un dictionnaire universel*, which he published in 1684 as the controversy was in its earliest stages. "The terms of all the sciences and the arts"—philosophy and medicine, civil and canon law, mathematics, astronomy and astrology, music, architecture, poetry and rhetoric, painting and sculpture, war, falconry and fish, natural curiosities, and moral principles—would be handled along with the etymologies and meanings of "French words old and new." Over three hundred pages of examples follow.[33] Furetière's first edition appeared posthumously in 1690 and opens with an essay by Bayle, who defended the work from its Parisian detractors as constituted by different priorities, less linguistic and more scientific.[34] Ultimately, the Académie decided to expand the scope of its own work and deputed the playwright Thomas Corneille (1625–1709) to the task. The resulting *Dictionnaire des arts and des sciences*, a work of two volumes, reached the press in 1694. These were joined to the Académie's language dictionary as a third and fourth volume in 1696.[35]

Several entries related to magic in Furetière's dictionary compose a background against which to judge his treatment of Albert. Furetière's entry on mage echoes Moréri's: a *mage* is a wise man and philosopher from the East, especially Persia, akin to a druid in Gaul; a magician (*magicien, -enne*) works in league with diabolic forces. Furetière offered Agrippa von Nettesheim as an example of a magician. Magic itself is defined as the art that pretends to achieve amazing and wonderful things. Furetière followed Naudé and Moréri in distinguishing three kinds of magic, natural, white, and black: Natural magic offers secrets for doing extraordinary things through the manipulation of natural causes, and Giambattista della Porta (d. 1615) is proposed as its exemplary practitioner. White magic has the same effects but involves the invocation of good angels. In contrast, black magic involves the invocation of demons to circumvent the ordinary working of nature. Furetière warned that mathematics can be mistaken for black magic, as in the case of Gerbert of Aurillac. Alchemy is proposed as synonymous with chemistry except in the hands of certain "idiots, charlatans, and searchers for the philosopher's stone."[36] To the extent that astrology proposes that the speculative study of the effects and influences of the stars allow the prediction of the future, it is "a vain and uncertain science." Astronomers and astrologers should never be, by Furetière's reckoning, confused.[37] His use of *science* in the customary early modern sense refers to all bodies of genuine knowledge and is not particularly associated with the natural sciences.[38] While, Furetière never cited Naudé, certain common themes associate them: magic can be distinguished between a natural kind that makes an almost ordinary way of tapping the forces of nature and involves nothing beyond human ingenuity and another kind that requires the help of spiritual assistance, a kind that, for its rarity, needs little elaboration.[39]

Furetière, never planning to encompass much biography in his work, assigned no entry to Albert in either the *Essais* or *Le Dictionaire*. Instead Furetière drew Albert into multiple individual entries. In the *Essais*, for example, Albert appears under "Dragon." Albert, Furetière remarked with allusion to several passages in Albert's *De animalibus*, described "a sea dragon, similar to a snake with short wings and very quick movements, and so venomous that it kills with its bite."[40] This entry reappears in the *Dictionnaire*, which also included nineteen additional references to the friar, deployed as an authority on the characteristics of natural objects. Most of these new entries pertain to birds—for example, the cormorant, the gyrfalcon, and the bearded falcon—and minerals—for example, borax and chrysolite; the details were, in fact, taken from his *De animalibus* and *De mineralibus*. Furetière drew attention to Albert's own reputed research in some entries. For example, he implied *De secretis mulierum* as Albert's work in the entry on *fetus*, and he offered Albert's brazen head as an example in the entries *machine*, *parlant*, and *teste*. In short, Furetière implicitly rejected the claim that the friar practiced magic, as he understood it. He made his esteem most direct under the headword *lumière*. After proposing a series of scientific, practical, and metaphorical understandings of the word, Furetière remarked that the term could be applied to "great men who have enlightened the church and the sciences." He offered three examples: Ambrose of Milan, for the church; Thomas Aquinas, for the academy; and Albert the Great, who was in all things "one of the grand *lumières* of his century."[41]

The ink was scarcely dry on the first edition of *Le Dictionaire universel* (1690) when the author of its preface began expressing his own interest in the new genre. Bayle, like Furetière, preceded his encyclopedia with a prospectus, the *Projet et fragmens d'un dictionnaire critique* (A plan and samples of a critical dictionary) (1692).[42] It comprised an explanation of guiding principles to the composition of such a compendium—the *projet*—followed by four hundred pages of sample entries—the *fragmens*. Bayle emphasized in the former the importance of accuracy through the proper testing and use of sources. He expressed ideas of historical accuracy and skepticism that recall Naudé's treatment of history in the *Apologie*, especially a shared interest in testing authority and a shared aspiration to a history writing free of prejudicial influences. Historical truth, Bayle argued, has a validity no less than mathematical truth: "It is my contention that historical truth can be pushed to a greater degree of certainty than that allowed of geometric truth; of course, both kinds of truth will be considered according to the kind of certainty that is peculiar to them."[43] Both arrive at truth claims more reliably than theology.[44] Bayle gave a respectful nod to *Le Grand Dictionnaire* and the standard it set, but also drew attention to what he regarded as the failings of particular articles.[45] The *Projet* indicates the skepticism toward received judgment and confidence in history as a means of arriving at genuine truth that Bayle shared with Naudé.

Both the first and the second editions of Bayle's *Dictionnaire historique et critique*, appearing in 1697 and 1702, include entries on Albert.[46] The second edition adds to the first several notes that contain information the author attributed to a frequent correspondent, the poet and philologer Bernard de La Monnoye (1641–1728), who belonged to the same learned, historically skeptical circles that had inspired Naudé a generation earlier.[47] The entry has three parts: a first, comprising biographical details; a second, treating claims about Albert's work and writing, most extensively about the practice of magic, that Bayle presented as untrue; and third, offering a summary of Albert's learning. Bayle introduced the second section with reference to Moréri's handling of similar problems in *Le Grand Dictionnaire*. Bayle followed Moréri's interpretations, but also made a few pointed corrections, such as of Moréri's misdating of Albert's exhumation. Bayle's familiarity with the sources about Albert's life and work is apparent throughout; he addressed the writings of "Albert's apologists" Peter of Prussia, Trithemius, and especially Naudé in detail. Despite Bayle's obvious regard for Naudé—the *Apologie* and other works appear throughout *Le Dictionaire historique*—the librarian is no more protected than Moréri from Bayle's critical eye. Again, it is mainly biographical errors that Bayle drew attention to, such as Naudé's misdating of Albert's entrance into the Dominican order and his incorrect assertion that Albert never left Cologne as a friar.[48] Bayle added in the revision of 1702 his disappointment at Naudé for his eccentric use of the term "android" for the brazen head, a point he took from La Monnoye (fig. 6).[49]

Bayle used the notes—eight in the first edition, ten in the second—to embellish points made tersely in the main text, in particular to treat Albert's unseemly writings and activities. He rejected Albert's midwifery with reference to Peter of Prussia's fifteenth-century argument, and he reproduced a lengthy quotation from the *Apologie* rejecting Albert's invention of gunpowder and artillery. He followed Naudé in rejecting Michael Maier's association of the early Dominicans with alchemical knowledge and quoted Albert's own words taken from the *De mineralibus* to exclude most alchemical pseudepigrapha from any credible list of Albert's writings.[50] He rejected Albert's authorship of the *De mirabilibus* and the *Speculum* on the authority of Naudé, Gianfrancesco Pico, and Delrio; like

THE ENCYCLOPEDIC ALBERT

Fig. 6. Frontispiece for the Amsterdam edition (1721) of Naudé's *Apologie*. The caption reads, "But they are so wickedly impious that it is actually from you that they derive their proof of this great charge: I shall appear to have been a close party to such a misdeed precisely because I am steeped in your learning and trained in your ways." [Boethius, *Consolation of Philosophy*, LCL 74:156]

Naudé, he proposed that Roger Bacon had authored the *Speculum*, a work he promised was less objectionable than it was often made out to be.[51] Still following Naudé, Bayle suggested that the supposed brazen head might have actually been a statue used for anatomical reference rather than a speaking machine.[52] Regarding the winter feast in the cloister gardens with the German king, Bayle appealed to a more recent handling of it by the Jesuit Théophile Raynaud (1583–1663), who included Albert's alleged practice of magic in a book on kinds of and defenses against calumny.[53]

In addition to the full entry on Albert in *Le Dictionaire historique*, Bayle deployed the friar philosopher as an authoritative source elsewhere in the volume. He cited Albert in the entry on Aristotle for the friar's suggestion that Stagirite had been expelled from Athens on account of his good morals.[54] He paired Albert and Roger Bacon in an entry on the latter for reputedly having constructed a talking head.[55] He compared Albert's treatment of the magi at the nativity in Matthew 2 to that of Girolamo Cardano (1501–1576) in the latter's entry.[56] He drew another comparison between the legends of Albert and of a certain Hierophile, an ancient doctor, unknown except for the story of his teaching medicine to a woman, Agnodice, illicitly. She, the story went, disguised herself as a man to practice it. This of course brought to mind the accusation of Albert's disguise as a woman to learn midwifery.[57] Bayle referred to Albert in the entry on the early sixteenth-century historian Albert Krantz so that he could scoff at an Oxford professor's confusing the two.[58] Bayle drew a sympathetic parallel between Tomás Sánchez (1550–1610), a Spanish Jesuit theologian, and Albert in the former's entry: Both priests' thought, Bayle explained, had been misunderstood and condemned but only after neither could defend himself. In Sánchez's case, church authorities had placed parts of a treatise on marriage on the Index of Forbidden Books; Albert's case remains unspecified.[59] Finally, Bayle made a quick reference to Albert in the entry on Baruch Spinoza for identifying pantheists before the Dutch philosopher: "Among the Christians there have been similar heretics. In the beginning of the thirteenth century, for example, a certain David of Dinant made no distinction between God and raw material. It is a mistake to say that before him no one had ever come up with this dream. Doesn't Albert speak of a philosopher who came up with it?" Bayle then quoted a passage from Albert's *Physica* on Alexander the Epicurean.[60] In these last two instances, Bayle's attempt at drawing a sympathetic parallel, between Albert and Sánchez and then Albert and Spinoza, are left frustratingly ambiguous beyond the allusion to what Bayle took as an ill-founded accusation of magic against Albert and the presupposition that Albert's theological and philosophical writing were orthodox.

Albert's Magic Through a Confessional Lens

Unencumbered by knowledge of Bayle's project, Henri Basnage de Beauval (1656–1710), a Huguenot refugee in Holland since the Edict of Fontainebleau in 1685, took to the task of revising Furetière's earlier work. His significant revisions first appear in the sixth edition of 1701, the year before Bayle's own revised *Dictionnaire* (the second edition).[61] Basnage was responsible for three more editions until the ninth and final edition of the dictionary appeared in 1727, like Furetière's first edition, posthumous to the editor.[62] Basnage used his editorial influence to amend Furetière's Catholic perspective on certain topics.[63] He removed, for example, references to Calvinists as heretics and elaborated the history and doctrine of Lutheranism.[64] The editors of France's premier Jesuit journal of letters at the time, *Les Mémoires de Trévoux*, took issue with such changes. Notably, the revisions and controversy are important not for throwing an alteration into relief but, rather, a consistency: Basnage revised Furetière's sketch of magic scarcely at all.[65] And the same can be said of the entry on magic in the new encyclopedia that emerged as the Catholic response to the Basnage edition, the *Dictionaire de Trévoux*. Formally known as the *Dictionnaire universel françois et latin*, it was never an official publication of the Jesuit order even though several Jesuits collaborated on its production until the order's dissolution in France by royal decree in 1764. There were nine editions of *Trévoux* in the eighteenth century. The first, in 1704, is little more than a modestly amended version of Basnage's own 1701 revision of Furetière's work; from the second edition onward, more substantial revisions were incorporated with each edition.[66] Throughout, *Trévoux*'s entry on magic followed Furetière's as closely as had Basnage's.

The tight relationship between Furetière, Basnage, and the editors of Trévoux is in evidence specifically on the matter of Albert and magic. We can take four emblematic editions of what may be called the Furetière tradition to demonstrate this point, specifically Furetière's own work (1690) as Ur-text; Basnage's first revision of it (1701); the first *Trévoux* (1704), largely taken from Basnage; and then the last *Trévoux* (1752) before the suppression of the Jesuit order. We have already seen that the editors pointed to Albert repeatedly as a respected authority on animals and minerals—for example, in entries on borax, dragons, the bearded vulture, and the bustard—and such claims remain as constant through time as across editorial perspectives. Mechanical references are likewise constant and consistent: Albert's supposed speaking brazen head, for example, is deployed as an example in multiple entries such as in *articulé*, *machine*, and *parlant*.

Theological themes promise to be more controversial. Anything Basnage had to say about "scholastics" would assuredly come under the most careful scrutiny of the Catholic editors of *Trévoux*. Yet even there, the repetition vastly outweighs amendment: Basnage repeated and expanded generously Furetière own earlier entry. The Calvinist pastor repeated the Catholic priest's opening definition that emphasized "reason" and "argument" in scholastic theology and contrasted it, fairly enough, to the "positive" theology of the early Christian theologians and their councils. Furetière proposed that Thomas Aquinas was "the founder of scholastic philosophy, following the method of Averroes." Basnage replaced the reference to Averroes with Aristotle and highlighted Albert's contribution, about which Furetière had written nothing. Basnage elaborated to explain scholasticism's development in three phases and placed Albert at the turn of "early" to "middle" scholasticism. He characterized the third phase as a reaction against Aquinas that "achieved little success" and remarked of the third phase, "These intellects became even more subtle, and the school became increasingly concerned with frivolous matters. They let themselves get heated up over pure formalities and argued over mere shadows. Their methods produced a mere jumble of opinions, which suffocated any good taste in letters that remained." Basnage pointed ecumenically to the sources of what he had added, citing the Jesuit poet René Rapin (1621–1687) in criticizing the quality of late scholastic writing and quoting the Maurist spiritual writer François Lamy (1635–1711) that "scholasticism is a fastidious and persnickety science." He cited the Calvinist theologian Lambert Daneau (1530–1595) for what history he added.[67]

Against all retrospective expectations, the *Dictionnaire de Trévoux* of 1704 reproduced the entry on the scholastics without amendment, including all references to Albert, as did the edition of 1752.[68] These similarities blunt the surprise when we find in the entries on topics related to magic few differences across the four editions. In the entries on "alchymie," "chymie" is offered as its near synonym regardless of the fruitless efforts spent searching for the philosopher's stone. The transmutation of metals is, the entries allow, in some contexts better referred to as alchemy in the sense of being a subfield of chemistry. The struggle over Paracelsus on the matter of alchemy that had so consumed Naudé is nowhere to be found.[69] Astrology is distinguished from astronomy in its own entry. The former is the conjectural science that judges the effects and influences of the stars and predicts future events; the latter, the science that measures and seeks to understand the movements of the stars, their size, their distance, and their eclipses. The former is an "art of trickery"; the latter, a science "certain, sublime, and highly expressive of human genius." Ptolemy (100–170), Cardano, and Regiomontanus (1436–1476) are named among infamous astrologers; Ptolemy (again), Nicolaus Copernicus (1473–1543), Tycho Brahe (1546–1601), Johannes

Kepler (1571–1630), and Giovanni Domenico Cassini (1625–1712), among great astronomers.[70] Demons and the diabolical appear in each dictionary, including in entries related to necromancy, a "detestable art," for which the biblical *pythonisse*—the medium at Endor in 1 Samuel—is the prime example.[71] The brief entry "occulte" offers necromancy as an example of the "vain and forbidden" occult sciences, which also include "Kabbalah and magic." The occult, by Furetière's reckoning, also offers cover for "bad philosophers who cannot discover the cause of an effect, of a disease, [and who] say that it comes from an occult virtue, an occult property, an occult cause, or an occult quality." Basnage in 1701 and *Trévoux* in 1704 repeat Furetière on this point, and the *Trévoux*'s edition of 1721 reinforces it yet further, adding "occult qualities are a resource for ignorant philosophers, who cannot ascertain the cause of a given effect which they wish to explain."[72]

Finally, there are a set of definitions regarding magic and related fields. Again, there are more similarities than differences, and emendations are few. One in which a criticism of Albert is added in later editions is the entry on horoscopes. Furetière explained in the 1690 edition that "drawing up a nativity" concerned "predictions about people's lives and fortunes," and likewise about those of "a city, the states, and grand enterprises."[73] Basnage's 1701 edition shortens discussion of nativities but concludes that "in the past, people were so infatuated with horoscopes that Albert the Great had the temerity to draw one of Jesus Christ."[74] The origins of the claim derive from such a horoscope in the *Speculum astronomiae*, which was commonly ascribed to Albert.[75] Trévoux simply repeats the entry with the claim in its first addition and augments it in later editions with a pair of couplets by the Jesuit poet Jean-Antoine du Cerceau (1670–1730): "I am not a great Astrologer, / and I know little of the art of lying, / though this art is very much in vogue; / I am much less able to construct a horoscope than an eclogue."[76]

All include the headwords *mage*, *magicien*, and *magie*. Furetière's definition of a mage focused on the term's presumed eastern origins, associated in particular with the Persians. Mages function sometimes like philosophers, sometimes like priests, sometimes like court advisers. *Trévoux* 1704 expanded the definition with reference to the magi in Matthew's Gospel. Later editions of *Trévoux* devoted increasing space to considerations of the etymological origins of the word. A *magicien* is defined across the dictionaries as one who achieves "extraordinary things" with the aid of diabolical power. They offer Cornelius Agrippa as an example of a male magician; Circe, of a female one. Echoing Naudè, they continue, "In ignorant centuries good philosophers were misunderstood as magicians." Basnage added reference to Circe's sorcery against Ulysses in Homer's epic. *Trévoux* elucidated historical confusions between "magicians" and "mathematicians."[77]

Furetière's entry on magic includes a general definition of magic as "the science that teaches how to do surprising and wonderful things." He divided magic into natural magic (i.e., achieving "extraordinary effects" through "natural causes") white magic (whose effects follow the invocation of angels), and black magic (whose effects follow through demons). Furetière reiterated—through the example of Pope Sylvester II and the analysis of the Polish Dominican history writer Abraham Bzovius (1567–1637)—that there is often much confusion between black magic and mathematics. Basnage amended and expanded Furetière's definition. Magic is perhaps, he allowed, applied to certain kinds of wisdom, and "natural magic" may apply to innocent familiarity with minerals. But thanks to the attachment of mages to "astrology, divination, enchantment, and wicked deeds," magic has become an "odious term" and can only signify an "odious and disgusting science." The challenge, as Basnage saw it, was distinguishing between what element of magic is charlatanry and what element amounts to outright diabolism. He underscored the ambiguity in the story of pharaoh's magicians in Exodus as to the source and nature of their power, sketched the disagreement between Reginald Scot (1538–1599) and King James of Scotland (1566–1625), and he quoted the treatment of satirist Lucian (second century CE) by the poet Guillaume de Brébeuf (1618–1661). Furetière's earlier definitions of white and black magic were left untouched. The editors of *Trévoux* reproduced Basnage's version, adding several sentences from Cornelius Agrippa on the different kinds of magic: natural, celestial, and ceremonial. The addition, signed Mascur, reinforces the convictions that magic is real and that natural magic is innocent.[78]

The *Dictionaire universel* and its two traditions of amendment, in the hands of the Calvinist Basnage and the Catholics of Trévoux, share a common interest in Albert as a scholastic thinker, representative of the best of intellectual traditions even if historically no longer current. There is a natural magic that does not deserve reproach and must be distinguished from other sorts of magic that are illusory or if real, diabolical. The similarities across eighteen combined editions of these two encyclopedias—one initiated by a Catholic priest and revised by Calvinist theologians and a second initiated in Catholic circles against the Calvinist revision to the first—undermine the conventional wisdom of distinctively Protestant and Catholic stances toward magic and superstition in the early modern period. In short, the naturalizing of magic, the confidence in the pursuit of natural causes to natural effects, grows.

Encyclopedias beyond the Francophone world addressed Albert's reputation for magic in similar ways and with similar sources, sometimes cited, sometimes not. Ephraim Chambers's *Cyclopaedia* in 1728 was a decisive contribution to the genre in the Anglophone world, and set the precedent there for using the word "encyclopedia."[79] Albert features in this work as the creator of an android; an expert in minerals, flora, and fauna; and a magician, falsely accused on account of his reputed casting of a horoscope of Christ, a claim derived from Basnage's revision of Furetière as well as *Trévoux*. Chambers followed Basnage's lead entries on magi and magic as well.[80] Not until the nineteenth century did an edition offer examples: "down to the 18th century, magic was greatly studied in Europe ... a grand and mysterious science, by means of which the secrets of nature could be discovered, and a certain godlike power acquired over the 'spirits.' ... The principal students and professors of magic during the period ... were Pope Sylvester II, Albertus Magnus, Roger Bacon, Raymond Lull, Pico della Mirandola, Paracelsus, Cornelius Agrippa, Trithemius, Van Helmont, and Jerome Cardan."[81] The list could easily have been taken from Naudé's *Apologie*, which had been available in English translation since 1657.[82] Another widely disseminated Anglophone example was Thomas Dyche's *New General English Dictionary* (1735). His treatment of Albert and magic is derivative of the *Cyclopaedia*.[83]

In proportion to the expansive size of the era's preeminent German-language encyclopedia, Albert's appearance in Zedler's *Univeral-Lexicon* (Leipzig, 1731–54), which comprised 284,000 entries in sixty-four volumes plus four supplements, was slight. A biographical entry hides among a group of five bishops of Regensburg sharing the name Albert.[84] The entry's author is unidentified; its content is neither traceable to an earlier encyclopedia nor remarkable.[85] The author justified the cognomen "magnus" with a vague reference to Albert's teaching and writing. He was, the anonymous author remarked, "an uncommonly accomplished mathematician [*Mathematicus*] and chemist [*Chymicus*]." Neither confirmation nor denial accompanies many episodes in Albert's life that contributed to his shady reputation for magic. The brazen head—"a statue in the form of a man, which was able to move and speak"—was simply one of many fascinating machines that Albert designed and would recall to eighteenth-century readers the many creative automata of their own day. In the *Universal-Lexicon*'s version of the story, Thomas Aquinas broke the brazen head, not because its logorrhea disturbed his studies, but because he mistakenly believed it worked through sorcery [*Zauberey*]). The entry relates Albert's apprenticeship as a midwife and his alleged discovery of the philosopher's stone. The friar's bibliography is outlined at the end with reference to the Jammy edition and the identification of several commonly misascribed titles, such as the *De secretis mulierum* and *De mirabilibus*. A bibliography offers the titles of Albert's theological and natural philosophical works, sometimes with a few descriptive words. The entry's perspective on Albert's philosophical standing follows the era's leading-edge work on the history of philosophy, Jakob Brucker's *Critical History of Philosophy* (1742–44). Brucker situated Albert at the opening stage of high medieval scholasticism's corruption, which he blamed on the turgid metaphysics and finicky logic that the scholastics, including Albert, had extracted from Aristotle. Brucker's disdain took form in the *Universal-Lexicon* as a silence on any specifics of Albert's philosophical conclusions. Naudé, the "famous French *polyhistor*," features prominently in this article's notes. Naudé's own biographical article as well offers an overview of his curriculum vitae, highlights his employment by three cardinals, and compiles a list of titles he wrote or edited. No special attention is drawn to the sixth entry on this list, the *Apologie*.[86]

The light touch of the *Universal-Lexicon*'s handling of Albert's reputed practice of magic stands in contrast to the *Universal-Lexicon*'s expansive treatment of magic in general. The encyclopedia includes separate, long entries on magic (*Magie*) and on sorcery (*Zauberey*) but draws a porous line between them.[87] Editors dedicate independent entries to two important subfields of magic, necromancy and witchcraft, while also further handling the topics in the larger entries on magic and sorcery.[88] While *Zauberey* is by definition demonic and necessarily evil, *Magie* is defined ambivalently, encompassing forms that could be either demonic or not. The article on *Magie* approaches the topic etymologically, historically, and philosophically. It includes a sprawling history of magic that is devoted to three main areas of antiquity: Greek philosophical history, Greek literary history, and biblical history. The principal practices and practitioners are sketched for each. A separate entry on the *magus* focuses on the Middle Eastern origins of the word.[89] Primeval magic was, by Zedler's reckoning, wholesome, and the knowledge of the mages was simply wisdom. The admixture of astrology, divination, and other satanic ways of knowing to pristine magic corrupted it. The *Universal-Lexicon*'s history of magic follows Naudé's lead through the European Middle Ages and the early modern period. The *Universal-Lexicon* presents magic as practices that can take one of two forms: one composing sound knowledge and moral use of forces in the natural world; another requiring the involvement of demonic powers. The article offers that there are other ways to classify kinds of magic. It describes a "French" model that follows Naudé in dividing magic into divine, white, natural, and black, as well as Agrippa proposal of dividing magic into natural, celestial, and ceremonial kinds. It further distinguishes between pure and impure magic. Additional subentries address magic that is superstitious, curious, artificial, necessary, Adamic, poetic, practical, and true. Natural, black, and white magic also receive brief entries of their own.[90]

In contrast, *Zauberey* requires the participation of demons by definition. Sorcery itself, the author explained, is "one of the most thoroughly harmful vices to be found under the sun, thus explaining the length of the article."[91] Indeed, the 105 columns devoted to *Zauberer* and *Zauberey* dwarf the seventeen devoted to magic.⁹² Sorcery divides into divinatory (i.e., the uncovering of hidden knowledge, especially the future), and the practical (the doing of evil to another). The entry considers how sorcery works, whether it is real, and how to understand it from distinct biblical, theological, philosophical, and jurisprudential perspectives. The witch trials, it should be recalled, were in decline but still ongoing in eighteenth-century, German-speaking Europe. The entry on sorcerers (*Zauberer*) defines them as practitioners of black magic. The article proposes a French hypothesis that the German word *Zauber* has roots in the Greek word *diabolos*. To the question whether sorcerers make pacts with the devil, the author remarked, "Some say yes, and others no. There are important reasons on both sides, and we leave it to the reader's judgment." He then alerted the reader that the article will conclude with a statement from a specialist who finds more against than for the idea.⁹³ (The article on witchcraft accepts the satanic compact more readily.⁹⁴) After reviewing the medieval history of sorcery, the author suggested that it was a common accusation by lazy priests and monks against the philosophically sophisticated. On this point, he reproduced Naudé's argument and offered Albert as a case in point. Elaborating beyond Naudé, the author proposed that the unseasonable feast in the cloister garden could be explained by a medieval prototype of the orangeries that were increasingly common in eighteenth-century Europe.⁹⁵ The entry concludes by returning to the issue of the demonic pact. The promised specialist is left unnamed, but his arguments take up a substantial seven columns.⁹⁶

Comparative analysis of Albert's and magic's treatment across multiple revisions of five major, rival encyclopedias, spanning the late seventeenth to late eighteenth centuries (Moréri, Furetière, Bayle, Chambers, and Zedler), plus two arguably autonomous derivations of Furetière (Basnage and *Trévoux*), points to three critical points of compatibility, regardless of national, philosophical, and theological differentiations among them: First, while they all maintained a distinction between natural and diabolic magic, contemporary and historical, Albert the Great was no longer regarded as a noteworthy practitioner of either. Second, neither praised nor censured for the practice of a magic broadly conceived to include alchemy, astronomy, and divination, Albert ever-less inspired the need to be exonerated from false charges of having practiced magic or occult sciences. And third, Albert was regarded as a scholarly authority worth citing in the presentation of natural qualities associated with natural objects. These three insights in the world of European learning in the period conventionally known as the Enlightenment allow for a fairly expedited treatment of the material presented at the beginning of this chapter, taken from what began in 1728 as a modest project to translate Chambers's *Cyclopaedia* and which since its completion in 1772 has been called the siege engine of the Enlightenment, Diderot and d'Alembert's *Encyclopédie*.

Enlightened Albert

The *Encyclopédie*'s treatment of Albert harmoniously draws from and develops what had for all intents and purposes become the encyclopedic standard on the topic. It features a biographical introduction to Albert in the article on the scholastics, multiple references to him in other entries, and significant entries on magic and related topics. Diderot himself authored the article on the scholastics. Scholasticism found itself in Diderot's crosshairs both as Europe's maladroit appropriation of Aristotle, whose ongoing influence Diderot lamented, and as a distinctively medieval and Catholic approach to philosophy and theology, which he scorned. Diderot's review of scholasticism,[97] like that in the *Universal-Lexicon*, follows Brucker's history of philosophy. Albert is grouped with Aquinas, Bacon, and Bonaventure, who together constituted a second phase of scholasticism and the beginning of its decline. What Brucker expressed with distaste, Diderot held in unrestrained contempt as he questioned whether the scholasticism of Peter Lombard, which had so profoundly disfigured Christianity, had any noteworthy antecedents in the early church or whether its mode of rationality was simply inherited in its unredeemably desiccated form from the Arabs. In the anonymous article on theology elsewhere in the *Encyclopédie*, scholasticism is further disparaged, and with reference to Albert: referring to the ecclesiastical historian and priest Claude Fleury (1640–1723), the article complains, "For who today reads Alexander of Hales or Albert the Great?" Indeed, what is "great" about him "beyond the size and number of his volumes."[98]

Diderot's biographical sketch of Albert, however, is not as severe: Diderot described Albert as "a man who knew almost everything that could be known" and as a teacher of the writings of Aristotle, courageous in the face of "papal proscription," likely an allusion to the controversies over Aristotelian and Averroist teachings in thirteenth-century Paris. No one, Diderot continued, knew Peripatetic dialectic and metaphysics better than Albert, but in his application of them to theology he advanced its corruption. Diderot lauded the breadth with which Albert mastered various areas of natural philosophy, mentioning in particular mathematics, mechanics, metallurgy, and lithology. Diderot reported Albert's design of a talking automaton and Aquinas's destruction of it, but without magical, astral, or demonic innuendo. His reference to the cloister garden feast is oblique: "He seems to have known how to obtain fruit in all seasons." He concluded with a swipe at the Jammy edition as "twenty-one large volumes that we no longer read."[99]

Outside of this longest single passage, Albert appears elsewhere in the *Encyclopédie* as a source and example. He is named in the article "android" for reputedly making one;[100] in "Aristotelianism" for having, along with Peter

Lombard and Aquinas, successfully reversed the effects of Bernard of Clairvaux's opposition to it;[101] in "astronomy" for having written the *Speculum* and for the invention of remarkable machines, otherwise unspecified;[102] and in "horoscopes" for supposedly casting one of Christ, as was earlier reported in the *Cyclopedia*.[103] One *Encyclopédie* contributor disposed to Albert was Gabriel-François Venel (1723–1775), who composed numerous articles for the *Encyclopédie* on chemistry, medicine, and related subjects. He ranked Albert just behind Roger Bacon as the twin masters of medieval chemistry. He praised them for having delved into "nearly every area of human knowledge" and attained in an era of "the most profound ignorance" a breadth of understanding that deserves to be admired even "in our own enlightened century."[104] The *Encyclopédie* raises only two components of Albert's long historical problem with magic: the story of his creating a talking head, and his engagement with the more dubious aspects of astrology in authoring the *Speculum astronomiae*. But in fact, it presents neither as problems of magic, superstition, or the occult. The brazen head is in the final analysis an example of mechanical prowess, and the *Speculum* is never more than an evaluative compendium of practices and treatises. The *Encyclopédie*'s contributors were less concerned with his being a magician than with his being an Aristotelian, and even then, in particular fields of natural philosophy and as a compiler of information about the natural world, they took the opportunity not just to use him as a credible source but also to praise him.

The absence of consideration of Albert's magical thinking, or even the attempt to defend him from it as a calumny, is all the more noteworthy when one considers how extensively the *Encyclopédie* deals with magic and related themes. Both magic and divination constitute their own domains in the *Encyclopédie*. Specific additional entries can be found, for example, on *conjuration* (3:885), *démonographe* (4:821), *goetie* (7:730), *magicien* (9:850), *maléfice* (9:994), *nécromancie* (11:69), *nécyomantie* (11:71), *occult* (11:332), *sorcellerie* (15:368), *sorciers* (15:369), and *theurgie* (16:278). The range of specified topics and some inconsistencies on particular points between them can be explained with reference to the diversity of the large group of thinkers who contributed to the *Encyclopédie*.[105]

Magic is defined as an "occult science or art, a way to learn to do things that appear beyond human power." Antoine-Noé de Polier de Bottens (1713–1783), an accomplished philologist and a leading Calvinist in Lausanne, is the likely author of the unsigned article, published in December 1765. Polier offered a history of magical practices to explain magic's transformation from the study of wisdom by ancient Chaldeans into an "illusory and despicable field of learning" in his own day and encompassing "astrology, prediction, spell-casting, and witchcraft."[106] Systematic presentation follows the historical overview: magic is related to and distinguished from religion, on the one side, and the knowledge of natural causes and the advance of technological expertise, on the other. While the article's overarching structure mimics in this respect what encyclopedias had described from Moréri to Zedler, Polier emphasized certain distinctive points. He regretted that the term *magic* was applied at all to human ingenuity and considered *natural magic* a particularly unfortunate nomenclature: "the limits of this so-called natural magic are narrowing every day.... And if Europe were to ever fall back into the barbarity from which it has finally emerged, we will seem to these future barbarians as magicians as well."

Regarding demonic magic, he called its aims absurd: only true philosophy "has dispelled humanity of these humiliating chimeras." He rejected with none of the *Universal-Lexicon*'s hesitation the possibility of diabolical pacts as the product of superstition and fanaticism, a mere expression of humanity's brutality toward its own. The solution to such misshapen thinking, by Polier's reckoning, is to be found in rational philosophy; in this respect Naudé's *Apologie*, he opined, took a less meaningful, less effective route by trying to exonerate the learned with lawyerly zeal instead of trying to overcome the underlying superstition with unrelenting reason. "Fear," he concluded, "is the daughter of ignorance, which in turn produces superstition, ... a fruitful source of errors, illusions, phantoms, and an overheated imagination that creates goblins, werewolves, ghosts and demons, which all jostle together in the mind.... No magic is so bad as that of the falsely devout."[107]

A Disappearing Act

Perhaps Polier made an unnecessary straw man out of a thinker who laid groundwork for his own position; straw men, of course, are not closely rationed in the *Encyclopédie*. Polier's rhetorical point, however, clarifies what the early modern encyclopedias reveal. From Naudé to Polier and through the encyclopedias between them, there was shared conviction that derogatory accusations of magic are unreliable. How the accusation gets handled changed: Naudé treated it as a calumny to refute; the encyclopedists increasingly treated it as something to ignore, and if reported, then not with animus but as a curiosity. These developments coincided with changing understandings of magic, especially a resharpening of the lines drawn between natural magic and any other kind of magic, lines that the sixteenth-century friars had all but erased.

The natural sciences and theology, the encyclopedists affirmed, have a history, and magic has been a part of that history. The historicizing insight was not the pure invention of the encyclopedists. Albert himself claimed as much in his treatment of the magi in his commentary on Matthew 2, and Naudé's exonerations depended on a historicized perspective on what accusers were naming magic. The development reflected in the encyclopedias had to do with new ambiguities about natural magic, pulled as the term was between more natural philosophical senses and inherently wicked ones. This tossed up for grabs, yet again, disciplines customarily understood as peripheral to the natural sciences, such as alchemy and astrology, and made expressions like "occult sciences" more useful and more ambiguous at the same time. As for diabolical magic, the encyclopedias tended to contain less and less about diabolical magic, with the notable exceptions of the *Universal-Lexicon*. While Zedler published more than anyone else on diabolical magic, he also went furthest in extracting it from any natural form. Polier took the matter a step further in defining, or really denouncing, "natural magic" as a cover for that which could be explained through genuine natural philosophy but had not yet. Polier insinuated, in a paraphrase of a yet-to-be articulated theological outlook, the notion of a natural magic of the gaps. Such reckoning reinforces a paradox we have seen from the beginning and that cuts across the relevant articles in the *Encyclopédie*— namely, that natural magic could denote either misunderstood natural phenomena or that nature was inherently magical.[108] Polier, in contrast, upended earlier treatments of demonic magic, from superstitious and idolatrous in practice to superstitious and fanatical in identification.

This changing frame affected judgment of Albert as a philosopher and magician. The earlier encyclopedists reliably started with Naudé's interpretation of magic as an accusation that misconstrued great accomplishment, a misconstrual that good history writing could expose. Naudé's apologetics laid the groundwork for the encyclopedists' increasingly sober reflections on Albert's accomplishments and the ease with which they could note and dismiss the accusation of magic. It was a framing and set of standards that in the end allowed Albert, as benighted as his Aristotelianism may have been,[109] to be a candle in the darkness of a barbarous age. While the *Encyclopédie* expressed that final judgment with singular clarity, a clarity consonant with its hostility to Aristotelianism, it is more significant to note the shared ambivalence toward the magical among the encyclopedias and the shared readiness to judge Albert on the merits of an engagement with the natural world that accepted it as natural and rational, even if also in part incorrect. While Catholic and Calvinist, Jesuit and Jansenist, and secular factions undeniably understood one another as rivals, they still shared an ambivalence toward magic, a disdain for superstition, and a historicized view of philosophy, natural philosophy, and magic. The encyclopedias that emerged demonstrate these harmonies not through intuited resonances among editorial principles but in the very texts and explanations that they contained. In this respect they follow lines of understanding the complexities of the Enlightenment that highlight its sources in theological discourses and soften the distinction between Enlightenment and Counter-Enlightenment that earlier generation took as self-evident.[110] The customary dividing lines do not allow for the extrapolation of how magic in general, and Albert's in particular, would be handled differently. Instead what comes into focus are the similarities: thus the libertine Naudé could inspire the priest Moréri, the priest Furetière could take from and expand on Moréri, the Calvinist Basnage could leave the Catholic Furetière unamended, the Jesuits could make Basnage's text their own, Zedler could offer a survey of the landscape without editorial comment, and under cover of derisive rhetoric, Diderot and Polier could do to the Jesuits what the Jesuits had done to the Calvinists. The end result is an Albert whom encyclopedists presented as no longer a magician, real or defamed, but a philosopher and naturalist, and for his day a remarkable one.

EPILOGUE
THE DISENCHANTED ALBERT

Late eighteenth-century treatments of Albert's investigations of the natural world without concern for magic moved his reputation across a significant threshold. Worry about and inquiry into his magical engagements were effectively marginalized in scientific, philosophical, and theological discourse. While the encyclopedic consensus did not dispel the image of Albert as a magician, when it appeared, it was disconnected from the writings and debates we have pursued over the preceding chapters. The aim of this epilogue is to evaluate the lingering associations of Albert to magic, and their absence, and to offer some reflections on the implications of Albert's seven-century-long reputational instability for the question of disenchantment. Taken as a case study, the history of Albert's reputation offers evidence against a putatively self-evident, linear progression for how learned European culture changed in its thinking about what magic is, whether it is real, and (if it is) how it works and whether it is good to practice.

Three nineteenth-century treatments of Albert's expertise in magic and the natural sciences offer benchmarks against which to assess the effects of the eighteenth-century encyclopedic consensus. These are found in belles lettres, esotericism, and hagiography, which are here treated in sequence. Mary Shelley created and then deployed an early post-Enlightenment, literary Albert in her *Frankenstein*. Her reference to Albert in the first pages of the novel signals the disreputability of the protagonist's early scientific education. While the boy Victor Frankenstein reads "with delight" Albert's "wild fancies," disillusion strikes quite literally one day when a bolt of lightning reduces an oak tree on the family property to a "blasted stump." A visiting "man of great research" explains the destruction in terms of electricity and thereby throws "into the shade Cornelius Agrippa, Albertus Magnus, and Paracelsus, the lords of [Victor's] imagination." Some years later at the university in Ingolstadt, when he admits the scientific inspirations of his youth, his accomplished "professor of natural philosophy" responds in shock, "Every instant that you have wasted on those books is utterly and entirely lost. You have burdened your memory with exploded systems and useless names. . . . I little expected, in this enlightened and scientific age, to find a disciple of Albertus Magnus and Paracelsus. My dear sir, you must begin your studies entirely anew."[1] As the reader comes to learn, Frankenstein's new studies lead to their own problems. Shelley's appeal is thus a double-edged sword. Albert represents a bad natural science that a new science properly surpasses in, for example, the explanatory power of electrical theory, but not in any capacity to curb the corrupting power of human ambition. Shelley made no reference to the historical Albert, his writings, or five centuries of dispute over him: His name alone is Shelley's handy glyph for what is irrational, superstitious, and antiquarian. Her treatment of Frankenstein's scientific ambitions rings of the Romantic reaction to Enlightenment rationalism, even as her use of Albert as a literary device does not signal the valorizing medievalism, also associated with Romanticism, of a time when humankind was better connected to the natural world and the spiritual was taken seriously.

The esoteric version of Albert as a magician is the cognate of the literary one. Here the term *esoteric* encompasses nineteenth-century occult movements that shared an enthusiasm for, or at least interest in, a real or constructed notion of science's "prehistory" and are associated with such authors as Éliphas Lévi Zahed (1810–1875) and H. P. Blavatsky (1831–1891). Such movements are also commonly associated with Romantic reactions to scientism, as also in some recent scholarship, as evidence for failed disenchantment, a retrenched enchantment, or even reenchantment. The esoteric Albert pairs with the literary Albert in that both offered a contrast to modern rationality, but neither had much to do with the Albert argued over in the preceding chapters. Some nineteenth-century learned attempts to determine a history of science found in Albert legitimate, if unusual, success at understanding the workings of nature; others, found in him license to practice magic in new forms. In his *On Old and New Magic* (1820), for example, Georg Conrad Horst (1769–1832), a theologian and occasional correspondent with Johann Wolfgang von Goethe, allowed for medieval magic such as Albert's to have achieved genuinely "deep insights into nature" and absolved it from any semblance of diabolism.[2] In his *New Miracle Showcase* (1839), the mathematician and precision engineer Johann Heinrich Moritz von Poppe (1776–1854) analyzed medieval natural magic in conjunction with "alchemy, chemistry, physics, the secrets and powers of nature, magnetism, sympathy, and related sciences," to determine its rationality, even as he recounted with skeptical fascination Albert's invention of a speaking head (fig. 7).[3] The brazen head also inspired the fascination of Éliphas Lévi, the above-mentioned esotericist, in his *Dogma and Ritual*

EPILOGUE 143

Fig. 432.—*The Talking Head of Albertus Magnus.*

ACOUSTICS.

Fig. 7. "The Talking Head of Albertus Magnus." From John Henry Pepper, *Cyclopaedic Science Simplified* (London: F. Warne, 1869), p. 473, fig. 432. This image introduces Pepper's chapter on acoustics. The illustration retains in the upper frame the fury of the surprised monk who destroys the brazen head as demonic but offers in the lower frame a new explanation for how, through a tube, Albert could speak through the head from below.

(1861).[4] In his *History of Magic* (1844) the Austrian physician Joseph Ennemoser (1787–1854) drew attention to Albert's acknowledgment of practicing magic, linked him to Bacon and Aquinas for recognizing magic's potential value, and made muddled but approving reference to Albert's study of the Kabbalah.[5] In his *History of Magic* (1870) the esotericist Paul Christian (Jean-Baptiste Pitois [1811–1872]) pointed to Albert, among other medieval prelates, as evidence of the church's openness to occult practices with the implication that such practices should enjoy the same sanction in the present.[6] The literary and esoteric Albert modeled something intentionally opposite from the rationalism and skeptical empiricism we saw in Naudé and the encyclopedias but also quite different from the Albert we see in the thirteenth century.

Simultaneous to Paul Christian's appeal to Albert as justification for his own esoteric practices, the bishops in Germany appealed to Rome in a new attempt to win Albert's canonization. This time its advocates succeeded, though the process took six decades to complete. In the course of it, the third Albert, a new hagiographical one, reemerged: the Albert who was at last raised to the altar had the form of a holy scientist. Already in the seventeenth century, various ecclesiastical authorities had given approval to Albert's limited veneration, in effect making him a blessed. Pope Gregory XV permitted Albert's veneration in the diocese of Regensburg in 1622; Pope Urban VIII, in the friar's hometown of Lauingen in 1631; and Pope Clement X, to the friar preachers worldwide in 1670. Albert's veneration had become so common in Germany by the nineteenth century that its bishops, convened at the First Vatican Council (1869–70), decided to pursue matters a step further and requested that Albert be declared a "doctor of the church." By 1870 popes had bestowed this title to saints in recognition of their contributions to Christian learning seventeen times. The German bishops likely anticipated in this gesture a political benefit at home. In the mid-nineteenth century the Catholic Church across Germany was under pressure from formidable, state-sponsored programs of secularization that took their most aggressive form in Otto von Bismarck's Kulturkampf (1871–78). If honored as a doctor of the church, Albert—German, Catholic, learned in natural sciences and theology, and a founder of, arguably, Germany's first institution of higher learning—could serve as a strong countersymbol against an antipathy toward Catholicism as antipatriotic and superstitious. Imagine the bishops' surprise when the responsible cardinal reminded them in his initial rejection of their petition that such declarations were to follow rather than precede a candidate's canonization.[7]

German devotees consequently mobilized behind Albert's canonization once again. Earlier works of historical scholarship were republished and sometimes translated into other languages.[8] Major Catholic figures in German politics and letters were recruited to the effort: the nineteenth-century philosopher and leader of the Center Party Georg Friedrich Freiherr von Hertling (1843–1919), for example, published a new intellectual biography of Albert,[9] and the esteemed twentieth-century medievalist Martin Grabmann (1875–1949) included a lengthy analysis of Albert in his extended project on the thirteenth-century world of ideas.[10]

Albert's reputation for magic could not be avoided altogether in the renewed biographical research. This time, however, new appreciation of what the magical arts may have been and new approaches in the historical scholarship on premodern science made dismissing any apprehension of his magic easy as never before. The new biographers—most prominently the Dominican Paulus von Loë, the Jesuit Franz Pelster, the onetime Dominican Heribert Scheeben—presented magic as protoscience where they could. Where they could not, they placed the magical under the rubric of legend: Joachim Sighart explained in his 1857 biography of Albert the suspicion of magic to be a confused understanding of Albert's expert understanding of the natural world and dismissed specific anecdotes as uneducated storytelling, a twist on Naudé's earlier approach. Seven decades later Scheeben isolated all consideration of magic in an appendix titled "Albert in the Legends."[11] In an era of exuberance for the critical edition, Albert's works were edited and published once more. The brothers Borgnet, diocesan priests of Reims, revised Jammy's collection lightly, not always to its betterment.[12] The Borgnet edition (1890–1899) excluded several disputed writings, such as the *Semita recta*. But other writings, like the *Speculum astronomiae*, remained in it. Tellingly, in the canonization acta of 1931 and related ecclesiastical documentation, Albert's practice of magic appeared only with reference to Peter of Prussia's vita, in which, it will be recalled, refutation of Albert's practice of magic had been a driving concern.[13] The derivative treatment in the acta gives yet more and different testimony of what the eighteenth-century reinterpretation of Albert's practice of magic had accomplished.

Pope Pius XI (r. 1931–39) canonized Albert equipollently, that is, after an abbreviated process, on 16 December 1931, and declared him a doctor of the church at the same time.[14] Whether Albert's reputation as a magician had ever been a genuine impediment to his canonization, as Peter and others had proposed, is far from certain. Canonization was so rare—no single pope presided over more than twelve such ceremonies before the nineteenth century—that the question that should puzzle is not why someone is not canonized but why someone ever is. In any event, magic was not an issue in the process that ultimately succeeded. Pius's decisions to canonize favored the learned saints of earlier eras. He had already canonized the author of the principal sixteenth-century Catholic catechism, Peter Canisius (1521–1597), and the revered seventeenth-century theologian and spiritual author Robert Bellarmine (1542–1621). He had declared them, along with the mystic John of the Cross (1542–1591), doctors of the church as well. His successor, Pius XII (r. 1939–58), added to Albert's titles "patron of all who cultivate the natural sciences" in 1941. This Pius underlined the timeliness of his declaration, two years into renewed world war, "when contemporary advances in the sciences are lamentably employed not in praise of God and for the welfare of humanity, but to rain down the calamities of war on city and countryside."[15] If command over the natural world could go wrong, Pius insinuates, blame should to be laid at the feet of the twentieth century, not the thirteenth.

In the literary Albert, esotericist Albert, and canonized Albert, we find three ways of handling Albert's reputation as a magician. On the one hand, each treats it differently: the association with magic made him irrational and antiquarian for Mary Shelley but a seeker of deeper truth for Paul Christian and his esotericist allies. Albert's ecclesiastical life-writers took another route by highlighting the kernel of the scientific in his writing and relegating the rest to legend. Following the encyclopedic line of thinking most closely, they were silent on his problematic "verif[ication] of the truth ... with the magical arts"[16] and highlighted instead his accomplishments as a keen observer of the natural world, however surpassed his findings had subsequently become. The editors of each of the three opera omnia have taken a similar approach.

On the other hand, the hagiographic Albert is not unique in its dependence on the thinking that had rendered Albert's work on magic immaterial. Shelley was attempting to chart a third way of engagement with the natural world by rejecting her titular protagonist's confidence in modern science's unlimited potentials no less than Albert's and Paracelsus's occultism. The esotericists looked exactly to what the encyclopedists had bracketed out in Albert and others to validate what, by their lights, the philosophes had misconceived about the natural world in the first place. What none of these factions did was return to the actual debates about what Albert had thought, written, or practiced. Those questions and that kind of engagement were apparently no longer necessary or proper. The magical Albert of the nineteenth century, as also its absence, emerged in reaction to the earlier thinking about magic, but could and did take multiple, incongruous forms.

Thus we return to the question whether Albert's protean reputation as a magician sheds light on the hypothesis of the West's disenchantment, understood as the process of cultural rationalization that led to Western modernity. To the extent the preceding chapters have sketched a coherent history, two questions drove this project forward: one, having to do with what the magical arts were that Albert worked with, and the other, having to do with what sense later thinkers made of Albert's engagement with magic. The history follows four points on which Albert's engagement with magic became contested, in some contexts elevating Albert's fame and in other lights defaming him.

Those points were, first, that Albert devoted himself most to a kind of magic that had to do with phenomena apprehensible within the natural world. The magical arts were by his reckoning fundamentally natural in that their causes and effects were encompassed in the natural world, a world created by God and open to rational discovery. They encompassed a body of knowledge and a set of skills that relied on the rational influences of celestial spheres on the terrestrial world and human society. They had nothing to do with special divine intervention (miracles), nor necessarily with the demonic. Second, a telltale of Albert's naturalizing approach to the magical arts was his recurrent use of the verb *experiri*, a verb he used throughout his natural philosophical writings to indicate a hands-on experience within the natural world. Magic, for Albert, was something to study and practice, not something only to read about. Third, Albert took a discrete, disaggregated approach to what other thinkers treated in aggregation. What can be achieved with particular minerals marked in certain ways at opportune celestial moments, by Albert's reckoning, is different from what can be achieved by following recipes in an alchemical handbook, as also using an herb medicinally and empowering it with incantations. The underlying theory and activity are different enough to merit distinct analyses. Fourth, Albert distinguished "magic" as it fell under either philosophical or theological scrutiny. Practices that incorporated the ritual invocations of demons and other ceremonies warranted philosophical reflection to the extent that their operation resembled the magical arts proper, but the invocation of demons was a moral problem, not a natural one, and so foremost was proper to theological reflection. Those commentators in his own day and after who did not follow these ground rules adopted other understandings of what magic was and appealed to Albert as endorsement of other ideas—about what immaterial entities could do in a material world, how mastery of the natural world was achieved, and what powers humans could acquire with the aid of demons—which had the effect of enchanting Albert.

Chapters 2 to 5 then chart four critical moments in which these summary points were reinterpreted and with them Albert's reputation as a magician. Each time, the treatment of Albert's life and reputation is shown to be as much shaped by how magic itself was understood differently in each context as what Albert had actually written about magic. In chapter 2, Albert was taken to endorse all sorts of magical theories and practices, which themselves fell sometimes inside, sometimes outside Albert's own understanding of magical arts. In subsequent chapters, the protagonists rejected Albert's reputation for magic in two cases as unfounded in his writing, first for moral reasons and then out of philosophical skepticism. In the third case, the encyclopedists rejected it as irrelevant to his accomplishments, understood as science in a historicizing manner. From Albert's own thinking and reactions to it, the study of Albert's reputation as a magician distills to two lessons in the flexibility of meaning, one having to do with what Albert was understood to have written and done; the other having to do with the word *magic*. These are the variables that shaped Albert's ever-changing reputation as a magician.

Whether this pliability matters brings us back to the concerns of the contemporary historians first raised in the introduction. Alexandra Walsham and Isabelle Draelants, it will be recalled, expressed qualms about reliance on historical teleology: the former rejected malformed assessments of how intellectual categories evolved from the Middle Ages to the present day,[17] and the latter, historical narratives that trace "the progress of the sciences away from superstition" and the structuralist's presumption of the "distinctions between science and magic."[18] A comparison of the lack of superstitious interests in Albert's *De mineralibus*,[19] the superstitious view of powers shaping nature in the fifteenth-century alchemical handbook *Compositum de compositis*,[20] and the concern for the diabolical corruption of Christian society in Peter of Prussia's *Legenda litteralis*[21] bolsters those admonitions. The chronicle of Albert's reputation for magic simply does not support the idea of a tidy progress of ideas, the onward march of scientific knowledge, or the ineluctable diminishment of enchanted thinking. Instead, along with Naudé's seventeenth-century appeal for a skeptical approach to sources and an appreciation that to be incorrect is not to be irrational, Albert's reputation as a magician is best accounted for when a multiplicity of discourses of magic—often simultaneous, sometimes interacting, and always destabilizing, and which range from the polemical to the forensic and from the ostracizing to the valorizing—can also be accounted for.[22]

Michael Bailey's concept of oscillations and Jason Ā. Josephson-Storm's concept of inverted disenchantment further order the instability of Albert's magical reputation in the debate over disenchantment and modernity. Both Bailey and Josephson-Storm refer with approval to the theorist of science studies, Bruno Latour.[23] His analysis of modernity and rejection of the European disenchantment thesis as a myth has attracted many historians of religion, magic, and ideas. Latour's rejection of that myth, with the myth's derogatory implications for medieval intellectual life, clears the ground for Bailey to develop his nuanced alternative approach to superstition. Bailey grounds his approach on Latour's diagnosis of modernity's false cleft between the natural-scientific and the sociopolitical and its exclusion of the spiritual from both, and thereby he evades the historiographical problem of abrupt change—the medieval is a superstitious age, the modern is a rational one. Bailey thus exposits oscillations in the West between superstition and skepticism.[24] Josephson-Storm starts with a similar diagnosis of modernity and proceeds to make a critical step beyond it: the goal is not simply to demythologize modernity's myth of disenchantment but to draw into relief the myth of modernity itself. The implications for Albert are clear: there should be no expectation that treatment of his writings on or practice of the magical arts would follow a clear line of development, nor that "modernity" respond to them in a coherent way.

Emphasis on the "naturalizing" component of disenchantment in its many forms draws into relief three central findings in *Disenchanting Albert the Great*: first, Albert strove to keep explanations for phenomena in the natural world natural, even when he offered those explanations through and according to magical arts. Second and in contrast to the first, Albert became the object of "enchantment" in his own day and in the centuries immediately following by those who used him as endorsement of magic well beyond what he had defined as such or accepted as valid and good. Third, the silence with which the encyclopedists, as well as the nineteenth-century hagiographers, treated his discussion of magic and his acknowledgment of having relied on it gives evidence of another disenchantment, either by means of silence or by laying blame at the feet of uneducated legend-spinners. At each stage, contemporary conceptions of magic loomed large in the assessment of Albert's writings, often larger than what Albert himself defined as such. While the history of Albert begins with Albert's reliance on magical arts and ends with their erasure, and while it begins enchanted and ends disenchanted, the story in between is messy. Albert's treatment of the magical arts, however naturalizing it was, laid the groundwork for an ever-more enchanted Albert during his life and posthumously. By twists and turns that enchantment gets undone: the Albert who had worked as a philosopher to disenchant the cosmos but who ended up himself enchanted was at long last disenchanted and recognized as the master of natural knowledge such as he had aspired to in the first place. The history of Albert and his reputation as a magician thus offers an object lesson in disenchantment and its ambiguities.

NOTES

INTRODUCTION

1. "Cuius veritatem etiam nos ipsi sumus experti in magicis." Alb., *De anima* 1.2.6 (ed. Colon. VII/1.32). The Albertus-Magnus-Institut dates the treatise to 1254–57. Albertus-Magnus-Institut, "Zeittafel."

2. The dating of Albert's writings and timeline of his life are taken from the following: Grabmann, *Mittelalterliches Geistesleben*, 2:287–412; Weisheipl, "Albert the Great"; Weisheipl, "Life and Works"; Resnick, "Albert the Great"; Albertus-Magnus-Institut, "Zeittafel."

3. Albert's commentaries generally take the same title as the corresponding Aristotelian work. See the list of abbreviations in the front matter. As a convention in *Disenchanting Albert the Great*, Albert's works are referred to in the text with their Latin titles, with an English translation offered only at the first reference. The most important works by other authors are referred to the same way. Other titles, whether originally in Latin or a vernacular, appear in the text in English translation and in the notes in the original language.

4. Weisheipl, "Albert the Great," 499.

5. "Aliter autem ab omnibus praemissis sentit doctor meus Dominus Albertus episcopus quondam Ratisbonensis, vir in omni scientia adeo divinus, ut nostri temporis stupor et miraculum congrue vocari possit, et in magicis expertus, ex quibus multum dependet huius materiae scientia. Dicit enim apparitiones angelorum non fieri per assumptionem corporum, sed per species corporum, quas sensibus corporalibus ingerunt modo supra exposito." Ulrich von Strassburg, *De summo bono* 4.3.9.9 (4:142, ll. 178–83).

6. "Fuit enim illis diebus regens et legens apud Coloniam dominus Albertus Ratisponensis episcopus de ordine Predicatorum, magnus in nigromantia, maior in philosophia, sed maximus in theologia." De Beke, "Chronica," 438–39.

7. E.g., this very moral concludes the poem "Es war ein Kung," 208.

8. Aurelius Augustinus, *De civitate dei* 21.6–8, 14; *De doctrina christiana* 2.20.30.

9. Isidore, *Etymologies* 8.9.9. Passages taken from Isidorus Hispalensis, *Etymologiarum sive Originum libri xx*; Isidorus Hispalensis, *Etymologies*.

10. Marrone, "William of Auvergne on Magic"; Marrone, "Magic and Natural Philosophy."

11. Draelants, "Notion of Properties," 179.

12. Burnett, "Two Approaches," 73.

13. Boudet, "'Nigromantia,'" 446–50; Burnett, "Talismans"; Draelants, "Notion of Properties," 176–79; Marrone, "Magic and Natural Philosophy," 288–89.

14. "Maligni spiritus." "Tenth *Titulus*," in Alfonsi, *Dialogue Against the Jews*, 221–28. See Ducay, "La renovación," 137. Ducay also alerts the reader to the connections between what Alfonsi wrote and what Gerbert and Gregory VII were accused of (*supra*).

15. Gundissalinus, *De divisione philosophiae*, 76. Draelants, "Notion of Properties," 176–79; Marrone, "Magic and Natural Philosophy," 287–88; Draelants, "'Magica,'" 498–502.

16. North, "Astronomy and Astrology," 2:456–59, 473–78; Rutkin, "Astrology," 3:541–47, 552–58; Donahue, "Astronomy," 3:562–64, 577–81.

17. Newman, "From Alchemy," 3:499-502; Newman, "Medieval Alchemy," 2:386.
18. Weill-Parot, Les "images astrologiques," 6.
19. See Kieckhefer, Magic in the Middle Ages. See also Davies, Magic; Bailey, Magic and Superstition.
20. E.g., Bailey, "Meanings of Magic"; Bailey, "Age of Magicians."
21. Walsham, "Migrations of the Holy," 253-54.
22. Henry, "Fragmentation of Renaissance Occultism," 8-10.
23. The exchange among four historians of magic—Richard Kieckhefer, Claire Fanger, Bernd-Christian Otto, and David L. d'Avray—in the first section of Page and Rider, *Routledge History of Medieval Magic* (15-67) concisely lays out the contours of the debate and signals the range of values at stake. Analyzing the contours of the debate over magic's definition in the work of three Continental scholars—Alain de Libera, Paolo Lucentino, and Paola Zambelli—Mandosio faulted all of them for their confidence in presupposing a single determining force behind the historical development of medieval and Renaissance magic ("Problèmes et controverses"). Cf. Zambelli, *L'ambigua natura*; Lucentini, "Sulla questione"; de Libera, "La face cachée."
24. Draelants, "Notion of Properties," 174.
25. His terms, "Ausgrenzung" and "Aufwertung." See Otto, *Magie*, 15-27, 617-20. See also Otto, "Historicising 'Western Learned Magic'"; Otto, "Discourse Historical Approach."
26. De Libera, *Métaphysique*, 19, 19n23. De Libera has rejected Albert's practice of magic with his alternative translation for *sumus experti* in this passage "'as we know, who have read everything.'"
27. Bailey, *Fearful Spirits*, 223-51, esp. 223.
28. Kors, *Naturalism and Unbelief*; Kors, *Atheism*; Kors, *Epicureans and Atheists*. See also Burson, "Process, Contingency"; Burson, "Theological Revolution," 15-18; Coleman, "Resacralizing the World"; Coleman, *Virtues of Abandon*; Tricoire, "Triumph of Theocracy," 71-85.
29. Josephson-Storm, *Myth of Disenchantment*, 1-8, 41-62.
30. His guide to libraries is Naudé, *Advis*. His volume on sorcerers is Naudé, *Apologie*.
31. D'Aurillac, *Correspondance*; d'Aurillac, *Opera mathematica*. See Guyotjeannin and Poulle, *Autour de Gerbert d'Aurillac*.
32. William of Malmesbury, *Gesta regum anglorum*, 2:167-69, 172. See Ricklin, "Der Philosoph"; Truitt, "Celestial Divination"; Riché, *Gerbert d'Aurillac*.
33. Sigebert of Gembloux, *Chronica* (995 CE), in Pertz, *Chronica et annales*, 353.
34. For analysis of the interplay of learning and necromancy in the emergence of Gerbert's medieval reputation, see Ricklin, "Der Philosoph"; Truitt, "Celestial Divination," 204-12.
35. E.g., "Veniens autem ad mare per incantationes, dyabolo accersito perpetuum illi pascitur homagium, si se ab illo qui denuo insequebatur defensatum ultra pelagus eveheret." Vincentius Bellovacensis, "De Gerberto papa et primis eius studiis in nigromantia," in *Speculum Historiale* 25.98 (taken from the edition of the Douay version [He] available online: http://atilf.atilf.fr/bichard/).
36. Power has freshly revised and partly upended the historiography of Bacon's practice of magic and place in the history of science; see Power, "Mirror for Every Age." See also Power, *Roger Bacon*; Johnson, "Preaching Precedes Theology." Cf. Molland, "Roger Bacon as Magician"; Williams, "Roger Bacon," 57-73; Thorndike, "Some Medieval Conceptions," 134-38.
37. "Rogerus Bakon, Anglus, Minoritani nominis quoque Oxoniensis doctor, Prestigiator ac Magus necromanticus, non in virtute Dei, sed in operatione malorum spirituum Oxonii ad nasum aeneum, scholasticorum domicilium, mirabilia magna fecisse traditur." Bale, *Illustrium Maioris Britanniae scriptorum*, 114^v-115^r.
38. Power, "Mirror for Every Age," 659-60.
39. Power, "Mirror for Every Age," 662-63.
40. Power, "Mirror for Every Age," 665-66, 671.
41. "La faveur du pape ne réduisit pas ses ennemis à l'inaction: ils s'adressèrent à son général qui condamna sa doctrine, supprima ses ouvrages, et le jetta au fond d'un cachot. On ne sait

s'il y mourut ou s'il en fut tiré: quoi qu'il en soit, il laissa après lui des ouvrages dont on ne devoit connoître tout le prix que dans des tems bien postérieurs au sien. Roger ou frere Bacon cessa d'être persécuté et de vivre en 1294, à l'âge de 78 ans." Diderot and d'Alembert, *Encyclopédie* 3:429–30, 14:775.

42. Apono, *Conciliator controversiarum*.
43. Vescovini, *Pietro d'Abano*.
44. *Differentia* 71: "Utrum forma specifica dicta tota substantia rei sit substantia, necne," de Apono, *Conciliator controversiarum*, 107ʳ–109ʳ. The correspondences to Albert's De mineralibus are drawn out here; see Weill-Parot, "Pietro d'Abano," 5–8. See also Delaurenti, "Pietro d'Abano," 39–52; Vescovini, "Pietro d'Abano."
45. Thorndike, "Relations of the Inquisition," 339.
46. Vescovini, "Pietro d'Abano," 607–15. See also Thorndike, *History of Magic*, 2:938–47.
47. Peter of Abano (Pseudo), "'Annulorum experimenta'"; Boudet, "Magie et illusionnisme," 247–69.
48. "Elucidarius magice," in Agrippa von Nettesheim, *De occulta philosophia* (1992), 583–89.
49. See Véronèse, "Pietro d'Abano."
50. "Sunt et alia plura, superstitiosa volumina huic Petro inscripta, quorum sit auctor quicumque fuerit. Vanus et superstitiosus erat per omnia." Trithemius, "Antipali maleficiorum," 298.
51. Naudé, *Apologie*, 380–91.
52. Diderot and d'Alembert, *Encyclopédie*, 3:429–30, 14:775.
53. Weill-Parot, "Cecco d'Ascoli," 225–29; Beccarisi, "Cecco d'Ascoli," 134–51; del Fuoco, "Il processo."
54. Weill-Parot, "Cecco d'Ascoli," 233–35; Weill-Parot, "I demoni"; Giansante, "La condanna"; del Fuoco, "Il processo."
55. Naudé, *Apologie*, 303, 343.
56. Tiraboschi, *Storia della letteratura italiana*, 5:1159–67.
57. "Nimiam curam apposuit, majorem quam christianum doctorem expediebat, nihil addendo de pietate fidei, ita et in approbatione quorumdam librorum astronomiae." Gerson, "Trilogium astrologiae theologizatae," 107.
58. E.g., Albertus Magnus (Pseudo), *Les admirables secrets*.
59. Davies, *Grimoires*, 57, 98–99.
60. "Cet ouvrage et le suivant ont été faussement attribuez à celui qu'on en fait l'Auteur. Ils ne laissent pas pour cela d'etre d'un grand credit chez les sots." Bordelon, *L'histoire des imaginations extravagantes*, 15.
61. Naudé, *Apologie*.
62. Diderot and d'Alembert, *Encyclopédie*.

CHAPTER 1

1. Baldner, "Albertus Magnus," 327–30.
2. "Est igitur necessario concedendum animam physico motu per se vel per accidens proprie nequaquam moveri. Et sic manifesta est solutio omnium eorum quae inducta sunt ex Platonis opinionibus." Alb., *De anima* 1.2.6 (ed. Colon. VII/1.32.19–23).
3. "Sed id quod omnino destruere totam istam disputationem videtur, est, quod ab antiquo Trismegisto et Socrate postea et nunc a divinis et incantatoribus communiter asseritur, quod scilicet dii incorporei existentes, quos angelos vel daemones vocant, et animae exutae a corporibus moveantur de loco ad locum; cuius veritatem etiam nos ipsis [sic] sumus experti in magicis." Alb., *De anima* 1.2.6 (ed. Colon. VII/1.32.24–31). The Jammy edition prints "ipsi" rather than "ipsis"; the Borgnet and Cologne editions include the terminal s. Several manuscripts I have inspected show no terminal s. Here I treat the s as a mistake, as do, e.g., Anzulewicz, "Magie," 419n411; de Libera, *Métaphysique*, 19n23.

4. Kahlos, "Early Church," 154–59, 162–64, 167.

5. "Magica in philosophiam non recipitur, sed est extrinsecus falsa professione, omnis iniquitatis et malitiae magistra, de vero mentiens, et veraciter laedens nimos." Hugh of Saint Victor, *Didascalicon*, 6.15, p. 132.

6. Albert's works are being digitized. The Aschaffendorff Verlag makes the text, but not the apparatus, of the Cologne edition available online by subscription. The Borgnet edition has been digitized and, as the Alberti Magni E-Corpus, is maintained by Bruno Tremblay at St. Jerome's University in Waterloo, Ontario: albertusmagnus.uwaterloo.ca. A recent effective use of the digitization can be found in the analysis of Albert's references to Hermes Trismegistus in Porreca, "Albertus Magnus."

7. Weill-Parot, *Les "images astrologiques,"* 268–70; Weill-Parot, "Imprinting Powers," 50–51, 62–63; Boudet, *Entre science et nigromancie*, 223–25; Rutkin, "Astrology and Magic"; Rutkin, *Sapientia astrologica*, 283–92.

8. Jeck, *"Materia, forma substantialis"*; Jeck, "Albert der Große"; Jeck, "Virtus Lapidum." See also *De cael.* and *De fato*, e.g., as well as the early and late theological works, *Super Sent.* and *Summa*.

9. Siraisi, "Medical Learning."

10. Especially, Palazzo, "Albert the Great's Doctrine."

11. Sturlese, "Saints et magiciens."

12. E.g., Petzoldt, "Albertus Magnus"; Petzoldt, "Albertus Mag(n)us."

13. "[Albert] nowhere in his commentaries on Aristotle or other works of natural science really stops and discusses magic at any length." Thorndike, *History of Magic*, 2:1555.

14. De Libera, *Métaphysique*, 19.

15. "Sie ist vielmehr ein Wissen um die in der Natur wirkenden Kräfte als das Werkzeug der supralunaren Intelligenz und die Kunst, sich derer zu bedienen." Anzulewicz, "Magie," 428–29.

16. *Magica* (in many grammatical forms) appears in the following philosophical texts: *De nat. loci*, *Mineral.*, *De anima*, *Somn. vig.*, *De mot. anim.*, *De veget.*, *De animal.*, and *De fato*; and in the following theological texts: *Super Sent.*, *Super Luc.*, *Super Ioh.*, and *Summa*.

17. E.g., "Aut secundum quod est in usu, et sic quaedam artes pestiferae sunt sicut illorum qui sapientes sunt, ut faciant mala sicut nigromantici, et quaedam aliae, quarum usus est in nocumentum proximi aut in iniuriam dei." Alb., *Super Ethica* 6.6 (ed. Colon. XIV, 432, 2–6). The Borgnet and Cologne editions do not hold to a strict or consistent distinction in their use of "necromancia" to denote divination with the aid of spirits and "nigromancia," conjuration of demons. Neither do the medieval manuscripts themselves. Albert's stance toward the referent, however, was conceptually consistent insofar as he allowed for a natural necromancy and condemned the conjuration of demons and the rituals required for such. Regarding the lexical complexities, see Boudet, "'Nigromantia'"; Draelants, "'Magica,'" 466–69.

18. "Si enim per invocationes, conjurationes, sacrificia, suffumigationes, et adorationes fiunt, tunc aperte pactum initur cum daemone, et tunc est apostasia oris ibi. Si autem non fit nisi opere simplici, tunc est apostasia operis: quia illud opus exspectatur a daemone: et exspectare aliquid a daemone vel velle aliquid percipere per ipsum, semper est fidei contumelia, et ideo apostasia." Alb., *Super Sent.* 2.7.12 (Borgn. 27:164).

19. See Kieckhefer, "Rethinking How to Define Magic," 17–18.

20. Hellmeier, *Anima et intellectus*, 147; Twetten and Baldner, "Introduction."

21. "De loco ad locum." Alb., *De anima* 1.2.6 (ed. Colon. VII/1.32.29–30).

22. "Sed de his nos disputabimus in scientia de natura deorum." Alb., *De anima* 1.2.6 (ed. Colon. VII/1, 31–33).

23. Albert referred to a book of Hermes as *De natura deorum*, most likely the *Aesclepius*: e.g., Alb., *De cael.* 1.1.2 (ed. Colon V/1, 4, 86–87); *De causis et proc.* 1.4.1 (ed. Colon XVII/2, 43, 58–59); *Summa* 1.18.70.1 (Borgn. 31:727a). See Jeck, "Albert der Große," 125n110.

24. The apparatus of the Cologne edition offers this interpretation. Cicero, *De natura deorum* 1.1.13.33 (LCL 268:34–37). Linking the two possibilities, Cicero remarked on a Mercury

(Hermes), the fifth of five so-named personages who fled into exile in Egypt for killing Argus, gave the Egyptians "leges et litteras," and was named by them Theuth. See *De natura deorum* 3.22.56 (LCL 268:340–41).

25. "Quae philosophiae primae pars quaedam est et ab Aristotele edita est." Alb., *De anima* 1.2.6 (ed. Colon. VII/1, 35–39).

26. "Tales enim substantiae non sunt proportionales spatio, per quod est motus per aliquam quantitatem vel indivisibile quantitatis, quod sit in eis, et ideo neque mensura motus ipsarum neque motus ipse ex principiis physicis causari potest. Hic autem de physicis loquimur tantum, ostendentes physice immobilem esse animam contra eos qui ex principiis, quae ipsi physica esse dicebant, causare voluerunt motum animae et dixerunt animam movere seipsam." Alb., *De anima* 1.2.6 (ed. Colon. VII/1, 32, 39–44).

27. Alb., *Metaph.* (ed. Colon. XVI).

28. "Et sic intelligentiae dicuntur dii participatione apud philosophos sicut etiam angeli et sancti apud theologos." Alb., *Super Eth.* 10.15 (ed. Colon. XIV/2, 766, 43–56).

29. De Boer, *Science of the Soul*, 15–17; Hasse, *Avicenna's "De anima"*; Hasse, "Early Albertus"; Averroës (Ibn Rushd), *Commentarium*.

30. "De obiectionibus sophisticis, ex quibus probari videtur, quod mundi sunt multi." Alb., *De cael.* 1.3.7 (ed. Colon. V/1, 69).

31. On the intelligences in relation to the celestial spheres and their influences on the terrestrial world, e.g., Alb., *Mineral* 2.1.3 (Borgn. 5:27b); *De mot. anim.* 1.1.3 (Borgn. 9:261b–263b).

32. Alb., *De anima* 1.1.1 (ed. Colon. VII/1, 1, 34–2, 17).

33. Grant, "Medieval and Renaissance Scholastic Conceptions," 9–12.

34. On the relationship of astrology and astronomy to mathematics, see Price, "InterpretingAlbert," 410–18, esp. 418. On the significance of "influences" to astrological theory, see Rutkin, "Astrology and Magic," 465.

35. Alb., *Metaph.* 11.1.6–8 (ed. Colon. XI, 465–71).

36. E.g., in the sections "Et est digressio declarans ea quae sunt dicta de period" in *De generatione et corruption* and "De quaestione, utrum caelum movetur ab anima vel a natura vel ab intelligentia" in the metaphysical treatise *De causis et proc.* Alb., *Gen. Corr.* 2.3.5 (ed. Colon. V/2, 206–7) and *De causis et proc.* 1.4.7 (ed. Colon. XVII/2, 52–55). See also Alb., *Phys.* 8.2.4 (ed. Colon. IV/2, 592–96) and *Metaph.* 11.1.3 (ed. Colon. XVI, 462–63); Weisheipl, "Celestial Movers," 156.

37. "Et ideo caeli motus non dicitur naturae motus, sed intelligentiae, quia si esset naturae motus, caelum in loco suo non moveretur, eo quod nullum naturalium corporum movetur in loco suo, sed potius cum est extra ipsum, movetur ad ipsum et quiescit in ipso. Huius autem in libro de caelo et mundo habemus ostendere rationes plures et perspectas." *Phys.* 2.1.2 (ed. Colon. IV, 78, 57–64).

38. Alb., *Mineral.* 2.3.3 (Borgn. 5:51a–52b); *De causis prop.* 1.2.2 (ed. Colon. V/2.64.1–6, 65.18–23); *De causis et proc.* 2.2.22 (ed. Colon. XVII/2.116.66–80).

39. Alb., *Mineral.* 2.1.3 (Borgn. 5:27b) and *Somn. vig.* 3.2.5 (Borgn. 9:202b–203a).

40. The challenge is a straightforward but important one: to translate rather than transliterate a word central to the historical matter at hand yet commonly used and differently understood today. On the general issue of "experience" in medieval natural philosophy, see Bénatouïl and Draelants, *"Expertus sum."*

41. In Alb., *De animal.*, in fact, the verb "sum" only appears (and some 41 times) in conjunction with "expertus."

42. Draelants tracked this notion across Albert's writings with particular attentiveness to medieval differences between *experientia* and *experimenta* ("Expérience et autorité," 89–99). See also Barker, "Experience."

43. See note 26 to chapter 1.

44. "Nos autem experti sumus veritatem esse in arte interpretandi somnia, et quae sit veritas utrum necessaria vel contingens: et si contingens, quam rationem contingentis habeat, inferius determinabimus." Alb., *Somn. vig.* 3.1.8 (Borgn. 9:189a).

45. "Et ideo comprehendit subtilem vaporem elevatum et convertit ipsum in pruinam, et praecipue quando iuvatur frigus aëris in respectu alicuius planetae frigidi sicut Saturni. Experti enim sumus sensibiliter Saturnum habere virtutem magnam in hoc, et haec est causa, quare frequenter fructus in flore destruitur in vere." Alb., *Meteora* 2.1.9 (ed. Colon. VI/1.49.3–9).

46. "Oportet autem scire, quod quatuor modi insitionum sunt possibiles, quos in natura nostrarum plantarum sumus experti optime provenire, et cito mutare plantam a silvestritate et sapore et figura." Alb., *De veget.* 7.1.10 (Meyer, 624).

47. "Ego etiam expertus sum pisces fugere odorem sulfuris et cupri et lini in aqua putrefacti, et si non patet eis locus fugae, moriuntur ex odore eos corrumpente." Alb., *De animal.* 4.2.1 (Stadler, 1:396.3–5).

48. "In naturae enim operibus visu proprio didici." Alb., *Mineral.* 3.2.6 (Borgn. 5:81b).

49. "Tantum enim duritiae habet in rostro, quod nucem amigdali positam in foramine arboris perforat, cum sit durissima, et comedit nucleum: et hoc saepius experti sumus in ponendo nucem amigdali in foramine quod fecit, rediit enim et perforavit eam nobis videntibus." Alb., *De animal.* 8.2.3 (Stadler 1:597).

50. "Similiter autem expertus sum de ferro et aere et stanno et plumbo, sed haec a substantia lapidis non vidi distincta, sed ab expertis in talibus pro certo didici, quod frequenter distincta, a substantia lapidis inveniuntur sicut inveniuntur auri grana inter arenas." Alb., *Mineral.* 3.1.1 (Borgn. 5:60a).

51. "Et non possunt haec ex principiis physicis probari: sed oportet ad hoc scire astronomiam et /55b/magicam et necromanticas scientias, de quibus in aliis considerandum est." Alb., *Mineral.* 2.3.5 (Borgn. 5:55a–b).

52. "Omnibus his diversitatibus executis, ut bene et subtiliter consideremus ea, quae dicta sunt; oportet conjecturas facere et experimenta, ut cognoscamus naturam arborum per se, et quodlibet genus arboris secundum arborum diversitatem. Et huiusmodi coniecturas oportet etiam facere in herbis minutis et etiam in oleribus et in fruticibus et fungorum generibus, licet sit valde difficile et dispendiosum. Valet tamen ad hoc nobis, ut consideremus, quid de his dixerunt antiqui experti, et inspiciamus libros, quos conscripserunt de his, ut bene quidem dicta accipiamus. Per nos enim haec omnia vix vel nunquam bene experiri possemus." Alb., *De veget.* 1.2.12 (Meyer, 100–101).

53. "Earum autem, quas ponemus, quasdam quidem ipsi nos experimento probavimus, quasdam autem referimus ex dictis eorum, quos comperimus non de facili aliqua dicere nisi probata per experimentum. Experimentum enim solum certificat in talibus, eo quod de tam particularibus naturis syllogismus haberi non potest." Alb., *De veget.* 6.1.1 (Meyer, 339–40).

54. "Ut experimentum probetur, ita quod in nullo fallat." Alb., *Ethica* 6.2.25 (Borgn. 7:442b).

55. "Dixit autem Hermes, quod, si plantae, sicut rosae, in terra fimata et humectata sanguine hominis plantentur, et retentus fuerit in eis succus praedicto modo, quod egreditur ad lentum ignem in hieme. Hoc non probatum est a nobis per experimentum." Alb., *De veg.* 4.4.3 (Meyer 285).

56. "Aiunt etiam hunc lapidem capiti mulieris dormientis suppositum, statim eam movere ad amplexum mariti sui si casta est. Si autem est adultera, prae nimio timore phantasmatum dicitur cadere de lecto." Alb., *Mineral.* 2.2.11 (Borgn. 5:41a).

57. Alb., *Mineral.* 1.1.1 (Borgn. 5).

58. Wyckoff, *Albertus Magnus*, 68. See also Riddle and Mulholland, "Albert." Regarding connections to magic and astronomy, see Rutkin, "Astrology and Magic," 492–97.

59. Draelants, "La science."

60. "Est autem principium in ipsa scientia omnia quaecumque fiunt a natura vel arte, moveri a virtutibus coelestibus primo." Alb., *Mineral.* 2.3.3 (Borgn. 5:51a).

61. As laid out, e.g., in Rutkin, "Astrology and Magic"; Price, "Interpreting Albert."

62. "Hinc est quod in scientia geomantiae figurae, punctorum ad imagines tales reduci praecipiuntur: quia aliter non sunt utiles. Hac ergo industria considerata primi praeceptores et professores physici gemmas et imagines metallicas ad imagines astrorum observatis temporibus quando vis coelestis fortissima ad imaginem eamdem esse probatur, ut puta coelestibus

multis virtutibus admixta, sculpi praecipiebant, et mira per tales imagines operabantur." Alb., *Mineral*. 2.3.3 (Borgn. 5:52a).

63. "Bonitatem doctrinae" and "nec sciri potest nisi simul et astronomia et magica et necromantiae scientiae sciantur." Alb., *Mineral*. 2.3.1 (Borgn. 5:48a) For an explanation of Albert's uses of the terms "astronomia" and "astrologia" and why *astronomia* is translated here as "astrology," see Price, "Interpreting Albert," 410–18. For a fuller analysis of Albert on talismans, see Weill-Parot, *Les "Images,"* 6, 268–70; Weill-Parot, "Imprinting Powers," 50–51, 62–63; Rutkin, *Sapientia astrologica*, 282–91.

64. Alb., *Mineral*. 2.3.3 (Borgn. 5:51a).

65. "In coelo autem juxta polum arcticum duae ursae pinguntur, in quarum medio disponitur draco tortuosus: et si hoc in lapide ad sapientiam et ingenium pertinente scriptum invenitur, juvabit astutiam et calliditatem et fortitudinem." Alb., *Mineral*. 2.3.5 (Borgn. 5:54a–54b).

66. Alb., *Mineral*. 2.3.3 (Borgn. 5:51a–b):

> His habitis, pro principio sumimus a dictis Philosophis, quod etiam alibi probandum est, figuras coelorum primas esse figuras, et ante omnium generatorum natura et arte figuras. Quod autem primum est genere et ordine generantium, absque dubio causalitatem suam per modum cuique congruum, omnibus influit sequentibus. Nos enim non intendimus hic de figuris mathematice sumptis, sed de figuris prout inducunt diversitatem generantium et generatorum in ordine et speciebus et natura formae et materiae suae: habebit igitur figura coelestis causalitatem in omni figura generata a natura, eo quod ars resolvitur in principium naturae: quia principium artis prout diximus, natura est secundum quod exivit a suo coelesti principio, cujus principium est intellectus practicus, sicut idem intellectus est principium artis, sicut diximus saepius in Coelo et Mundo et Physicis.

67. "Quod autem primum est genere et ordine generantium, absque dubio causalitatem suam per modum cuique congruum, omnibus influit sequentibus," Alb., *Mineral*. 2.3.3 (Borgn. 5:51b).

68. "Ex his autem de necessitate concluditur, quod si observare ad coelestem figuram imprimatur figura in materia per naturam vel artem, quod coelestis figurae aliqua vis influitur operi naturae et artis: et inde est, quod observare ad imagines coeli praecipiuntur fieri opera et exitus et introitus et incisio vestium et vestitura a Ptolemaeo sapiente." Alb., *Mineral*. 2.3.3 (Borgn. 5:51b–52a).

69. Alb., *Mineral*. 1.1.8 (Borgn. 5:11a), 2.1.3 (27b), 3.1.5 (66a).

70. Anzulewicz, "Magie," 426. "Ars imitator naturam in sua operatione": Aristotle, *Physics* 8.2. See Krause and Anzulewicz, "From Content," 196; Hödl, "'Opus'"; Weisheipl, "Axiom."

71. Zambelli, *"Speculum astronomiae" and Its Enigma*, 135. See Hackett, "Albert." The problem of its ambiguous authorship is addressed in the following chapter.

72. E.g., Aquinas, ST II-II, q. 96 a. 2. Thomas' critique became harsher over time. Weill-Parot, *Les "images astrologiques,"* 281–302; Weill-Parot, "Imprinting Powers," 64; Rutkin, *Sapientia astrologica*, 294–312.

73. "Quod si verum est, mirabile est valde, et absque dubio coelesti virtuti deputandum." Alb., *Mineral*. 2.2.10 (Borgn. 5:40a).

74. "Quas Hermes mirabiles esse dicit in lapidibus et etiam in plantis: per quas etiam naturaliter fieri posset quidquid fit scientis magicis, si virtutes illae bene cognoscerentur." Alb., *Mineral*. 2.2.10 (Borgn. 5:40a).

75. "Jaspis est lapis multorum colorum, et habet species decem: melior tamen est viridis translucens, rubeas habens venas, et in argento proprio locari habet, et in partibus multis invenitur. Expertum enim est quod stringit fluxum sanguinis et menstruorum. Aiunt etiam quod negat conceptum, et juvat partum: et quod gestantem se a luxuria prohibet. In magicis etiam legitur, quod si incantatus est, reddit gratum et potentem et tutum, et fugat febres et hydropisim." Alb., *Mineral*. 2.2.8 (Borgn. 5:39b).

76. "Virtus autem [magnetis] est mirabilis in attractione ferri, ita quod virtutem ejus transmittat in ferrum, ut illud etiam attrahat: et aliquando multae acus hoc modo suspensae ad se invicem videntur. . . . In magicis autem traditur quod phantasias mirabiliter commovet, principaliter seu praecipue si consecratus obsecratione et charactere sit, sicut docetur in magicis. Ferunt etiam hoc cum mulsa acceptum curare hydropisim. Aiunt etiam hunc lapidem capiti mulieris dormientis suppositum, statim eam movere ad amplexum mariti sui si casta est. Si autem est adultera, prae nimio timore phantasmatum dicitur cadere de lecto." Alb., *Mineral.* 2.2.11 (Borgn. 5:40b–41a).

77. "Et valet divinantibus: propter quod a magicis quaeritur." Alb., *Mineral.* 2.2.17 (Borgn. 5:46a).

78. Alb., *De veget.* 6.2.1 (Meyer, 475):

> Sunt autem multi alii effectus lapidum et plantarum, qui experimento sciuntur vel accipiuntur in eisdem, in quibus student magici, et mira per eos operantur. Et hoc intendit Plato, dicens formas separatas per se esse moventes. Non enim voluit dicere separatas, quae nullo modo coniunctae sunt secundum esse; sed potius separatas dixit, quae, licet sint in materia, non tamen movent per hoc, quod sunt in materia, sed per virtutem intellectualium formarum, id est, superiorum, quae per se movent, et non per qualitates aut per mixturas elementorum. Et istae operationes sunt, quae nec compositorum elementorum sunt, nec compositionis ipsius secundum se, sed sunt formarum, secundum quod influxae sunt ab intellectualibus et separatis substantiis. Ad harum igitur trium naturarum indagationem qualitates et compositiones et operationes specierum ponimus plantarum, specialiter inducentes de quibusdam, ut ex his per similem indagationis modum de aliis curiosior expertor inveniat.

79. Wölmer, "Albert," 221–27; Meyer, *Nicolai*, xii–xxviii; Kirk, "Passage," 5.

80. Wölmer, "Albert," 225.

81. "Expertum enim est a nobis, ita crescere ficulneas et cypressos, et alia plurima genera arborum. . . . Quod autem expressissime in haec extrema per diversitatem declinat, est id, quod vocatur arbor trifolii, et arbor, quae vocatur arbor malvae, quae pro certo experti sumus primo esse herbam tenellam, et postea fere per omnia media transeundo efficiuntur magnae arbores ad longitudinem forte duodecim pedum vel plurium." Alb., *De veget.* 1.2.5 (Meyer, 78).

82. "Illum autem modum jam experti sumus, quod, cum inseruntur flagra persici in pruni vel cini trucum sive stipitem, quod mutantur ambarum arborum naturae, et fiunt escula majora et meliora quam sint alia escilla." Alb., *De veget.* 5.1.7 (Meyer, 317). Elsewhere on grafting, see Alb., *De veget.* 7.1.10 (Meyer, 624).

83. "Hoc autem iam experti sumus in vitibus, sub quibus sarmenta et paleae et ovorum testae congestae fumabant ad gemmas et ad flores et fructus: et multae ex his perierunt omnino, quarundam autem gemmae inutiles effectae sunt, et quarundam flores; siquae autem aliquid uvarum protulerunt, omnino postea aruit et exsiccatum est." Alb., *De veget.* 7.1.2 (Meyer, 595).

84. "Nos autem experti sumus, quod melius proveniunt, si mense septembri sicut et triticum serantur, et citius habentur herbae in futura aestate." Alb., *De veget.* 7.2.2 (Meyer, 643).

85. Alb., *De veget.* 1.1 (Meyer, 1–52).

86. "Sed quod oportet adjungere, est, quod etiam quaedam habere videntur effectus divinos, quos hi, qui in magicis student, magis insectantur: sicut betonica divinationem praebere dicitur, et verbena quae amorem, et ea, quae vocatur herba meropis, quae dicitur aperire seras clausas." Alb., *De veget.* 5.2.6 (Meyer, 338).

87. "Dicunt autem, qui magicis student, quod tauri ferocissimi ficulneis alligati citius mansuescunt." Alb., *De veget.* 6.1.19 (Meyer, 389).

88. "Magicis autem studentes dicunt, quod semen eius, in potu haustum, extinguit libidinem et feminas facit infecundas." Alb., *De veget.* 6.1.33 (Meyer, 449).

89. "Qui autem magicis insudant, dicunt, quod radix piri, et praecipue styptici et tarde maturi, portata et ligata super mulierem, impedit conceptum; et si mulier parturiens super se, vel iuxta, pira habuerit, difficulter parit." Alb., *De veget.* 6.1.30 (Meyer, 434).

90. "Est autem frigida et sicca, utilitates multas habet in medicinis et magicis, et praecipue contra fistulam et vulnera et ulcera." Alb., *De veget.* 6.2.2 (Meyer, 482).
91. Alb., *De veget.* 6.1.30 (Meyer, 434).
92. "Est autem omnium eorum, qui in nigromantia student, sententia, quod dii, qui invocantur per characteres et sigilla et sacrificia, faciliores se exhibent et exaudibiliores in oblatione thuris" in the entry on *Boswellia serrata* (Indian olibanum), Alb., *De veget.* 6.1.34 (Meyer, 458).
93. "Hanc multum quaerunt nigromantici sicut et verbenam, dicentes, eam habere signa divinationis, quando decerpitur adiurata carmine Aesculapii." Alb., *De veget.* 6.2.3 (Meyer, 484).
94. "Qui autem student incantationi et physicis ligaturis, dicunt, quod ebenus nigra cunis alligatur, ut infantem phantasmata non terreant." Alb., *De veget.* 6.1.18 (Meyer, 384).
95. "Lignum autem eius quae-/406/-runt incantatores, ut faciant ex eo baculos pugilum, et dicunt ad hoc specialiter valere." Alb., *De veget.* 6.1.26 (Meyer, 405).
96. "Ferunt autem incantatores quod mulier, succum foliorum ejus bibens post fluxum suorum menstruorum, non concipiat, sed sterilis efficiatur." Alb., *De veget.* 6.1.30 (Meyer, 431).
97. Alb., *De animal.* 2.1.8 (Stadler, 259). See also Copenhaver, "Tale of Two Fishes," 382–83.
98. "De multis certificat melius aliis avibus." Alb., *De animal.* 8.2.4 (Stadler, 605). The *fraudius avis* is identified as the nuthatch (sitelle) in the 1803 *Nouveau dictionnaire*, 9:73.
99. "Et postquam in eis resederit huiusmodi spiritus, exit ex eis quiddam simile ei, quod exit aliquando cum embrionibus, quod vocatur hychomindez, quod interpretatur animal ingenii in nigromancia a Graecis, a Latinis autem medicis et nigromanticis vocatur harpa, et est frustum sicut bufo formatam et assimilatur stercori in substantia: et nigromantici quaerunt ipsum prae omnibus ad compellendum animos feminarum." Alb., *De animal.* 6.3.1 (Stadler, 483–84).
100. Leviticus 11:19; and Deuteronomy 14:18.
101. Sura 27, 20–24.
102. E.g., Aristophanes, *Birds* 13–19 (LCL 179:14–15); and Ovid, *Metamorphoses* 4.619–74 (LCL 42:332–35).
103. Alb., *De animal.* 2.1.6 (Stadler, 255).
104. Alb., *De animal.* 23.24 (Stadler, 1513).
105. Alb., *De animal.* 8.2.4 (Stadler, 604).
106. "Quae tota est avis praestigiosa et multa augurans, ut dicunt magi et augures." Alb., *Mineral.* 2.2.15 (Borgn. 5:44a).
107. "Upupam etiam et upupae membra et praecipue cerebrum et linguam et cor, multum quaerunt incantatores. Sed nos hic de hoc non intendimus: est enim alterius scientiae hoc proprium investigare." Alb., *De animal.* 23.24 (Stadler, 1513).
108. Degen, "Concepts," 373–81.
109. Delaurenti, "Pratiques," 353–59, 366–68; Delaurenti, "La fascination," 146–50.
110. Delaurenti, "La fascination," 139–46.
111. Alb., *Mineral.* 2.1.1 (Borgn. 5:24a).
112. Delaurenti, "Pratiques," 353–59, 371–72.
113. *De mot. anim.*, *De anima*.
114. Palazzo, "Scientific Significance"; Palazzo, "Albert the Great's Doctrine."
115. Palazzo, "Albert the Great's Doctrine."
116. "Sed necromantia est ars pestifera quoad suas operationes, et magis utitur experimentis, quam ratione, et vi daemonis utitur pro antidoto: et ideo Ecclesia condemnavit hanc omnino." Alb., *Super Sent.* 4.34.9 (Borgn. 30:337b).
117. "An maleficium sit excludendum per maleficium?" Alb., *Super Sent.* 4.34.9 (Borgn. 30:337b).
118. Aquinas, *De sortibus* III, STh II/2, q 95, a 3–8. STh II/2 quaestio 96, art. 2.
119. Jeck, "Platons Götter," 177–88.
120. Five commentaries on Pseudo-Dionysius's works are edited in volumes 36 and 37 of the ed. Colon.

121. De Libera, "Albert," 347n341. Reflecting the influence of the *Liber de causis* on Albert, see Alb., *De causis et proc.* (ed. Colon. XVII/2).

122. Lucentini, "L'ermetismo," 429-40.

123. Sturlese and Porreca disagree on how coherent Albert understood the authorship of the hermetic writings to have been; see Porreca, "Albertus Magnus"; Sturlese, "Saints et magiciens."

124. Sturlese, "Saints et magiciens," 618-20; Porreca, "Albertus Magnus"

125. See Collins, "Scholastics."

126. Alb., *Super Mt.* 2 (ed. Colon. XXI/1, 46, 19-20).

127. "Et nota, quod vocat illos magos, quia magi dicuntur sapientes et maxime in astrologia, quia illa scientia est de maximis rebus." Alb., *Super Dion. Epist.*, ep. 7 (ed. Colon. XXXVII/2, 512, 23-25). Albert's commentaries on the Pseudo-Dionysian corpus were completed by 1250.

128. "Magus enim et mathematicus et incantator et maleficus sive nigromanticus et ariolus et haruspex et divinator differunt." Alb., *Super Mt.* 2 (ed. Colon. XXI/1, 46, 21-23).

129. "Scientia de separatis et abstractis." Alb., *Super Mt.* c. 2 (ed. Colon. XXI/1, 46, 28-29).

130. On *mathematici*, *astronomi*, and *astrologi* according to Albert, see Price, "Interpreting Albert," 410-18, esp. 418.

131. "Aliter quam dictum est, trufator est et trutannus et abiciendus," 46.46-47.

132. Hugh of Saint Victor, "De magica et partibus eius." *Didascalicon* 6.15 (*Opera omnia* 810c-812b). Thorndike, "Some Medieval Conceptions," 111.

133. Isidore, *Etymologies* 8.9.9.

134. Isidore, *Etymologies* 8.9.25-28.

135. Daniel 1:4, 17.

136. "Arioli, et magi, et malefici, et Chaldaei." Daniel 2:2.

137. Alb., *Super Dan.* 2.2 (Borgn. 18:469a).

138. E.g., Alb., *Super Isa.* 7:6, 8:19, 44:25, 46:1 (ed. Colon. XIX, 104, 132, 455, 468).

139. "Quasi magistri, qui de universis philosophantur, magi tamen specialiter astronomi dicuntur, qui in astris futura rimantur." Alb., *Super Dan.* 1.20 (Borgn. 18:465b).

140. Calvet, *L'alchimie*, 86-88; Kibre, "Albertus Magnus on Alchemy"; Calvet, "Essai," 191.

141. Kibre, "Albertus Magnus on Alchemy," 187. E.g., Alb., *Mineral.* 1.1.5 (Borgn. 5:7a) 3.1.1 (59a), 3.1.9 (70b).

142. Alb., *Super Sent.* 2.7.8 (Borgn. 27:154b); *Super Ethica* 1.3 (ed. Colon. XIV, 15, 64-70).

143. "'Quod videlicet sciant artifices alchimiae species permutari non posse, sed similia his facere possunt, ut tingere rubeum citrino, ut aurum videatur: et album tingere, donec sit multum simile argento vel auro vel cui voluerint corpori. Caeterum autem quod differentia specifica aliquo tollatur ingenio, non credo possibile: sed exspoliatio accidentium non est impossibilis, vel saltem diminutio eorum.'" Compare Alb., *Mineral* 3.1.9 (Borgn. 5:70b-71a) with Avicenna (Ibn Sina), *De congelatione*, 54. See also Wyckoff, *Albertus Magnus*, 177, 279-85; Ps.-Avicenna, "Declaratio Lapidis Physici Avicennae filio suo Aboali" (*De conglutinatione lapidum*), in Manget, *Bibliotheca chemica curiosa*, 633-38.

144. On transmutation in Albert's writing, see Rinotas, "*Sciant artifices*"; Rinotas, "Alchemy and Creation."

145. "De transmutatione autem horum corporum et mutatione unius in aliud non est physici determinare, sed artis quae vocatur alchimia." Alb., *Mineral.* 3.1.1 (Borgn. 5:60a).

146. Alb., *Mineral.* 2.1.2 (Borgn. 5:26b).

147. Newman, "Brian Vickers," 485-97; Calvet, *L'alchimie*.

148. Kibre, "Albertus Magnus on Alchemy," 196-202; Calvet, *L'alchimie*, esp. 209-39.

CHAPTER 2

1. "Vir in omni scientia adeo divinus, ut nostri temporis stupor et miraculum congrue vocari possit, et in magicis expertus." Ulrich von Strassburg, *De summo bono* 4.3.9.9 (4:142, ll. 178-83).

2. "Et in magicis expertus, ex quibus multum dependet huius materiae scientia." Ulrich von Strassburg, *De summo bono* 4.3.9.9 (4:142, ll. 178–83).
3. See Palazzo, "Ulrich of Strasbourg's Philosophical Theology," 211–18.
4. Regarding Albert on the possibility of copulation and conception between humans and demons, see Alb., *Super Sent.* 2.8.5 (Borgn. 27:174), *Super Sent.* 3.37.10 (Borgn. 28:703), *Summa* 1.18.75.4 (Borgn. 31:790a–791a), and *De animal.* 17.1.5 (Stadler, 1165).
5. Albert Fries in Fries and Illing, "Albertus Magnus," 133.
6. For a recent exchange on this matter, see Hendrix, "How Albert the Great's "Speculum astronomiae'"; Hendrix, "Albert the Great." See also Burnett, review of *How Albert the Great's "Speculum astronomiae.'"*
7. Vitas fratrum ordinis praedicatorum c. XIII, § IX; c. XXIII, §7, in Gerardus de Fracheto, *Vitae fratrum ordinis praedicatorum necnon cronica ordinis ab anno mcciii usque ad mccliv*, 1, 187–88, 216–17. Cf. Paravicini Bagliani, "La légende médiévale," 298n299, 299.
8. Thomas of Cantimpré, *Bonum universale* 2.57 (563, ll. 576–77).
9. Thomas of Cantimpré, *Bonum universale* 2.1 (563, ll. 119–20).
10. "Aliter autem ab omnibus praemissis sentit doctor meus Dominus Albertus episcopus quondam Ratisbonensis, vir in omni scientia adeo divinus, ut nostri temporis stupor et miraculum congrue vocari possit, et in magicis expertus, ex quibus multum dependet huius materiae scientia. Dicit enim apparitiones angelorum non fieri per assumptionem corporum, sed per species corporum, quas sensibus corporalibus ingerunt modo supra exposito." Ulrich von Strassburg, *De summo bono*, 4.3.9.9 (4:142, ll. 178–83).
11. See the *Chronica maiora* by Matthew of Paris (1200–1259).
12. Palazzo, "Ulrich of Strasbourg's Philosophical Theology."
13. Salimbene of Parma, *Cronica*, 805, 806–8.
14. Thorndike, *History of Magic*, 3:45–47; Succurro, "*Liber Compostelle*"; Bagliani, "La légende médiévale," 302, 308–9. Hackett, "Albert the Great," 441–44; Paravicini Bagliani, *Le "Speculum Astronomiae*," 6.
15. "Ego quidem frater Bonaventura de Yseo ordinis minorum fuit amicus domesticus et familiaris fratris Alberti Theotonici de ordine predicatorum. Multa contulimus de scientiis et de experimentis secretis secretorum ut nigromanciae alchimiae et cetera." Florence, Bibliotheca Riccardiana, MS 119, fol. 143^v.
16. "Nam frater Albertus in diebus vitae suae habuit gratiam a domino papa propter eius famam sanctitatis intellectus prudentiae quod licite possit adiscere et examinare et scire et probare omnes artes scientiarum boni et mali laudando libros veritatis et damnando omnes libros falsitatis et erroris. Unde multum laboravit in complendo inceptos libros Aristotelis et novas compilationes librorum fecit de multis artibus scientiarum ut astrologiae geomanciae nigromantiae, lapidum preciosorum et experimentorum alchimiae." Munich, BSB, clm 23809, fol. 3^v. On Albert's acquisition of an attractive knife by the dark arts in clm 16126, see Scheeben, *Albertus Magnus* (1955), 204.
17. "Albertus et ipse ordinis Praedicatorum, Coloniensis domus eiusdem ordinis lector, vir undecumque doctissimus, multa et scripsisse fertur et scribere, sed primam partem Postillatum eius in Lucam, tamen fateor me vidisse. Et ut salva pace eius dictum sit, sicut a quibusdam dicitur, dum subtilitatem secularis Philosophie nimis sequitur, splendorem aliquantulum Theologicae puritatis obnubilat." Henry of Ghent (Pseudo), "De viris illustribus," 417–18. See also Henry of Ghent (Pseudo), "De scriptoribus ecclesiasticis," 2:125.
18. Grant, "Medieval Natural Philosophy"; Hackett, "*Ego expertus sum*"; Williams, "Roger Bacon in Context"; Power, *Roger Bacon*; Ingham, "Conjuring Roger Bacon"; Molland, "Roger Bacon as Magician."
19. "Et vere laudo eum plus quam omnes de vulgo studentium, quia homo studiosissimus est, et vidit infinita, et habuit expensum; et ideo multa potuit colligere utilia in pelago auctorum infinito." *Opus minus*, in Brewer, *Fr. Rogeri Bacon opera*, 327.
20. "Ille, qui fecit se auctorem" and "ille qui composuit tot et tam magna volumina de naturalibus." Hackett, "Attitude of Roger Bacon." Cf. Rutkin, "Astrology and Magic," 472n469.
21. Bacon, *Compendium* §72, pp. 69–72.

162   NOTES TO PAGES 51–55

22. Bacon, *Compendium* §73, pp. 70–71.
23. Hackett, "Attitude of Roger Bacon," 71.
24. Von Loë, "De vita et scriptis" (1900); von Loë, "De vita et scriptis" (1901); Paravicini Bagliani, "La légende médiévale."
25. Ptolomaeus Lucensis, *Historia* l. 22, c. 18 (561, ll. 563–14).
26. Guillelmus de Tocco, *Ystoria sancti Thome de Aquino*, 115–20.
27. Henricus de Hervordia, *Liber de rebus* c. 94 (195–96).
28. "Als er si vormalen dick het betwungen, ze ervaren haimlich sache, der christenhait zu guot." *Sächsische Weltchronik*, 2:326, 314–31; Menzel, *Die Sächsische Weltchronik*.
29. "Fuit enim illis diebus regens et legens apud Coloniam dominus Albertus Ratisponensis episcopus de ordine Predicatorum, magnus in nigromantia, maior in philosophia, sed maximus in theologia." De Beke, "Chronica," 438–39.
30. Papi, "Corsini, Matteo"; Polidori, *Rosaio della vita*, 14–16.
31. Wisdom 7:29 (English of the Douay-Rheims translation).
32. Ancient Greek astronomers—Hipparchus and Ptolemy, e.g.—estimated the precession of equinoxes to a period of thirty-six thousand years. Today the cycle is estimated at twenty-six thousand years.
33. Bowe, "Alexander's *Metaphysics* Commentary," 7–25.
34. Arnold, "Eschatological Imagination"; Landes, "Fear of an Apocalyptic Year 1000," 250, 259; Truitt, *Medieval Robots*, 69–88. See also Johnston, "Animating Statues."
35. William of Malmesbury, *Gesta regum anglorum*, §§167–72, pp. 279–95.
36. McEvoy, *Robert Grosseteste*, 19–30, 62–66, 76–95.
37. Gower, *Confessio Amantis*, xi–xii.
38. Gower, "Confessio Amantis," 4.234–43, p. 307.
39. Truitt, *Medieval Robots*, 89–91.
40. Bardney, "Vita Roberti Grosthed," 333.
41. Truitt, *Medieval Robots*, 69–70.
42. *Famous Historie of Fryer Bacon*.
43. The following works recount a number of stories about Albertus as a practitioner of the magical arts with little or no critical examination of their origins: Thoemes, *Albertus Magnus*, 151–70; Scheeben, *Albertus Magnus* (1932), 200–230; Petzoldt, "Albertus Magnus," 255–61. Somewhat more critical, Eckert, "Albert-Legenden." For consideration of the tales' folkloric origins, see Gottschall, "Albert's Contributions," 726–28.
44. "Es war ein Kung in Frankereich," in *Marners Golden Ton*, Heidelberg, cpg 392, 14^r–17^r. Also edited in Görres, *Altteutsche Volks- und Meisterlieder*, 195–208.
45. "Er kund gar wohl die schwarze Kunst, Zu ihr gewann er groß Lieb und Gunst." "Es war ein Kung," 196.
46. "Wann er dich führt zum Laden ein, So streich du dan die Hände dein Auch außen an die weiße Wand; So sieht mans dann am Morgen." "Es war ein Kung," 202.
47. "Ein Kneul Fadens hätt er bei ihm, Es mocht ihm helfen wohl darvon, Des freut er sich mit Schalle." "Es war ein Kung," 205.
48. "Er sprach: mein Jugend mich verführt, Das muß ich immer klagen." To that the king responded, "sei dir erlaubt, Wann man dir schlaget ab das Haubt; Was du darnach an mich begehrst, Mag ich die nit versagen." "Es war ein Kung," 206.
49. "Albertus war zu Regensburg; Sein Sach hat er verkehret. Er war ein Bischof, also rein, Sein Glaub erschein Da also weit, den rechten Grund er lehrte. Er nahm auch zu in der Geschrift, Ihn gewürdigt hat Gott großer Macht, Den edlen Bischof klare." "Es war ein Kung," 207.
50. "Wie er die Jungfrau hat gestehlt, Doch mag er seyn wohl auserwählt; Sein Sünd hat er wahrlich bereut, Dernach er sein Leib zwange. Mit Fasten, Wachen und Gebeth, So dient er Gott früh und spät, Er führt ein strenges Leben. Sein Sünd er wahrlich reuen thät. Er was so stet, Darum mag er wohl han das ewig Leben. Gott will, daß wir auch unsre Sünd Büßen, eh uns die Erd verschlündt, Daß wir an unserm letzten End Von Gott werden empfangen." "Es war ein Kung," 208.

51. Thomas of Cantimpré, *Bonum universale* 2.57 (550).
52. Martin Schleich, "Ein hübsch lied von einer kuenigin von Franckreich." See also Zapf, "Schleich, Martin."
53. Grund, "'Ffor to Make Azure,'" 26.
54. Grund, "'Ffor to Make Azure,'" 39.
55. Le Franc, *Le champion des dames*, 4:113–46, ll. 17377–8200. See Octavien de Guasco, *Dissertations historiques*, 68.
56. Le Franc, *Le champion des dames*, 4:129–30, ll. 17769–84. See also Le Franc, "Le champion des dames."
57. See Williams, "Roger Bacon and His Edition," 57–73; Gilbert, "Notes"; Eamon, *Science and the Secrets of Nature*, 45–53, 134.
58. Sannino, *Il "De mirabilibus mundi."*
59. Draelants and Sannino, "Albertinisme et hermétisme," 223–34, 250–51; Van der Lugt, "'Abominable Mixtures,'" 229.
60. Eamon, "Books of Secrets"; Davies, *Grimoires*, 38; Eamon, *Science and the Secrets of Nature*.
61. Thorndike, "Further Consideration," 419n411.
62. Draelants, "Commentaire," 32–103.
63. Ferckel, "Zur Bibliographie"; Kusche, "Zur *Secreta Mulierum*." Here the edition published in Amsterdam in 1740 is used: Albertus Magnus (Pseudo), "De secretis." For the critical edition, see Barragán Nieto, *El "De secretis mulierum."* See Thorndike, "Further Consideration," 427–43; Lemay, *Women's Secrets*, 1–47; Green, *Making Women's Medicine Masculine*, 209–11.
64. Albertus Magnus (Pseudo), "De secretis," 95–99.
65. Albertus Magnus (Pseudo), "De secretis," 47–60.
66. Thorndike, "Further Consideration," 427; Lemay, *Women's Secrets*.
67. Davies, *Grimoires*, 57; Crowther-Heyck, "Wonderful Secrets," 256–59.
68. Newman, "Medieval Alchemy." See also Newman, "What Have We Learned?"
69. "Quod si permiscueris aquam solam, fiet Luna: si coniunxeris ignem, rubefaciet, Domino concedente." Albertus Magnus (Pseudo), "Libellus de Alchimia," in Jammy, *Beati Alberti opera*, 21:g-17.
70. Halleux, "Albert le Grand et l'alchimie," 78; Calvet, "L'Alchimie," 129–33; Kibre, "Alchemical Writings," 500–502, 511–15.
71. Jammy, *Beati Alberti opera*, vol. 21; Borgn., vol. 37; Calvet, "L'Alchimie," 129–33. For the modern English translation, see Albertus Magnus (Pseudo), *Libellus de alchimia*.
72. Albertus Magnus (Pseudo), *"Alkimia minor."* See Kibre, *"Alkimia minor,"* 267–76; Calvet, "L'Alchimie," 133–36.
73. Albertus Magnus (Pseudo), *"De occultis naturae."* See Kibre, *"De occultis naturae"*; Kibre, "Albertus Magnus, *De occultis naturae*," 157–59; Calvet, "L'Alchimie," 136–41.
74. Albertus Magnus (Pseudo), *"Calistenus."* See Kibre, "Alchemical Tract," 303–9; Calvet, "L'Alchimie," 142–46.
75. Calvet, "L'Alchimie," 146–49; Kibre, "Alchemical Writings," 506.
76. Calvet, "L'Alchimie," 149–51; Kibre, "Alchemical Writings," 510.
77. Calvet, "L'Alchimie," 151–53; Kibre, "Alchemical Writings," 511.
78. The *Speculum*'s authorship will be given as Magister Speculi in the text. The latest critical edition is Albertus Magnus (Pseudo), *"Speculum astronomiae"* (1992). Assessment of the authorship problem can be found in Hackett, "Albert the Great"; Paravicini Bagliani, *Le "Speculum Astronomiae,"* 6; Paravicini Bagliani, "Albertus Magnus," 401–11. Cf. Hendrix, "Albert the Great"; Weill-Parot, *Les "images astrologiques,"* 6, 27–62, 279–80.
79. Paravicini Bagliani, *Le "Speculum Astronomiae,"* 6, 33.
80. "Tum, si mihi forte obicias *librum de licitis et illicitis* [Speculum astronomiae], in quo reicit quidem magos, astronomicos autem probat auctores, respondebo existimari quidem a multis esse illud opus Alberti, sed nec ipsum Albertum, nec libri inscriptionem usquequaque hoc significare, cum auctor ipse, quicumque demum fuerit, nomen suum consulto et ex professo

dissimulet.... Quae utique, aut non scripsit Albertus aut, si scripsit, dicendum est cum Apostolo: 'In iis laudo; in hoc non laudo,'" Pico della Mirandola, *Disputationes*, 1:94,98–11. See also Akopyan, "'Princeps aliorum,'" 100–104.

81. E.g., Pico's Dalmatian contemporary Federicus Chrysogonus (1472–1538) did this in his *Speculum astronomicum*; see Girardi-Karsulin, "Grisogonovo *Astronomsko zrcalo*," 29, 31–32, 35–36.

82. Jammy, *Beati Alberti opera*, vol. 5.

83. Hackett, "Albert the Great."

84. Geyer, "Das *Speculum astronomiae*," 95–101.

85. Magister Speculi is the proposal of Nicolas Weill-Parot. Charles Burnett has recently agreed with Scott E. Hendrix, who is "convinced about Albertus's authorship," that the scholarship would do well to "move on" from the latest debates over attribution (review of *How Albert the Great's "Speculum astronomiae,"* 221).

86. E.g., Albertus Magnus (Pseudo), *"Speculum astronomiae"* (1992), c. 2, pp. 212–19.

87. "Magis quod debeant reservari quam destrui." Albertus Magnus (Pseudo), *"Speculum astronomiae"* (1992), c. 17 (270).

88. Albertus Magnus (Pseudo), *"Speculum astronomiae"* (1992), c. 17 (270–73).

89. Weill-Parot, "Astral Magic."

90. "Unde Albertus magnus per utilem etiam tractatum edidit in quo vere astronomie et artis magice libros per eorum principia et fines distinxit ut astronomicam veritatem et magicam vanitatem ab invicem sequestraret." Petrus de Alliaco, *Concordantia*, a3^r.

91. "Libros astrologiae multum expedit discernere, quatenus appareat qui sunt et qui non sunt tolerandi. Composuit super hac re magnus Albertus opusculum quod appellatur Speculum Alberti, narrans quomodo temporibus suis voluerunt aliqui destruere libros Albumasar et quosdam alios. Videtur autem, salvo tanti doctoris honore, quod sicut in expondendis libris philosophicis, praesertim Peripateticorum, nimiam curam apposuit, majorem quam christianum doctorem expediebat, nihil addendo de pietate fidei, ita et in approbatione quorumdam librorum astronomiae, praesertim de imaginibus, de nativitatibus, de sculpturis lapidum, de caracteribus, de interrogationibus nimis ad partem superstitionum ratione carentium declinavit." Gerson, "Trilogium astrologiae theologizatae," 106–7. See Kaluza, "Gerson critique d'Albert le Grand," 174–75.

92. Ficino, *Liber de vita* 3.12.121–24, 3.18.127–42, 3.25.5–16, in Ficino, "Three Books," 304, 340, 380.

93. See Copenhaver, *Magic in Western Culture*, 531, 534–35, 539, 544–45, 554.

94. Quinlan-McGrath, *Influences*, 91.

95. Ficino, *Liber de vita* 3.20.21–35 in Ficino, "Three Books," 350.

96. Agrippa von Nettesheim, *De occulta philosophia* (1992), 505–7.

97. "Nam quod Alberto magno profundissimo rerum naturalium scrutatori contigit, ut propter miranda quae occulta virtute naturae operatus est, magus a vulgo sit habitus, mihi sum certus similiter contingere posse." Trithemius, *Polygraphiae libri sex*, 46–47. Arnold reported another such reference in a letter dated 10 May 1503 to Count John von Westerburg, reprinted in *De septem secundeis* (Strasbourg, 1610), 43–44; see Arnold, *Johannes Trithemius*, 23, 184, 197, 199. See also Baron, "Trithemius und Faustus." It also bears noting that front matter to Agrippa's *De occulta philosophia* included an exchange of letters with Trithemius (68–73).

98. Weyer, *De praestigiis daemonum* 2.6.

99. The subtitle to the printed edition explains it: *ars per occultam scripturam animi sui voluntatem absentibus aperiendi certa*. Trithemius, *Steganographia* (1606).

100. Gohory wrote under the pseudonym Leo Suavius. Suavius, *Theophrasti Paracelsi*, 250–51.

101. E.g., "Hanc naturalem Magiam non erubescit vir catholicus et sanctissimus Albertus Magnus dicere se fuisse secutum, et experientiis in ea multa comperiisse et quid oportet plura dicere. Dicant mihi isti Magistri, utrum hoc quod ego voco magiam naturalem, sit res prohibita, aut aliquid continens, quod sit contra fidem, hoc dicere non possunt, etiam volentes." And

"similiter cum legunt Albertum in experimento Magiae multum temporis consumpsisse, de magia naturali hoc intelligant, non de prohibita, ne exemplo tanti viri, illi se dedant, quod illi licuit sibi quoque licere praesumentes." Pico della Mirandola, "Apologia," 1:168–72.
102. Pomponazzi, *De incantationibus*.
103. Verardi, "La voie secrète," 618; Martin, *Subverting Aristotle*, 186.

CHAPTER 3

1. Meersseman, *Laurentii Pignon*, 57–59.
2. Luis de Valladolid, "Tabula Alberti Magni." See Scheeben, "Les écrits d'Albert le Grand"; Geyer, "Der alte Katalog"; Paravicini Bagliani, "La légende médiévale," 327–30.
3. Luis de Valladolid, "Historia de vita et doctrina."
4. Geyer, "Der alte Katalog," 399.
5. "Fecit librum, ubi improbavit scientias magicas nigromanticorum scilicet nigromantiam, geomantiam, ydromantiam, aerimantiam, pyromantiam, aruspiciam, horoscopicam, augurium, maleficia, sortilegia, praestigia." Luis de Valladolid, "Tabula Alberti Magni," 249, item 275.
6. Korner, *Chronica Novella*, 180–81.
7. Werner Rolevinck, *Tractatus de excellentiis domini Alberti Magni*, Berlin, Staatsbibliothek, Stiftung Preußischer Kulturbesitz, MS theol. lat. oct. 171, fols. 12^r–19^r, hereafter abbreviated EDA. This manuscript, the sole extant, is likely an autograph, dating to the late 1460s or early 1470s. See Holzapfel, *Werner Rolevincks Bauernspiegel*, 25; Marks, *Medieval Manuscript Library*, 1: 197; Stehkämper and Zender, *Albertus Magnus*, 33–34; Wolffgram, "Neue Forschungen," 151. See also Keil, "Rolevinck, Werner."
8. The authorship and dating of the Dominican works are clarified in Collins, "Albertus, *Magnus* or *Magus*?"
9. I draw from, revise, and expand on analysis of the Dominican hagiographical writings and the associations between them and both the diabolization of magic and the canonization effort that I first published as Collins, "Albertus, *Magnus* or *Magus*?"
10. Classen, "Werner Rolevinck's *Fasciculus Temporum*"; Gow, "(En)gendering Evil," 209–30; Mertens, "Landeschronistik"; Widder, "Westfalen und die Welt"; Graus, "Funktionen der spätmittelalterlichen Geschichtsschreibung," 46.
11. Buchholz, *Die Bibliothek*.
12. "Kaltyser, Peter," 19:490.
13. EDA, 13^r–13^v.
14. EDA, 14^r–15^v.
15. EDA, 16^r–17^v.
16. EDA, 18^r–19^v.
17. EDA, 19^r.
18. EDA, 15^r–v.
19. EDA, 19^v.
20. EDA, 19^r.
21. "Dicunt eum nonulli fuisse magicis artibus occupatum. alii eciam supersticiosa exercuisse. alii imaginibus astrologicis plus dedisse quam decuit doctorem canonicum. alii erilibus lacertis tunicas femineas inseruisse ad explicandum secreta mulierum. alii supra modum ipsum fuisse curiosum ad indaganda occulta omnis creature. ac vere alterum Salomonem disputasse de stellis de elementis de lapidibus et cetera usque ad ysopum qui exit de pariete. nec quidquam intactum ipsum reliquisse." EDA, 16^r.
22. "Vlricus eius discipulus hoc sentire videtur. libro xo tractatu. 3°. ca°. ix°. vbi sic dicit. Doctor meus dominus albertus episcopus quondam ratisponensis vir in dei scientia adeo divinus. ut nostri temporis stupor et miraculum congrue vocari possit. et in magicis expertus igitur non apparet quod fuit nigromanticus. Responsio. Ista obiectio seipsam soluit. quia si talis fuisset.

non eum taliter commendasset. videlicet supra omnes qui in diebus suis fuerunt. Nullo modo autem expertus fuerat in magicis. ibi eciam negat. quia libros illorum vidit." EDA, 16ᵛ.

23. "Ut autem ista magna clarescunt. Advertenda sunt verba ipsius quae ponit in libro qui dicitur 'Speculum alberti.' Ait enim, 'Multos libros nigromanticos inspexi. Sed quoniam eos abhorrui. Non extat nisi mihi perfecta memoria. Spiritus enim meus numquam requiescebat in eis. Tamen volui transeundo vidisse ut saltem non ignorarem qualiter esset miseris eorum sectatoribus irridendum et haberem de suo unde repellerem excusationes eorum.'" EDA, 17ʳ.

24. EDA, 18ʳ-18ᵛ.

25. "Cessent ergo vaniloquia. cessent obloquia. et iuxta apostolicam exhortationem non simus pueri sensibus sed innocentia. studeamusque illorum imitari vitam. quorum efferimus doctrinam. queramus in spiritu humilitatis et mansuetudinis per studia laboriosa exercitationem sudosam. aliquando peruenire mereamur ad conteplationem gloriosam et requiem *amamosam* (?)." EDA, 19ᵛ.

26. The principal studies of biographical materials pertaining to Albert are von Loë, "De vita et scriptis" (1900); von Loë, "De vita et scriptis" (1901); von Loë, "De vita et scriptis" (1902); Pelster, *Kritische Studien*, 16-27; Scheeben, *Albert der Große*, 27; Scheeben, "Zur Chronologie"; Paravicini Bagliani, "La légende médiévale."

27. Sommerlechner, *Stupor mundi?*, esp. 11.

28. Such as Gerhardus de Fracheto's *Vitas fratrum OP* and the *Rithmicum dictamen de Alberto episcopo*, both composed in 1260, and Bernhard of Gui's chronicle of the Order of Preachers. Also, biographical information from Thomas Cantimpré's *Bonum universale apum*, Tholomeus de Lucca's *Historia ecclesiae nova*, and Johannes de Colonna's *Liber de viris illustribus*. In 1380 Hermann von Minden incorporated Heinrich von Herford's work into his *Catalogus Episcoporum Mindensium*.

29. E.g., von Loë, "De vita et scriptis" (1900); von Loë, "De vita et scriptis" (1901); von Loë, "De vita et scriptis" (1902); de Gaiffier, "Bulletin"; Pelster, *Kritische Studien*; Scheeben, *Albert der Große*, 27; Schieffer, *Albertus Magnus*; Stehkämper and Zender, *Albertus Magnus*.

30. Ptolomaeus Lucensis, "Historia ecclesiastica nova," 1150, 1151, 1184.

31. Johannes de Columna, *De vita et moribus virorum illustrium, tam sanctorum quam aliorum philosophorum*. See Remigio Sabbadini, "Giovanni Colonna," 282-305.

32. Wolfenbüttel, Herzog August Bibliothek, Cod. Guelf. 11b Helmst, 145ᵛ-146. See also Henricus de Hervordia, *Liber de rebus*, 201-2.

33. *Legenda venerabilis domini Alberti Magn* is hereafter abbreviated LVA. The prologue begins, "Gloriosus Deus in sanctis suis cuius magnitudinis numerus non est, cum infinitus sit atque incomprehensibilis." I worked principally with the copy at the Universitäts- und Landesbibliothek Bonn under the shelf mark Ink 927.

34. For a report of the translation independent of a legend, see "Translatio b. Alberti Magni."

35. Meijer, *Dominikanenklooster*, 52. Likewise, Molhuysen, *Nieuw Nederlandsch Biografisch Woordenboek*, 1:1390. A necrology dated 1500 indicates his death on 30 July, Löhr, *Beiträge zur Geschichte*, document 858, p. 318.

36. "Sub aliis verborum coloribus ponendo." LLA, prologus, 2ᵛ. See Joachim Knape, *Poetik und Rhetorik*, 120, 205-6.

37. Magdalius, "Legenda compendiosa," A1ʳ-A5ʳ.

38. Magdalius, "Legenda compendiosa," Aiiʳ, Aiiiᵛ.

39. Magdalius, "Legenda compendiosa," Aiiiiʳ.

40. Magdalius, "Legenda compendiosa," Aiiiiᵛ-Avʳ.

41. See Collins, "Latin Hagiography in Germany"; Williams-Krapp, "Deutschsprachige Hagiographie."

42. In this regard: "pura ignorantia... vitiosissima invidia," LVA, bvᵛ-bviiᵛ.

43. "Perlegisse libros illos se testatur ut posset reprobare eosdem quod certissime peccatum non est sed virtutis operatio. Hoc enim facto caput Goliath proprio amputatum est gladio." LVA, ciiᵛ. See Grant, *Science and Religion*, 108.

NOTES TO PAGES 76–82   167

44. As, e.g., "ideo ipse Albertus determinative noluit loqui de ipsis sed disputative tantum in speculo prefato quasi diceret." LVA, dv^r.

45. "Malefici exhibere se mendaciter promittebant ex scientiis nimirum astronomie mathematice alchimie aliisque pluribus paucissis." LVA, bvi^r.

46. LVA, bviii^r, cf. LVA., dv^v. See in addition to the references in Kieckhefer, *Magic in the Middle Ages*, 12n3.

47. "Etiamsi aliquid observes in huiusmodi de scientia astronomie immiscens bona malis vera falsis hec est enim astutia diaboli ut facilius decipiat." LVA, ci^r.

48. "Quare et fictitiis suis revelationibus huiusmodi scientias divinitivas creditur tradidisse suis cultoribus admiscens aliqua observanda ex scientia astronomie ut minus appareat falsitas occultata et ideo recte de illis divinatoribus dicit ipse Albertus super illud Ysaie xliiii." LVA, cvi^v.

49. "Hic iam audisti Alberti testimonio pygmeos non esse homines sed de genere simiarum quos etiam negat habere intellectum. Sed quod huiusmodi monstra sint que loquuntur aliqua voce hominis idem Albertus experimento probat." LVA, diii^r–diii^v. Cf. Alb., *De animal.* 2.1.1 (Stadler, 228).

50. "Quia non sunt invente imagines huius nisi ad vana vel mala sicut ad mulieres seducendas vel seras aperiendas vel naves immobilitandas vel terrores inducendos." LVA, di^r.

51. "In astronomicis autem implicita et vicinitas est aliqua ad nigromanticas." LVA, cii^v.

52. LVA, div^r.

53. "Hec omnia tibi o lector per Albertum narrata cognosce ut scias impietatem nigromanticorum et abhorreas apostasie crimen incurrere." LVA, ciii^v.

54. "Vetule quedam et illi Egyptiaci." LVA, cv^r.

55. "Quia rationibus quibusdam se videretur defendere." LVA, cvi^v.

56. LVA, bviii^r.

57. LVA, aii^{r}ff.

58. LVA, cviii^v–div^v.

59. LVA, ciii^v–cv^r.

60. Scheeben, "Les écrits d'Albert le Grand," 260–63.

61. See Scheeben, "Les écrits d'Albert le Grand," 289–92.

62. Also known as the *Libellus de alchimia*. Kibre, "Albertus Magnus on Alchemy," 201; Kibre, "Alchemical Writings"; Albertus Magnus (Pseudo), *Libellus de alchimia*, 75–76.

63. "Hunc librum quidam alchimici putant esse Alberti sed falsissimum est quia ipse Albertus istum librum semitae rectae cum suis opinionibus damnat eo quod omnino contrarium sentit. . . . Item approbat omnia que albertus reprobat et stulta dicta esse dicit. Quare si inspexeris librum mineralium Alberti et etiam librum semitae recte dices iste liber mineralium damnat et elidit librum semite recte specialissime." LVA, dvii^v–dviii^r.

64. Nigromancy, aeromancy, chiromancy, geomancy, hydromancy, as well as the use of rings, divinations, characters, horoscopes enchantments, and suffumigations. LLA, 34^v–37^v.

65. "Alii autem illum obstetricem contra grammaticos epiceni generis vel communis fuisse mentiuntur." LLA, 35^r.

66. Lemay, *Women's Secrets*, 1.

67. "Nemo fidei catholice amplius nocet quam obstetrics." Kramer, "Institoris," 1.11 and 2.11. See Biller, "Childbirth in the Middle Ages"; Forbes, *Midwife and the Witch*, 112–38; Jerouschek, introduction to *Malleus Maleficarum*, xxxvii–xxxviii. See also Harley, "Historians as Demonologists." Concerning the authorship of the *De secretis mulierum*, see Lemay, *Women's Secrets*, 1–58; Siraisi, "Medical Learning," 381; Strunz, *Albertus Magnus*, 15, 48; Thorndike, *History of Magic*, 3:241; Thorndike, "Further Consideration."

68. See Puff, "Female Sodomy." Regarding the case of Joan of Arc, see Schibanoff, "True Lies."

69. LLA, 36^r.

70. "Sed numquid etiam omnium herbarum arborum aromatum ipse hortulanus et plantator fuit qui virtutes et proprietates illarum non ignoravit? Et ut omnia brevibus concludamus

numquid tot artium mechanicarum hic censendus est practicus quos super his edidit libros? Aut non nauta aut arator aut lanifex aut venator et sic de aliis ipse fuit? Minime nec valet adhuc perversorum argumentum si ad solas mulieres hec facta fuisse referant quoniam eadem ratione vincuntur ut supra." LLA, 36^(r-v). This argument of Rudolph's echoes a passage in Rolevinck's *De excellentiis* that highlights the numerous fields about which Albertus wrote knowingly but which he never practiced, such as sailing and building. Rolevinck, *De excellentiis*, 18^v.

71. In the standard handbook of logic in the later Middle Ages, Peter of Spain (later Pope John XXI) calls the enthymeme "an imperfect syllogism"; see Petrus Hispanus Portugalensis (Peter of Spain), *Tractatus*, 22, 56. As Ronald Witt puts it, "The contrast here is between a means of proof in which probable premises are used in order to establish a probable conclusion (the enthymeme) and a means of proof in which two premises are used to deduce a logical conclusion (the syllogism)." Witt, *In the Footsteps of the Ancients*, 74, 10n21.

72. "Quod si adhuc protervire audeant ad hoc breviter respondeant an non Augustinus Hieronymus Gregorius Ambrosius Thomas Aquinas et Bonaventura aliique sancti patres carnalium peccatorum diversarumque specierum illarum dicendi sunt actores quia de huiusmodi hominum peccatorum scribunt immunditiis? Nequaquam!" LLA, f36^v.

73. Saint Anatolius, bishop of Laodicea (d. ca. 282). Eusebius praised him for his learning in rhetoric, philosophy, the natural sciences, and mathematics. He opened a school for Aristotelian philosophy in his hometown of Alexandria. His feast day is 3 July. AASS July I:642ff. Eusebius, *Historia ecclesiastica* 7.32.14–19.

74. "Noverat enim solertissimus docotr Albertus huius scientiae utilitatem. Noverat etiam eiusdem scientiae utilitatem Julianus Augustus et apostata qui ne ipsi catholici se armis eorum scilicet paganorum per philosophie studium ad fidem seipsos fortius communirent philosophie studium ut in ecclesiastica historia legitur catholicis interdixit." LLA, 35^v–36^r.

75. See Collins, "Latin Hagiography in Germany"; Williams-Krapp, "Deutschsprachige Hagiographie."

76. Hillenbrand, "Die Observantenbewegung," 259, 271; Jerouschek, introduction to *Malleus Maleficarum*, xl, xli, xliv; von Loë, *Statistisches*, 15; Löhr, "Die zweite Blütezeit," 215–16; Schnyder, *Malleus Maleficarum*, 86 (item 138).

77. Boudet, *Entre science et nigromance*; Boudet, "'Nigromantia'"; Boudet and Weill-Parot, "Être historien des sciences"; Bailey, "From Sorcery to Witchcraft"; Bailey, "Witchcraft, Superstition, and Astrology"; Bailey, *Fearful Spirits*.

78. Boureau, *Satan hérétique*; Clark, *Thinking with Demons*; Stephens, *Demon Lovers*.

79. Bailey, "From Sorcery to Witchcraft"; Bailey, "Age of Magicians"; Cohn, *Europe's Inner Demons*; Kieckhefer, *European Witch Trials*; Peters, *Magician, the Witch*.

80. See Bailey, *Battling Demons*.

81. Duni, "Under the Devil's Spell," 16.

82. Bailey, "From Sorcery to Witchcraft," 977–88; Jerouschek, introduction to *Malleus Maleficarum*, xl–xli; Thorndike, *History of Magic*, 3:42, 4:249; Van Rooy, "Saint Albert le Grand," 3–5; Zambelli, "Scholastic and Humanist Views," 128. Disputing the Observance's special interest in demonology, witch-hunting, and inquisition is Tavuzzi, *Renaissance Inquisitors*, 200–202, 209–10; cf. Bailey, review of *Renaissance Inquisitors*, 821–22. Neil Tarrant (*Defining Nature's Limits*), however, develops the association between Dominicans and ecclesial concerns over the demonic, especially through such ecclesiastical organs as the Inquisition and the Index. Regarding Kramer's understanding of witchcraft and women's susceptibility to it, see Ayanna, "Witchcraft"; Herzig, "Witches, Saints, and Heretics."

83. See Gow, Desjardins, and Pageau, "Introduction."

84. Bailey, "From Sorcery to Witchcraft," 962.

85. Collins, *Reforming Saints*, 12, 19–50, 53–54.

86. Barthelmé, *La réforme dominicaine*; Hillenbrand, "Die Observantenbewegung"; Löhr, *Die Teutonia*, 1–40; Löhr, "Die zweite Blütezeit." For instruction from the master general to Sprenger in 1483 on not expelling unreformed friars, see Reichert, *Registrum litterarum*, 87.

87. Munich, Bayerische Staatsbibliothek, clm 3864, fols. 61, 105–26.

88. Hansen, *Quellen und Untersuchungen*, 371n373.
89. Hansen, *Quellen und Untersuchungen*, 401-2.
90. Löhr, "Die zweite Blütezeit," 229; Hillenbrand, "Die Observantenbewegung," 259. See also Walz, "Bestrebungen," 288-93.
91. "Cum esse possit et probabile mutum sit plures non canonizatos sanctis canonizatis aliquibus in beatitudine esse excellentiores et ex vite merito maiora posse impetrare." LVA, giii^v.
92. "Ob malorum prelatorum resistentiam . . . propter negligentiam fratrum." LVA, giii^r.
93. "Nec interdicitur tamen ab ecclesia immo ipsa admittit sanctis non canonizatis porrigere preces in privato si probabile est sanctos tales beatos esse." LVA, giv^v. "Legimus enim de magnis sanctis etiam non nisi partes multos valde annos est inventos vel miracula fecisse ut de beato Barnaba legitur similiter et de sancto Quintino martyre atque de sanctis Cassio et sociis eius in diocesi Coloniensi." LVA, gv^r.
94. LVA, jiii^r–jiii^v:

> Papa etiam Pius huius nominis secundus qui et Silvius Aeneas vir prudens et in multis expertus cuius ingenium scripta propria commendant de sanctitate Alberti non dubitans in epistola quam ad Turcum scribit admonendo de Christiana religione suscipienda. . . . Multi ex discipulis eius clarissimi evaserunt sed precipua est magni Alberti fama qui nullum doctrine genus ignorasse crditus est nec minor eo Thomas Aquinas fuit in litteris et si maior extitit sanctitate. Haec papa Piius. Supponit igitur, sanctum esse Albertum licet in hac parte Thomam quia ab ecclesia iam canonizatum pretulit. In quo autem gradu sanctitatis sunt et quis maior ipsorum soli Deo ad plenum notum est ipse enim ponderator est spirituum.

See Pius II (Aeneas Silvius Piccolomineus), *Orationes politicae et ecclesiasticae*, 2:23.

95. LLA, 2^v.
96. LVA, aiiii^r–bv^v; and LLA, 3^r–10^v.
97. "In propria persona pedester incedendo visitaverit non habens es in zona sed cum fratribus ostiatim panem mendicando apostolice perfectionis emulator factus est idem volens a fratribus per omnia obervari." LVA, fvii^v–fviii^r.
98. LVA, fviii^v. Also, LLA, 11^r–11^v.
99. "Timeretque de periculo quod alamannie episcopos ob temporalis dominii gravamen ad multa damnabilia quandoque pertrahit." LVA, hiv^r.
100. LVA, jvi^r–jvi^v. Rudolph addressed the matter as well, albeit less directly; see LLA, 21^r.
101. "Monumenta cultus B. Alberti Magni."
102. Regarding the success rate of petitions for canonization in the fifteenth century, see Wetzstein, *Heilige vor Gericht*, 28.
103. Tarrant, *Defining Nature's Limits*, 188, 196.
104. Baldini and Spruit, *Catholic Church and Modern Science*, 720-26.
105. See Tarrant, "Giambattista della Porta"; Campbell, Gianfrancesco, and Tarrant, "Alchemy and the Mendicant Orders," 202n209, 204; Tarrant, "Between Aquinas and Eymerich"; Tarrant, "Reconstructing Thomist Astrology"; Tarrant, *Defining Nature's Limits*, 19, 46, 50-56, 58, 78, 97, 188.
106. From an earlier generation of scholars, see Thorndike, "Further Consideration"; Kibre, "Albertus Magnus on Alchemy"; Kibre, "Further Manuscripts," 243-47; Kibre, "*Alkimia minor*"; Kibre, "Alchemical Tract." In more recent scholarship, see Grant, *History of Natural Philosophy*; Moran, *Distilling Knowledge*; Zika, *Exorcising Our Demons*, 91.
107. See Otto, *Magie*, 15-17, 617-20; Otto, "Discourse Historical Approach," 37-47.

CHAPTER 4

1. "S'il n'estoit assez cogneu par ses oeuvres, que son merite a esté si grand et sa doctrine si extraordinaire, que telle recompense pourroit sembler petite, si Trismegiste ne s'estoit

tellement reservé le titre de tres-grand qu'il n'a depuis lui esté comuniqué à personne." Naudé, *Apologie*, 516.
   2. Naudé, *Apologie*, 12–21.
   3. In this chapter the translations of Naudé's *Apologie* are the author's own, based on the Prévot edition of 1998 and checked against the first Paris edition of 1625. Parenthetical citations in this chapter refer to the page numbers from the Prévot edition, Naudé, "Apologie."
   4. Naudé, *Considérations politiques*, 148.
   5. Martin, *Subverting Aristotle*, 134–44.
   6. Rice, *Gabriel Naudé*, 63.
   7. Naudé, *History of Magick*; Naudé, "Schutz=Schrifft"; Naudé, *Über den Zauberglauben*. See also Horowitz, "Gabriel Naudé."
   8. Schino, *Batailles libertines*, 15–18; Schneider, *Dignified Retreat*, 1–39, 273–76, 308–16. His guide to the building library collections appeared shortly after the *Apologie*: Naudé, *Advis*; see also Mireaux, "Gabriel Naudé"; Blum, "Bibliotheca Memmiana"; Lancien, "'Der nützliche Gebrauch'"; Nelles, "Library as an Instrument of Discovery"; Rovelstad, "Two Seventeenth-Century Library Handbooks"; Delvaille, "Libertins du xvii siècle"; Grafton, "Libraries and Lecture Halls"; Suominen, "Gabriel Naudé."
   9. See Grafton, "Girolamo Cardano," esp. 337.
   10. Ovid, *Amores*, 1.2.
   11. Campanella, *De sensu rerum*, 260–369; Campanella, *Del senso*. See Schino, "Campanella," 393–431; Schino, *Batailles libertines*, 61–73; Bianchi, "*Libertas philosophandi*"; Lerner, *Tommaso Campanella*, 33–36.
   12. Campanella, *De sensu rerum*, 353 and 357. See also Paganini, "Wie aus Gesetzgebern," 55–61.
   13. Included here as well is Girolamo Cardano's claim that Averroes was also inspired by a demon.
   14. E.g., see Verardi, "Francesco Storella.'"
   15. Trithemius, *Steganographia* (1606); Arnold, *Johannes Trithemius*, 23, 180–200; Brann, *Trithemius and Magical Theology*, 7.
   16. Riolan, *Ad Libavi maniam*; Guibert, *Alchymia ratione*, 65–68, 75–78; Guibert, *De interitu alchymiae metallorum transmutatoriae tractatus* 11, 22–26, 94–96. See also Newman and Principe, "Alchemy Versus Chemistry," 44–47.
   17. Naudé, "Apologie."
   18. Huser, *Bücher und Schrifften*; Sudhoff, *Bibliographia Paracelsica*.
   19. See Bianchi, "Gabriel Naudé critique des alchemistes"; Kahn, *Alchimie et paracelsisme*, 587–89.
   20. Maier, *Symbola aureae mensae duodecim nationum*, 236–317.
   21. "Albert le Grand n'a iamais songe à le faire." Naudé, *Apologie*, 521.
   22. Guibert, *Alchymia ratione*, 65–68, 75–78. Guibert reiterated his rejection of alchemy with references again to Albert and Paracelsus, in Guibert, *De interitu alchymiae metallorum transmutatoriae tractatus*, 11, 22–26, 94–96.
   23. Robert Bellarmine had recently singled them out for censure as well; see Bellarmino, *De scriptoribus ecclesiasticis liber unus*, 199.
   24. "Il ne reste donc maintenant qu'à refuter l'erreur de ceux qui se sont presuadez que l'on pouvoit forger des testes d'airain sous certaines constellations, lesquelles rendoient par apres des responses, et servoient a ceux qui les possedoient de guide et de conduitte en toutes leurs affaires."
   25. See Truitt, *Medieval Robots*.
   26. Tostado, *Eccam vobis qui sacris litteris incumbitis studiosi*, 72^v. The passage in question pertains to Exodus 14. Tostado digressed to explain that astral component to the magic animating the figure.
   27. He was a kabbalist and author of *De harmonia mundi totius* (Venice: Bernardino de Vitalibus, 1525), translated into French by Guy le Fèvre de La Boderie in 1578.

28. *Speculum peregrinarum questionum* d. 3, c. 4, q. 3 (fol. 128ᵛ); see also d. 3, c. 7, q. 4 (fol. 165ʳ).

29. Naudé cited a letter to Martin Sandellio dated 1619, included in the letters prepared for press by Charles-Annibal Fabrot under the title "de magia" and appearing in Paris in 1623. Raguseus, *Epistolarum mathematicarum seu de divinatione libri duo* l. 2, ep. 6, pp. 372–431.

30. "Plusieurs autres qu'il seroit ennuyeux de specifier." Naudé, *Apologie*, 529.

31. "Quae veris addere falsa gaudet, et e minimo sua per mendacia crescit." Ovid, *Metamorphoses* 9.

32. Naudé, *Le Marfore*.

33. Horowitz, "Gabriel Naudé," 62; Bianchi, *Rinascimento e libertinismo*, 77–108.

34. Naudé, *Instruction*.

35. Horowitz, "Gabriel Naudé," 62; Bianchi, *Rinascimento e libertinismo*, 180–92.

36. Andreä, *Fama fraternitatis*.

37. Kahn, "Rosicrucian Hoax," 238.

38. Maier, *Themis aurea*.

39. Beeler, "Invisible College"; van Dülmen, *Die Utopie*; Peukert, *Das Rosenkreutz*; Yates, *Rosicrucian Enlightenment*.

40. Kahn, "Rosicrucian Hoax"; Kahn, *Alchimie et paracelsisme*.

41. Yates, *Rosicrucian Enlightenment*; Gilly, "Die Rosenkreuzer."

42. Boucher, *Couronne mystique*. See Smith, "Resisting the Rosicrucians."

43. Roberti, *Goclenius Heautonti morumenos*, 204–64.

44. Debus, *French Paracelsians*; Moran, "Paracelsianism."

45. Gaultier, *Table chronographique*.

46. Gaultier, *Table chronographique*, 875.

47. Garasse, *La doctrine curieuse*. See Godard de Donville, *Le Libertin*.

48. Viau and Bourgueil, *Le Parnasse des poètes satyriques*.

49. E.g., *Variétés historiques et littéraires*, 1:115–26 and 9:275–307.

50. Miller, *Peiresc's Europe*.

51. Kahn, "Rosicrucian Hoax," 274.

52. Kahn, "Rosicrucian Hoax," 277.

53. The authoritative account of the Rosicrucian hoax is to be found in Kahn, *Alchimie et paracelsisme*. For Naudé's role, see esp. 424–35, 470–82, 587–89. See also Kahn, "Rosicrucian Hoax."

54. Kahn, "Rosicrucian Hoax," 262–63.

55. Naudé, *Instruction*, 1–8.

56. Naudé, *Instruction*, 8–13.

57. Naudé, *Instruction*, 13–17.

58. Naudé, *Instruction*, 18–51.

59. Bianchi, "Gabriel Naudé critique des alchimistes"; Schino, *Battaglie libertines*, 16–17.

60. Naudé, *Instruction*, 53–58. See also Maier, *Symbola aureae mensae duodecim nationum*; Maier, *Themis aurea*; Maier, *Verum inventum*.

61. Godard de Donville, *Le Libertin*; Godard de Donville, "Théophile"; Kahn, "Rosicrucian Hoax," 283–85; Bianchi, *Rinascimento e libertinismo*, 190–92; Bianchi, "Gabriel Naudé critique des alchimistes."

62. Kahn, "Rosicrucian Hoax," 291–93.

63. Pintard, *Le libertinage érudit*, 156–78. Brian Copenhaver briefly handles Naudé, the tetrade, and the problem of magic, in "Occultist Tradition and Its Critics," 1:473–74. See also Paganini, "Ways of Clandestinity," 131.

64. Pintard, *Le libertinage érudit*, 127–208. See also Naudé, *Lettres*; Schiffman, *On the Threshold*, 25–27, 101; Copenhaver, "Nature Against Authority," 285–87, 317–28; Gouverneur, *Prudence et subversion libertine*; Martin, *Subverting Aristotle*, 126–33; Pietsch, "Libertinage érudit," 169–72; Schneider, *Dignified Retreat*, 247–98.

65. Sloan, "Descartes, the Sceptics"; Pantin, "New Philosophy," 100–102, 257.
66. See Burson and Matytsin, *Skeptical Enlightenment*; Matytsin, *Specter of Skepticism*.
67. Libertinage erudite, d'ecriture, and d'action. See also Wauters, *"Libertinage érudit."*
68. Pietsch, *"Libertinage érudit,"* 165–66.
69. Popkin, *History of Scepticism*, 96. On the origin of "secularizing" debates in religious controversy, see, e.g., Coleman, "Resacralizing the World."
70. E.g., Coleman, "Resacralizing the World"; Burson, "Theological Revolution."
71. See Gouverneur, *Prudence et subversion libertine*; Schneider, *Dignified Retreat*, 26.
72. Schino, *Batailles libertines*. (The first edition of this work appeared in Italian in 2014.) See also Godard de Donville, *Le Libertin*; Godard de Donville, "Libertinage"; Cavaillé, "Les libertins"; Cavaillé, "Libérer le libertinage."
73. "Qua nempe Angelico tendis super astra volatu / Cum nemo angelicis tantum sese efferat alis." In Naudé, *Apologie*, ci[r]. See also Hirai, *Jacques Gaffarel*.
74. "Livor Apollineis iamdudum infensus alumnis / sparserat ex Orco nigra venena suo / at qui conficiat Pythonem hunc, misit Apollo / Naudaeum; gaude vindice Musa tuo" (Angry envy had long sprinkled black poison from its own underworld on Apollonian students. But Apollo sent Naudé, who finished off this Python. Rejoice in your victory, O Muse). In Naudé, *Apologie*, cii[v].
75. "Je vous dirai pourtant avecque verité / Qu'en defendant si bien toute l'antiquité / Du crime qui vous fait ainsi prendre les armes / Vous passez pour sorciers vous memes parmi nous / Car, o doctes escrits, vous avez tant de charmes / Que nous sommes forcez de n'aimer plus que vous." In Naudé, *Apologie*, ciii[r]. Roberts, "Obscenity and the Politics of Authorship."
76. Garasse, *Nouveau jugement*, 106–43.
77. Garasse, *La doctrine curieuse*.
78. Garasse's work is understood to provide useful if indirect evidence for many provocative ideas circulating in early seventeenth-century France. For the premier twentieth-century historian of libertinage, Pintard, Garasse's association of libertinism with atheism is taken as important evidence of emergent atheism during the late Renaissance in French intellectual circles. Pintard, *Le libertinage érudit*.
79. Spargo, *Virgil the Necromancer*.
80. Garasse, *Nouveau jugement*, 121–28.
81. De Lancre, *L'incrédulité*.
82. De Lancre, *L'incrédulité*, 4. Here the work of Alfred Soman has been crucial to understanding the skepticism among judges of the Parlement of Paris toward accusations of and convictions for witchcraft, e.g., Soman, "Les procès." In short, De Lancre's concerns that judges were not taking the crime seriously were justified.
83. De Lancre, *L'incrédulité*, 13.
84. Weyer, *De praestigiis daemonum*; Weyer, *On Witchcraft*.
85. Bodin, *De la demonomanie des sorciers*; Bodin, *On the Demon-Mania of Witches*.
86. Delrio, *Disquisitionum magicarum*.
87. Gödelmann, *Disputatio de magis*; Gödelmann, *De magis*.
88. Gödelmann, *De magis*, 2.1.17 and 12.13.12–13. See also Lehmann and Ulbricht, "Motive und Argumente."
89. Autun (de Chevanes), *L'Incrédulité sçavante*, 935–1108.
90. Autun (de Chevanes), *L'Incrédulité sçavante*, 939–50.
91. Autun (de Chevanes), *L'Incrédulité sçavante*, 1086.
92. Naudé, *Lettres*, 67.
93. Raleigh, *History of the World*, 172.
94. Naudé, *Considérations politiques*, 148.
95. Bodin, *Methodus*; Vossius, *Ars historica*. See Soll, "Uses of Historical Evidence," 154; Schiffman, *On the Threshold*, 26; Kelley, "Theory of History," 755; Peach, "Contre l'histoire."

96. Naudé, *Causae Kempensis coniectio*. See Jaumann, "*Respublica litteraria*," 22–23.
97. Kelley, *Faces of History*, 211–16.

CHAPTER 5

1. "Systéme figuré des connoissances humaine" in Diderot, "Prospectus," 52.
2. D'Alembert, "Discours préliminaire," 1:i–xlv.
3. Diderot and d'Alembert, *Encyclopédie*, 17:718.
4. Kristeller, "Between the Italian Renaissance," 58.
5. Popkin, *History of Scepticism*, 80.
6. Bianchi, *Tradizione*, 50–57.
7. "Der geistige Führer der Aufklärung." Cassirer, *Die Philosophie*, 279.
8. Loveland, "Encyclopaedias and Genre," 171–72; Loveland, *European Encyclopaedia*, 2–36, 248–84.
9. Collison, *Encyclopaedias*, 4–16; Yeo, *Encyclopaedic Visions*, 1–32; Loveland, *European Encyclopaedia*, 71–89, 248–84, 321–57.
10. *Dictionnaire universel (Trévoux)* (1752), 1:1724–25, and 6:368; Diderot and d'Alembert, *Encyclopédie*, 2:330, and 14:770–77.
11. E.g., Opera omnia of Henry Suso, Johannes Tauler, and Jan van Ruusbroec were reprinted multiple times in the early modern period. Bonaventure and Arnold of Villanova were prominent high medieval exceptions to the sixteenth-century tendency against scholastics. For seventeenth-century developments in France, see Kors, *Atheism*, 86–88.
12. Aquinas, *Opera omnia*.
13. Gauslini, *Beatus Albertus Magnus*.
14. Longo, "Jammy, Pierre," 862–63; Jammy, *Veritates de auxilio gratiae*.
15. Lyonnaise publishers had recently produced the opera omnia of the scholastic Duns Scotus (1265/66–1308) and later, of the Franciscan scholastic Bonaventure (1221–1274). Regarding the publication of critical editions of medieval scholastics in seventeenth-century France, see Kors, *Atheism*, 86n10.
16. Malvenda, *Commentaria*.
17. *Index operum B. Alberti Magni*. See also Guy Patin to Claude Belin, Paris, 12 March 1646, letter 136 in Triaire, *Lettres de Gui Patin*, 1:498.
18. Lévesque, *Les frères*, 264; Meersseman, "Die neue Kölner," 107–14.
19. Jammy, *Beati Alberti opera*, 3:23.
20. Jammy, *Beati Alberti opera*, 1:i1^v–i2^r.
21. Jammy, *Beati Alberti opera*. The vita appears in 1:e1^r–e5^v.
22. Quétif and Échard, *Scriptores ordinis praedicatorum recensiti*.
23. Miller, "Louis Moréri's *Grand dictionnaire*," 13; Loveland, "Encyclopaedias and Genre," 171–72; Yeo, *Encyclopaedic Visions*, 17–18. Michel Foucault, remarking on the presumed "neutrality" of the alphabet as an organizing principle to knowledge, called the *Grand Dictionnaire* the first of its kind. Foucault, *Les mots*, 53n51.
24. Moréri, *Le Grand Dictionnaire* (1674); Moréri, *Le Grand Dictionnaire* (1681).
25. E.g., Jean Cibenius Alemand's *Lexicon historicum ac poeticum* (1544), Charles Estienne's *Dictionarium historicum ac poeticum* (1553), Juigné-Broissinière's *Dictionnaire théologique, historique, poétique, cosmographique et chronologique* (1644), and Estienne Paul Boyer's *Bibliothèque universelle* (1649). Moréri, *Le Grand Dictionnaire* (1674), a2^r–a3^r.
26. Moréri, *Le Grand Dictionnaire* (1692).
27. Moréri, *Le Grand Dictionnaire* (1674), 65.
28. Moréri, *Le Grand Dictionnaire* (1681), 1:120–21.
29. Louis Moréri, *Le Grand Dictionnaire* (1759), 1:269.
30. Moréri, *Le Grand Dictionnaire* (1674), 852.

31. Moréri, *Le Grand Dictionnaire* (1692), 3:408.
32. Moréri, *Le Grand Dictionnaire* (1718), 4:402.
33. Furetière, *Essais*.
34. Furetière, *Dictionaire universel* (1690).
35. Corneille, *Dictionnaire des arts et des sciences*.
36. Furetière, *Dictionaire universel* (1690), 1:G4ᵛ.
37. Furetière, *Dictionaire universel* (1690), 1:S1ʳ.
38. Furetière, *Dictionaire universel* (1690), 3:500.
39. Furetière, *Dictionaire universel* (1690), 2:510–11.
40. Furetière, *Essais*, 62–63.
41. Furetière, *Dictionaire universel* (1690), 2:497.
42. Bayle, *Projet*, *1ʳ–***4ᵛ.
43. Bayle, *Projet*, ***1ʳ. See Cassirer, *Die Philosophie*, 271–72.
44. See van Bunge, "Bayle's Skepticism Revisited," 292–315; Sommer, "Zur 'Geschichtsphilosophie,'" 92.
45. See, e.g., the text and notes of the entries on Balbus, Cassius Severus, and Erasmus in Bayle, *Projet*, 79, 147, 248.
46. Bayle, *Dictionaire* (1697), 1:164–67; Bayle, *Dictionaire* (1702), 1:137–39. Here I will cite the 1702 edition and draw attention to the 1697 edition only when they diverge. Two footnotes—I and K—are added to the latter edition: I addresses Albert's height; K addresses the authorship of the *De secretis mulierum*. La Monnoye is today popularly known, if at all, through his Christmas carols, which include "Patapan."
47. Anderson, "Sallengre," 266–68.
48. Bayle, *Dictionaire* (1702), 138–39nH.
49. Bayle, *Dictionaire* (1702), 139nK. See Isaac Bullart and Jacques Ignace Bullart, *Académie*, 145–49.
50. Bayle, *Dictionaire* (1702), 137nE.
51. Bayle, *Dictionaire* (1702), 138nF-I.
52. Bayle, *Dictionaire* (1702), 138nF-II.
53. Raynaud, *Hoplotheca contra ictum calumniae*, 148–50, 361–62. Bayle's relatively long and sometimes droll entry on Raynaud as "one of the most famous and learned Jesuits of the seventeenth century." Bayle, *Dictionaire* (1702), 3:2544–49.
54. Bayle, *Dictionaire* (1702), 1:359nR.
55. Bayle, *Dictionaire* (1702), 1:429nA.
56. Bayle, *Dictionaire* (1702), 1:765.
57. Bayle, *Dictionaire* (1702), 2:1559, 1560nB.
58. Bayle, *Dictionaire* (1702), 2:1736nE.
59. Bayle, *Dictionaire* (1702), 3:2660nC.
60. Bayle, *Dictionaire* (1702), 3:2767, 2767nA; Alb., *Phys*. 1.3.13 (ed. Colon. IV/1, 64, 34–46).
61. Furetière, *Dictionnaire universel* (1701).
62. Furetière, *Dictionnaire universel* (1727).
63. A year before his exile in consequence of the Edict of Fonainebleau (1685), Basnage made his resentments against Catholicism explicit in *Tolérance des religions*. See Turcan, "Les particularités," 96; Marcil-Lacoste, "Hypothéses," 212n219; Behnke, *Furetière*; Ross, "Antoine Furetière's *Dictionnaire universel*," 64.
64. His editorial principles in this regard can be derived from Basnage, *Tolerance*.
65. Furetière, *Dictionnaire universel* (1727), X2ʳ–X2ᵛ.
66. Behnke, *Furetière*, 60–85, 104–20.
67. Furetière, *Dictionnaire universel* (1701), 3:Oooo1ᵛ.
68. *Dictionnaire universel (Trévoux)* (1704), 3:FFfiiʳ–FFfiiᵛ; *Dictionnaire universel (Trévoux)* (1752), 6:1368.

69. Furetière, *Dictionnaire universel* (1701), 1:M2^v; *Dictionnaire universel (Trévoux)* (1704), 1:Hi^v.

70. Furetière, *Dictionnaire universel* (1701), 1:Dd4^v; *Dictionnaire universel (Trévoux)* (1704), 1:Sii^v.

71. Furetière, *Dictionnaire universel* (1701), 2:MMMmmm1^v, 2^r; *Dictionnaire universel (Trévoux)* (1704), 2:*bii^v.

72. Furetière, *Dictionaire universel* (1690), 2:DDDdd1^r; Furetière, *Dictionnaire universel* (1701), 3:B2^r; *Dictionnaire universel (Trévoux)* (1704), 2:Aiv^r; *Dictionnaire universel (Trévoux)* (1721), 4:217–18.

73. "On appelle aussi cela, dresser une nativité, quand il s'agit de predictions sur la vie et la fortune des hommes, car on fait aussi les horoscopes des villes, des Estats, des grandes entre prises, etc." Furetière, *Dictionnaire universel* (1690), Ee2^v.

74. "On etoit autrefois tellement infatué d'oroscopes, qu'Albert le grand eut la temerité de tirer celui de Christ." Furetière, *Dictionnaire universel* (1701), 2:Ttt2^r.

75. See Albertus Magnus (Pseudo), *Speculum astronomiae* (1977), 36–37.

76. "Je ne suis pas grand Astrologue, / et je sçais peu l'art de mentir, / Quoique cet art soit fort en vogue; / Je m'entends bien moins a batir un horoscope qu'une Eglogue." *Dictionnaire universel (Trévoux)* (1752), 4:971.

77. Furetière, *Dictionaire universel* (1690), 2:SSs2^v–SSs3^r; Furetière, *Dictionnaire universel (1701)*, 2:Fffff4^r–Fffff4^v; *Dictionnaire universel (Trévoux)* (1704), 2:Xi^v; *Dictionnaire universel (Trévoux)* (1752), 5:46–50.

78. *Dictionnaire universel (Trévoux)* (1721), 3:35.

79. Chambers, *Cyclopaedia* (1728). See Loveland, "Encyclopaedias and Genre," 172; Yeo, "Solution," 61–72.

80. Chambers, *Cyclopaedia* (1728), 2:6A2^r–6A2^v.

81. Chambers, *Encyclopaedia*, 6:257.

82. Naudé, *History of Magick*.

83. Dyche, *New General English Dictionary*, 1:Yy2^r, Kkk1^v.

84. Loveland, *European Encyclopaedia*, 272–73.

85. Löffler, "Wer schrieb den Zedler?," 265–83.

86. For Brucker on Albert, see Brucker, *Historia*, 2.2:787–98. For Brucker's influence on the *Universal-Lexicon*, see Hanegraaff, "Power," 252–73.

87. Zedler, *Universal-Lexicon*, 23:1169–73 and 61:38–142.

88. Zedler, *Universal-Lexicon*, 12:1978–95 and 23:1538–41. See also Essler, *Zauber*.

89. Zedler, *Universal-Lexicon*, 19:234–37.

90. Zedler, *Universal-Lexicon*, 19:288–304.

91. Zedler, *Universal-Lexicon*, 61:62.

92. Zedler, *Universal-Lexicon*, 61:38–142.

93. Zedler, *Universal-Lexicon*, 61:41.

94. Zedler, *Universal-Lexicon*, 12:1978–95.

95. Zedler, *Universal-Lexicon*, 61:46.

96. Zedler, *Universal-Lexicon*, 61:54–61.

97. Diderot and d'Alembert, *Encyclopédie*, 14:770–77.

98. Diderot and d'Alembert, *Encyclopédie*, 16:250.

99. Diderot and d'Alembert, *Encyclopédie*, 14:773.

100. Diderot and d'Alembert, *Encyclopédie*, 1:448.

101. Diderot and d'Alembert, *Encyclopédie*, 1:665.

102. Diderot and d'Alembert, *Encyclopédie*, 1:789.

103. Diderot and d'Alembert, *Encyclopédie*, 8:311.

104. Diderot and d'Alembert, *Encyclopédie*, 3:429–30.

105. Josephson-Storm, *Myth of Disenchantment*, 51–58.

106. Diderot and d'Alembert, *Encyclopédie*, 9:852.

107. Diderot and d'Alembert, *Encyclopédie*, 9:854.
108. Josephson-Storm, *Myth of Disenchantment*, 57.
109. Cf. Edelstein, "Aristotelian Enlightenment," 187–204.
110. Burson, "Refracting the Century," 227–46; Schmidt, "Light," 268–90.

EPILOGUE

1. The story of the oak appears in chapter 1 of the 1818 version, chapter 2 of the 1831 revision. Shelley, *Frankenstein*, 32–36.
2. Horst, *Von der alten und neuen Magie*, 25.
3. Von Poppe, *Neuer Wunder-Schauplatz*, 37, 66.
4. Lévi, *Dogme et rituel*, 252, 356. See also Otto, "Catholic 'Magician.'"
5. Ennemoser, *Geschichte der Magie*, 72, 727.
6. Christian, *L'Histoire de la magie*, 16–20.
7. "Quod unum ex essentialibus requisitis deest ad hoc ut Beatus Albertus Magnus possit inter Ecclesiae Doctores recenseri, nempe insignis sanctitas eo sensu intellect ut ipsius nomen inscriptum esse deberet in Martyrologio Romano." "Monumenta cultus B. Alberti Magni," 364.
8. Sighart, *Albertus Magnus*; Sighart, *Albert the Great*.
9. Von Hertling, *Albertus Magnus*; von Hertling, "Albert der Große."
10. Grabmann, "Der Einfluss Alberts."
11. E.g., Sighart, *Albertus Magnus*, 12, 69, 71; Scheeben, *Albertus Magnus*, 200–230.
12. Bernard Geyer, a theologian at the University of Bonn and a priest of the archdiocese of Cologne, instigated the newest as yet incomplete opera omnia known as the Cologne edition. In 1951, the tricentenary of the Jammy edition, the Cologne edition's first published volume included a work omitted from both earlier opera omnia, the *De bono*. The Cologne edition, now about three-fourths complete, will ultimately comprise more than seventy titles in forty-one volumes. See Meersseman, "Die neue Kölner," 107–14; Stegmüller, *Analecta upsaliensia*, 169, 170.
13. Postulator General of the Order of Preachers, *Esposizione*; Laurentus, "Colonien"; Postulator General of the Order of Preachers, *Esposizione . . . Supplemento*; Quentin, *Inquisitio*.
14. Pius XI, "In thesauris sapientiae."
15. Pius XII, "Ad Deum," 89–91, esp. 90.
16. "Cuius veritatem etiam nos ipsi sumus experti in magicis." Alb., De anima 1.2.6 (ed. Colon. VII/1.32).
17. Walsham, "Migrations of the Holy," 253–54.
18. Draelants, "Notion of Properties," 174.
19. See chapter 1.
20. See chapter 2.
21. See chapter 3.
22. Otto, *Magie*, 1–36; Otto, "Historicising 'Western Learned Magic.'"
23. The book both refer to is Latour, *Nous n'avons jamais été modernes*; Latour, *We Have Never Been Modern*.
24. Bailey, *Fearful Spirits*, 246–49.

BIBLIOGRAPHY

Agrippa von Nettesheim, Heinrich Cornelius. *De occulta philosophia libri tres.* Cologne: Johann Soter, 1533.
———. *De occulta philosophia libri tres.* Edited by V. Perrone Compagni. Leiden: Brill, 1992.
Akopyan, Ovanes. "'Princeps aliorum' and His Followers: Giovanni Pico della Mirandola on the 'Astrological Tradition' in the *Disputationes adversus astrologiam divinatricem*." In *Debating the Stars in the Italian Renaissance*, edited by Ovances Akopyan, 72–105. Leiden: Brill, 2020.
Albertus Magnus (Pseudo). *Les admirables secrets.* Cologne: Le Dispensateur des Secrets, 1696.
———. "Alkimia minor." *Isis* 32 (1940): 276–300.
———. "Calistenus." *Isis* 35 (1944): 309–16.
———. "De occultis naturae." *Osiris* 13 (1958): 159–83.
———. "De secretis mulierum libellus." In *De secretis mulierum libellus... De virtutibus herbarum... De Mirabilibus mundi... adjectum est ob materiae similitudinem Michaelis Scoti, philosophi de Secretis naturae opusculum*, 3–118. Amsterdam, 1740.
———. *Libellus de alchimia.* Edited by Virginia Heines. Berkeley: University of California Press, 1958.
———. "Speculum astronomiae." In *The "Speculum astronomiae" and Its Enigma*, edited by Paola Zambelli, 203–73. Dordrecht: Kluwer Academic, 1992.
———. *Speculum astronomiae.* Edited by Stefano Caroti, Michela Pereira, Stefano Zamponi, and Paola Zambelli. Pisa: Domus Galilaeana, 1977.
Albertus-Magnus-Institut. "Zeittafel: Chronologie nach derzeitigem Forschungsstand." In *Albertus Magnus und sein System der Wissenschaften: Schlüsseltexte in Übersetzung Lateinisch–Deutsch*, edited by Hannes Möhle, 28–31. Münster: Aschendorff, 2011.
Alembert, Jean le Rond d'. "Discours préliminaire." In *Encyclopédie; ou, Dictionnaire raisonné des sciences, des arts, et des métiers, par une société de gens de lettres*, 1:i–xlv. Paris: André le Breton et al., 1751.
Anderson, Brom. "Sallengre, La Monnoye, and the 'Traité.'" In *Heterodoxy, Spinozism, and Free Thought in Early Eighteenth-Century Europe*, edited by Silvia Berti, Françoise Charles-Daubert, and Richard H. Popkin, 255–71. Dordrecht: Kluwer Academic, 1996.
Andreä, Johann Valentin. *Fama fraternitatis (1614); Confessio fraternitatis (1615).* Quellen und Forschungen zur württembergischen Kirchengeschichte 6. Stuttgart: Calwer Verlag, 1994.
Anzulewicz, Henryk. "Magie im Verständnis Alberts des Grossen." In *Mots médiévaux offerts à Ruedi Imbach*, edited by Iñigo Atucha, Dragos Calma, Catherine König-Pralong, and Irene Zavattero, 419–31. Turnhout: Brepols, 2011.
Apono, Petrus de. *Conciliator controversiarum, quae interphilosophos et medicos versantur.* Venice: Iuntas, 1565.
Arnold, Benjamin. "Eschatological Imagination and the Program of Roman Imperial and Ecclesiastical Renewal at the End of the Tenth Century." In *The Apocalyptic Year 1000*,

edited by Richard Allen Landes, Andrew Colin Gow, and David C. Van Meter, 270-88. Oxford: Oxford University Press, 2003.

Arnold, Klaus. *Johannes Trithemius (1462-1516)*. Quellen und Forschungen zur Geschichte des Bistums und Hochstifts Würzburg 23. Würzburg: Kommissionsverlag Ferdinand Schöningh, 1991.

Autun (de Chevanes), Jacques d'. *L'Incrédulité sçavante et la crédulité ignorante, au sujet des magiciens et des sorciers*. Lyon: Jean Molin, 1671.

Averroës (Ibn Rushd). *Commentarium magnum in Aristotelis "De anima libros."* Edited by F. Stuart Crawford. Cambridge, MA: Mediaeval Academy of America, 1953.

Avicenna (Ibn Sina). *"De congelatione et conglutinatione lapidum" Being Sections of the Kitâb al-Shifâ*. Edited by E. J. Holmyard and D. C. Mandeville. Paris: Paul Geuthner, 1927.

Ayanna, Amiri. "Witchcraft, Heinrich Kramer's *Nuremburg Handbook*, and *Ecclesiasticus*: The Construction of the Fifteenth-Century Civic Sorceress." In *Magic and Magicians*, edited by Albrecht Classen, 565-90. Berlin: Walter de Gruyter, 2017.

Bacon, Roger. *Compendium of the Study of Philosophy*. Edited and translated by Thomas S. Maloney. Auctores Britannici medii aevi. Oxford: Published for the British Academy by Oxford University Press, 2018.

Bailey, Michael D. "The Age of Magicians: Periodization in the History of Magic." *Magic, Ritual, and Witchcraft* 3, no. 1 (2008): 1-28.

———. *Battling Demons: Witchcraft, Heresy, and Reform in the Late Middle Ages*. University Park: Penn State University Press, 2003.

———. *Fearful Spirits, Reasoned Follies: The Boundaries of Superstition in Late Medieval Europe*. Ithaca, NY: Cornell University Press, 2013.

———. "From Sorcery to Witchcraft: Clerical Conceptions of Magic in the Later Middle Ages." *Speculum* 76, no. 4 (2001): 960-90.

———. *Magic and Superstition in Europe: A Concise History from Antiquity to the Present*. Lanham, MD: Rowman and Littlefield, 2007.

———. "The Meanings of Magic." *Magic, Ritual, and Witchcraft* 1, no. 1 (2006): 1-23.

———. Review of *Renaissance Inquisitors*, by Michael Tavuzzi. *Catholic Historical Review* 94 (2008): 821-22.

———. "Witchcraft, Superstition, and Astrology in the Late Middle Ages." In *Chasses aux sorcières et démonologie*, edited by Martine Ostorero, Georg Modestin, and Kathrin Utz Tremp, 349-66. Florence: SISMEL, 2010.

Baldini, Ugo, and Leen Spruit, eds. *Catholic Church and Modern Science: Documents from the Archives of the Roman Congregations of the Holy Office and the Index*. Vol. 1, *Sixteenth-Century Documents*. Fontes Archivi Sancti Officii Romani 5. Rome: Libreria editrice vaticana, 2009.

Baldner, Steven. "Albertus Magnus: Matter, Motion, and the Heavens." *Thomist* 78 (2014): 327-50.

Bale, John. *Illustrium Maioris Britanniae scriptorum*. Ipswich: D. van der Straten, 1548.

Bardney, Richard. "Vita Roberti Grosthed, episcopi Lincolniensis." In *Anglia sacra, sive Collectio historiarum*, edited by Henry Wharton, 325-48. London: Richard Chiswell, 1691.

Barker, Mark J. "Experience and Experimentation: The Meaning of *Experimentum* in Aquinas." *Thomist* 76, no. 1 (2012): 37-71.

Baron, Frank E. "Trithemius und Faustus: Begegnungen in Geschichte und Sage." In *Johannes Trithemius: Humanismus und Magie im vorreformatorischen Deutschland*, edited by Richard Auernheimer and Frank E. Baron, 39-60. Munich: Profil, 1991.

Barragán Nieto, José Pablo, ed. *El "De secretis mulierum" atribuido a Alberto Magno: Estudio, edición crítica y traducción*. Textes et études du Moyen âge 63. Porto: Brepols, 2012.

Barthelmé, Annette. *La réforme dominicaine au XVe siècle en Alsace et dans l'ensemble de la Province de Teutonie*. Strasbourg: Heitz, 1931.

Basnage de Beauval, Jacques. *Tolérance des religions*. Rotterdam: Henry de Graef, 1684.

Bayle, Pierre. *Dictionaire historique et critique*. Rotterdam: Reinier Leers, 1697.

———. *Dictionaire historique et critique*. 2nd, rev. ed. Rotterdam: Reinier Leers, 1702.

———. *Projet et fragmens d'un dictionnaire critique*. Rotterdam: Reinier Leers, 1692.

Beccarisi, Alessandra. "Cecco d'Ascoli filosofo." In *Cecco d'Ascoli*, edited by Antonio Rigon, 134–51. Rome: Istituto superiore di studi medioevali, 2007.

Beeler, Stanley W. "The Invisible College: A Study of the Three Original Rosicrucian Texts." PhD dissertation, University of Alberta, 1989.

Behnke, Dorothea. *Furetière und Trévoux: Eine Untersuchung zum Verhältnis der beiden Wörterbuchserien*. Lexicographica. Tübingen: M. Niemeyer Verlag, 1996.

Beke, Johannes de. "Chronica, 1247–1256, excerpta." In *Hermannus Altahensis und andere Geschichtsquellen Deutschlands im dreizehnten Iahrhundert*, edited by Johannes Friedrich Boehmer, 432–39. Fontes rerum Germanicarum. Stuttgart: J. G. Cotta, 1845.

Bellarmino, Roberto Francesco Romolo. *De scriptoribus ecclesiasticis liber unus*. Lyon: Horace Cardon, 1613.

Bénatouïl, Thomas, and Isabelle Draelants, eds. *"Expertus sum": L'expérience par les sens dans la philosophie naturelle médiévale*. Micrologus' Library 40. Florence: SISMEL, 2011.

Bianchi, Lorenzo. "Erudition, critique et histoire chez Gabriel Naudé (1600–1653)." In *Philologie und Erkenntnis*, edited by Ralph Häfner, 35–55. Tübingen: Max Niemeyer, 2001.

———. "Gabriel Naudé critique des alchimistes." In *Alchimie et philosophie à la Renaissance*, edited by Jean-Claude Margolin and Sylvain Matton, 405–21. De Pétrarque à Descartes. Paris: J. Vrin, 1993.

———. *"Libertas philosophandi et République des Lettres: France et Italie à travers les relations entre Naudé et Campanella."* In *Les premiers siècles de la république européenne des lettres*, edited by Marc Fumaroli, 342–63. Paris: Alain Baudry, 2005.

———. *Rinascimento e libertinismo: Studi su Gabriel Naudé*. Naples: Bibliopolis, 1996.

———. *Tradizione libertina e critica storica: Da Naudé a Bayle*. Milan: Franco Angeli, 1988.

Biller, Peter. "Childbirth in the Middle Ages." *History Today* 36 (August 8, 1986): 42–49.

Blum, Rudolf. "Bibliotheca Memmiana: Untersuchungen zu Gabriel Naudés *Advis pour dresser une bibliotheque*." In *Bibliotheca docet*, edited by Siegfried Joost, 209–32. Amsterdam: Erasmus-Buchhandlung, 1963.

Bodin, Jean. *De la demonomanie des sorciers*. Paris: Jacques du Puys, 1580.

———. *Methodus ad facilem historiarum cognitionem*. Paris: Martin Juvenes, 1566.

———. *On the Demon-Mania of Witches*. Renaissance and Reformation Texts in Translation. Toronto: Centre for Reformation and Renaissance Studies, 1995.

Boer, Sander Wopke de. *The Science of the Soul: The Commentary Tradition on Aristotle's "De anima," c. 1260–c. 1360*. Ancient and Medieval Philosophy. Leuven: Leuven University Press, 2013.

Bonaventure. *Opera omnia*. 7 vols. Lyon: Philippe Borde, Laurent Arnaud, et Pierre Borde, 1668.

Bordelon, Laurent. *L'histoire des imaginations extravagantes de Monsieur Oufle*. Amsterdam: Estienne Roger, Pierre Humbert, Pierre de Coup, et les Freres Chatelain, 1710.

Boucher, Jean. *Couronne mystique, ou Armes de piété contre toute sorte d'impiété, hérésie, athéisme, schisme, magie et mahométisme*. Tournay: A. Quinqué, 1623.

Boudet, Jean-Patrice. *Entre science et nigromance: Astrologie, divination et magie dans l'Occident médiéval (XIIe–XVe siècle)*. Histoire ancienne et médiévale. Paris: Publications de la Sorbonne, 2006.

———. "Magie et illusionnisme entre Moyen Age et Renaissance: Les *Annulorum experimenta* attribués à Pietro d'Abano." In *Médecine, astrologie et magie*, edited by Jean-Patrice Boudet, Franck Collard, and Nicolas Weill-Parot, 247–93. Florence: SISMEL, 2013.

———. "'Nigromantia': Brève histoire d'un mot." In *Geomancy and Other Forms of Divination*, edited by Alessandro Palazzo and Irene Zavaterro, 445–62. Florence: SISMEL, 2017.

Boudet, Jean-Patrice, and Nicolas Weill-Parot. "Être historien des sciences et de la magie médiévales aujourd'hui: Apports et limites des sciences sociales." In *Être historien du Moyen âge au XXIe siècle*, 199–228. Paris: Publications de la Sorbonne, 2008.

Boureau, Alain. *Satan hérétique: Histoire de la demonologie (1280–1330)*. Paris: Odile Jacob, 2004.

Bowe, Geoffrey S. "Alexander's *Metaphysics* Commentary and Some Scholastic Understandings of Automata." *ΣΧΟΛΗ [Schole]* 14 (2020): 7–25.

Brann, Noel L. *Trithemius and Magical Theology: A Chapter in the Controversy over Occult Studies in Early Modern Europe*. Western Esoteric Traditions. Albany: State University of New York Press, 1999.

Brewer, J. S., ed. *Fr. Rogeri Bacon opera quaedam hactenus inedita*. London: Longman, Green, Longman, and Roberts, 1859.

Brucker, Jakob. *Historia critica philosophiae*. Leipzig: Breitkopf, 1742–44.

Buchholz, Franz. *Die Bibliothek der ehemaligen Kölner Kartause*. Cologne: Bibliothekar-Lehrinstitut, 1957.

Bullart, Isaac, and Jacques Ignace Bullart. *Académie des sciences et des arts, contenant les vies, & les éloges historiques des hommes illustres, qui ont excellé en ces professions depuis environ quatre siècles parmy diverses nations de l'Europe*. Amsterdam: Elzevier, 1682.

Bunge, Wiep van. "Bayle's Skepticism Revisited." In *Enlightened Religion: From Confessional Churches to Polite Piety in the Dutch Republic*, edited by Joke Spaans and Jetze Touber, 292–315. Leiden: Brill, 2019.

Burnett, Charles. Review of *How Albert the Great's "Speculum astronomiae" Was Interpreted*, by Scott E. Hendrix. *Magic, Ritual and Witchcraft* 7, no. 2 (2012): 220–22.

———. "Talismans: Magic as Science? Necromancy Among the Seven Liberal Arts." In *Magic and Divination in the Middle Ages*, 1:1–15. Aldershot: Variorum, 1994.

———. "Two Approaches to Natural Science in Toledo of the Twelfth Century." In *Christlicher Norden—Muslimischer Süden*, edited by Matthias M. Tischler and Alexander Fidora, 69–80. Münster: Aschendorff, 2011.

Burson, Jeffrey D. "Process, Contingency, and Cultural Entanglement: Toward a Post-Revisionism in Enlightenment Historiography?" *Journal of the Western Society for French History* 47 (2021): 1–13.

———. "Refracting the Century of Lights: Alternate Genealogies of Enlightenment in Eighteenth-Century Culture." In *Let There Be Enlightenment*, edited by Anton M. Matytsin and Dan Edelstein, 227–46. Baltimore: Johns Hopkins University Press, 2018.

———. "Theological Revolution and the Entangled Emergence of Enlightenment Secularization." In *Between Secularization and Reform*, edited by Anna Tomaszewska, 15–45. Leiden: Brill, 2022.

Burson, Jeffrey D., and Anton M. Matytsin, eds. *The Skeptical Enlightenment: Doubt and Certainty in the Age of Reason*. Oxford University Studies in the Enlightenment 3. Liverpool: Liverpool University Press, 2019.

Calvet, Antoine. *L'alchimie au Moyen âge XIIe–XVe siècles*. Études de philosophie médiévale. Paris: Librairie philosophique J. Vrin, 2018.

———. "L'Alchimie du Pseudo-Albert le Grand." *Archives d'histoire doctrinale et littéraire du Moyen Age* 79 (2012): 115–60.

———. "Essai sur la constitution et la transmission de corpus alchimiques latins aux XIIIe–XVe siècles: Albert le Grand, Thomas d'Aquin, Roger Bacon." *Micrologus* 27 (2019): 191–204.

Campanella, Tommaso. *Del senso delle cose e della magia*. Edited by Germana Ernst. Biblioteca filosofica Laterza. Rome: Laterza, 2007.

———. *De sensu rerum et magia libri quatuor*. Frankfurt: Egenolff Emmel, 1620.

Campbell, Andrew, Lorenzo Gianfrancesco, and Neil Tarrant. "Alchemy and the Mendicant Orders of Late Medieval and Early Modern Europe." *Ambix* 65, no. 3 (2018): 201–9.
Cassirer, Ernst. *Die Philosophie der Aufklärung*. Tübingen: J. C. B. Mohr (Paul Siebeck), 1932.
Cavaillé, Jean-Pierre. "Libérer le libertinage: Une catégorie à l'épreuve des sources." *Annales: Histoire, Sciences sociales* 64 (2009): 45–78.
———. "Les libertins: L'Envers du Grand Siècle." *Les Cahiers du Centre de Recherches Historiques: Archives* 28–29 (2002): 1–22.
Chambers, Ephraim. *Cyclopaedia; or an Universal Dictionary of Arts and Sciences*. 2 vols. London: James and John Knapton et al., 1728.
———. *Cyclopaedia; or an Universal Dictionary of Arts and Sciences*. 5th ed. 2 vols. London: W. Innys et al., 1743.
———. *Encyclopaedia: A Dictionary of Universal Knowledge for the People*. London: W. and R. Chambers, 1864.
Christian, Paul. *L'Histoire de la magie, du monde surnaturel, et de la fatalité*. Paris: Furne, Jouvet et Cie., 1870.
Clark, Stuart. *Thinking with Demons: The Idea of Witchcraft in Early Modern Europe*. Oxford: Clarendon Press, 1997.
Classen, Albrecht. "Werner Rolevinck's *Fasciculus Temporum*." *Gutenberg-Jahrbuch* 81 (2006): 225–30.
Cohn, Norman. *Europe's Inner Demons: An Enquiry Inspired by the Great Witch-Hunt*. London: Book Club Associates, 1993.
Coleman, Charly. "Resacralizing the World: The Fate of Secularization in Enlightenment Historiography." *Journal of Modern History* 82, no. 2 (2010): 368–95.
———. *The Virtues of Abandon: An Anti-Individualist History of the French Enlightenment*. Stanford, CA: Stanford University Press, 2014.
Collins, David J. "Albertus, *Magnus* or *Magus*? Magic, Natural Philosophy, and Religious Reform in the Late Middle Ages." *Renaissance Quarterly* 63, no. 1 (2010): 1–44.
———. "Latin Hagiography in Germany, 1450–1550." In *Hagiographies: Histoire internationale de la littérature hagiographique latine et vernaculaire en Occident des origines à 1550*, edited by Guy Philippart, 4:522–82. Turnhout: Brepols, 2006.
———. *Reforming Saints: Saints' Lives and Their Authors in Germany, 1470–1530*. Oxford Studies in Historical Theology. Oxford: Oxford University Press, 2008.
———. "Scholastics, Stars, and Magi: Albert the Great on Matthew 2." In *The Sacred and the Sinister: Studies in Medieval Religion and Magic*, edited by David J. Collins, S.J., 257–78. University Park: Penn State University Press, 2019.
Collison, Robert Lewis. *Encyclopaedias: Their History Throughout the Ages—A Bibliographical Guide with Extensive Historical Notes to the General Encyclopaedias Issued Throughout the World from 350 B.C. to the Present Day*. New York: Hafner, 1964.
Copenhaver, Brian P. *Magic in Western Culture from Antiquity to the Enlightenment*. Cambridge: Cambridge University Press, 2015.
———. "Nature Against Authority: Breaking Away from the Classics." In *Renaissance Philosophy*, edited by Brian P. Copenhaver, 285–328. Oxford: Oxford University Press, 1992.
———. "The Occultist Tradition and Its Critics." In *The Cambridge History of Seventeenth-Century Philosophy*, edited by Daniel Garber and Michael Ayers, 1:454–512. Cambridge: Cambridge University Press, 1998.
———. "A Tale of Two Fishes: Magical Objects in Natural History from Antiquity Through the Scientific Revolution." *Journal of the History of Ideas* 52, no. 3 (1991): 373–98.
Corneille, Thomas. *Dictionnaire des arts et des sciences*. Paris: Jean Baptiste Coignard et veuve, 1694.
Crowther-Heyck, Kathleen. "Wonderful Secrets of Nature: Natural Knowledge and Religious Piety in Reformation Germany." *Isis* 94, no. 2 (2003): 253–73.
Davies, Owen. *Grimoires: A History of Magic Books*. Oxford: Oxford University Press, 2009.

---. *Magic: A Very Short Introduction*. Oxford: Oxford University Press, 2012.
Debus, Allen G. *The French Paracelsians: The Chemical Challenge to Medical and Scientific Tradition in Early Modern France*. Cambridge: Cambridge University Press, 1991.
Degen, Andreas. "Concepts of Fascination, from Democritus to Kant." *Journal of the History of Ideas* 73, no. 3 (2012): 371–93.
Fuoco, Maria Grazia del. "Il processo a Cecco d'Ascoli: Appunti intorno al cancelliere di Carlo di Calabria." In *Cecco d'Ascoli*, edited by Antonio Rigon, 218–37. Rome: Istituto superiore di studi medioevali, 2007.
Delaurenti, Béatrice. "La fascination et l'action à distance: Questions médiévales (1230–1370)." *Médiévales* 50 (2006): 137–54.
---. "Pietro d'Abano et les incantations: Présentation, édition et traduction de la *differentia* 156 du *Conciliator*." In *Médecine, astrologie et magie*, edited by Jean-Patrice Boudet, Franck Collard, and Nicolas Weill-Parot, 39–106. Florence: SISMEL, 2013.
---. "Pratiques médiévales de réécriture: La cas de la doctrine avicennienne du pouvoir de l'âme en dehors du corps." *Aevum* 90 (2016): 351–76.
Delrio, Martin Antoine. *Disquisitionum magicarum*. Leuven: Gerard Rivius, 1599–1600.
Delvaille, Bernard. "Libertins du xvii siècle." *Revue des Deux Mondes* (2005): 58–67.
Dictionnaire universel françois et latin (Trévoux). 1st ed. Trévoux: Estienne Ganeau, 1704.
Dictionnaire universel françois et latin (Trévoux). 2nd ed. Paris: Florentin Delaulne et al., 1721.
Dictionnaire universel françois et latin (Trévoux). 7th ed. Paris: La Compagnie des libraires associés, 1752.
Diderot, Denis. "Prospectus de 'l'Encyclopédie.'" In *Oeuvres de Denis Diderot*, edited by Jacques-André Naigeon, 3:3–220. Paris: Desray et Deterville, 1798.
Diderot, Denis, and Jean le Rond d'Alembert, eds. *Encyclopédie; ou, Dictionnaire raisonné des sciences, des arts, et des métiers, par une société de gens de lettres*. 28 vols. Paris: André le Breton, 1751–72.
Donahue, William. "Astronomy." In *The Cambridge History of Science*, edited by Katharine Park and Lorraine Daston, 3:562–95. Cambridge: Cambridge University Press, 2006.
Draelants, Isabelle. "Commentaire." In *Le "Liber de virtutibus herbarum, lapidum et animalium" (Liber aggregationis): Un texte à succès attribué à Albert le Grand*, 9–208. Florence: SISMEL, 2007.
---. "Expérience et autorités dans la philosophie naturelle d'Albert le Grand." In *"Expertus sum,"* edited by Thomas Bénatouïl and Isabelle Draelants, 89–122. Florence: SISMEL, 2011.
---. "'Magica vero sub philosophia non continetur': Statut des arts magiques et divinatoires dans les encyclopédies et leurs 'auctoritates' (1225–1260)." In *Geomancy and Other Forms of Divination*, edited by Irene Zavaterro and Alessandro Palazzo, 463–518. Florence: SISMEL, 2017.
---. "The Notion of Properties: Tensions Between *Scientia* and *Ars* in Medieval Natural Philosophy and Magic." In *The Routledge History of Medieval Magic*, edited by Sophie Page and Catherine Rider, 169–86. London: Routledge, 2019.
---. "La science encyclopédique des pierres au 13e siècle: L'apogée d'une veine minéralogique." In *Aux origines de la géologie de l'Antiquité au Moyen Âge*, edited by C. Thomasset, J. Ducos, and J.-P. Cambon, 91–139. Paris: Champion, 2010.
Draelants, Isabelle, and Antonella Sannino. "Albertinisme et hermétisme dans une anthologie en faveur de la magie, le *Liber aggregationis*: Prospective." In *Mélanges offerts à Hossam Elkhadem*, edited by F. Daelemans, J. M. Duvosquel, Robert Halleux, and David Juste, 223–55. Brussels: Archives et Bibliothèques de Belgique, 2007.
Ducay, Maria Jesús Lacarra. "La renovación de las artes liberales en Pedro Alfonso: El papel innovador de un judío converso en el siglo XII." In *De Toledo a Huesca: Sociedades medievales en transición a finales del siglo XI (1080–1100)*, edited by Carlos Laliena Corbera and Juan F. Utrilla Utrilla, 131–38. Zaragoza: Institución Fernando el Católico, 1998.

Dülmen, Richard van. *Die Utopie einer christlichen Gesellschaft Johann Valentin Andreae (1586–1654). Kultur und Gesellschaft.* Stuttgart-Bad Cannstatt: Frommann-Holzboog, 1981.

Duni, Matteo. *Under the Devil's Spell: Witches, Sorcerers, and the Inquisition in Renaissance Italy.* Villa Rossa Series: Intercultural Perspectives on Italy and Europe. Florence: Syracuse University Press, 2007.

Duns Scotus, Johannes. *Opera omnia quae huiusque reperiri potuerunt, collecta, recognita, notis, scholiis et commentariis illustrata.* Edited by Luke Wadding. 12 vols. Lyon: Laurence Durand, 1639.

Dyche, Thomas. *A New General English Dictionary.* Vol. 1. London: Richard Ware, 1735.

Eamon, William. "Books of Secrets in Medieval and Early Modern Science." *Sudhoffs Archiv* 69, no. 1 (1985): 26–49.

———. *Science and the Secrets of Nature: Books of Secrets in Medieval and Early Modern Culture.* Princeton, NJ: Princeton University Press, 1994.

Eckert, Willehad Paul. "Albert-Legenden." In *Albert der Grosse: Seine Zeit, sein Werk, Seine Wirkung,* edited by Albert Zimmermann, 1–23. Miscellanea mediaevalia. Berlin: Walter de Gruyter, 1981.

Edelstein, Dan. "The Aristotelian Enlightenment." In *Let There Be Enlightenment,* edited by Anton M. Matytsin and Dan Edelstein, 187–204. Baltimore: Johns Hopkins University Press, 2018.

"Effroyables pactions faites entre le diable et les prétendus invisibles, avec leurs damnables instructions, perte déplorable de leurs escoliers, et leur miserable fin." In *Variétés historiques et littéraires,* edited by Édouard Fournier, 9:275–307. Paris: Pagnerre, 1859.

Ennemoser, Joseph. *Geschichte der Magie.* 2 vols. Leipzig: F. A. Brockhaus, 1844.

Essler, Michaela. *Zauber, Magie und Hexerei: Eine etymologische und wortgeschichtliche Untersuchung sprachlicher Ausdrücke des Sinnbezirks Zauber und Magie in indogermanischen Sprachen.* Norderstedt: BoD, 2017.

"Es war ein Kung in Frankereich." In *Altteutsche Volks- und Meisterlieder aus den Handschriften der Heidelberger Bibliothek,* edited by Joseph Görres, 195–208. Frankfurt: Gebrüder Wilmans, 1817.

"Examen sur l'inconnue et nouvelle caballe des frères de la Rozée-Croix, habituez depuis peu de temps en la ville de Paris: Ensemble l'histoire des moeurs, coustumes, prodiges et particularitez d'iceux." In *Variétés historiques et littéraires,* edited by Édouard Fournier, 1:115–26. Paris: Pagnerre, 1855.

The Famous Historie of Fryer Bacon. London: G. Purslowe, 1627.

Ferckel, Christian. "Zur Bibliographie der *Secreta mulierum.*" *Archiv für Geschichte der Medizin* 7 (1913): 47–48.

Ficino, Marsilio. "Three Books on Life." In *Three Books on Life: A Critical Edition and Translation with Introduction and Notes,* edited by Carol V. Kaske and John R. Clark, 92–460. Binghamton, NY: Medieval and Renaissance Texts and Studies, 1989.

Forbes, Thomas Rogers. *The Midwife and the Witch.* New Haven, CT: Yale University Press, 1966.

Foucault, Michel. *Les mots et les choses: Une archéologie des sciences humaines.* Paris: Gallimard, 1966.

Fracheto, Gerardus de. *Vitae fratrum ordinis praedicatorum necnon cronica ordinis ab anno mcciii usque ad mccliv.* Monumenta Ordinis Fratrum Praedicatorum Historica 1. Leuven: Charpentier & Schoonjans, 1896.

Fries, Albert, and Kurt Illing. "Albertus Magnus." *Verfasserlexikon* 1 (1978): 124–39.

Furetière, Antoine. *Dictionaire universel, contenant generalement tous les mots françois tant vieux que modernes, et les termes de toutes les sciences et des arts.* 3 vols. The Hague: Arnoud et Reinier Leers, 1690.

---. *Dictionnaire universel, contenant generalement tous les mots françois tant vieux que modernes, et les termes des sciences et des arts.* Edited by Jacques Basnage de Bauval. 2nd ed. 3 vols. The Hague: Arnoud et Reinier Leers, 1701.

---. *Dictionnaire universel, contenant generalement tous les mots françois tant vieux que modernes, et les termes des sciences et des arts.* Edited by Jacques Basnage de Bauval and Jean Brutel de la Riviere. 4 vols. The Hague: Pierre Husson et al., 1727.

---. *Essais d'un dictionnaire universel.* 1684.

Gaiffier, Badouin de. "Bulletin des publications hagiographiques: Albert le Grand." *Analecta bollandiana* 51 (1933): 183–90.

Garasse, François. *La doctrine curieuse des beaux esprits de ce temps combattue et renversée.* Paris: S. Chappellet, 1623.

---. *Nouveau jugement de ce qui a été dict et escrit pour et contre le livre de "La doctrine curieuse" des beaux esprits de ce temps.* Paris: J. Quesnel, 1625.

Gaultier, Jacques. *Table chronographique de l'estat du christianisme.* Lyon: Pierre Rigaud, 1621.

Gauslini, Bernardino. *Beatus Albertus Magnus gente teutonicus, natione Suevus, patria Lauengensis, episcopus Ratisbonae, ex familia Praedicatorum recens laudibus illustratus.* Venice: G. Valentino, 1630.

Gerbert d'Aurillac. *Correspondance.* Edited by Pierre Riché and Jean-Pierre Callu. 2 vols. Les classiques de l'histoire de France au moyen age. Paris: Les Belles Lettres, 1993.

---. *Opera mathematica.* Edited by Nicolaus Bubnov. Berlin: Friedländer, 1899.

Gerson, Jean. "Trilogium astrologiae theologizatae." In *Œuvres complétes*, edited by Palémon Glorieux, 10:90–109. Paris: Desclée, 1973.

Geyer, Bernhard. "Der alte Katalog der Werke des Heiligen Albertus Magnus." *Studi e Testi* 122 (1946): 398–413.

---. "Das *Speculum astronomiae*, kein Werk des Albertus Magnus." *Münchener Theologische Zeitschrift* 4 (1953): 95–101.

Giansante, Massimo. "La condanna di Cecco d'Ascoli: Fra astrologia e pauperismo." In *Cecco d'Ascoli*, edited by Antonio Rigon, 184–99. Rome: Istituto superiore di studi medioevali, 2007.

Gilbert, Allan H. "Notes on the Influence of the *Secretum secretorum*." *Speculum* 3, no. 1 (1928): 84–98.

Gilly, Carlos. "Die Rosenkreuzer als europäisches Phänomen im 17. Jahrhundert und die verschlungenen Pfade der Forschung." In *Rosenkreuz als europäisches Phänomen im 17. Jahrhundert*, edited by Carlos Gilly, 19–56. Amsterdam: Pelikaan, 2001.

Girardi-Karsulin, Mihaela. "Grisogonovo *Astronomsko zrcalo* (Speculum astronomicum) i Zrcalo astronomije (Speculum astronomiae) Alberta Velikog." *Prilozi za Istrazivanje Hrvatske Filozofske Bastine* 71-72 (2010): 29–37.

Godard de Donville, Louise. "Libertinage." In *Dictionnaire du Grand siècle*, edited by François Bluche, 873–74. Paris: Librairie Arthème Fayard, 2005.

---. *Le Libertin des origines à 1665: Un produit des apologètes.* Biblio. Paris: Papers on French Seventeenth Century Literature, 1989.

---. "Théophile, les 'Beaux Esprits' et les Rose-Croix." In *Correspondances: Mélanges offerts à Roger Duchêne*, edited by Wolfgang Leiner, 143–54. Tübingen: Gunter Narr, 1992.

Gödelmann, Johannes Georg. *De magis, veneficis, et lamiis.* Frankfurt: Nicolaus Basse, 1591.

---. *Disputatio de magis, veneficis, maleficis et lamiis.* Frankfurt: Christopher Corvinus, 1584.

Görres, Joseph, ed. *Altteutsche Volks- und Meisterlieder aus den Handschriften der Heidelberger Bibliothek.* Frankfurt: Gebrüder Wilmans, 1817.

Gottschall, Dagmar. "Albert's Contributions to or Influence on Vernacular Literatures." In *A Companion to Albert the Great*, edited by Irven Michael Resnick, 725–57. Leiden: Brill, 2013.

Gouverneur, Sophie. *Prudence et subversion libertines: La critique de la raison d'État chez François de la Mothe Le Vayer, Gabriel Naudé et Samuel Sorbière*. Libre pensée et littérature clandestine. Paris: H. Champion, 2005.
Gow, Andrew Colin. "(En)gendering Evil: Sinful Conceptions of the Antichrist in the Middle Ages and the Reformation." In *Normative Zentrierung / Normative Centering*, edited by Rudolf Suntrup and Jan R. Veenstra, 147–58. Frankfurt: Peter Lang, 2002.
Gow, Andrew Colin, Robert B. Desjardins, and Francois V. Pageau. "Introduction: The Arras Witch Treatises in Context." In *The Arras Witch Treatises*, edited by Andrew Colin Gow, Robert B. Desjardins, and Francois V. Pageau, 1–18. University Park: Penn State University Press, 2016.
Gower, John. *Confessio Amantis*. Edited by Russell A. Peck. Medieval Academy Reprints for Teaching 9. Toronto: University of Toronto Press, 1980.
———. "Confessio Amantis." In *The Complete Works: The English Works*, edited by G. C. Macaulay, vol. 4. Oxford: Clarendon Press, 1901.
Grabmann, Martin. "Der Einfluss Alberts des Grossen auf das mittelalterliche Geistesleben." *Zeitschrift für katholische Theologie* 25 (1928): 153–82, 313–56.
———. *Mittelalterliches Geistesleben*. 3 vols. Munich: Max Hueber, 1926–56.
Grafton, Anthony. "Girolamo Cardano and the Tradition of Classical Astrology." *Proceedings of the American Philosophical Society* 142 (1998): 323–54.
———. "Libraries and Lecture Halls." In *The Cambridge History of Science*, edited by Katharine Park, and Lorraine Daston, 3:238–50. Cambridge: Cambridge University Press, 2006.
Grant, Edward. *A History of Natural Philosophy: From the Ancient World to the Nineteenth Century*. New York: Cambridge University Press, 2007.
———. "Medieval and Renaissance Scholastic Conceptions of the Influence of the Celestial Region on the Terrestrial." *Journal of Medieval and Renaissance Studies* 17, no. 1 (1987): 1–23.
———. "Medieval Natural Philosophy: Empiricism Without Observation." In *The Dynamics of Aristotelian Natural Philosophy from Antiquity to the Seventeenth Century*, edited by C. Leijenhorst, C. Lüthy, and J. M. M. H. Thijssen, 141–68. Leiden: Brill, 2002.
———. *Science and Religion, 400 B.C. to A.D. 1550: From Aristotle to Copernicus*. Baltimore: Johns Hopkins University Press, 2006.
Graus, František. "Funktionen der spätmittelalterlichen Geschichtsschreibung." In *Geschichtsschreibung und Geschichtsbewußtsein im späten Mittelalter*, edited by Hans Patze, 11–56. Vorträge und Forschungen. Sigmaringen: Thorbecke, 1987.
Green, Monica Helen. *Making Women's Medicine Masculine: The Rise of Male Authority in Pre-Modern Gynaecology*. Oxford: Oxford University Press, 2008.
Grund, Peter. "'Ffor to Make Azure as Albert Biddes': Medieval English Alchemical Writings in the Pseudo-Albertan Tradition." *Ambix* 53, no. 1 (2006): 21–42.
Guasco, Octavien de. *Dissertations historiques, politiques et litteraires*. Vol 1. Tournai: la Veûve D. Varle, 1756.
Guibert, Nicolaus. *Alchymia ratione et experientia ita demum viriliter impugnata et expugnata*. Strasbourg: Lazarus Zetner, 1603.
———. *De interitu alchymiae metallorum transmutatoriae tractatus*. Toul: Sebastian Philippe, 1614.
Guillelmus de Tocco. *Ystoria sancti Thome de Aquino (1318–1323)*. Edited by Claire Le Brun-Gouanvic. Studies and Texts. Toronto: Pontifical Institute of Medieval Studies, 1996.
Gundissalinus, Dominicus. *De divisione philosophiae*. Edited by Alexander Fidora and Dorothée Werner. Freiburg: Herder, 2007.
Guyotjeannin, Olivier, and Emmanuel Poulle, eds. *Autour de Gerbert d'Aurillac*. Paris: École des chartes, 1996.
Hackett, Jeremiah M. G. "Albert the Great and the *Speculum astronomiae*: The State of the Research at the Beginning of the Twenty-First Century." In *A Companion to Albert the Great*, edited by Irven Michael Resnick, 437–49. Leiden: Brill, 2013.

———. "The Attitude of Roger Bacon to the *Scientia of Albertus Magnus*." In *Albertus Magnus and the Sciences*, edited by James A. Weisheipl, 53–72. Toronto: Pontifical Institute of Mediaeval Studies, 1980.

———. "*Ego expertus sum*: Roger Bacon's Science and the Origins of Empiricism." In *"Expertus sum,"* edited by Thomas Bénatouïl and Isabelle Draelants, 145–74. Florence: SISMEL, 2011.

Halleux, Robert. "Albert le Grand et l'alchimie." *Revue des sciences philosophiques et théologiques* 66 (1982): 57–80.

Hanegraaff, Wouter J. "The Power of Ideas: Esotericism, Historicism, and the Limits of Discourse." *Religion* 43, no. 2 (2012): 252–73.

Hansen, Joseph, ed. *Quellen und Untersuchungen zur Geschichte des Hexenwahns und der Hexenverfolgung im Mittelalter*. Bonn: C. Georgi, 1901.

Harley, David N. "Historians as Demonologists: The Myth of the Midwife-Witch." *Social History of Medicine* 3, no. 1 (1990): 1–26.

Hasse, Dag Nikolaus. *Avicenna's "De anima" in the Latin West the Formation of a Peripatetic Philosophy of the Soul, 1160–1300*. London: Warburg Institute, 2000.

———. "The Early Albertus Magnus and His Arabic Sources on the Theory of the Soul." *Vivarium* 46, no. 3 (2008): 232–52.

Hellmeier, Paul D. *Anima et intellectus: Albertus Magnus und Thomas von Aquin über Seele und Intellekt des Menschen*. Beiträge zur Geschichte der Philosophie und Theologie des Mittelalters. Münster: Aschendorff Verlag, 2011.

Hendrix, Scott E. "Albert the Great, the *Speculum astronomiae*, and Astrology." *Studies in Medieval and Renaissance History* 15 (2018): 155–95.

———. *How Albert the Great's "Speculum astronomiae" Was Interpreted and Used by Four Centuries of Readers: A Study in Late Medieval Medicine, Astronomy, and Astrology*. Lewiston, NY: Edwin Mellen Press, 2010.

Henricus de Hervordia. *Liber de rebus memorabilioribus sive chronicon*. Edited by August Potthast. Gottingen, 1859.

Henry, John. "The Fragmentation of Renaissance Occultism and the Decline of Magic." *History of Science* 46, no. 1 (2008): 1–48.

Henry of Ghent (Pseudo). "De scriptoribus ecclesiasticis." In *Bibliotheca ecclesiastica*, edited by Johann Albert Fabricius, 2:117–40. Hamburg: Christian Liebezeit and Theodor Christoph Felginer, 1718.

———. "De viris illustribus." In *De illustribus ecclesiae scriptoribus*, edited by Suffridus Petrus, 396–431. Cologne: Maternus Cholinus, 1580.

Hertling, Georg Freiherr von. "Albert der Große." In *Wetzer und Welte's Kirchenlexikon oder Encylopädie der katholischen Theologie und ihrer Hülfswissenschaften*, edited by Joseph Hergenröther and Fraz Kaulen, 1:414–19. 2nd, rev. ed. Freiburg: Herder, 1882.

———. *Albertus Magnus: Beiträge zu seiner Würdigung*. Cologne: J. P. Bachem, 1880.

Herzig, Tamar. "Witches, Saints, and Heretics: Heinrich Kramer's Ties with Italian Women Mystics." *Magic, Ritual, and Witchcraft* 1, no. 1 (2006): 23–55.

Hillenbrand, Eugen. "Die Observantenbewegung in der deutschen Ordensprovinz der Dominikaner." In *Reformbemühungen und Observanzbestrebungen im spätmittelalterlichen Ordenswesen*, edited by Kaspar Elm, 219–72. Berlin: Duncker & Humblot, 1989.

Hirai, Hiro, ed. *Jacques Gaffarel: Between Magic and Science*. Bruniana & Campanelliana Supplementi 39. Pisa: Fabrizio Serra, 2014.

Hödl, Ludwig. "'Opus naturae est opus intelligentiae': Ein neuplatonisches Axiom im aristotelischen Verständnis des Albertus Magnus." In *Averroismus im Mittelalter und in der Renaissance*, edited by Friedrich Niewöhner and Loris Sturlese, 132–48. Zurich: Spur Verlag, 1994.

Holzapfel, Egidius. *Werner Rolevincks Bauernspiegel: Untersuchung und Neuherausgabe von "De regimine rusticorum."* Freiburger theologische Studien 76. Basel: Herder, 1959.

Horowitz, Maryanne Cline. "Gabriel Naudé's *Apology for Great Men Suspected of Magic*: Variations in Editions from 1625 to 1715." In *Histories of Heresy in Early Modern Europe: For, Against, and Beyond Persecution and Toleration*, edited by J. C. Laursen, 61–75. New York: Palgrave Macmillan, 2002.
Horst, Georg Konrad. *Von der alten und neuen Magie: Ursprung, Idee, Umfang, und Geschichte*. Mainz: Florian Kupferberg, 1820.
Hugh of Saint Victor. *Didascalicon de studio legendi*. Edited by Charles Henry Buttimer. Washington, DC: Catholic University Press, 1939.
Huser, Johannes, ed. *Bücher und Schrifften des ... Philippi Theophrasti Bombast von Hohenheim, Paracelsi genannt*. Basel: Conrad Waldkirch, 1589–91; Strasbourg: Zetzner, 1605.
———. *Opera omnia*. Edited by J. P. Migne. Patrologia Latina 176. Paris: Garnier Fratres, 1880.
Index operum B. Alberti Magni ... desumptus ex iis quae R. P. F. Bernardinus Gausolinus in laudem dicti typis dedit anno 1630 ... omnia ejusdem opera continens, quorum, vel in historiis vel in diversis bibliothecis memoria conservatur; nunc novo prælo excusus pro editione integra, quam curante reverendissimo Patre F. Thoma Turco generali ejusdem ordinis hoc anno 1646 inceperunt DD. Claudius Prost, Petrus et Claudius Rigaud fratres, Hieronymus de la Garde, et Joannes Antonius Huguetan bibliopolae Lugdunenses.... Paris: G. Sassier, 1646.
Ingham, Patricia Clare. "Conjuring Roger Bacon." In *The Medieval New: Ambivalence in an Age of Innovation*, edited by Patricia Clare Ingham, 48–72. Philadelphia: University of Pennsylvania Press, 2015.
Isidorus Hispalensis. *Etymologiarum sive Originum libri xx*. Edited by W. M. Lindsay. Oxford: Clarendon Press, 1911.
———. *The Etymologies*. Edited by Stephen A. Barney, W. J. Lewis, J. A. Beach, and Oliver Berghof. Cambridge: Cambridge University Press, 2006.
Jammy, Pierre, ed. *Beati Alberti Magni Ratisbonensis episcopi ordinis praedicatorum opera*. 21 vols. Lyon: Claudius Prost et al., 1651.
———. *Veritates de auxilio gratiae, ab erroribus et falsis opinionibus vindicatae*. Grenoble: Pierre Fremon, 1659.
Jaumann, Herbert. "*Respublica litteraria*: Partei mit einem Programm der Parteilosigkeit: Gegen das anachronistische Mißverständnis eines mehrdeutigen Konzepts der Frühen Neuzeit." *Aufklärung* 26 (2014): 17–30.
Jeck, Udo Reinhold. "Albert der Große über die Natur der Metalle: Ein Beitrag zur Geschichte des Hermetismus in der Philosophie des 13. Jahrhunderts." *System und Struktur* 6 (1998): 121–37.
———. "*Materia, forma substantialis, transmutatio*: Frühe Bemerkungen Alberts des Großen zur Naturphilosophie und Alchemie." *Documenti e studi sulla tradizione filosofica medievale* 5 (1994): 205–40.
———. "Platons Götter im lateinischen Mittelalter: Ein Beitrag zur Rezeption des platonischen Timaios bei Augustin, Calcidius und Albertus Magnus." *Bochumer philosophisches Jahrbuch für Antike und Mittelalter* 14 (2011): 157–90.
———. "Virtus Lapidum: Zur philosophischen Begründung der magischen Wirksamkeit und der physikalischen Beschaffenheit kostbarer Mineralien in der Naturphilosophie Alberts des Grossen." *Early Science and Medicine* 5 (2000): 33–46.
Jerouschek, Günter. Introduction to *Malleus Maleficarum (1487) von Heinrich Kramer (Institoris)*, v–lv. Hildesheim: Georg Olms Verlag, 1992.
Johnson, Timothy J. "Preaching Precedes Theology: Roger Bacon on the Failure of Mendicant Education." *Franciscan Studies* 68 (2010): 83–95.
Johnston, Sarah Iles. "Animating Statues: A Case Study in Ritual." *Arethusa* 41, no. 3 (2008): 445–77.
Josephson-Storm, Jason Ā. *The Myth of Disenchantment: Magic, Modernity, and the Birth of the Human Sciences*. Chicago: University of Chicago Press, 2017.

Kahlos, Maijastina. "The Early Church." In *The Cambridge History of Magic and Witchcraft in the West*, edited by David J. Collins, 148–82. Cambridge: Cambridge University Press, 2015.

Kahn, Didier. *Alchimie et paracelsisme en France à la fin de la Renaissance 1567–1625*. Cahiers d'Humanisme et Renaissance. Geneva: Droz, 2007.

———. "The Rosicrucian Hoax in France (1623–1624)." In *Secrets of Nature*, edited by William Royall Newman and Anthony Grafton, 235–344. Cambridge, MA: MIT Press, 2001.

"Kaltyser, Peter." In *Allgemeines Lexikon der bildenden Künstler von der Antike bis zur Gegenwart (Ingouville-Kauffungen)*, edited by Hans Vollmer, 19:490. Leipzig: E. A. Seemann, 1926.

Kaluza, Zénon. "Gerson critique d'Albert le Grand." *Freiburger Zeitschrift für Philosophie und Theologie* 45 (1998): 169–206.

Keil, G. "Rolevinck, Werner." In *Die deutsche Literatur des Mittelalters: Verfasserlexikon*, edited by Wolfgant Stammler and Karl Langosch, 8:140–53. 2nd, rev. ed. Berlin: Walter de Gruyter, 1992.

Kelley, Donald R. *Faces of History: Historical Inquiry from Herodotus to Herder*. New Haven, CT: Yale University Press, 1998.

———. "The Theory of History." In *The Cambridge History of Renaissance Philosophy*, edited by Charles B. Schmitt, Quentin Skinner, Eckhard Kessler, and Jill Kraye, 746–61. Cambridge: Cambridge University Press, 1988.

Kibre, Pearl. "Albertus Magnus, *De occultis naturae*: Latin Text." *Osiris* 13 (1958): 157–83.

———. "Albertus Magnus on Alchemy." In *Albertus Magnus and the Sciences*, edited by James A. Weisheipl, 187–202. Toronto: Pontifical Institute of Mediaeval Studies, 1980.

———. "An Alchemical Tract Attributed to Albertus Magnus." *Isis* 35, no. 4 (1944): 303–16.

———. "Alchemical Writings Ascribed to Albertus Magnus." *Speculum* 17, no. 4 (1942): 499–518.

———. "The *Alkimia minor* Ascribed to Albertus Magnus." *Isis* 32, no. 2 (1940): 267–300.

———. "The *De occultis naturae* Attributed to Albertus Magnus." *Osiris* 11 (1954): 23–39.

———. "Further Manuscripts Containing Alchemical Tracts Attributed to Albertus Magnus." *Speculum* 34, no. 2 (1959): 238–47.

Kieckhefer, Richard. *European Witch Trials: Their Foundations in Popular and Learned Culture, 1300–1500*. Berkeley: University of California Press, 1976.

———. *Magic in the Middle Ages*. 3rd ed. Cambridge: Cambridge University Press, 2022.

———. "Rethinking How to Define Magic." In *The Routledge History of Medieval Magic*, edited by Sophie Page and Catherine Rider, 15–25. London: Routledge, 2019.

Kirk, G. S. "A Passage in *De plantis*." *Classical Review* 6, no. 1 (1956): 5–6.

Knape, Joachim. *Poetik und Rhetorik in Deutschland, 1300–1700*. Gratia: Bamberger Schriften zur Renaissanceforschung. Wiesbaden: Harrassowitz, 2006.

Korner, Hermann. *Chronica Novella*. Edited by Jakob Schwalm. Göttingen: Vandenhoeck & Ruprecht, 1895.

Kors, Alan Charles. *Atheism in France, 1650–1729*. Princeton, NJ: Princeton University Press, 1990.

———. *Epicureans and Atheists in France, 1650–1729*. New York: Cambridge University Press, 2016.

———. *Naturalism and Unbelief in France, 1650–1729*. New York: Cambridge University Press, 2016.

Kramer, Heinrich "Institoris." In *Malleus Maleficarum*, edited by Christopher S. Mackay, 1:83–103. Cambridge: Cambridge University Press, 2006.

Krause, Katja, and Henryk Anzulewicz. "From Content to Method: The *Liber de causis* in Albert the Great: Western Scholarly Networks and Debates." In *Reading Proclus and the "Book of Causes,"* edited by Dragos Calma, 1:180–208. Leiden: Brill, 2019.

Kristeller, Paul Oskar. "Between the Italian Renaissance and the French Enlightenment: Gabriel Naudé as an Editor." *Renaissance Quarterly* 32, no. 1 (1979): 41–72.

Kusche, B. "Zur *Secreta Mulierum*-Forschung." *Janus: Revue internationale de l'histoire des sciences, de la medecine, de la pharmacie, et de la technique* 62 (1975): 103–23.
Lancien, Christina. "'Der nützliche Gebrauch einer großen Bibliothek' Vorschläge zum Bibliotheksaufbau von Gabriel Naudé und Gottfried Wilhelm Leibniz." *Bibliothek Forschung und Praxis* 14 (1990): 113–31.
Lancre, Pierre de. *L'incrédulité et mescréance du sortilège.* Paris: Nicolas Buon, 1622.
Landes, Richard Allen. "The Fear of an Apocalyptic Year 1000: Augustinian Historiography, Medieval and Modern." In *The Apocalyptic Year 1000*, edited by Richard Allen Landes, Andrew Colin Gow, and David C. Van Meter, 243–70. Oxford: Oxford University Press, 2003.
Latour, Bruno. *Nous n'avons jamais été modernes: Essai d'anthropologie symétrique.* Paris: La Découverte, 1991.
———. *We Have Never Been Modern.* Translated by Catherine Porter. Cambridge, MA: Harvard University Press, 1993.
Laurentus, C. "Colonien. seu Ordinis Praedicatorum Canonizationis beati Alberti Magni Ordinis Praedicatorum et Episcopi Ratisbonensis." *Analecta sacri ordinis Fratrum Praedicatorum* 39 (1931): 212.
Le Franc, Martin. *Le champion des dames.* Edited by Robert Deschaux. 4 vols. Paris: Champion, 1999.
———. "Le champion des dames—Livre IV, vv. 17377–18200." In *L'imaginaire du sabbat: Edition critique des textes les plus anciens (1430 c.–1440 c.)*, edited by Martine Ostorero, Agostino Paravicini Bagliani, Kathrin Utz Tremp, and Catherine Chène, 439–508. Cahiers lausannois d'histoire médiévale. Lausanne: Université de Lausanne, 1999.
Lehmann, Hartmut, and Otto Ulbricht. "Motive und Argumente von Gegnern der Hexenverfolgung von Weyer bis Spee." In *Vom Unfug des Hexen-Processes*, edited by Hartmut Lehmann and Otto Ulbricht, 1–14. Wiesbaden: Harrossowitz, 1992.
Lemay, Helen Rodnite, ed. *Women's Secrets: A Translation of Pseudo-Albertus Magnus' "De secretis mulierum" with Commentaries.* Albany: State University of New York, 1992.
Lerner, Michel-Pierre. *Tommaso Campanella en France au XVIIe siècle.* Istituto italiano per gli studi filosofici lezioni della Scuola di studi superiori in Napoli. Naples: Bibliopolis, 1995.
Lévesque, Jean Donatien. *Les frères prêcheurs de Lyon: Notre Dame de Confort, 1218–1789.* Lyon: Mainoz, 1978.
Lévi, Éliphas. *Dogme et rituel de la haute magie.* Vol. 1. Paris: Germer Baillière, 1861.
Libera, Alain de. "Albert le Grand et Thomas d'Aquin Interprètes du *Liber de Causis*." *Revue des Sciences philosophiques et théologiques* 74 (1990): 347–78.
———. "La face cachée du monde." *Critique* 59 (2003): 430–48.
———. *Métaphysique et noétique Albert le Grand.* Edited by Jean-François Courtine. Problèmes et controverses. Paris: J. Vrin, 2005.
Loë, Paulus von. "De vita et scriptis b. Alberti Magni." *Analecta bollandiana* 19 (1900): 257–84.
———. "De vita et scriptis b. Alberti Magni." *Analecta bollandiana* 20 (1901): 273–316.
———. "De vita et scriptis b. Alberti Magni." *Analecta bollandiana* 21 (1902): 361–71.
———. *Statistisches über die Ordensprovinz Teutonia.* Quellen und Forschungen zur Geschichte des Dominikanerordens in Deutschland 1. Leipzig: Otto Harrassowitz, 1907.
Löffler, Katrin. "Wer schrieb den Zedler? Eine Spurensuche." *Leipziger Jahrbuch zur Buchgeschichte* 16 (2007): 265–83.
Löhr, Gabriel M. *Beiträge zur Geschichte des Kölner Dominikanerklosters im Mittelalter.* Quellen und Forschungen zur Geschichte des Dominikanerordens in Deutschland 16–17. Leipzig: Otto Harrassowitz, 1922.

———. *Die Teutonia im fünfzehnten Jahrhundert: Studien und Texte vornehmlich zur Geschichte ihrer Reform*. Quellen und Forschungen zur Geschichte des Dominikanerordens in Deutschland 19. Leipzig: Otto Harrassowitz, 1924.

———. "Die zweite Blütezeit des Kölner Dominikanerklosters (1464–1525)." *Archivum Fratrum Praedicatorum* 19 (1949): 208–54.

Longo, C. "Jammy, Pierre." In *Dictionnaire d'histoire et de géographie ecclésiastiques*, edited by Roger Aubert and Jean-Pierre Hendrickx, 862–63. Paris: Letouzey et Ané, 1997.

Loveland, Jeff. "Encyclopaedias and Genre, 1670–1750." *Journal for Eighteenth-Century Studies* 36, no. 2 (2013): 159–75.

———. *The European Encyclopaedia from 1650 to the Twenty-First Century*. Cambridge: Cambridge University Press, 2019.

Lucentini, Paolo. "L'ermetismo magico nel secolo XIII." In *Sic itur ad astra*, edited by Menso Folkerts and Richard Lorch, 409–50. Wiesbaden: Harrassowitz, 2000.

———. "Sulla questione della magia nella storia del peniero medievale." *Giornale critico della filosofia italiana* 82 (2004): 257–74.

Luis de Valladolid. "Historia de vita et doctrina Alberti Magni." *Subsidia hagiographica* 1 (1889): 96–105.

———. "Tabula Alberti Magni aliorumque scriptorum ordinis Praedicatorum." *Archivum Fratrum Praedicatorum* 1 (1931): 243–50.

Magdalius, Jacobus. "Legenda compendiosa et metrica domini Alberti magni." In *Legenda litteralis Alberti*, A'-ii-r–B'-i-r. Cologne: Johannes Koelhoff de Lubeck, 1490.

Maier, Michael. *Symbola aureae mensae duodecim nationum. Hoc est, Hermaea seu Mercurii festa*. Frankfurt: Anton Humm, 1617.

———. *Themis aurea, hoc est, de legibus fraternitatis R[osea] C[rucis]*. Frankfurt: Lucas Jennis, 1618.

———. *Verum inventum, hoc est Munera Germaniae*. Frankfurt: Lucas Jennis, 1619.

Malvenda, Tomas. *Commentaria in Sacram Scripturam, una cum nova de verb ad verbum ex hebr. translatione*. 5 vols. Lyon: C. Prost, 1650.

Mandosio, Jean-Marc. "Problèmes et controverses: À propos de quelques publications récentes sur la magie au Moyen Âge et à la Renaissance." *Aries* 7 (2007): 207–25.

Manget, Jean-Jacques, ed. *Bibliotheca chemica curiosa*. Vol. 1. Geneva: Chouet, G. de Tournes, et al., 1702.

Marcil-Lacoste, Louise. "Hypothèses sur l'historicité du savoir philosophique." *Proceedings of the American Catholic Philosophical Association* 52 (1978): 204–12.

Marks, Richard Bruce. *The Medieval Manuscript Library of the Charterhouse of St. Barbara in Cologne*. 2 vols. Analecta Cartusiana. Salzburg: Institut für Englische Sprache und Literatur der Universität Salzburg, 1974.

Marrone, Steven P. "Magic and Natural Philosophy." In *The Routledge History of Medieval Magic*, edited by Sophie Page and Catherine Rider, 287–98. London: Routledge, 2019.

———. "William of Auvergne on Magic in Natural Philosophy and Theology." In *Was ist Philosophie im Mittelalter?*, edited by Jan A. Aertsen and Andreas Speer, 741–48. Miscellanea Mediaevalia. Berlin: Walter de Gruyter, 1998.

Martin, Craig. *Subverting Aristotle: Religion, History, and Philosophy in Early Modern Science*. Baltimore: Johns Hopkins University Press, 2014.

Matytsin, Anton M. *The Specter of Skepticism in the Age of Enlightenment*. Baltimore: Johns Hopkins University Press, 2016.

McEvoy, James J. *Robert Grosseteste*. Oxford: Oxford University Press, 2000.

Meersseman, Gilles, ed. *Laurentii Pignon catalogi et chronica, accedunt catalogi stamsensis et upsalensis scriptorum O.P.* Monumenta ordinis praedicatorum 18. Rome: Institutum historicum fratrum praedicatorum, 1936.

———. "Die neue Kölner (1951) und die erste Lyoner (1651) Gesamtausgabe der Werke Alberts des Großen." *Divus Thomas: Jahrbuch für Philosophie und spekulative Theologie* 30 (1952): 102–14.

Meijer, G. A. *Dominikanenklooster en Statie te Nijmegen*. Nijmegen, 1892.
Menzel, Michael. *Die Sächsische Weltchronik: Quellen und Stoffauswahl*. Vorträge und Forschungen. Sigmaringen: J. Thorbecke, 1985.
Mertens, Dieter. "Landeschronistik im Zeitalter des Humanismus und ihre spätmittelalterlichen Wurzeln." In *Deutsche Landesgeschichtsschreibung*, edited by Franz Brendle, Dieter Mertens, Anton Schindling, and Walter Ziegler, 19–31. Stuttgart: Steiner, 2001.
Meyer, E. H. F. *Nicolai Damasceni "De plantis" libri duo Aristoteli vulgo adscripti*. Leipzig: Leopold Voss, 1841.
Miller, Arnold. "Louis Moréri's *Grand dictionnaire historique*." In *Notable Encyclopedias of the Seventeenth and Eighteenth Centuries*, edited by Frank A. Kafker, 13–52. Oxford: Voltaire Foundation, 1981.
Miller, Peter N. *Peiresc's Europe: Learning and Virtue in the Seventeenth Century*. New Haven, CT: Yale University Press, 2000.
Mireaux, Émile. "Gabriel Naudé et la bibliothèque mazarine." *Revue des Deux Mondes (1829–1971)* 22 (1954): 353–62.
Molhuysen, P. C. *Nieuw Nederlandsch Biografisch Woordenboek*. Vol. 1. Leiden: A. W. Sijthoff's uitgevers-maatschappij, 1911.
Molland, A. George. "Roger Bacon as Magician." *Traditio* 30 (1974): 445–60.
"Monumenta cultus B. Alberti Magni." *Analecta sacri ordinis Fratrum Praedicatorum* 3 (1897): 349–65.
Moran, Bruce T. *Distilling Knowledge: Alchemy, Chemistry, and the Scientific Revolution*. New Histories of Science, Technology, and Medicine. Cambridge, MA: Harvard University Press, 2005.
———. "Paracelsianism." In *Dictionary of Gnosis and Western Esotericism*, edited by Wouter J. Hanegraaff, 915–22. Leiden: Brill, 2006.
Moréri, Louis. *Le Grand Dictionnaire historique, ou Le mélange curieux de l'histoire sacrée et profane*. Lyon: Jean Girin et Barthelemy Riviere, 1674.
———. *Le Grand Dictionnaire historique, ou Le mélange curieux de l'histoire sacrée et profane*. 2 vols. Lyon: Jean Girin et Barthelemy Riviere, 1681.
———. *Le Grand Dictionnaire historique, ou Le mélange curieux de l'histoire sacrée et profane*. Edited by Jean Le Clerc. Utrecht: Francois Halma, Guillaume vande Water, et al., 1692.
———. *Le Grand Dictionnaire historique, ou Le mélange curieux de l'histoire sacrée et profane*. Paris: Denis Mariette, 1718.
———. *Le Grand Dictionnaire historique, ou Le mélange curieux de l'histoire sacrée et profane*. Edited by Etienne-Francois Drouet. Paris: Les libraires associés, 1759.
Naudé, Gabriel. *Advis pour dresser une bibliothèque*. Paris: François Targa, 1627.
———. *Apologie pour tous les grands personnages qui ont esté faussement soupçonnez de magie*. Paris: François Targa, 1625.
———. "Apologie pour tous les grands personnages qui ont été faussement soupçonnés de magie." In *Libertins du XVIIe siècle*, edited by Jacques Prévot, 137–380. Bibliothèque de la Pléiade. Paris: Gallimard, 1998.
———. *Causae Kempensis coniectio pro curia Romana*. Paris: Sebastian and Gabriel Cramoisy, 1651.
———. *Considérations politiques sur les coups d'Etat*. Le Temps et l'histoire. Paris: Les Éditions de Paris, 1989.
———. *The History of Magick by way of Apology for All the Wise Men Who Have Unjustly Been Reputed Magicians from the Creation to the Present Age*. Translated by John Davies. London: John Streater, 1657.
———. *Instruction à la France sur la vérité de l'histoire des frères de la Rose-Croix*. Paris: F. Julliot, 1623.
———. *Lettres de Gabriel Naudé à Jacques Dupuy (1632–1652)*. Edited by Phillip J. Wolfe. Edmonton: Lealta / Alta Press, 1982.

———. *Le Marfore, ou Discours contre les libelles: Quae tanta Insania Cives?* Paris: Louis Boulenger, 1620.

———. "Schutz=Schrifft, worin alle vornehmen Leute, die der Zauberey fälschlich beschuldiget sind, vertheidiget werden." In *Kurtze Lehr=Sätze von dem Laster der Zauberey*, edited by Christian Thomasius, 1–268. Halle: Renger, 1704.

———. *Über den Zauberglauben und andere Schwärmereien; oder Vertheidigung berühmter Männer, die von ihren Zeitgenossen für Zauberer gehalten worden.* Leipzig: Weygand, 1787.

Nelles, Paul. "The Library as an Instrument of Discovery: Gabriel Naudé and the Uses of History." In *History and the Disciplines*, edited by Donald R. Kelley, 41–57. Rochester, NY: University of Rochester Press, 1997.

Newman, William R. "Brian Vickers on Alchemy and the Occult: A Response." *Perspectives on Science* 17, no. 4 (2009): 482–506.

———. "From Alchemy to 'Chymistry.'" In *The Cambridge History of Science*, edited by Katharine Park and Lorraine Daston, 3:497–517. Cambridge: Cambridge University Press, 2006.

———. "Medieval Alchemy." In *The Cambridge History of Science*, edited by David C. Lindberg, Ronald L. Numbers, and Roy Porter, 2:385–403. Cambridge: Cambridge University Press, 2013.

———. "What Have We Learned from the Recent Historiography of Alchemy?" *Isis* 102, no. 2 (2011): 313–21.

Newman, William R., and Lawrence M. Principe. "Alchemy Versus Chemistry: The Etymological Origins of a Historiographical Mistake." *Early Science and Medicine* 3 (1998): 32–65.

North, John D. "Astronomy and Astrology." In *The Cambridge History of Science*, edited by David C. Lindberg, Ronald L. Numbers, and Roy Porter, 2:456–84. Cambridge: Cambridge University Press, 2013.

Otto, Bernd-Christian. "A Catholic 'Magician' Historicises 'Magic': Éliphas Lévi's *Histoire de la Magie*." In *History and Religion: Narrating a Religious Past*, edited by Bernd-Christian Otto, Susanne Rau, and Jörg Rüpke, 419–43. Berlin: Walter de Gruyter, 2015.

———. "A Discourse Historical Approach Towards Medieval Learned Magic." In *The Routledge History of Medieval Magic*, edited by Sophie Page and Catherine Rider, 37–47. London: Routledge, 2019.

———. "Historicising 'Western Learned Magic': Preliminary Remarks." *Aries* 16, no. 2 (2016): 161–240.

———. *Magie: Rezeptions- und diskursgeschichtliche Analysen von der Antike bis zur Neuzeit. Religionsgeschichtliche Versuche und Vorarbeiten.* Berlin: Walter de Gruyter, 2011.

Paganini, Gianni. "The Ways of Clandestinity: Radical Cartesianism and Deism in Robert Challe (1659–1721)." In *Between Secularization and Reform*, edited by Anna Tomaszewska, 131–59. Leiden: Brill, 2022.

———. "Wie aus Gesetzgebern Betrüger werden: Eine philosophische Archäologie des 'radikalen' Libertinismus." In *Radikalaufklärung*, edited by Jonathan I. Israel and Martin Mulsow, 49–91. Berlin: Suhrkamp, 2014.

Page, Sophie, and Catherine Rider, eds. *The Routledge History of Medieval Magic.* Routledge Histories. London: Routledge, 2019.

Palazzo, Alessandro. "Albert the Great's Doctrine of Fascination in the Context of his Philosophical System." In *Via Alberti*, edited by Ludger Honnefelder, Hannes Möhle, and Susana Bullido del Barrio, 135–215. Münster: Aschendorff, 2009.

———. "The Scientific Significance of Fate and Celestial Influences in Some Mature Works by Albert the Great: *De fato, De somno et vigilia, De intellectu et intelligibili, Mineralia*." In *Per perscrutationem philosophicam: Neue Perspektiven der mittelalterlichen Forschung*, edited by A. Beccarisi, R. Imbach, and P. Porro, 55–78. CPTMA Beiheft. Hamburg: Felix Meiner, 2008.

———. "Ulrich of Strasbourg's Philosophical Theology: Textual and Doctrinal Remarks on 'De summo bono.'" In *Schüler und Meister*, edited by Andreas Speer and Thomas Jeschke, 205–42. Berlin: Walter de Gruyter, 2016.

Pantin, Isabelle. "New Philosophy and Old Prejudices: Aspects of the Reception of Copernicanism in a Divided Europe." *Studies in the History and Philosophy of Science* 30, no. 2 (1999): 237–62.

Papi, Anna Benvenuti. "Corsini, Matteo." In *Dizionario Biografico degli Italiani*, edited by Alberto Maria Ghisalberti, 29:644–47. Rome: Istituto della Enciclopedia italiana, 1983.

Paravicini Bagliani, Agostino. "La légende médiévale d'Albert le Grand (1270–1435): Premières recherches." *Micrologus* 21 (2013): 295–367.

———. "Le 'Speculum astronomiae': Enquête sur les manuscrits." In *Albertus Magnus*, edited by Walter Senner, 401–11. Berlin: Akademie Verlag, 2001.

———. *Le "Speculum Astronomiae," une énigme? Enquête sur les manuscrits*. Micrologus' Library 6. Florence: SISMEL: Edizioni del Galluzzo, 2001.

Peach, Trevor. "Contre l'histoire et les historiens: *Les Succinctz adversaires* de Charles de la Ruelle (1572–1574)." *Bibliothèque d'Humanisme et Renaissance* 65 (2003): 69–82.

Pelster, Franz. *Kritische Studien zum Leben und zu den Schriften Alberts des Großen*. Stimmen der Zeit, Ergänzungsheft: Forschungen 4. Freiburg: Herder, 1920.

Pepper, John Henry. *Cyclopaedic Science Simplified*. London: Frederick Warne, 1869.

Pertz, Georg Heinrich, ed. *Chronica et annales aevi Salici*. Monumenta Germaniae Historica. Scriptores (in Folio) 6. Hannover: Hahn, 1844.

Peters, Edward M. *The Magician, the Witch, and the Law*. Philadelphia: University of Pennsylvania Press, 1978.

Petrus Alfonsi. *Dialogue Against the Jews*. Edited by Irven Michael Resnick. Washington, DC: Catholic University of America Press, 2006.

Petrus de Abano (Pseudo). "'Annulorum experimenta.'" In *Médecine, astrologie et magie*, edited by Jean-Patrice Boudet, 270–86. Florence: SISMEL, 2013.

Petrus de Alliaco. *Concordantia astronomiae cum theologia*. Augsburg: Erhard Ratdolt, 1490.

Petrus Hispanus Portugalensis [Peter of Spain]. *Tractatus*. Philosophical Texts and Studies 22. Assen: Van Gorcum, 1972.

Petzoldt, Leander. "Albertus Magnus." *Enzyklopädie des Märchens* 1 (1977): 255–61.

———. "Albertus Mag(n)us: Albert der Grosse und die magische Tradition des Mittelalters." In *Verführer, Schurken, Magier*, edited by Ulrich Müller, and Werner Wunderlich, 27–46. Mittelaltermythen (Mittelaltermythen). St. Gallen: UVK, 2001.

Peukert, Will-Erich. *Das Rosenkreutz*. 2nd, rev. ed. Pansophie 3. Berlin: Erich Schmidt, 1973.

Pico della Mirandola, Giovanni. "Apologia." In *Opera Omnia*, 1:114–240. Basel: Officina Henricpetrina, 1572.

———. *Disputationes adversus astrologiam divinatricem a cura*. Edited by Eugenio Garin. 2 vols. Edizione nazionale dei classici del pensiero italiano. Florence: Vallecchi, 1946–52.

Pietsch, Andreas. "*Libertinage érudit*, Dissimulation, Nikodemismus: Zur Erforschung gelehrter Devianz." In *Diskurse der Gelehrtenkultur in der Frühen Neuzeit*, edited by Herbert Jaumann, 163–96. Berlin: Walter de Gruyter, 2016.

Pintard, René. *Le libertinage érudit dans la première moitié du XVIIe siècle*. 2nd, rev. ed. Geneva: Slatkine, 2000.

Pius II (Aeneas Silvius Piccolomineus). *Orationes politicae et ecclesiasticae*. Edited by Joannes Dominicus Mansi. 3 vols. Lucca: Ph. M. Benedini, 1755–59.

Pius XI. "In thesauris sapientiae." *Acta apostolicae sedis* 24 (1932): 5–16.

Pius XII. "Ad Deum." *Acta apostolicae sedis* 34 (1942): 89–91.

Polidori, Filippo-Luigi, ed. *Rosaio della vita trattato morale attribuito a Matteo de' Corsini e composto nel MCCCLXXIII*. Florence: Societa Poligrafica Italiana, 1845.

Pomponazzi, Pietro. *De incantationibus*. Edited by V. Perrone Compagni. Lessico intellettuale europeo. Florence: Olschki, 2011.

Popkin, Richard H. *The History of Scepticism from Savonarola to Bayle*. Oxford: Oxford University Press, 2003.
Poppe, Johann Heinrich Moritz von. *Neuer Wunder-Schauplatz*. Stuttgart: J. Scheible, 1839.
Porreca, David. "Albertus Magnus and Hermes Trismegistus: An Update." *Mediaeval Studies* 72 (2010): 245–81.
Postulator General of the Order of Preachers, ed. *Esposizione e documentazione storica del culto tributato lungo il corso dei secoli al B. Alberto Magno, Vescovo e Confessore dell'Ordine Domenicano*. Rome: Scuola Tipografica Missionaria Domenicana, 1930.
―――, ed. *Esposizione e documentazione storica del culto tributato lungo il corso dei secoli al B. Alberto Magno, Vescovo e Confessore dell'Ordine Domenicano: Supplemento*. Rome: Scuola Tipografica Missionaria Domenicana, 1931.
Power, Amanda. "A Mirror for Every Age: The Reputation of Roger Bacon." *English Historical Review* 121, no. 492 (2006): 657–92.
―――. *Roger Bacon and the Defence of Christendom*. Cambridge Studies in Medieval Life and Thought. Cambridge: Cambridge University Press, 2013.
Price, Betsy Barker. "Interpreting Albert the Great on Astronomy." In *A Companion to Albert the Great*, edited by Irven Michael Resnick, 397–436. Leiden: Brill, 2013.
Ptolomaeus Lucensis. "Historia ecclesiastica nova." In *Rerum Italicarum Scriptores*, edited by G. Muratori, 11:754–1242. Milan: Societas Palatina, 1727.
―――. *Historia ecclesiastica nova*. Edited by Ottavio Clavuot and Ludwig Schmugge. Monumenta Germaniae Historica, Scriptores. Hannover: Hahnsche Buchhandlung, 2009.
Puff, Helmut. "Female Sodomy: The Trial of Katherina Hetzeldorfer (1477)." *Journal of Medieval and Early Modern Studies* 30, no. 1 (2000): 41–61.
Quentin, H. (Relator Generalis). *Inquisitio iussu sanctissimi domini nostri Pii papae xi peracta de vita b. Alberti Magni o.p. episcopi Ratisbonensis et de cultu ei praestito*. Sacred Conregation of Rites, Historical Section. Rome: Typi polyglotti Vaticani, 1931.
Quétif, Jacobus, and Jacobus Échard. *Scriptores ordinis praedicatorum recensiti*. Paris: J. B. Christopher Ballard, 1719–23.
Quinlan-McGrath, Mary. *Influences: Art, Optics, and Astrology in the Italian Renaissance*. Chicago: University of Chicago Press, 2013.
Raguseus, Georgius. *Epistolarum mathematicarum seu de divinatione libri duo*. Paris: Nicolas Buon, 1623.
Raleigh, Walter. *The History of the World*. London: Walter Burre, 1614.
Raynaud, Théophile *Hoplotheca contra ictum calumniae*. Lyon: Philippe Borde et al., 1650.
Reichert, Benedictus Maria, ed. *Registrum litterarum: Salvi Cassettae (1481–1483), Barnabae Saxoni (1486)*. Quellen und Forschungen zur Geschichte des Dominikanerordens in Deutschland 7. Leipzig: Otto Harrassowitz, 1912.
Resnick, Irven Michael. "Albert the Great: Biographical Introduction." In *A Companion to Albert the Great*, edited by Irven Michael Resnick, 1–11. Leiden: Brill, 2013.
―――, ed. *A Companion to Albert the Great: Theology, Philosophy, and the Sciences*. Leiden: Brill, 2013.
Rice, James V. *Gabriel Naudé, 1600–1653*. Studies in Romance Literatures and Languages. Baltimore: Johns Hopkins University Press, 1939.
Riché, Pierre. *Gerbert d'Aurillac: Le pape de l'an mil*. Paris: Fayard, 1987.
Ricklin, Thomas. "Der Philosoph als Nekromant: Gerbert von Aurillac (Sylvester II.) und Vergil im europäischen Hochmittelalter." *Interfaces* 1 (2015): 236–64.
Riddle, John M., and James A. Mulholland. "Albert on Stones and Minerals." In *Albertus Magnus and the Sciences*, edited by James A. Weisheipl, 203–34. Toronto: Pontifical Institute of Mediaeval Studies, 1980.
Rinotas, Athanasios. "Alchemy and Creation in the Work of Albertus Magnus." *Conatus* 3 (2018): 63–74.
―――. "The *Sciant artifices* in the Work of Albert the Great: Towards Two Kinds of Transmutation?" *Early Science and Medicine* 27 (2022): 57–82.

Riolan, Jean. *Ad Libavi maniam Ioannis Riolani responsio*. Paris: Adrian Perier, 1606.
Roberti, Johannes. *Goclenius Heautonti morumenos*. Luxembourg: Hubertus Reulandt, 1618.
Roberts, Hugh. "Obscenity and the Politics of Authorship in Early Seventeenth-Century France: Guillaume Colletet and the *Parnasse des poetes satyriques* (1622)." *French Studies* 68 (2014): 18–33.
Ross, Walter W. "Antoine Furetière's *Dictionnaire universel*." In *Notable Encyclopedias of the Seventeenth and Eighteenth Centuries*, edited by Frank A. Kafker, 53–67. Oxford: Voltaire Foundation, 1981.
Rovelstad, Mathilde V. "Two Seventeenth-Century Library Handbooks, Two Different Library Theories." *Libraries and Culture* 35, no. 4 (2000): 540–56.
Rutkin, H. Darrel. "Astrology." In *The Cambridge History of Science*, edited by Katharine Park and Lorraine Daston, 3:541–62. Cambridge: Cambridge University Press, 2006.
———. "Astrology and Magic." In *A Companion to Albert the Great*, edited by Irven Michael Resnick, 451–505. Leiden: Brill, 2013.
———. *Sapientia astrologica: Astrology, Magic and Natural Knowledge, ca. 1250–1800*. Archimedes: New Studies in the History and Philosophy of Science. Cham: Springer International, 2019.
Sabbadini, Remigio. "Giovanni Colonna, biografo e bibliografo del secolo XIV." *Atti della Reale Accademia di Scienze di Torino* 46 (1911): 282–305, 830–59.
Sächsische Weltchronik. Deutsche Chroniken und andere Geschichtsbücher des Mittelalters 2. Hannover: Hahn, 1877.
Salimbene of Parma. *Cronica*. 2 vols. Corpus christianorum continuatio mediaevalis. Turnhout: Brepols, 1998–99.
Sannino, Antonella. *Il "De mirabilibus mundi" tra tradizione magica e filosofia naturale*. Micrologus' Library. Florence: SISMEL, 2011.
Scheeben, Heribert Christian. *Albert der Große: Zur Chronologie seines Lebens*. Quellen und Forschungen zur Geschichte des Dominikanerordens in Deutschland 27. Leipzig: Otto Harrassowitz, 1931.
———. *Albertus Magnus*. Religiöse Schriftenreihe der Buchgemeinde Bonn 8. Bonn: Buchgemeinde, 1932.
———. *Albertus Magnus*. Cologne: J. P. Bachem, 1955.
———. "Les écrits d'Albert le Grand d'après les catalogues." *Revue Thomiste*, n.s., 14 (1931): 260–92.
———. "Zur Chronologie des Lebens Alberts des Großen." *Divus Thomas* 10 (1932): 363–418.
Schibanoff, Susan. "True Lies: Transvestism and Idolatry in the Trial of Joan of Arc." In *Fresh Verdicts on Joan of Arc*, edited by Bonnie Wheeler and Charles T. Wood, 31–60. New York: Routledge, 2014.
Schieffer, Rudolf. *Albertus Magnus: Mendikantentum und Theologie im Widerstreit mit dem Bischofsamt*. Lectio Albertina 3. Münster: Aschendorffsche Verlagsbuchhandlung, 1999.
Schiffman, Zachary Sayre. *On the Threshold of Modernity: Relativism in the French Renaissance*. Studies in Historical and Political Science. Baltimore: Johns Hopkins University Press, 1991.
Schino, Anna Lisa. *Batailles libertines: La vie et l'œuvre de Gabriel Naudé*. Translated by Stéphanie Vermot-Petit-Outhenin. Libre pensée et littérature clandestine. Paris: Honoré Champion éditeur, 2020.
———. "Campanella tra magia naturale e scienza nel giudizio di Gabriel Naudé." *Physis* 22 (1980): 393–431.
Schleich, Martin. "Ein hübsch lied von einer kuenigin von Franckreich." In *Die kleineren Liederdichter des 14. und 15. Jahrhunderts*, edited by Thomas Cramer, 3:1254–61. Munich: W. Fink, 1982.
Schmidt, James. "Light, Truth, and the Counter-Enlightenment's Enlightenment." In *Let There Be Enlightenment*, edited by Anton M. Matytsin and Dan Edelstein, 268–90. Baltimore: Johns Hopkins University Press, 2018.

Schneider, Robert Alan. *Dignified Retreat: Writers and Intellectuals in the Age of Richelieu.* Oxford: Oxford University Press, 2019.
Schnyder, André, ed. *Malleus Maleficarum von Heinrich Institoris (alias Kramer) unter Mithilfe Jakob Sprengers aufgrund der dämonologischen Tradition zusammengestellt.* Göppingen: Kümmerle, 1993.
Shelley, Mary Wollstonecraft. *Frankenstein; or, The Modern Prometheus.* New York: Puffin Books, 2020.
Sighart, Joachim. *Albert the Great, of the Order of Friar-Preachers: His Life and Scholastic Labours.* Translated by T. A. Dixon. London: R. Washbourne, 1876.
———. *Albertus Magnus: Sein Leben und seine Wissenschaft.* Regensburg: Manz, 1857.
Siraisi, Nancy G. "The Medical Learning of Albertus Magnus." In *Albertus Magnus and the Sciences,* edited by James A. Weisheipl, 379–404. Toronto: Pontifical Institute of Mediaeval Studies, 1980.
Sloan, Phillip R. "Descartes, the Sceptics, and the Rejection of Vitalism in Seventeenth-Century Physiology." *Studies in the History and Philosophy of Science* 8, no. 1 (1977): 1–28.
Smith, William Bradford. "Resisting the Rosicrucians: Theories on the Occult Origins of the Thirty Years' War." *Church History and Religious Culture* 94, no. 4 (2014): 431–43.
Soll, Jacob. "The Uses of Historical Evidence in Early Modern Europe: Introduction." *Journal of the History of Ideas* 64, no. 2 (2003): 149–57.
Soman, Alfred. "Les procès de sorcellerie au parlement de Paris (1565–1640)." *Annales: Histoire, Sciences sociales* 32 (1977): 790–814.
Sommer, Andreas Urs. "Zur 'Geschichtsphilosophie' in Bayles "Dictionnaire historique et critique."" *Aufklärung* 16 (2004): 79–94.
Sommerlechner, Andrea. *Stupor mundi? Kaiser Friedrich II. und die mittelaltelriche Geschichtsschreibung.* Publikationen des historischen Instituts beim österreichischen Kulturinstitut in Rom: Abhandlungen 2. Vienna: Österreichische Akademie der Wissenschaften, 1999.
Sonnini, Charles S. *Nouveau dictionnaire d'histoire natuelle, appliquée aux arts.* 24 vols. Paris: Crapelet, 1803–4.
Spargo, John Webster. *Virgil the Necromancer.* Studies in Virgilian Legends. Cambridge, MA: Harvard University Press, 1934.
Speculum peregrinarum questionum. Lyon: Scipio de Sabiano, 1534.
Stegmüller, Friedrich. *Analecta upsaliensia: Theologiam medii aevi illustrantia.* Uppsala Universitets Årsskrift 1. Uppsala: A. B. Lunequistska, 1953.
Stehkämper, Hugo, and Matthias Zender, eds. *Albertus Magnus: Ausstellung zum 700. Todestag.* Cologne: Stadt Köln Historisches Archiv, 1980.
Stephens, Walter. *Demon Lovers: Witchcraft, Sex, and the Crisis of Belief.* Chicago: University of Chicago Press, 2002.
Strunz, Franz. *Albertus Magnus: Weisheit und Naturforschung im Mittelalter.* Menschen, Völker, Zeiten 15. Vienna: Karl König, 1925.
Sturlese, Loris. "Saints et magiciens: Albert le Grand en face d'Hermès Trismégiste." *Archives de Philosophie* 43 (1980): 615–34.
Suavius, Leo. *Theophrasti Paracelsi philosphiae et medicinae utriusque universae compendium.* Basel: Peter Perna, 1568.
Succurro, Maria Chiara. "The *Liber Compostelle* Attributed to Friar Bonaventura of Iseo: The Textual Tradition of a Thirteenth-Century Alchemical Encyclopedia." *Ambix* 63, no. 3 (2016): 199–216.
Sudhoff, Karl. *Bibliographia Paracelsica.* Graz: Akademische Druck, 1958.
Suominen, Vesa. "Gabriel Naudé: A Librarian and a Libertin Between the Huguenot Wars and the Enlightenment." *Informaatiotutkimus* 38 (2019): 24–48. https://doi.org/10.23978/inf.79889.
Tarrant, Neil. "Between Aquinas and Eymerich: The Roman Inquisition's Use of Dominican Thought in the Censorship of Alchemy." *Ambix* 65, no. 3 (2018): 210–31.

---. *Defining Nature's Limits: The Roman Inquisition and the Boundaries of Science.* Chicago: University of Chicago Press, 2022.

---. "Giambattista della Porta and the Roman Inquisition: Censorship and the Definition of Nature's Limits in Sixteenth-Century Italy." *British Journal for the History of Science* 46 (2013): 601–25.

---. "Reconstructing Thomist Astrology: Robert Bellarmine and the Papal Bull *Coeli et terrae*." *Annals of Science* 77 (2020): 26–49.

Tavuzzi, Michael. *Renaissance Inquisitors: Dominican Inquisitors and Inquisitorial Districts in Northern Italy, 1474–1527*. Studies in the History of Christian Traditions. Leiden: Brill, 2007.

Thoemes, Nikolaus. *Albertus Magnus in Geschichte und Sage: Festschrift zur sechsten Säcularfeier seines Todestages am 15. November 1880*. Cologne: J. P. Bachem, 1880.

Thomas Aquinas. *Opera Omnia*. Edited by Vincenzo Giustiniani and Tomás Manrique. 17 vols. Rome: Bladus & Osmarinus, 1570.

Thomas of Cantimpré. *Bonum universale de apibus*. Douay: Balthazar Beller, 1627.

Thorndike, Lynn. "Further Consideration of the *Experimenta*, *Speculum astronomiae*, and *De secretis mulierum* Ascribed to Albertus Magnus." *Speculum* 30, no. 3 (1955): 413–43.

---. *A History of Magic and Experimental Science*. 8 vols. London: Macmillan, 1923–58.

---. "Relations of the Inquisition to Peter of Abano and Cecco d'Ascoli." *Speculum* 1, no. 3 (1926): 338–43.

---. "Roger Bacon and Experimental Method in the Middle Ages." *Philosophical Review* 23, no. 3 (1914): 271–98.

---. "Some Medieval Conceptions of Magic." *Monist* 25, no. 1 (1915): 107–39.

Tiraboschi, Girolamo. *Storia della letteratura italiana*. 9 vols. Modena: Presso la Societa' Tipografica, 1771–82.

Tostado, Alfonso. *Eccam vobis qui sacris litteris incumbitis studiosi, tantopere exoptatam super Exodum interpretatione fidissimam*. Venice: Peter Liechtenstein, 1528.

"Translatio b. Alberti Magni, anno 1483." *Analecta sacri ordinis Fratrum Praedicatorum* 3 (1897): 349–51.

Triaire, Paul, ed. *Lettres de Gui Patin, 1630–1672*. Paris: H. Champion, 1907.

Tricoire, Damien. "The Triumph of Theocracy: French Political Thought, God, and the Question of Secularization in the Age of Enlightenment." In *Between Secularization and Reform*, edited by Anna Tomaszewska, 68–100. Leiden: Brill, 2022.

Trithemius, Johannes. "Antipali maleficiorum." In *Paralipomena opusculorum*, edited by Joannes Busaeus, 273–426. Cologne: Johannes Wulffraht, 1624.

---. *Polygraphiae libri sex*. Cologne: Johannes Birckmann and Werner Richwin, 1564.

---. *Steganographia*. Frankfurt: Johannes Berner, 1606.

---. *Steganographia*. Edited by Wolfgang Ernst Heidel. Nuremburg: Johannes Frederick Rudiger, 1721.

Truitt, Elly Rachel. "Celestial Divination and Arabic Science in Twelfth-Century England: The History of Gerbert of Aurillac's Talking Head." *Journal of the History of Ideas* 73 (2012): 201–22.

---. *Medieval Robots: Mechanism, Magic, Nature, and Art*. The Middle Ages. Philadelphia: University of Pennsylvania Press, 2015.

Turcan, Isabelle. "Les particularités de la première édition du *Dictionnaire de Trévoux* en 1704." In *Quand le dictionnaire de Trévoux rayonne sur l'Europe des lumières*, edited by Isabelle Turcan, 95–102. Paris: Harmattan, 2009.

Twetten, David, and Steven Baldner. "Introduction to Albert's Philosophical Work." In *A Companion to Albert the Great*, edited by Irven Michael Resnick, 165–72. Leiden: Brill, 2013.

Ulrich von Strassburg. *De summo bono*. Hamburg: Felix Meiner, 1989–.

Van der Lugt, Maaike. "'Abominable Mixtures': The *Liber vaccae* in the Medieval West, or the Dangers and Attractions of Natural Magic." *Traditio* 64 (2009): 229–77.

Van Rooy, R. P. "Saint Albert le Grand et la Magie." *Bulletin mensuel de la Société Albert-le-Grand* 6 (1940): 2-24.
Verardi, Donato. "Francesco Storella e l'Aristotele 'negromante.'" *Bruniana & Campanelliana* 25 (2019): 541-49.
———. "La voie secrète de l'albertisme: François Storella, Jean-Baptiste della Porta et l'aristotélisme magique à Naples au XVIe siècle." *Revue des sciences philosophiques et théologiques* 102 (2018): 611-22.
Véronèse, Julien. "Pietro d'Abano magicien à la Renaissance: Le cas de l'*Elucidarius magice* (ou *Lucidarium artis nigromantice*)." In *Médecine, astrologie et magie*, edited by Jean-Patrice Boudet, Franck Collard, and Nicolas Weill-Parot, 295-330. Florence: SISMEL, 2013.
Vescovini, Graziella Federici. "Pietro d'Abano: *Il Conciliatore* tra magia e scienza." *Medicina nei Secoli* 20 (2008): 607-40.
———, ed. *Pietro d'Abano: Trattati di astronomia—"Lucidator dubitabilium astronomiae," "De motu octavae sphaerae" e altre opere*. Il mito e la storia 3. Padua: Ed. Programma, 1992.
Viau, Théophile de, and Georges Bourgueil. *Le Parnasse des poètes satyriques*. Paris: Passage du Nord-Ouest, 2002.
Vossius, Gerardus Joannes. *Ars historica, sive de Historiae et historices natura historiaque scribendae praeceptis, commentatio*. Leiden: Johannes Maire, 1623.
Walsham, Alexandra. "Migrations of the Holy: Explaining Religious Change in Medieval and Early Modern Europe." *Journal of Medieval and Early Modern Studies* 44, no. 2 (2014): 241-80.
Walz, Angelus M. "Bestrebungen zur Heiligsprechung Alberts des Großen in alter und neuer Zeit." *Divus Thomas* 10 (1932): 287-304.
Ward, Laviece C. "Werner Rolevinck and the *Fasciculus Temporum*: Carthusian Historiography in the Late Middle Ages." In *Normative Zentrierung / Normative Centering*, edited by Rudolf Suntrup and Jan R. Veenstra, 209-30. Frankfurt: Peter Lang, 2002.
Wauters, Tim. "*Libertinage érudit* and Isaac Vossius: A Case Study." *Journal for Early Modern Cultural Studies* 12, no. 2 (2012): 37-53.
Weill-Parot, Nicolas. "Astral Magic and Intellectual Changes (Twelfth-Fifteenth Centuries): 'Astrological Images' and the Concept of 'Addressative' Magic." In *The Metamorphosis of Magic from Late Antiquity to the Early Modern Period*, edited by Jan N. Bremmer and Jan R. Veenstra, 167-87. Leuven: Peeters, 2002.
———. "Cecco d'Ascoli and Antonio da Montolmo: The Building of a 'Nigromantical' Cosmology and the Birth of the Author-Magician." In *The Routledge History of Medieval Magic*, edited by Sophie Page and Catherine Rider, 225-36. London: Routledge, 2019.
———. "I demoni della Sfera: La 'nigromanzia' cosmologico-astrologica di Cecco d'Ascoli." In *Cecco d'Ascoli*, edited by Antonio Rigon, 103-34. Rome: Istituto superiore di studi medioevali, 2007.
———. *Les "images astrologiques" au Moyen Age et à la Renaissance: Spéculations intellectuelles et pratiques magiques, XIIe-XVe siècle*. Sciences, techniques et civilisations du Moyen Age à l'aube des Lumières 6. Paris: Honoré Champion Éditeur, 2002.
———. "Imprinting Powers: The Astrological Seal and Its Doctrinal Meanings in the Latin West." In *Seals: Making and Marking Connections Across the Medieval World*, edited by Brigitte Miriam Bedos-Rezak, 49-72. Leeds: Arc Humanities Press, 2018.
———. "Pietro d'Abano et l'occulte dans la nature: Galien, Avicenne, Albert le Grand et la *differentia* 71 du *Conciliator*." In *Médecine, astrologie et magie*, edited by Jean-Patrice Boudet, Franck Collard, and Nicolas Weill-Parot, 21-38. Florence: SISMEL, 2013.
Weisheipl, James A. "Albert the Great and Medieval Culture." *Thomist* 44, no. 4 (1980): 481-501.
———. "The Axiom 'Opus naturae est opus intelligentiae' and Its Origins." In *Albertus Magnus: Doctor universalis, 1280/1980*, edited by Gerbert Meyer and Albert Zimmermann, 441-64. Mainz: Matthias-Grünewald-Verlag, 1980.

---. "The Celestial Movers in Medieval Physics." In *Nature and Motion in the Middle Ages*, edited by William Carroll, 143–75. Washington, DC: Catholic University Press, 1985.
---. "The Life and Works of St. Albert the Great." In *Albertus Magnus and the Sciences*, edited by James A. Weisheipl, 13–51. Toronto: Pontifical Institute of Mediaeval Studies, 1980.
Wetzstein, Thomas. *Heilige vor Gericht: Das Kanonisationsverfahren im europäischen Spätmittelalter*. Forschungen zur kirchlichen Rechtsgeschichte und zum Kirchenrecht 28. Cologne: Böhlau, 2004.
Weyer, Johann. *De praestigiis daemonum et incantationibus ac veneficiis*. Basel: Johannes Oporinus, 1563.
---. *On Witchcraft*. Translated by John Shea. Edited by Benjamin G. Kohl and H. C. Erik Midelfort. Asheville, NC: Pegasus Press, 1998.
Widder, Ellen. "Westfalen und die Welt: Anmerkungen zu Werner Rolevinck." *Westfälische Zeitschrift* 141 (1991): 93–122.
William of Malmesbury. *Gesta regum anglorum*. Edited by R. A. B. Mynors, R. M. Thomson, and M. Winterbottom. 2 vols. Oxford: Clarendon Press, 1998–99.
Williams, Steven J. "Roger Bacon and His Edition of the Pseudo-Aristotelian 'Secretum secretorum.'" *Speculum* 69, no. 1 (1994): 57–73.
---. "Roger Bacon in Context: Empiricism in the High Middle Ages." In *"Expertus sum,"* edited by Thomas Bénatouïl and Isabelle Draelants, 123–44. Florence: SISMEL, 2011.
Williams-Krapp, Werner. "Deutschsprachige Hagiographie von ca. 1350 bis ca. 1550." In *Hagiographies: Histoire internationale de la littérature hagiographique latine et vernaculaire en Occident des origines à 1550*, edited by Guy Philippart, 1:267–88. Corpus Christianorum. Turnhout: Brepols, 1994.
Witt, Ronald G. *In the Footsteps of the Ancients: The Origins of Humanism from Lovato to Bruni*. Studies in Medieval and Reformation Thought 74. Leiden: Brill, 2000.
Wolffgram, Hugo. "Neue Forschungen zu Werner Rolevincks Leben und Werken." *Westfälische Zeitschrift* 50 (1892): 127–61.
Wölmer, Gilla. "Albert the Great and His Botany." In *A Companion to Albert the Great*, edited by Irven M. Resnick, 221–67. Leiden: Brill, 2013.
Wyckoff, Dorothy, ed. *Albertus Magnus: Book of Minerals*. Oxford: Clarendon Press, 1967.
Yates, Frances Amelia. *The Rosicrucian Enlightenment*. London: Routledge, 1972.
Yeo, Richard. *Encyclopaedic Visions: Scientific Dictionaries and Enlightenment Culture*. Cambridge: Cambridge University Press, 2001.
---. "A Solution to the Multitude of Books: Ephraim Chambers's 'Cyclopaedia' (1728) as 'the Best Book in the Universe.'" *Journal of the History of Ideas* 64 (2003): 61–72.
Zambelli, Paola. *L'ambigua natura della magia: Filosofi, streghe, riti nel Rinascimento*. Milan: Il Saggiatore, 1991.
---. "Scholastic and Humanist Views of Hermeticism and Witchcraft." In *Hermeticism and the Renaissance*, edited by Ingrid Merkel and Allen G. Debus, 125–53. Washington, DC: Folger Shakespeare Library, 1988.
---. *The "Speculum astronomiae" and Its Enigma: Astrology, Theology, and Science in Albertus Magnus and His Contemporaries*. Boston Studies in the Philosophy of Science 135. Dordrecht: Kluwer Academic, 1992.
Zapf, Volker. "Schleich, Martin." In *Die deutsche Literatur des Mittelalters: Verfasserlexikon*, 2nd, rev. ed., edited by Wolfgant Stammler and Karl Langosch, 4:2931–33. Berlin: Walter de Gruyter, 2012.
Zedler, Johann Henrich, ed. *Grosses vollständiges Universal-Lexicon aller Wissenschafften und Künste*. 64 vols. Leipzig: Zedler, 1731–54.
Zika, Charles. *Exorcising Our Demons: Magic, Witchcraft, and Visual Culture in Early Modern Europe*. Studies in Medieval and Reformation Thought 91. Leiden: Brill, 2003.

INDEX

Titles of works are more commonly listed under the author's name. Illustrations are indicated by italics.

Académie Française, 124
Agrippa von Nettesheim, Heinrich Cornelius, 16, 64–65, 96, 99, 104, 124, 131, 132, 133, 134, 141
Ailly, Pierre d', 64
Albert the Great
  aging, 68–70
  as Albertus Coloniensis (Albert of Cologne), 2
  as Albertus Teutonicus (Albert the German), 2, 73, 86
  as bishop, 47, 49, 51, 55, 75, 85, 88, 89, 95, 100, 101, 104, 144
  and the Blessed Virgin Mary, 68–70, 75, 87, 121
  canonization, xvi, 3, 120, 145, 146; call for, fifteenth century, 18, 20, 71–75, 85, 86–87, 88–92; call for, nineteenth century, 144
  De anima, 1, 18, 23, 24, 26, 27, 29, 31, 35, 39, 44, 46, 47, 49, 59, 121
  De animalibus, 31, 32, 35, 37, 38, 59, 121, 125
  De caelo et mundo, 27, 28, 33
  De causis proprietatibus elementorum, 33
  De generatione et corruptione, 27, 33
  De mineralibus, 8, 24, 31, 32–33, 34, 35, 37, 43, 47, 55, 58, 60, 61, 63, 65, 79, 80, 104, 121, 124, 126, 148
  De natura deorum, proposed but unwritten work, 29
  De somno et vigilia, 31
  De vegetabilibus, 8, 31, 32, 35, 37, 121
  death, 68–70, 74
  as "the Great," 2, 19, 73, 94, 101, 133
  indices of works, 68–69, 79, 92, 104, 121
  on the Index of Prohibited Books, 90–91, 128
  Metaphysica, 28
  Meteora, 31
  and midwifery, 80, 82, 85, 90, 117, 126, 128, 133
  opera omnia, 60, 61, 62, 117, 120–21, 123, 146
  Parva naturalia, 27
  Physica, 27, 30, 33, 128
  pseudepigraphal works attributed to, 3, 10, 18, 43, 47, 55–56, 57–62, 67, 79, 95, 103, 104, 126
  Sentences, commentary on Peter Lombard's, 8, 26, 39, 43, 46
  Speculum astronomiae, possible authorship of, 34, 47, 50, 62–66, 69, 70, 73, 78, 104, 121, 126, 128, 131, 137, 145
  Summa theologiae, 8, 39
  Super Danielem, 42
  Super Ethica, 28, 43
  Super Isaiam, 42
  Super Mattheum, 40–41, 138
  Super Sententiarum (see *Sentences*)
  translation of remains, xvi, 74, 88, 89
Albert the Great (Pseudo)
  Alkimia minor, 61
  Calistenus, 61
  Compositum de compositis, 61, 148
  De mirabilibus mundi, 58–59, 79, 104, 126, 133
  De occultis naturae, 61
  De secretis mulierum, 59, 79, 82, 90, 104, 125, 133
  Experimenta Alberti, 47, 58
  Libellus de alchimia, 61
  Liber aggregationis, 58–59
  Liber de virtutibus herbarum, lapidum, et animalium, 58–59, 79
  Propositiones artis alchemiae, 61
  Secreta Alberti, 58
  Secretorum tractatus, 61
  Semita recta, 56, 60–61, 79–80, 121, 145
  Speculum astronomiae (*see* Magister Speculi)
alchemy, 2, 25, 40, 42–43, 44, 45, 47, 49–50, 55–56, 57, 58, 60–62, 66, 88, 106, 135, 139, 147
  as a laboratory or experimental practice, 9–10, 19, 31, 56, 60, 61, 62
  in the history of science, 9, 148
  medical, 102, 109

alchemy *(continued)*
  as an object of suspicion, 7, 10, 27, 48, 77–78, 80, 84, 85, 91, 95, 101, 102–4, 126
  as a science, 6, 43, 60, 77, 91–92, 102, 116, 124, 130, 142
Alembert, Jean le Rond d', 14, 20–21, 116, 118, 119, 135
  See also *Encyclopédie*
Alexander of Hales, 50–51, 73, 136
Alfonsi, Petrus, 6
Apologie pour tous les grands personnages faussement soupçonnez de magie. See Naudé, Gabriel
apostasy, 26, 78, 84–85, 89
Anatolius of Laodicea, 83
angels, 1, 4, 15, 23, 28, 44, 46, 49, 55, 65–66, 97–98, 99, 111, 114, 124, 132
Anzulewicz, Henryk, 25, 34
Apuleius, 64
Aquinas, Thomas, 2, 7, 34, 35, 39, 45, 47, 49, 51, 64, 73, 75, 79, 81, 82, 88, 100–101, 104, 105, 112, 120, 121, 125, 130, 133, 136, 137, 144
Arabic, 48, 57, 61
  influences on Latin Western thought, 5, 6, 7, 16, 40, 58, 102, 136
  See also Islam
Aristotelian, 1, 7, 27–28, 32, 40, 43, 65, 96, 101, 136–37, 139
Aristotle, 1, 6, 15, 23, 27–28, 32, 34, 35, 38, 39, 40, 42, 48, 50, 51, 53, 57, 59, 60, 65, 69, 99, 101, 105, 128, 130, 134, 136
  De anima, 1, 23, 27
Arnold (Pseudo), 61
Arnold of Villanova, 65, 91, 102–3, 116
Arnold of Saxony, 32
Asclepius, 28, 36, 40
astrology (and astronomy), 6, 15, 29, 31, 33, 34, 40–42, 50, 60, 63, 69, 77, 92, 95, 98, 101, 105, 111, 113, 124, 135, 139
  distinction with astronomy, 33, 34, 63, 64, 124, 130
  distinction with diabolical mantics, 77–78
  judicial, 6, 53, 63, 104
  mathematical, 33, 41–42, 63, 99
  as an object of suspicion, 4, 6–7, 16–17, 18, 26, 40–42, 62, 73, 77–78, 84, 85, 98, 104, 131, 132, 134, 137
astronomy. See astrology
atheism, 11, 104, 107, 108, 110
Augustine of Hippo
  on magic, 4, 23, 26, 45, 57, 77
  as moral example, 72
automata, 53, 54, 64, 66, 95, 98, 99, 104–5, 116, 117, 123, 125, 126, 128, 129, 133, 136, 137, 142, *143*
Autun (de Chevanes), Jacques d'. See Chevanes, Jacques de

Avicenna, 15, 30, 32, 36, 38, 43, 59, 60, 61, 65, 98

Bacon, Francis, 97, 98, 104
Bacon, Roger, 12, 13–15, 16, 45, 48, 53, 54, 57, 61, 65, 101, 102, 105, 116, 123, 128, 133, 136, 137, 144
  Compendium of the Study of Philosophy, 51
  criticism of Albert, 50–51, 70
  On the Faults Occasioned by the Study of Theology, 104
  "On the Secret Works of Art and Nature and the Nullity of Magic," 13
  Opera, 50
  Opus maius, 13
  Opus minor, 50
  Opus tertium, 13
Bailey, Michael D., 11, 148–49
Bale, John, 14
Bardney, Richard, 54
Bartholomew of England, 32
Basnage de Beauval, Henri, 129–30, 131, 132, 133, 135, 140
Bayle, Pierre, 111, 117–18, 119, 124, 125–29, 135
Beke, Johannes de, 2, 52
Bellarmine, Robert, 122, 146
Benno of Osnabrück, 12–13
Bible, 17, 39, 41–42, 44, 57, 69, 71, 78, 79, 97–98, 108, 135
  Daniel, 40, 42, 79
  Exodus, 132
  Genesis, 78, 113
  as history, 97, 113, 134
  Isaiah, 42, 52, 77
  Matthew, 40, 42, 63, 123, 128, 131, 138
  Samuel, 76, 131
Bismarck, Otto von, 144
Blavatsky, H. P., 142
Bodin, Jean, 112, 114
Bonaventure of Iseo, 48, 49, 50
  Liber compostelle, 49–50
Bonaventure of Bagnoregio, 73, 136, 173n11, 173n15
Bordelon, Laurent, 19
Borromeo, Federico, 91
Boucher, Jean, 107, 108
brazen head. See automata
Brucker, Jakob, 133–34, 136
Buridan, Johannes, 55

Calvinism, 107, 122, 129, 130, 132, 137, 139, 140
Campanella, Tommaso, 98, 99, 114
Canisius, Peter, 145
Cardano, Girolamo, 97, 98, 99, 128, 130
Carthusians
  Charterhouse of Saint Barbara, 71–72, 86

Hermann of Appledorn, 72
interest in Albert the Great, 71–72, 75, 88
Kaltyser, Peter, 72, 86
Ryckel, Denis, 72
    See also Dionysius (Pseudo); Rolevinck, Werner
Catholic, 3, 54, 65, 83, 107–8, 110, 112, 119, 129, 130, 132, 136, 139, 140, 144, 145
Cecco of Ascoli, 12, 16–17
celestial
    bodies, 6, 7, 28, 29, 30, 33, 34, 35, 41, 44
    influences, 5, 6–7, 8, 11, 15, 25, 29–30, 33–34, 36, 38, 40, 44, 52–54, 59–60, 61–65, 75, 85, 124, 130, 147
    movements, 6, 15, 28–30, 33, 35, 41, 53, 63, 99, 130
    powers, 14, 33–35, 36, 54, 60, 64
    spheres, 28, 29–30, 44, 147
Celestine V. See Morrone, Peter
Chacón, Alfonso, 90
Chambers, Ephraim, 118, 132–33, 135
Charron, Pierre, 108
Chevanes, Jacques de, 112–13
Cicero, 28
Colletet, Guillaume, 111
Cologne, 48, 62, 71, 74, 75, 83, 84, 86, 87, 88–90, 95–96, 102, 126
Comestor, Peter, 78
Commines, Philippe de, 114
confessionalization, 129
Corneille, Thomas, 124
Corsini, Matteo, 52–53, 54
    The Rosebush of Life, 52
cross-dressing. See Albert the Great: and midwifery
curiosity, 76, 85
Cyclopaedia. See Chambers, Ephraim

Dee, John, 14
Delrio, Martin Anthony, 94, 104, 105, 112, 126
demonic. See demons; diabolical
demons, 5, 6, 8, 13, 15, 17, 23, 26, 28, 29, 39, 40, 41, 43, 44, 45, 46, 48, 49, 51–51, 55, 57, 65, 66, 78, 93, 98, 99, 105, 113, 123, 124, 131, 132, 134, 138, 147
Descartes, René, 110
diabolical
    alchemy as, 43, 48
    assistance, 8, 14, 17, 25–26, 35, 40, 52, 53, 54, 63, 66, 78, 84, 99, 107, 114, 123, 131, 147
    commerce with, 45, 49, 57, 77, 89, 99
    conjuring, 4, 5–6, 12–13, 16–17, 26, 37, 41, 54, 93, 137
    demonology, 17, 94, 99, 101, 104, 112, 137
    diabolism, 14, 39, 66, 108, 132, 142
    forces, 89, 124, 148
    influence, 63, 64, 143, 147
    inspiration, 40, 48
    interest in, 60, 131
    intervention, 11, 15, 38–39, 65, 84, 98, 99, 105, 107, 136, 147
    invocation, 45, 63, 84, 93, 124, 147
    magic, 8, 12, 18, 36, 37, 38, 39, 47, 69, 70, 83, 84, 85, 96, 97, 98, 99, 101, 103, 112, 114, 123, 132, 134, 135, 138, 139
    nigromancy as, 5, 26, 39, 41, 52, 70, 77
    pacts, 78, 135, 138
    participation, 4, 77, 134
    powers, 14, 57, 64, 66, 78, 111, 131, 134
    temptation, 75, 77
    theory of, 65, 94, 111–2
    understanding of magic as, 1, 4, 9, 12, 14, 15, 17, 25, 45, 65, 71, 85, 91, 93, 113, 134
dictionary. See encyclopedia
Dictionaire universel, le. See Furetière, Antoine
    See also Basnage de Beauval, Henri
Diodati, Elie, 110
Dictionnaire des arts and des sciences. See Corneille, Thomas
Dictionnaire de Trévoux, 21, 129, 130, 131, 132, 133, 135
Dictionnaire historique et critique. See Bayle, Pierre
Diderot, Denis, 14, 20–21, 116, 118, 119, 135–36, 140
    See also *Encyclopédie*
Dionysius (Pseudo), 40, 72
disenchantment, 11–12, 21–22, 45, 93, 141, 142, 146, 148–49
divination, 5, 6, 16, 24, 25, 35, 36, 38, 39, 41, 42, 47, 50, 53, 63, 69, 77, 78, 84, 92, 112, 114, 116, 132, 134, 135
    augury, 37, 38, 41
    diviners, 4, 23, 28, 40, 41, 42
    divini, 4
    geomancy, 50, 63, 69, 78, 98
    mantic arts, 77, 98, 112
    in the *Speculum Astronomiae*, 69, 78
    See also nigromancy
Dominicans, 1, 9, 16, 18, 21, 33, 47, 48, 49, 51, 59, 60, 61, 62, 69, 70, 71, 73, 74, 75, 90, 95, 96, 105, 115, 120, 121, 126, 132, 145
    chapter at Pfortzheim, 74, 83, 86, 90
    Observance movement, 83–84, 86–87, 88–89, 91–93
    priory of the Holy Cross, Cologne, 74, 86
    See also *individual names*
Draelants, Isabelle, 9, 148
Dupin, Louis-Ellies, 122, 123
Dupuy, Jacques, 108, 110, 111
Dupuy, Pierre, 110, 111

Echard, Jacques, 121
encyclopedia, 20–21, 117, 118–20, 122, 123, 125, 132–33, 138, 139, 141, 146, 148, 149
encyclopedic. *See* encyclopedia
Encyclopédie, 14, 16, 17, 116–17, 118, 119, 135–37, 139
Enlightenment, 11, 110, 111, 117, 118, 119–20, 139, 142
Ennemoser, Joseph, 144
envy, 38, 76, 80, 95
Erasmus of Rotterdam, 97, 107
Etymologies. See Isidore of Seville
Esotericism, 141, 142, 144, 146
Eusebius of Caesarea, 82–83
experimentation
  in alchemy, 7, 43
  experimental science, 13, 14
  experiri in Albert's work, 30–32, 44, 147
  in pseudepigraphal works, 59, 62
Eymeric, Nicholas, 84

Farabi, al-, 6
fascination, 25, 38–39
Ficino, Marcilio, 16, 64, 114
Franciscans, 48, 55, 103, 105
Frazer, James G., 26
Frederick II (Holy Roman Emperor), 49, 73
Furetière, Antoine, 124–25, 129, 130, 131, 132, 133, 135, 140

Gaffarel, Jacques, 111
Galen, 15, 38, 59, 60, 102, 103
Garasse, François, 107–8, 111, 112
Gassendi, Pierre, 110
Gaultier, Jacques, 107, 108
Gauslini, Bernardino, 120, 121
Geber of Spain (Jabir), 33, 61, 102
Geber (Pseudo), 61, 102
  Height of Perfection, 60
Gerard de Frachet, 48
Gerbert of Aurillac (Sylvester II), 12–13, 53, 100, 105, 124, 132, 133
Germa the Babylonian, 33
Gerson, Jean, 114
  criticism of Albert, 18, 64, 66, 70, 104
Geyer, Bernard, 62
Goclenius, Rudolph, 107
Gödelmann, Georg von, 101, 112
gods
  of ancient philosophy, 23, 27–29
  conjuring, 36
  false, 4, 28, 29
goetia. *See* magic: demonic
Gohory, Jacques, 65
Golden Legend, 57
Gower, John, 53–54

Grabmann, Martin, 145
Grand Albert, the (also *Le Grand Albert*), 19, 19, 60
Grand Dictionaire historique, le. See Moréri, Louis
  See also Leclerc, Jean
Greene, Robert, 14
Gregory VII, 13, 100
Grosseteste, Robert, 53–54, 95, 101, 105
Guibert, Nicholas, 104
Guicciardini, Francesco, 114
Gundissalinus, Dominicus, 6, 34, 70
  On the Divisions of Philosophy, 6
  See also nigromancy

Hackett, Jeremiah, 51
Henry, John, 9
Henry of Ghent (Pseudo)
  De viris illustribus, 50
Henry of Herford, 51
  Liber de memorialioribus, 74
heresy
  association of magic with, 1, 4, 70, 85
  heresies, 76, 78, 85, 89, 103, 107, 108, 128
Hermes Trismegistus, 23, 25, 28, 32, 33, 35, 39, 40, 61, 64, 65, 94
Hermetica, 40
  See also Hermes Trismegistus
Hertling, Georg Friedrich Freiherr von, 145
Hippocrates, 32
Historia de vita et doctrina Alberti Magni. See Luis de Valladolid
historicism, 95, 96–97, 105, 106, 109, 113, 114, 125–26, 138–39, 148
history, as a genre or method. *See* historicism
Holbach, Paul-Henri, Baron d', 116
Homer, 111, 131
hoopoe, 37–38, 59
Horst, Georg Conrad, 142
Hugh of Saint Victor, 23, 41
Huguenot, 108

Ibn al-Jazzar, 58
Ibn Hayyan, Jabir, 102
images, science of, 6, 7, 15, 25, 33, 41, 73, 101
incorporeal entities, 1, 2, 23, 26, 28, 29, 40
Index, Sacred Congregation of, 90–91, 128
Innocent VIII, 84
Inquisition, 84, 85
  Roman, 90–91
  Spanish, 108
Isidore of Seville, 4, 6, 41, 42
  The Etymologies, 4, 41
Islam
  al-Andalus, 13
  Dar al-Islam, 6

Islamic influences on Latin Western thought, 15, 17, 30, 35, 43, 58, 65, 77, 102, 106
Prophet Muhammad, 99

James I and VI of England and Scotland, 114, 132
Jammy, Pierre, 121, 123, 133
Jerome, 72, 79
Jesuits, 21, 108, 109, 110, 111, 112, 121, 122, 128, 129, 130, 139, 140, 145
Jews. *See* Judaism
John XXII, 17
John of Colonna
  De viris illustribus, 74
John of Rupescissa, 103, 104
Josephson-Storm, Jason Ā., 11, 148–49
Judaism
  antisemitism, 6, 105
  in the Bible, 42
  Jewish Scholars, 6, 35, 65, 78, 98
Julian, 83
Justin Martyr, 83

Kabbalah, 65, 98, 105, 106, 116, 131, 144
Kaltyser, Peter, 72, 86
Kelley, Donald, 114
Kempis, Thomas, 114
Kircher, Athanasius, 110
Korner, Hermann, 69–71
Kors, Alan Charles, 11
Kramer, Henry "Institoris", 84–85, 168n82
  Malleus maleficarum, 83–84, 90
Kristeller, Paul O., 110, 117

La Monnoye, Bernard de, 126
La Mothe Le Vayer, François de, 110
Labbé, Pierre, 121
Lancre, Pierre de, 94, 105, 111–12
Latour, Bruno, 148
Le Franc, Martin, 57
Leclerc, Jean, 121, 123
Legenda litteralis Alberti magni. *See* Rudolf of Nijmegen
Legenda venerabilis domini Alberti magni. *See* Peter of Prussia
Lesser Albert, the (also *Le petit Albert*), 19
Lévi Zahed, Éliphas, 142
Libera, Alain de, 10, 25, 152n23, 152 n26
Libertinism, 110, 117, 140
Lombard, Peter, 8, 26, 39, 45, 46, 136–37
Luis de Valladolid, 18, 68–71, 74, 76, 79, 87
Lull, Raymond, 65, 133
Lull, Raymond (Pseudo), 61
Luther, Martin, 103, 107
Lutheranism, 129

Magdalius, Jacobus, 71, 75, 83, 85, 90
magic
  in accounts of Albert's life, 2–3, 18, 46–53, 55, 72, 76, 92–93, 145
  angelic (theurgic), 64, 97–98, 112, 114, 137
  anthropological approaches to, 8
  black, 55, 113, 116, 123, 124, 132, 134, 135
  boundaries with religion, 4, 7–8, 118, 122, 137
  boundaries with science, 6, 7–9, 13, 15, 25, 30, 31, 33, 35, 43, 44, 83, 148
  challenges of defining, 4
  demonic (goetia), 98, 101, 103, 112, 114, 137, 138, 139
  diabolical, 83, 84, 85, 96, 97, 99, 123, 133–35, 139
  divine, 97–98, 114, 134
  magi, 4, 33, 41–42
  Magi (biblical), 40–41, 42, 63, 99, 123, 128, 131, 138
  magia, 4, 26, 44
  malificii, 4
  maleficium, 39, 84, 137
  natural, 4–5, 6, 7, 13, 26, 44, 65, 67, 69, 95, 96, 97, 98, 101, 105, 112, 114, 115, 116, 123, 124, 125, 132, 134, 135, 138, 139, 142
  naturalizing approach to, 11, 15, 21, 25, 26, 33, 34, 35, 37, 38–39, 44, 45, 48, 66, 93, 132, 147, 149
  sociological approaches to, 8
  sorcery (*see under* magic: black, demonic, diabolical, etc.)
  white, 13, 124, 132, 134
  See also alchemy; astrology; divination; nigromancy; witchcraft
Magister Speculi, 34, 50, 63–64, 65, 69, 73, 78, 104, 126–28, 131, 137
Magor the Greek, 33
Maier, Michael, 103, 106, 109, 126
Malleus maleficarum. *See* Kramer, Henry
Malvenda, Tomas, 121
mantic arts. *See* divination
Marbod of Rennes, 32
Mersenne, Marin, 110
Mesmes, Henri de, 97
Montaigne, Michel de, 108, 117
Moréri, Louis, 119, 122–23, 124, 126, 135, 138, 140
Morrone, Peter (Celestine V), 88
Murner, Thomas, 55
Muslim. *See* Islam

Naudé, Gabriel, 12, 110–11, 115, 130, 145
  Apologie, 16, 20, 94–106, 109, 111–2, 113, 114, 120, 125, 126, 127, 133, 134, 138
  assessments of historical figures, 14, 16, 17
  as a historian, 20, 95–97, 99, 103, 105–6, 109, 113, 114, 117, 125–6, 138–39, 148

Naudé, Gabriel *(continued)*
  Instruction à la France, 106, 107, 108–9, 113
  as a source for later encyclopedists, 20, 117, 123, 124, 126–8, 131, 133, 134, 135, 138, 139, 140
natural philosophy, 4, 5, 8, 22, 25, 27, 37, 44, 45, 48, 50–51, 53, 54, 57, 59, 66, 69, 77, 78, 84, 91–92, 93, 95, 96, 98, 107, 110, 112, 113, 114, 115, 116, 136, 137, 139, 142, 147
natural science, 1, 6, 7, 8, 20, 21, 22, 25, 27, 30, 44, 54, 58, 95, 96, 100, 119, 124, 138, 142, 144, 146, 148
  relationship to alchemy, 43
necromancy. *See* nigromancy
Nicolaus of Damascus, 35–36
Nider, John, 84
nigromancy (also necromancy)
  Albert's expertise in, 2, 24, 26, 36–37, 44, 45, 47, 76, 80, 91, 93
  Albert's reputation for, 5, 9, 16, 49, 50, 52, 70, 90, 122
  and astronomy, 69
  Boundaries with sciences, 5–6, 44, 59, 77–78, 85, 91
  as conjuration of the dead, 5, 41
  demonic, 5, 7, 9, 26, 36–37, 39, 41, 52, 60, 63, 70, 77, 91, 93, 99
  and encyclopedias, 122, 123, 131, 134, 137
  and Homer, 111
  meaning, 5–6
  Penalties for, 16–17
  as physics, 6, 33, 34, 52, 59, 70
  and talismans, 34–35
  and Virgil, 111
  and witchcraft, 84
Numa Pompilius, 12, 96, 99

obstetrics. *See* Albert the Great: and midwifery
On Ecclesiastical Writers (unknown author), 48
Order of Preachers. *See* Dominicans
Otto, Bernd-Christian, 10
Ovid, 37, 98, 105, 120

Paracelsian. *See* Paracelsus
Paracelsus, 102, 103, 104, 107, 108, 109, 130, 133, 141–42, 146
Patin, Guy, 102, 111, 113
Paul of Aegina, 60
Peiresc, Nicolas-Claude Fabri de, 108, 110
Peter of Abano, 12, 15–16, 65, 91
Peter of Prussia, 71, 74–80, 82, 83, 85, 87, 88, 89, 90, 104, 113, 121, 126, 145
Peter of Trau, 13
philosophes, 110, 146
physics. *See* natural philosophy
Picatrix, 65

Pico della Mirandola, Gianfrancesco, 104, 126
Pico della Mirandola, Giovanni, 16, 62, 65, 101, 104, 123, 133
  Disputations Against Divinatory Astrology, 62
Pintard, René, 110, 117
Pitois, Jean-Baptiste, 144, 146
Pius XI, 145–46
Pius XII, 146
Platearius, Matthaeus, 36
Plato, 39, 40, 64
Platonists, 64, 98
Pliny, 60
Plutarch, 97
Polier de Bottens, Antoine-Noé de, 137–38, 139, 140
Pomponazzi, Pietro, 65–66
Popkin, Richard, 110, 117
Poppe, Johann Heinrich Moritz von, 142
Porphyry, 64, 99
Porta, Giambattista della, 124
Proclus, 40
Protestant, 107, 108, 109, 110, 119, 129, 132
pseudepigrapha. *See* Albertus Magnus; Albertus Magnus (Pseudo)
Ptolemy, 15, 33, 34, 53, 130
Ptolemy of Lucca, 51
  Historia ecclesiastica nova, 51, 74

Quétif, Jacques, 121
Quintilian, 97
Quran, 37

Raleigh, Walter, 113–14
Rapin, René, 130
Raymond of Capua, 86
Raynaud, Théophile, 128
Regensburg, diocese of, 74, 75, 85, 88, 90, 95, 100, 101, 104, 133, 144
Renaissance, 43, 64, 65, 66, 71, 106, 111, 117, 120
Rinck, Peter, 72
ritual, 7, 17, 26, 39, 45, 63, 93, 123, 142, 147
  See also magic
Roberti, Johannes, 107, 108
Rolevinck, Werner, 71–74, 75, 76, 80, 85, 86, 87, 88
Romanticism, 3, 142
Rosicrucians, 106–7, 108, 109, 113
Rudolf of Nijmegen, 71, 74–75, 80–83, 85, 86, 87, 88, 90, 121
Ryckel, Denis, 72

Sacrobosco, Johannes de, 16
Sánchez, Tomás, 128
Savonarola, Michele, 15–16, 99
Saxon World Chronicle, 51–52

Scaliger, Julius Caesar, 17, 98
scholastic, 4, 8, 14, 16, 21, 28, 30, 38, 40, 74, 76, 102, 116, 130, 132, 134, 136
Schino, Anna Lisa, 117
Schleich, Martin, 55
Secreta secretorum, 57
Seneca, 97
Shelley, Mary, 141–42, 144, 146
Sigebert of Gembloux, 13
Sleiden, Johann, 114
Socrates, 17, 23, 28, 39, 40, 52, 99
sorcery. *See* magic: demonic; magic: diabolical
Speculum astronomiae. See Magister Speculi
    See also Albert the Great; *Speculum astronomiae*, possible authorship of
Sprenger, Jacob, 83, 84, 85–86, 88–89, 90
Spinoza, Baruch, 128
stars, science of. *See* astrology
suffumigation, 24, 26
Sylvester II. *See* Gerbert of Aurillac

Tabula Alberti magni See Luis de Valladolid
Tacitus, 97
talismans, 11, 15, 25, 33–35, 63, 64, 79
Tebith, 33
Tereus of Thrace, 37
theurgy. *See* magic: angelic
Thomas of Cantimpré, 32, 48, 50, 51, 55, 68
    The Book of Bees, 48–49, 55
    De apibus, 74
Thorndike, Lynn, 25, 63
Thucydides, 97
Tiraboschi, Girolamo, 17
Tostado, Alonso, 105
Tractatus de excellentiis Alberti magni. See Rolevinck, Werner

Trithemius, Johannes, 12, 16, 65, 101, 104, 122, 123, 126, 133
    Steganographia, 12
Turco, Thomas, 121

Ulrich of Strasbourg, 2, 9, 46, 47, 48, 49, 50, 65, 66, 73, 79
    De summo bono, 46, 74
Universal-Lexicon. See Zedler, Johann Heinrich

Vanini, Lucilio, 108
Viau, Théophile de, 108, 111
Vincent of Beauvais, 13
Vinet, John, 84
Virgil, 99, 105, 111, 112
vitae, 47, 51, 68–69, 71, 74–76, 78–79, 82, 83, 84, 85, 86–88, 89, 90, 91, 121, 145, 146
Vossius, Isaac, 110, 114

Walsham, Alexandra, 9, 148
Weber, Max, 21
Weyer, Johannes, 65, 112
William of Auvergne, 5, 26, 44, 45, 65, 67
William of Holland (king of Germany), 52
William of Malmesbury, 13, 53
William of Tocco, 51
witchcraft (maleficia), 4, 39, 57, 60, 69, 134, 137
    and nigromancy, 84
    persecution, 18, 83–85, 94, 111, 112, 135
    See also magic: *maleficium*

Zauberey, 133–35
    See also magic
Zedler, Johann Heinrich, 118, 133, 135, 138, 139, 140

THE MAGIC IN HISTORY SERIES

FORBIDDEN RITES
A Necromancer's Manual of the Fifteenth Century
Richard Kieckhefer

CONJURING SPIRITS
Texts and Traditions of Medieval Ritual Magic
Edited by Claire Fanger

RITUAL MAGIC
Elizabeth M. Butler

THE FORTUNES OF FAUST
Elizabeth M. Butler

THE BATHHOUSE AT MIDNIGHT
An Historical Survey of Magic and Divination in Russia
W. F. Ryan

SPIRITUAL AND DEMONIC MAGIC
From Ficino to Campanella
D. P. Walker

ICONS OF POWER
Ritual Practices in Late Antiquity
Naomi Janowitz

BATTLING DEMONS
Witchcraft, Heresy, and Reform in the Late Middle Ages
Michael D. Bailey

PRAYER, MAGIC, AND THE STARS IN THE ANCIENT AND LATE ANTIQUE WORLD
Edited by Scott Noegel, Joel Walker, and Brannon Wheeler

BINDING WORDS
Textual Amulets in the Middle Ages
Don C. Skemer

STRANGE REVELATIONS
Magic, Poison, and Sacrilege in Louis XIV's France
Lynn Wood Mollenauer

UNLOCKED BOOKS
Manuscripts of Learned Magic in the Medieval Libraries of Central Europe
Benedek Láng

ALCHEMICAL BELIEF
Occultism in the Religious Culture of Early Modern England
Bruce Janacek

INVOKING ANGELS
Theurgic Ideas and Practices, Thirteenth to Sixteenth Centuries
Edited by Claire Fanger

THE TRANSFORMATIONS OF MAGIC
Illicit Learned Magic in the Later Middle Ages and Renaissance
Frank Klaassen

MAGIC IN THE CLOISTER
Pious Motives, Illicit Interests, and Occult Approaches to the Medieval Universe
Sophie Page

REWRITING MAGIC
An Exegesis of the Visionary Autobiography of a Fourteenth-Century French Monk
Claire Fanger

MAGIC IN THE MODERN WORLD
Strategies of Repression and Legitimization
Edited by Edward Bever and Randall Styers

MEDICINE, RELIGION, AND MAGIC IN EARLY STUART ENGLAND
Richard Napier's Medical Practice
Ofer Hadass

PICATRIX
A Medieval Treatise on Astral Magic
Translated with an introduction by Dan Attrell and David Porreca

MAKING MAGIC IN ELIZABETHAN ENGLAND
Two Early Modern Vernacular Books of Magic
Edited by Frank Klaassen

THE LONG LIFE OF MAGICAL OBJECTS
A Study in the Solomonic Tradition
Allegra Iafrate

KABBALAH AND SEX MAGIC
A Mythical-Ritual Genealogy
Marla Segol

SORCERY OR SCIENCE?
Contesting Knowledge and Practice in West African Sufi Texts
Ariela Marcus-Sells

SPECULUM LAPIDUM
A Renaissance Treatise on the Healing Properties of Gemstones
Camillo Leonardi; translated with an introduction by Liliana Leopardi

THE CHILD WITCHES OF OLAGUE
The Child Witches of Olague
Lu Ann Homza